INSIDERS' GUIDE® TO
MYRTLE BEACH AND THE GRAND STRAND

Help Us Keep This Guide Up to Date

Every effort has been made by the authors and editors to make this guide as accurate and useful as possible. However, many things can change after a guide is published—establishments close, phone numbers change, facilities come under new management, etc.

We would love to hear from you concerning your experiences with this guide and how you feel it could be improved and be kept up to date. While we may not be able to respond to all comments and suggestions, we'll take them to heart and we'll also make certain to share them with the authors. Please send your comments and suggestions to the following address:

The Globe Pequot Press
Reader Response/Editorial Department
P.O. Box 480
Guilford, CT 06437

Or you may e-mail us at:

editorial@GlobePequot.com

Thanks for your input, and happy travels!

Insiders' Guide®
to Myrtle Beach

and the Grand Strand

SEVENTH EDITION

By Kimberly Allyson Duncan
and
Lisa Tomer Rentz

Guilford, Connecticut
An imprint of The Globe Pequot Press

Front cover photograph: Wendell Metzen, Index Stock
Back cover and spine photographs: Myrtle Beach Area Chamber of Commerce

Maps created by XNR Productions Inc. © The Globe Pequot Press.

ISBN: 0-7627-2681-4

Manufactured in the United States of America
Seventh Edition/First Printing

Contents

Directory of Maps

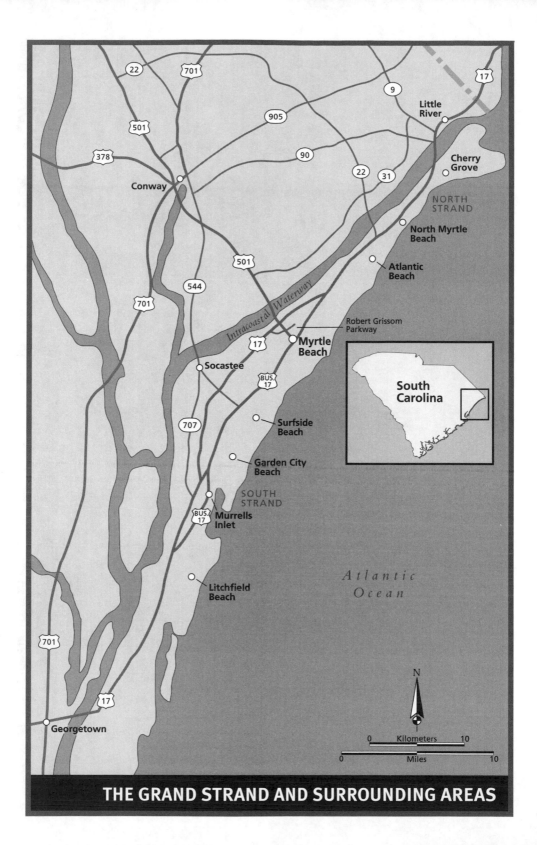

THE GRAND STRAND AND SURROUNDING AREAS

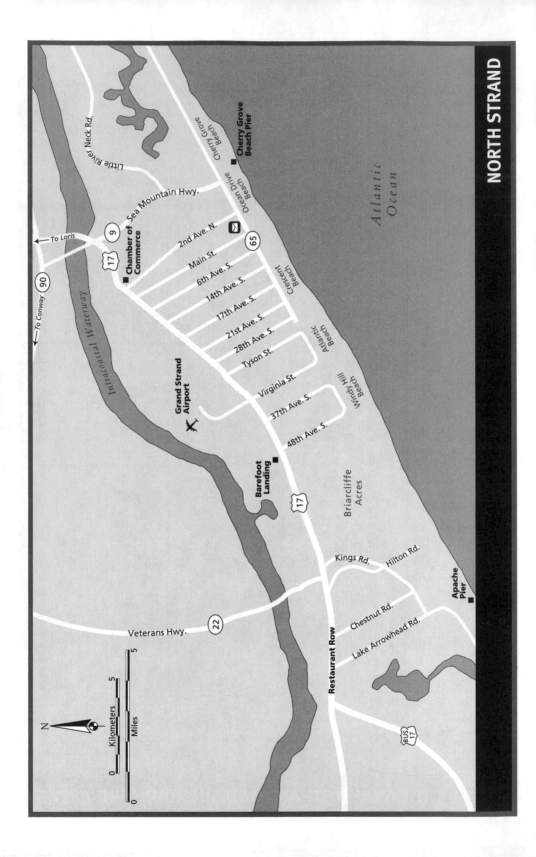

Atlantic
Ocean

Cherry Grove Beach Pier
Cherry Grove Beach

Ocean Drive Beach

Little River Neck Rd.

Chamber of Commerce

Sea Mountain Hwy.

To Loris

9

17

90
To Conway

2nd Ave. N.

65

Main St.

6th Ave. S.

14th Ave. S.

17th Ave. S.

21st Ave. S.

28th Ave. S.

Tyson St.

Crescent Beach

Intracoastal Waterway

Grand Strand Airport

Virginia St.

37th Ave. S.

48th Ave. S.

Atlantic Beach

Windy Hill Beach

Barefoot Landing

17

Briarcliffe Acres

Kings Rd.

Hilton Rd.

Veterans Hwy.

22

Restaurant Row

Chestnut Rd.

Lake Arrowhead Rd.

Apache Pier

BUS 17

N

Kilometers
0 5

Miles
0 5

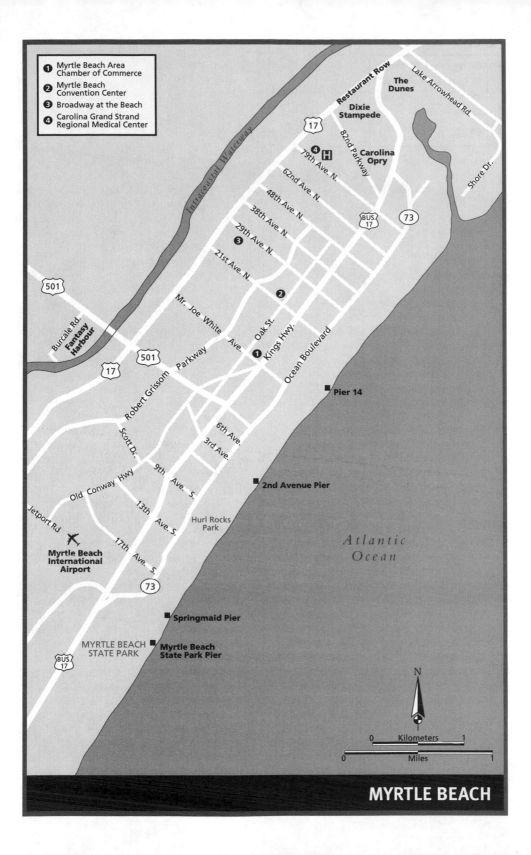

MYRTLE BEACH

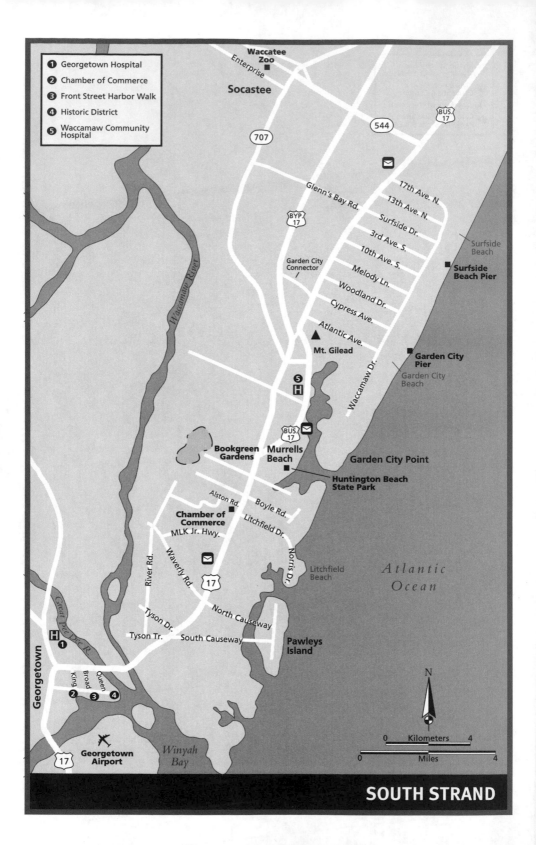

SOUTH STRAND

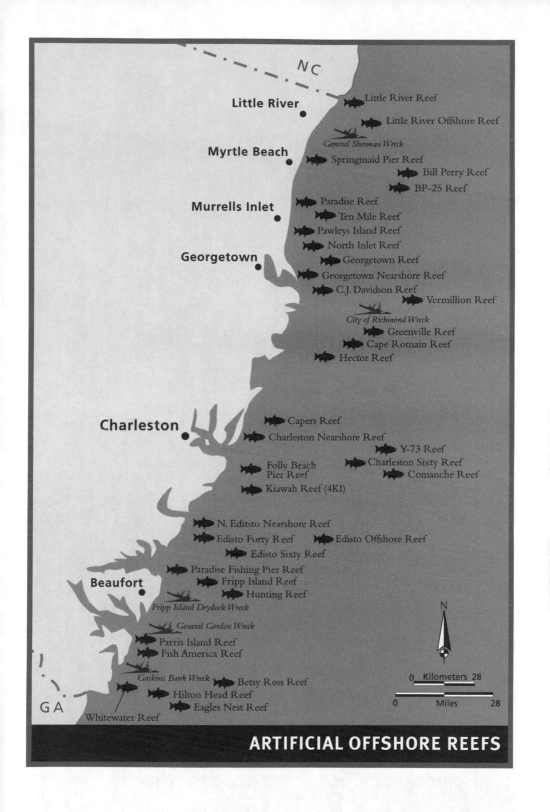

ARTIFICIAL OFFSHORE REEFS

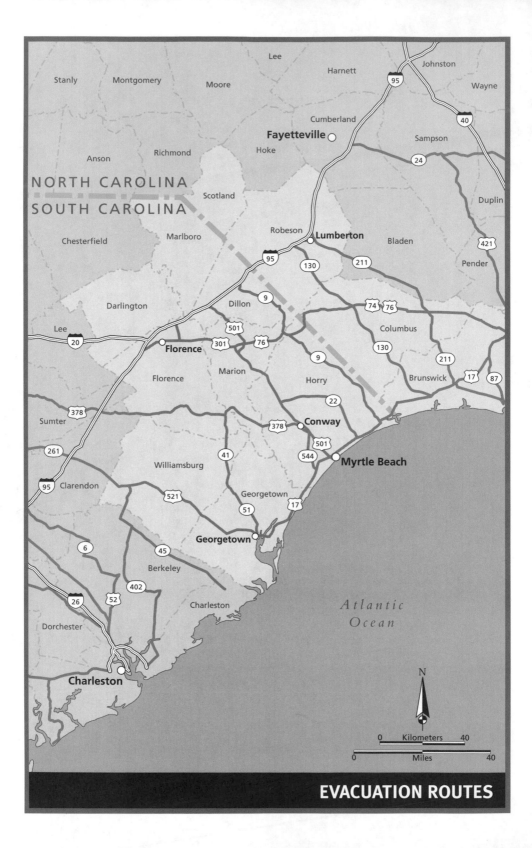

EVACUATION ROUTES

Preface

Don't think of your trip to Myrtle Beach in terms of how long it will take you to get here—the few hours from Columbia or the all-day drive from Pennsylvania. Rather, think of what you are gaining on this sandy adventure: incomparable ocean views and sultry breezes, mounds of all-you-can-eat crab legs, your highest score on a video game or lowest in golf, a perfect memento to wear back home, or (and probably most of all) a touch of that Southern sunshine that will slow you down to the comfortable pace of the local drawl.

As you've probably heard by now (with nearly 14 million visitors annually, word can't help but spread), the Grand Strand has a lot more to offer than its wide, fun-filled beach. You should definitely spend your afternoons there, laying out, reading, crabbing, shelling, and swimming—you know, all the traditional beach things Myrtle Beach provides so well. But what should you do in the cool mornings? What if it's raining? What if your child asks about the area's flora and fauna or history? Which golf courses allow walking? With your special tastes in consideration, where should you stay? And, where should you eat?

When you arrive, you'll see plenty of signs pointing you in many different directions; the multitude of businesses along U.S. Highway 17 compete with each other in everything from price to visibility. But with *Insiders' Guide to Myrtle Beach and the Grand Strand*, you'll be prepared for, if not knowledgeable of, the new surroundings. As Insiders we have crafted a guide to the Grand Strand specifically for people who want to enjoy themselves; even though we're not necessarily on vacation here, we heartily agree the Grand Strand is about enjoying yourself.

There are many ways to accomplish this, from strolling the beach and eating grilled meals to playing the most exclusive golf clubs and experiencing fine dining. With this Insiders' look at the Grand Strand, we hope we are helping you come up with the right combination and ensuring that you'll come back to try out a new one next year.

We looked at all the possibilities, trying to think of the most significant Insiders' tip to make your excursion as comfortable as possible, and this is the one that leapt to our minds first: Do not underestimate the value of a good sunscreen!

Acknowledgments

I am extremely fortunate and grateful for a group of friends that keep me sane—even when deadlines loom and my attitude is less than exemplary. Kelly, Gail, Troi, Kim, Sherri—I love each of you and cherish the fact that you have confidence in my abilities. I am also grateful to my nine-year-old daughter, Madison, future president of the United States, for an older-than-her-years understanding of her mother's busy work life. Thank you for loving me so unselfishly. I also want to say thank you to my beautiful niece, Kaela, for being exactly who you are. You are enormously important to me. It would be remiss of me not to thank my father for teaching me to love words. My life is infinitely richer because of his gift. And, last but not least, I extend my gratitude to Mother for a genetic dose of creativity that helps me weave words in ways that comfort me when nothing else can.

I would also like to acknowledge the contributions of Lisa Tomer Rentz for her work on the previous edition.

— Kimberly Allyson Duncan

How to Use This Book

This incredible 60-mile stretch of beach from Little River to Georgetown, appropriately dubbed the Grand Strand, is a vacationer's mecca. There's so much going on in any given area that, oftentimes, people need not wander beyond a 2-mile radius from their hotel to keep busy all day and night. We hope that this guide to South Carolina's favorite coastal resort will help you effectively plan your next visit here, your relocation, or your retirement. One thing is sure, this guide will give you a true Insiders' view of the Grand Strand from those of us who live, work, and play here.

In producing the *Insiders' Guide to Myrtle Beach and the Grand Strand,* we have tried to lead you through the dizzying options of things to see and do. The chapters on Shopping, Restaurants, Nightlife, Annual Events, Entertainment, Attractions, Kidstuff, and Arts and Culture should be good starting points for planning your activities. If you still have time and energy, the chapter on Day Trips can direct you to nearby sites of interest. The last thing we want is for you to get lost around here, so we've provided a Getting Here, Getting Around chapter as well as a variety of maps of the overall area, including main arteries and roadways.

We also have used the regional headings of the North Strand, Myrtle Beach, and the South Strand in the chapters to orient you and save you travel time. By breaking out these areas, you can pinpoint people, places, and things closest to you. Basically the North Strand is anywhere from the village of Little River to Myrtle Beach proper. Lake Arrowhead Road and the Restaurant Row section of the Grand Strand will be your landmarks of note that you have passed from the North Strand into Myrtle Beach proper.

The Myrtle Beach section of the Strand continues southward until you see the signs denoting Surfside Beach. Surfside marks the starting point of the South Strand entries in this book, encompassing Garden City Beach, Murrells Inlet, Litchfield Beach, Pawleys Island, and Georgetown. Road signs let you know that once you've hit the Murrells Inlet area, you've traveled from Horry County into Georgetown County.

This guide contains several listings from sister regions, which we call Beyond the Strand. As a geographical heading, Beyond the Strand lends itself to areas within Horry or Georgetown Counties that are considered inland and usually denote areas west of the Intracoastal Waterway.

Whether you're staying for a weekend, a week, or permanently, this guide will help you find suitable accommodations or a roof over your head; check out the chapters on Accommodations and Real Estate.

To make financial planning easier, we've coordinated a dollar-sign key to give you a price range for places to eat and stay. However, prices quoted in this guide are subject to change, and each establishment reserves the right to make those changes without prior notice. Also we do apologize here and now if you should contact any place mentioned in this guide only to find it out of business. As is typical of a resort area, there is so much new market competition here that it's not unusual for a certain percentage of businesses to close their doors each year.

Other chapters provide vital information on child care, education, local laws, retirement, and medical care.

When using the Insiders' Guide, you'll come across a lot of cross-referencing. We do this to give you the most complete information possible. For example, you may be reading an entry in the Attractions chapter that refers you to the Kidstuff chapter for more information. The Kidstuff chapter may include the same entry, but it's written from the perspective of relating to children's interests. In this way you'll be able to get the whole scoop on a place, what there is for adults and for children.

Please note that the area code for the Coastal and Pee Dee regions of South Carolina is 843 (which replaced an 803 code in 1998).

This (843) area code includes the South Carolina counties of Beaufort, Charleston, Chesterfield, Colleton, Darlington, Dillon, Florence, Georgetown, Horry, Jasper, Marion, Marlboro, and Williamsburg. It will also take in most of Berkeley County and parts of Clarendon, Dorchester, and Lee Counties.

We hope *Insiders' Guide to Myrtle Beach and the Grand Strand* will give you a real feel for this area and the opportunity to experience it to the fullest. With this information in hand, you'll fit right in as if you've been beachcombing all your life.

Area Overview

North Strand
Little River
North Myrtle Beach
Myrtle Beach
South Strand

Most people think of the Grand Strand as the coast of South Carolina; technically The Strand is an island with a 60-mile oceanfront and three roads connecting it to the mainland (four if you count U.S. Highway 17 connections in both the North and South Strands). Surrounded on the north and the west by the Intracoastal Waterway, a Roosevelt-era shipping lane, the east by the Atlantic Ocean, and on the south by Winyah Bay, the Grand Strand can be basically shut off from the outside motoring world by closing four bridges.

The Grand Strand is named so for a reason: The wide strand accommodates people of every type at various activities including swimming, sunbathing, seashelling, volleyball playing, Sea-Dooing, fishing, parasailing, boating, and more. The communities are first and foremost beach oriented. All the houses and buildings are designed for optimum views of the water. One street inland, Myrtle Beach goes beyond sand in your shoes and provides restaurants, shopping, golf, and many other diversions.

Considered one of the nation's top vacation destinations, the Grand Strand hosts nearly fourteen million visitors annually. The increasing number of attractions, theaters, outlet malls, shopping centers, ecotourism opportunities, and golf courses attracts visitors throughout the year. The Myrtle Beach Area has received these positive national reviews:

• The American Bus Association's "Hottest Up-and-Coming Destination"—for five consecutive years.

• AAA travel managers named the Myrtle Beach Area the second most popular travel destination for the summer of 1999.

• The Myrtle Beach Area is consistently recognized by *Southern Living* as a favorite family vacation destination.

• Independent tourism researchers list Myrtle Beach among the nation's top vacation spots for retirees age fifty-five and older.

• In the past several years, both the *Wall Street Journal* and *Money* magazine have listed Myrtle Beach among America's top spots for retirement.

Stretching far beyond just the city limits of Myrtle Beach, the Grand Strand reaches from the North Carolina border, beachcombing southward more than 60 miles to the historic, oak-lined avenues of Georgetown, where five rivers meet to form Winyah Bay. This 60-mile stretch includes the latest high-tech amusements to more than 115 golf courses to world-class entertainment theaters and superstars to family beaches to almost-untouched beach wilderness. Amazingly, one can drift just slightly off the beaten path and find salt marshes, classic Spanish moss, hammocks, ghost tales, and historic legends that make the Disney Channel seem dull.

So you have plenty to do. Visit the world-famous Pavilion and ride every ride. Smell the salt water dancing with the scents of fresh cotton candy and mustard-coated corn dogs. Sift your toes into the sand as the surf laps at your ankles. Take a marsh cruise, go deep-sea fishing, or windsurf. Fall asleep in the sun. Swim and sail and dine and dance. Play a few rounds of golf. Hobnob with country music stars, or just relax and enjoy.

Up and down the Strand, piers stretch into the ocean, providing opportunities for fishing, romantic strolls, and gazing into the horizon. PHOTO: COURTESY OF MYRTLE BEACH AREA CHAMBER OF COMMERCE

North Strand

Tourist development of the North Strand began around 1937 with a log cabin–type motel. Except for some serious destruction from Hurricane Hazel in 1954, these little beach communities have maintained their individual identities while creating a greater presence as North Strand entities.

Although minimal but steady erosion has prompted a renourishment project on a 25-mile stretch of beach between North Myrtle Beach and Garden City Beach (see the related Close-up in the Beach Information chapter), many folks who call the North Strand home boast that they still have the world's widest beach. While the claim is disputable, no one will deny that their beach is remarkably wide—especially when the tide is at low ebb. Unlike many South Carolina beaches, this section of sand still offers plenty of room to bask in the sun, take long walks, mastermind sand castles, and play volleyball and paddle ball, even when the tide is high.

The sand of the North Strand is packed firm; driving cars on the beach used to be popular but is now prohibited. But bikes are allowed and make for a breezily enjoyable ride. Bicycles and a three-wheeled, low-riding style of bike can be rented along the North Strand, so avoid the hassle of bringing your own. The three-wheelers are a comic and attention-getting mode of travel; you sit in a semireclined position and pedal with your feet out front. It's awkward at first, but with a little coordination and some concentration, you'll get the knack quickly. Although these big trikes have hand grips, you steer using your feet and the sway of your body. Attachments allow you to pull the kids along.

Little River

Where the Carolinas meet, the sun smiles on the charming fishing village of Little River. Nestled beneath the twisted arms of weathered oaks, you'll discover an unhurried and uncommon side of the Grand Strand. From clutches of cheerful shops, an unexpected array of merchandise spills forth. You can also schedule a deep-sea fishing excursion, take a cruise down the Intracoastal Waterway, or hang around and chat with tanned dock workers while they haul in a day's catch. Restaurants, marinas, and fresh seafood abound. Water is the undisputed king, and everyone is subject to its rule. Like the rest of the North Strand, Little River is growing rapidly, but it's still possible to discover marvelous pockets of solitude in this historic fishing village.

Each spring thousands of people make a pilgrimage to Little River on the weekend in May when the horseshoe area of the beloved waterfront hosts the famous Blue Crab Festival (see the Annual Events chapter). This daylong event—Little River's finest—showcases live entertainment, oodles of arts and crafts displays, and an abundance of fresh, delectable seafood.

North Myrtle Beach

North Myrtle Beach, home of the state's shimmy-in-your-well-worn-Weejuns dance, the Shag, makes up the largest section of the North Strand. The city was established in the 1960s when legendary South Carolina Congressman John Jenrette (then a state legislator) argued that the four smaller communities of Cherry Grove, Ocean Drive, Crescent Beach, and Windy Hill would prosper if they merged into a single municipality.

Condominiums and small motels are typical oceanfront accommodations, but you can still find front-row cottages. Their suitability for house parties, coupled with North Myrtle Beach's long-standing party-hearty reputation, make it a mainstay for Shaggers, collegiate men and women, and arcade-loving kids.

From mid-May, when exams end at many institutions, until mid-June, you'll find North Myrtle overflowing with celebrating students from far and wide. On Easter weekend alone, an estimated 75,000 to 90,000 kids flock to the beach

Insiders' Tip

Always take time to stop at visitor centers or chamber of commerce offices when you're new in town or just visiting. The staff can point you in the direction of fun and may know of special events or have coupons for you to use.

for dancing and romancing. Over the years police have been forced to become especially strict about public drinking. Consequently many college kids have found themselves singing the jailhouse blues instead of dancing on the Strand. Jenrette, who served as the first town judge, still enjoys telling of his escapades trying not to jail many a young drinking party-seeker in the early days of North Myrtle. Even today, for those willing to demonstrate a little self-control, one visit will confirm an irrefutable truth: There's no better place on the eastern seaboard to celebrate the end of another school year.

Cherry Grove, just south of Little River, is one of several communities that compose North Myrtle Beach. Sea Mountain Highway is the only way into Cherry Grove from U.S. 17, so watch the signs carefully. Cherry Grove has its share of oceanfront condominiums and motels, but away from the ocean you'll find rows of houses on pilings lining serpentine channels and inlets. Many Cherry Grove residents and tourists handpick this section of the Strand because they relish the joys of catching, cleaning, and cooking their own seafood.

From dawn to dusk, Cherry Grove's Hogg Inlet bustles with folks shrimping and fishing, crabbing with chicken necks, and dutifully tending their fish pots. Pa-

The Grand Strand teems with entertainment and attractions, but cruise "off-the-beaten-path" and you'll find a slow, sweet side of South Carolina's Lowcountry. PHOTO: COURTESY OF THE LOWCOUNTRY COMPANION

tient anglers troll, seeking out the day's best fishing spots. At night they gig for flounder. You'll be glad to know Hogg Inlet has a public boat landing, so you don't have to own a home on the creek to partake of the inlet's bounty. In recent years Hogg Inlet has also become a late-night hangout and parking spot for young locals wanting a secluded smooching area.

Along U.S. 17 the communities known as Ocean Drive, Crescent Beach, Atlantic Beach, and Windy Hill run together in a hard-to-distinguish blur. In fact if you're not a local, it's nearly impossible to know when you've passed from one community into the next. On the ocean you'll find more motels and condominiums in Ocean

Drive and Crescent Beach. Ocean Drive is best known as the place where the world-famous dance the Shag originated. Accordingly, Main Street Ocean Drive boasts several clubs where beach music will never go out of style.

Although not technically a part of the city of North Myrtle Beach, Atlantic Beach sits between the Windy Hill and Crescent Beach communities. Historically Atlantic Beach was known as the "black beach" because during Jim Crow years it was the only beach on the southern Atlantic seaboard open to African Americans. Separated for years from the rest of North Myrtle Beach by oceanfront chain-link fences, today Atlantic Beach has a few small motels, nightspots, and lots of cottages, and it is still primarily an African-American community.

Where North Myrtle ends Briarcliffe Acres begins, sheltered by a wall of tall pine trees. Moderately upscale and almost solely residential, you're likely to miss this tiny town if someone doesn't point it out. The easy way to find it is to look for Colonial Mall on the west side of the highway.

One of the North Strand's many delights is Barefoot Landing, a top-ranked tourist attraction. On U.S. 17 and inland from Windy Hill Beach, this charming variation of a shopping center includes shops nestled around a 27-acre freshwater lake. Barefoot Landing is home to more than 100 specialty and retail shops, factory direct stores, more than 1,000 feet of floating dock, a boardwalk, and a handful of waterfront restaurants. Attractions include the Barefoot Carousel, *Barefoot Princess Riverboat*, Alligator Adventure, The Alabama Theatre, and the House of Blues.

The North Strand wraps up with the Grand Strand's famed Restaurant Row. Like a string of fine pearls, an impressive selection of restaurants lines either side of U.S. 17. Seafood, of course, is the natural specialty, but hearty steaks, spicy ribs, Italian favorites, Japanese options, and even down-home country cooking can be found along this renowned strip. During summer dinner hours, nearly every restaurant sports a long line of eager patrons, but you're sure to find the food worth the wait. Highway traffic is especially heavy during that dinner rush, which starts as early as 5:00 P.M. and continues until around 8:00 P.M.

Closest to Myrtle Beach is the unincorporated Shore Drive community. Highly developed and densely populated, this is an area of high-rise hotels and condominiums, retiree homes, a nearly constant flow of renters and time-share purchasers, and a couple of upscale residential communities.

Myrtle Beach

The Grand Strand revolves around the city of Myrtle Beach. The resort area first became popular here, and everything seems to spiderweb outward from Myrtle Beach. Though Pawleys Island was a long-standing resort for the wealthy, it was Myrtle Beach that made the Strand accessible to the general population. The largest, most developed, and most popular of the beaches, Myrtle Beach is so dominant that most locals refer to it simply as "The Beach." Even folks living south in Surfside or Garden City and those living north in Ocean Drive or Cherry Grove still tell outsiders that they live "at Myrtle Beach."

In years past the area has been billed the Seaside Golf Capital of the World, the Campground Capital of the World, and the Miniature Golf Capital of the World—on top of all the other hoopla about the Strand.

Myrtle Beach once was even home to the world's largest sand sculpture. As part of a Sun Fun Festival (see the Annual Events chapter) promotion, Myrtle Beach challenged the city of Long Beach, Washington, to a sand castle–building competition. Hundreds of volunteers rallied Southern pride to create a sand sculpture that stretched for 86,536 feet—more than 16 miles! The feat landed the city in the *Guinness Book of World Records* in 1991 (Long Beach has since recaptured the record).

The tourism experts say that Myrtle Beach's greatest attractions are still the Atlantic Ocean and the beautiful beaches. But in the past few years so many other things have sprung up that it is hard for even Insiders to keep track of the latest attraction. In addition to shopping, amusement parks, miniature golf, water parks, waterway cruises, live-entertainment theaters, and golf, there is a constant quest among promoters to find even greater ways to satisfy visitors and residents alike. Whether it's the family beach, golfer's paradise, the country music and live-entertainment haven, the food, the shopping, the amusements, the attractions... whatever the draw, Myrtle Beach seems to provide something for everyone.

Even old-timers are amazed at the development that has transformed Myrtle Beach.

The *Wall Street Journal* recently declared

that the state bird of South Carolina is evolving into the "construction crane" because of Myrtle Beach. Myrtle Beach once was a summer vacation resort catering to blue-collar factory workers primarily in North and South Carolina and Tennessee. In fact, even Generation-X locals can remember when the only real tourist season was during July when the textile mills closed for vacation. But the face of Myrtle Beach has rapidly changed, becoming a mixture of blue-collar workers, northern mid-management retirees, upscale golfers, families, and a whole new demographic of white-collar vacationers.

During the past several years, the Strand's 120-plus golf courses have helped expand the spring and fall shoulder seasons in the tourism industry to make Myrtle Beach a nine-month resort. More than four million rounds of golf are played in the area each year.

Still, the average visitor to the Myrtle Beach area is an ocean-seeking vacationer. Almost 40 percent of nearly fourteen million annual visitors live within a day's drive to the beach. Myrtle Beach is approximately halfway between New York City and Miami.

Myrtle Beach's main drag is Ocean Boulevard (known locally as the Boulevard), the street that literally runs along the ocean. The Boulevard is divided east-west by numbered streets (30th Avenue South to First Avenue South and then First Avenue North to 82nd Avenue North).

Unofficially Myrtle Beach is divided into four areas. The south end of the Boulevard is a solid line of accommodations—some large, some small. The mid-portion of the Boulevard features venues for entertainment and activities, including the Myrtle Beach Pavilion and Ripley's Believe It or Not! Museum. Beginning around 32nd Avenue North, there is an exclusive residential district where permanent and summer residents coexist in beautiful homes. From 52nd Avenue northward, motels and condominiums dominate the beachfront.

Heading directly west from the midportion of the Boulevard, along 21st Avenue North, you will cross U.S. Highway 17 Business, also called Kings Highway and the primary home for shopping centers, a mall, and regular nonresort businesses. Farther west is Oak Street, primarily a business district. About 3 miles from the ocean, you will hit U.S. Highway 17 Bypass; locals know it as simply the Bypass, and many have come to call it the "former Bypass" because of traffic backups. On 21st Avenue North, between Oak Street and the Bypass, you will find Broadway at the Beach, one of the most significant developments at Myrtle Beach during the past decade.

The beaches of the Grand Strand are public; in fact, law specifically designates how many feet apart public access areas must be, based on development density. Thanks to the vision of Myrtle Beach officials, many of the city's public access areas have parking available. The city has erected blue and yellow signs along the Boulevard to help visitors recognize these access sites. Wheelchair access to the beach is also provided; through the efforts of several area civic clubs, beach services now offer specially designed wheelchairs that are easy to maneuver on the sand.

Myrtle Beach hosts many annual festivals. Two of the most popular are the Sun Fun Festival, usually held the first full weekend in June, and the Canadian-American Days festival, held in March to

Insiders' Tip

Pay attention to North and South indicators on numbered street names. For example: Not only is 30th Avenue North 60 streets north of 30th Avenue South in Myrtle Beach, but there is also another set of 30th avenues, North and South again, in North Myrtle Beach.

A wide, white ribbon of shoreline is the Grand Strand's most striking natural resource. PHOTO: COURTESY OF MYRTLE BEACH AREA CHAMBER OF COMMERCE

coincide with spring break for Canadian students.

The fifty-plus-year-old Sun Fun Festival originally served as an official kickoff for the summer season. Even now that Myrtle Beach is a year-round tourist destination, the traditional Sun Fun Festival continues to offer four days of nonstop fun in early June. The famous festival frequently attracts national media attention to the beauty and bikini contests, sand castle–building, a huge parade, children's games, musical and theatrical performances, cookouts, sailing regattas, and much more.

Canadian-American Days offers a jam-packed agenda, too. "Can-Am," as locals call it, was developed in recognition of thousands of Canadian tourists who were already visiting the beach every spring. More than 40 years ago, the chamber of commerce decided to launch a Canadian advertising campaign to extend the beach season by encouraging even more north-ern visitors during the otherwise slow time. During this 10-day festival, banks willingly exchange currency, and some businesses even offer an exchange rate at par. Radio, television, and newspapers headline Canadian news.

See the Annual Events chapter for details on both of these events.

South Strand

The South Strand includes Surfside Beach, Garden City Beach, Murrells Inlet, Litchfield Beach, and Pawleys Island. Compared with the rest of the Grand Strand, the South Strand subscribes to a more leisurely pace and lifestyle, with less neon and glitter as well as a low-key nightlife with just as much allure. Many praise this stretch of land, with its rich marshland, uninhabited beaches, bountiful inlets, and maritime forest, as the Carolina coast's finest treasure. For those same reasons, South Strand residents cherish their privacy and work vigilantly to protect the area's resources.

The town of Surfside was incorporated in 1964 with 881 residents. Today, having officially changed its name to Surfside Beach and billing itself as "the family beach," the town's year-round population is more than 4,500. Immediately adjacent to Myrtle Beach and most like it in nature, Surfside Beach has become a destination unto itself—mostly for RV park visitors and hotel guests who like a little more solitude than Myrtle Beach offers.

U.S. 17 in Surfside is lined with restaurants, beach shops, and attractions, including the Legends In Concert show of celebrity impersonators. Accommodations along Surfside's oceanfront differ somewhat from those in Myrtle Beach. Fewer high-rises tower above the sun-drenched beaches, and cottages and condominiums treasure comfort.

Directly south of Surfside Beach, Garden City Beach is a family-oriented retreat sporting hundreds of residential homes, summer cottages, and condominiums. Surf fishing reels in many participants along this beach, which is also a favorite retreat for beachcombers. Garden City Beach is also one of the Grand Strand's most popular retirement destinations, with large controlled-access senior-citizen communities dominating the area.

The point where Atlantic Avenue punctuates Ocean Boulevard is the only area in Garden City that resembles the glittery expanses of Myrtle Beach. Here you'll find arcades and carnival-style food vendors. As for quieter pursuits, walking Garden City's pier is a popular pastime, particularly when a silvery Carolina moon is riding high.

The North Jetty of Garden City was built in 1979 with rocks weighing up to 200 pounds each. It extends 3,445 feet from the shore and stabilizes the inlet across the ocean so commercial and recreational boats won't bog down. The jetty ensures ideal boating conditions, regardless of tidal action, which is especially important for those who fish commercially and rely on the sea's bounty to make a living.

South of Garden City is Murrells Inlet, the oldest fishing village in South Car-

olina. Murrells Inlet is home to anglers, writers, poets, and more legends and ghost stories than any other part of the Grand Strand. Mickey Spillane, who created the detective character Mike Hammer, lives in the Inlet, as do a dozen other nationally known novelists, poets, and musicians, all of whom love the small-town atmosphere of being able to walk into a fish market or an antiques shop without being mobbed.

Fishing in the creeks and waterways of Murrells Inlet has been a way of life for generations, and the quiet community trumpets itself as the Seafood Capital of South Carolina. Best known to tourists for dozens of seafood restaurants in a 3-mile stretch, Murrells Inlet also is home to numerous antiques shops, fresh seafood markets, and Captain Dick's, one of the Grand Strand's best marinas (see the Boating chapter).

The journey south on U.S. 17 from Murrells Inlet to Litchfield is a quick, pretty trip. Densely wooded areas line the highway and give a sense of traveling back in time, a sensation deliberately cultivated by locals. Carefully manicured landscapes adorn the median along the main highway. Once known as Magnolia Beach, the popular resort of Litchfield Beach takes its name from Litchfield Plantation, a rice plantation on the Waccamaw River. The manor house is one of the few still-standing plantation homes surrounded by majestic oaks. Open as a country club and a bed-and-breakfast, Litchfield Plantation is now classified as a small world-class luxury hotel.

Litchfield's quaint shops, outstanding restaurants, and various accommodations are reasonably new compared to the historic resort of Pawleys Island, slightly south of Litchfield. The beaches of Litchfield and Pawleys are among the widest, most litter-free, and best-preserved on the South Carolina coast; however, much of the property is private, and you'll find only a few points of public beach access. Though the points are clearly marked, parking is limited.

Pawleys Island proclaims itself the oldest resort area in America. Even in the 1700s the tiny barrier island was a summer retreat for wealthy plantation owners

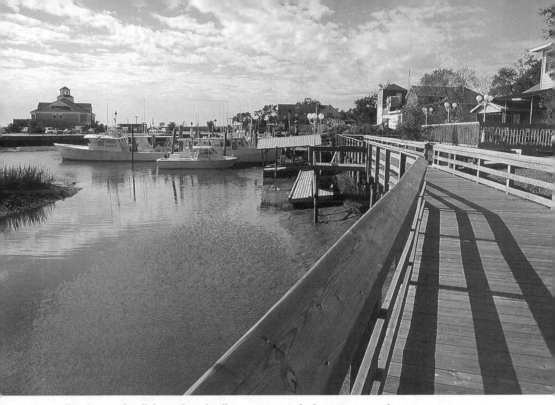

Murrells Inlet Marshwalk boasts boardwalks, marinas, seafood restaurants, and more. PHOTO: COURTESY
OF MYRTLE BEACH AREA CHAMBER OF COMMERCE

and their families. Despite storms and the ravages of time, many of their cottages, weatherworn and rustic looking, still remain. Hence for many years, locals have termed their island "arrogantly shabby." As a matter of fact, bumper stickers, T-shirts, and tourism brochures for Pawleys Island all have adopted that description.

Today Pawleys is known for its low-key lifestyle, handmade hammocks, and sightings of the Gray Man, a friendly ghost who warns of impending hurricanes. The cherished lifestyle is carefully protected by islanders. The 2-mile island was incorporated as a town in 1984 and in recent years has made for one of the most colorful political stories in South Carolina's history, with their struggle to restrict local building codes and prevent construction of high-rise condominiums and hotels. They have been successful. A few bed-and-breakfast inns flourish, offering a taste of beach living as it used to be: simple, unassuming, and perfectly tranquil.

South of Pawleys Island and at the foot of the Grand Strand is Georgetown, a shipping community that was once called Little Charleston. With a Revolutionary War–era flavor; the narrow, brick streets; and its well-preserved, two-centuries-old churches and homes, the flavor of the town really is colonial. A bell-towered Rice Museum dominates the center of town and features exhibits that track the antebellum history of the plantation heyday.

In recent years the little community has grappled with pollution problems stemming from wastewater discharge from International Paper and a steel mill that have long replaced the shipping, slaving, and rice industries. Still, there is enough flavor left of the old colonial town and enough old-style bed-and-breakfast residences that the visitor seeking to step back in time will find a paradise in Georgetown.

Myrtle Beach and the Grand Strand Vital Statistics

Nicknames: "The Grand Strand"—the extra wide beach and grouping of all the beach towns such as Little River, Windy Hill, Myrtle Beach, Garden City, and Pawleys Island.

"The Independent Republic"—Horry County, because of historical events such as the signing of secession papers in Conway (the county seat), and Horry County's geographic separation, with rivers and marshes separating it from the rest of the state.

Mayor of Myrtle Beach: Mark S. McBride

Population: (Horry & Georgetown County) 252,426 (permanent residents)

Area: The Grand Strand—60 miles of coast, from Little River to Georgetown

Average Temperatures: July—air 88, water, 80;
January—air 56, water 50

Average Days of Sunshine: Sunny, 216; rainy, 72; average humidity at 1:00 P.M., 57 percent

Major University: Coastal Carolina University

Important Dates in History:
    1730: The city of Georgetown is planned
    1779: South Carolina joins Union
    1900: Burroughs and Collins Company constructs a railway to the beach
    1901: First hotel, the Seaside Inn, is built
    1936: Intracoastal Waterway is opened to boaters
    1954: Hurricane Hazel
    1989: Hurricane Hugo
    1997: Beach Renourishment Project begins; area's first museum of art opens

Major Area Employers: Burroughs and Chapin, AVX

Famous Sons and Daughters: Vanna White, Alabama (started as Wild Country at the Bowery)

Major Airport: Myrtle Beach International Airport

Major Roadways:
Ocean Boulevard: runs parallel to ocean throughout most of Grand Strand.
U.S. Highway 17 Business (King's Highway) and Bypass: also runs parallel to the ocean a little farther inland.
U.S. Highway 501: from Florence, into Conway and on into the heart of the Grand Strand. To get to North Strand leave U.S. 501 to take S.C. Highway 90.
Interstate 40 East (to U.S. 17 South): for travelers coming from eastern North Carolina.
Interstates 95 and 20: for those coming from the west into Florence.

Driving Laws:
To obtain a driver's license you must be at least 18 years of age; to obtain a permit, age 14; new residents may use old licenses for up to 90 days. Seat belts and child safety restraints required. Headlights must be on when use of wipers is necessary.

Alcohol Laws: Drinking age is 21. Sale of alcohol prohibited on Sundays. Beer and wine available at grocery stores; liquor sold at ABC stores marked with large red dots.

Sales Tax: 5 percent South Carolina sales tax; 16 cents per gallon gasoline tax; maximum of $300 tax on purchase of vehicles.

Hospitality Tax: 2.5 percent hospitality fee charged on prepared food, admissions, and overnight accommodations of less than 90 days.

Tourism Information:
Myrtle Beach Area Chamber of Commerce
1200 North Oak Street
Myrtle Beach, SC 29577
(800) 356–3016

North Myrtle Beach Chamber Office
213 Highway 17 North
North Myrtle Beach, SC 29582
(843) 249–3519

South Strand Office
3410 Highway 17 South
Murrells Inlet, SC 29576-0650
(843) 651–1010

Georgetown Chamber of Commerce
1001 Front Street
Georgetown, SC 29442
(843) 546–8436

When the tide is low, rent a bike and enjoy a cruise down the sun-scrubbed shoreline. PHOTO: COURTESY OF
THE LOWCOUNTRY COMPANION

Getting Here, Getting Around

A vacation in Myrtle Beach is wonderful. It can calm even the most tense soul. So while you're sitting in traffic with the kids squabbling in the back seat, just remind yourself how nice your vacation is going to be.

Close your eyes and think about those gorgeous beaches with the sun shimmering on the water; feel that cool salt air wafting across your face; and imagine yourself floating over the crisp clear waves. Now say to yourself every 5 or 10 minutes, "It really is worth it." Because it is.

Most likely, the only distasteful part of your trip will be getting here and, possibly, getting around in places once you're here. Don't fret—this chapter should help.

Getting Here

By Automobile

The popularity of the Grand Strand has soared, with an estimated 13.7 million visitors pouring in every year. Although dramatic road improvements are under way, Grand Strand roads have not kept pace with the area's popularity. But take it from those of us who have lived here for years: It's easy to avoid traffic snarls if you travel at the right times of day and night. Plan your trip so that you will be driving U.S. Highway 501 into Myrtle Beach before 7:00 A.M. or after 7:00 P.M. Monday through Thursday. Also, stay off beach exit roads right after hotel checkout time on Saturdays and Sundays. You will be much better off to check out of your room, put the bags in the car, and hang around town until late afternoon. That way you can also get in one extra afternoon on the beach, which is far more pleasant than bumper-to-bumper driving.

If you're coming to the Grand Strand from eastern North Carolina, you might want to try Interstate 40 east or U.S. Highway 17 south to Wilmington, North Carolina. At Wilmington head southbound on U.S. 17. You should expect traffic to be moving pretty slowly along that stretch, unless you heed our previous advice and travel it early morning or late evening.

From Charleston take U.S. 17 north. It could be crowded at peak traffic times.

If you're traveling north on Interstate 95, take exit 170 (clearly marked "Myrtle Beach"), near Florence. Take U.S. Highway 76 to U.S. 501 and follow it the rest of the way. Vacationers heading to North Strand beaches—Little River, Crescent Beach, Ocean Drive, Atlantic Beach, and Windy Hill—should veer to the left at Marion, cross two lanes of U.S. 501, and continue on U.S. 76. At Nichols take a right onto S.C. Highway 9.

If you're traveling Interstate 20, follow the signs toward Florence. The road will merge into I-95 north and bypass Florence. Then take exit 170, same as if you'd come the whole way on I-95. If you're traveling south on I-95, take exit 193 at Dillon. Head toward Latta, then take U.S. 501. If you're going to North Myrtle Beach, you can take S.C. 9 all the way from Dillon.

If you're going to the South Strand, you might want to take S.C. Highway 544. You'll turn to the right off U.S. 501 about 4 or 5 miles out of Conway. If you opt to continue on U.S. 501, you will connect with the U.S. 17 Bypass at the overpass about 10 miles out of Conway, just after the bridge at the Waccamaw Pottery complex. U.S. 501 and the U.S. 17 Bypass are much easier roads to travel than S.C. 544, but they'll add a few miles to your trip, and traffic is usually bad between 7:00 A.M. to 7:00 P.M. or when it's raining. It's a toss-up. The route you pick will probably depend on what kind of road you prefer.

From Conway, most people will take U.S. 501. You'll find it most frustrating on Saturdays between about 11:00 A.M. and 3:00 P.M.

If you're traveling on U.S. 501 into Conway and your ultimate destination is on the north end of Myrtle Beach, use the opportunity to take a ride on Veterans Highway, Horry County's first major road project in 30 years. Originally known as the Conway Bypass, the new roadway stretches roughly 30 miles from U.S. 501 (west of Conway) to U.S. 17 near Barefoot Landing and the Colonial Mall. When the three-year construction project opened in May 2002, it was more than six months ahead of schedule and $300,000 under budget. In another decade or so, the South Carolina Department of Transportation estimates more than 70,000 vehicles will travel this route every day.

Coming South Via I–77

Coming to the Grand Strand via Interstate 77 from western North Carolina, West Virginia, Ohio, western Pennsylvania, Michigan, and, possibly, Canada can be a trying time. We've consulted a couple of travel-service offices for their best directions; but, when we tried those routes, we wound up spending a lot of time sitting in traffic. So here's a favored route of some transplanted Northerners who call Myrtle Beach home: Travel I–77 South through Charlotte, North Carolina, to Rock Hill, South Carolina. Just past Rock Hill, take exit 77 onto U.S. Highway 21 South. Stay on U.S. 21 for about 5 miles and exit east onto S.C. Highway 5. Stay on S.C. 5 for about 5 miles until you reach U.S. Highway 521. Head south on U.S. 521 to Lancaster. Outside of Lancaster take S.C. Highway 9 for about 3 miles to S.C. High-

way 903. Take S.C. 903 east for about 20 miles to S.C. Highway 151 and turn right. Stay on S.C. 151 for about 40 miles to Darlington. Just outside of Darlington, take U.S. Highway 52 toward Florence until it junctions with I–95. Take I–95 north and follow the instructions included in this chapter (see previous section) from that point.

It sounds confusing, we know, but pull out your map and highlight the route in advance. Even though the roads look like two-laners on most maps, you actually will travel four-laners most of the way, with the exception of the 60-mile or so stretch between Lancaster and McBee, South Carolina. Following these directions it should take about 3½ hours to get from Charlotte to Myrtle Beach. If you don't want to bother with the back roads, we understand. If you prefer interstate highways, stay on I–77 to Columbia, South Carolina, then take I–20 to Florence and follow the directions included in this chapter from that point. The advantage is traveling all interstates, but it might take a little longer.

Some relief possibly is in sight: West Virginia is building its first segment of what will be Interstate 73. This $31 million addition to the state's interstate system will run from Detroit to Charleston, South Carolina, and is expected to become a major thoroughfare for northern tourists traveling to the Grand Strand. But don't escalate your hopes just yet, the South Carolina portion isn't slated for construction for another decade or so, and other obstacles have recently come up. While West Virginia is busy with its portion of the highway, other states are still debating its route. Ohio is currently conducting impact studies. Conservationists are up in arms in South Carolina since the proposed route would cut a swath through the Francis Marion National Forest, and other sections infringe on historic sites and natural wetlands. Besides overcoming public objection, the state of South Carolina will have to cough up about $6 billion for its end of this interstate deal.

The Myrtle Beach International Airport is upgrading at breakneck speed. New gates, expanded flights, and added amenities are encouraging more airline traffic than ever before. PHOTO: COURTESY OF MYRTLE BEACH AREA CHAMBER OF COMMERCE

By Plane

In addition to services offered at the Myrtle Beach International Airport and the Grand Strand Airport (listed subsequently), private planes and corporate jets can access the Conway-Horry County Airport, off U.S. Highway 378, outside Conway, (843) 397-9111. The airport is home of the North American Institute of Aviation, an international pilot training school. Overnight tie down is $3.00. (See the Child Care and Education chapter for more information.)

Myrtle Beach International Airport
1100 Jetport Road, Myrtle Beach
(843) 448-1589

An $18-million renovation project recently put Myrtle Beach International Airport into the big-city league. The terminal grew from 50,000 square feet to 120,000, and an upper-level concourse was added.

Rainy days no longer bring a polite attendant with an umbrella out to the planes to walk passengers into the terminal. Two jetways now connect the planes to the terminal, so passengers need never get wet nor cold.

Scheduled jet service is provided by USAirways to and from its major hubs to nearly 200 domestic and international cities. Jet service is also provided by Atlantic Southeast Airline (ASA), a Delta connector with a number of flights daily to its hubs in Atlanta. Additionally, jet service is also provided by Continental, Midway, Spirit, and ComAir.

Direct flights to and from Myrtle Beach are available to Atlanta, Atlantic City, Buffalo, Charlotte, Chicago O'Hare, Cleveland, Detroit, Kansas City, New York Laguardia, Newark, and Raleigh, North Carolina.

Airline reservation numbers include: ASA/Delta/Comair, (800) 282-3424; Continental, (800) 525-0280; Spirit, (800) 772-7117; and USAirways, (800) 428-4322.

For private or charter aircraft, Myrtle Beach Aviation, the general fixed-base operator at Myrtle Beach International Airport, can be reached at (843) 477-1860.

You should be able to get to Myrtle Beach by air from just about anywhere in the United States. Unless you can book an express flight, you'll have to take a smaller commuter flight, probably from a major air terminal in Charlotte, North Carolina, or Atlanta.

Grand Strand Airport
33rd Avenue South and Terminal Avenue, North Myrtle Beach
(843) 272-5337

Horry County operates the Grand Strand Airport, where private aircraft and corporate jets can land. You don't have to notify anyone that you're coming, but be aware that all services close for business at 10:00 P.M.

You can leave your craft for several days while you enjoy the beach. The airport is about 1 block west of U.S. 17, pretty much in the heart of North Myrtle Beach.

The fixed-base operators at Grand Strand Airport is Ramp 66, which can be reached via telephone at (843) 272-5337

or (800) 433-8918 or via e-mail at ramp66@aol.com. Overnight tie-down is $7.00 per night. Fuel is also available.

If Ramp 66 staffers have time, and your accommodations aren't too far away, they will take you to your motel.

Ramp 66 also has its own car rental service, featuring all new cars. Customers can use a car for an hour for free. After that, it's $8.00 per hour. It also has weekly rates. If you're coming into the airport at odd hours, you need to take care of your car rental ahead of time. Ramp 66 is at your service seven days a week.

Loris–Twin Cities Airport
U.S. Highway 301

This is a public and unattended airport for training and landings for private aircraft.

Rental Cars

Eight companies including National, (800) 227-7368; Avis, (800) 831-2847; Hertz, (800) 654-3131; Budget, (800) 527-0700; Payless, (800) PAYLESS; Dollar, (800) 800-4000; and USave, (800) 441-3741, rent cars and vans at Myrtle Beach International. Other rental car offices in the Myrtle Beach area include Alamo, (800) 327-9633; Thrifty, (843) 626-6527; Rent-A-Wreck, (843) 626-9393; and Zippy Car Rental, (843) 448-1991. Coastal Cabs can take you to your hotel and provide a van by request; inquire at the Executive Coach Service booth.

By Bus

You should be able to get to Myrtle Beach on a Greyhound bus from just about any point in the United States. You'll find it easier during the summer, when more buses are scheduled. The station, at Oak Street and Seventh Avenue North, Myrtle Beach, is open from 10:00 A.M. to 2:00 P.M. and 3:30 to 7:00 P.M. Call (843) 448-2472 or (800) 231-2222 for details.

By Train

Don't count on riding the train to your Grand Strand vacation destination; Florence and Dillon are the two closest places Amtrak serves. The problem is you can't get to the Grand Strand from either of those cities unless you arrange for a vehicle or have friends who'll pick you up. If you decide to take the train to Florence or Dillon and then rent a car, there are two outlets that, with advance notice, can arrange for a vehicle to be at the station when you arrive. In Florence contact Carolina Car Rentals, (843) 665-0802; in Dillon, call Dillon Used Auto Parts Inc., (843) 774-5301.

Some folks used to ride Amtrak to Florence and catch the Greyhound bus to Myrtle Beach. However, bus service from Florence to Myrtle Beach was discontinued because not enough people used it.

Greyhound officials say it is possible that the Florence to Myrtle Beach bus will be put back into action during the tourist season, but don't count on it. They recommend calling ahead before you buy your train ticket.

By Boat

The most scenic and perhaps most peaceful way to get to the Grand Strand is by boat. The Intracoastal Waterway generally parallels the Atlantic Ocean for 1,200 miles from Boston to Key West, Florida.

In 1932 the Army Corps of Engineers dug a 20-mile canal, connecting Little River to the Waccamaw River. This portion goes right through the Grand Strand.

Boaters can tie up at Barefoot Landing for a day of shopping and dining and an evening of country music at the Alabama Theatre. There are numerous marinas along the waterway and the Waccamaw River, where boaters can spend the night, eat in a nice restaurant, buy groceries, or have their motors tuned up.

Many of the marinas have signs along the waterway telling you what CB radio channel to tune in to contact them.

Marinas along the Grand Strand include Hague Marina, just before Socastee, (843) 293-2141; Bucksport, a very popular docking spot, (843) 397-5566; Wacca Wache at Wachesaw Landing, (843) 651-2994 or (843) 651-7171 or (800)

Insiders' Tip

If you're traveling with your dog, your furry companion must be kept on a leash. In North Myrtle Beach the only beach access restrictions for pets are during the summer days, from 9:00 A.M. to 5:00 P.M. In Myrtle Beach and Surfside, sections are out of bounds for four-footed friends year-round.

395-6694; and Cedar Landing, in the Murrells Inlet area, (843) 651-8706. (See the Boating chapter for details about marinas.)

There is a city-owned marina in Conway, (843) 248-1711, on the Waccamaw River. If you're traveling south on the waterway, turn right at Enterprise Landing at Channel Marker 25. Then head north for about 9 miles. Some boaters choose this course to enjoy the river's beauty. It winds and has some sharp turns, so if your boat's length is 40 feet or more, you might not want to try it.

To navigate the waterway, it's a good idea to have a nautical chart. Such charts point out dangerous spots, marinas, and buoys and describe available services at the marinas.

You won't find the waterway as crowded as U.S. Highway 501, but it is a popular artery for travelers, recreational boaters, and water-skiers. Water routes can get crowded on weekends—especially the Waccamaw River.

The stretch between Conway and Bucksport is especially charming—a wonderful place to get back in touch with nature. Egrets build nests on the channel markers, and beautiful old trees overhang

A multitude of new road projects makes getting in and around the Grand Strand easier than ever.

PHOTO: COURTESY OF MYRTLE BEACH AREA CHAMBER OF COMMERCE

the water. If you're fortunate enough to travel at night, the moon glistens on the water, and you can spot campfires back in the woods. At times campers come to the riverbank and shout hearty hellos to the boaters.

Navigating the Strand Like a Local

Trying to navigate the Grand Strand can be a frustrating venture at first because there seem to be so many names for the same routes. You'll hear "17 Bypass," "Kings Highway," "the Boulevard" and a host of others. We're going to try to make sense of all this for you.

The first thing to remember is that all main arteries along the Grand Strand par-allel the Atlantic Ocean. Closest to the beach is Ocean Boulevard (a.k.a. the Boulevard or the 'Vard). Ocean Boulevard officially runs from Garden City Beach northward, breaks for 5 to 7 miles of pri-vate land and state park, and ends at Dunes Golf and Beach Club, 9000 Ocean Boulevard. It picks up again at 48th Av-enue South, at Windy Hill beach, and con-tinues northward to Cherry Grove beach.

Westward from Ocean Boulevard, the next main roadway is Kings Highway—commonly referred to as U.S. 17 or Busi-ness 17 (in Myrtle Beach). Kings Highway is the proper name for this road in Myrtle Beach. To make a mental note, just re-member that Kings Highway is also called "Business 17" because shops, restaurants, and attractions galore line both sides of this main artery. Kings Highway (U.S. 17) stretches the length of the Strand to Georgetown, then southward all the way through South Carolina. (*NOTE:* For this guide, we only use Kings Highway to refer to U.S. 17 Business in Myrtle Beach; otherwise, we defer to U.S. 17.)

Still moving west, you'll come across the racing traffic of U.S. 17 Bypass or Alternate 17. True to its name, this highway's purpose is to bypass traffic from Kings Highway. The Bypass reaches from Murrells Inlet northward until it merges with Kings Highway at Dixie Stampede just south of the Restaurant Row district. Once you've merged here, the road becomes U.S. 17.

If you really want to skip through town like a true native—anywhere from the Myrtle Beach International Airport to 48th Avenue North, in Myrtle Beach—here's how:

Leaving the Myrtle Beach International Airport, take the first right turn onto South Broadway (road signs read S.C. 15). As you proceed, South Broadway will turn into West Broadway at the stoplights. Keep in the center lanes that allow you to travel straight through this original downtown section of Myrtle Beach until you reach the third set of stoplights; then get in the left-turn lane. Turning left will put you on Oak Street; you'll wind through town to 38th Avenue North. Go straight through the 38th Avenue stoplights onto Pine Lakes Drive and pass through a lovely old residential section of Myrtle Beach all the way to 48th Avenue North.

Getting around in Myrtle Beach is easier thanks to the widening of 21st Avenue North between Kings Highway and U.S. 17 Bypass. Another project widened Oak Street to five lanes—four travel lanes and a turn lane—from 21st Avenue North at the Myrtle Beach Convention Center to 29th Avenue North. From 29th Avenue North to 38th Avenue North, the road was widened to three lanes—two travel lanes and a turn lane. The project also included the addition of curbs, gutters, and sidewalks. The Robert M. Grissom Parkway is a brand-new four-lane route from 48th Avenue North in Myrtle Beach to Harrelson Boulevard near the airport.

Several years ago the state pledged more than half a million dollars for road construction in Horry County. Veterans Highway is already open and the following projects are slated for the near future:

- constructing a Carolina Bays Parkway that will add four lanes from S.C. 9 to a bridge across the Intracoastal Waterway near 62nd Avenue North;
- constructing a Conway Perimeter Road between U.S. 378 and U.S. 501;
- completing a cloverleaf bypass from U.S. 501 to U.S. 17 Bypass;
- converting S.C. 544 to five lanes from Socastee to Conway;
- installing intersection improvements on U.S. 501, S.C. 90, and Secondary Roads 31 and 66;
- adding frontage roads from Forestbrook Road to the Intracoastal Waterway; and
- completing the Robert M. Grissom Parkway and an overpass above U.S. 501 at Waccamaw Pottery.

The wishes of residents and visitors who have long hoped for new and better roads along the Grand Strand are clearly being granted. The $900 million worth of

Insiders' Tip

Thanks to new milepost markers being installed along the length of U.S. 17 Business and Bypass, finding businesses and landmarks along the Grand Strand soon will be easier. The project will begin on the southern end of the Grand Strand with milepost marker number 185 at the Georgetown County line. It will end with number 221 at the North Carolina line. Numbered markers will be installed along both U.S. 17 Business and Bypass.

road construction means the process of traveling from one place to another is changing faster than a speeding bullet. For detailed and current project information, visit www.cityofmyrtlebeach.com.

Taxis

For easy, accessible travel it's always best to have an automobile when exploring the Grand Strand. Let's face it, to cover 60 miles of territory, any other mode of transportation will take considerable time. But there's nothing more expedient than a cab to simply get from point A to point B in good time. We warn you that taxi fares are not cheap around here. To give you an idea of the usual cost, a trip from Myrtle Beach International Airport to a Myrtle Beach destination around 21st Avenue North costs approximately $15. Try any of the following companies for service: American Cab, (843) 626–2222 or (843) 249–4909; Coastal Cab, (843) 448–4444; Race Cab, (843) 444–4000; or Southern Flyer Taxi, (843) 361–2464.

Public Transit

Once you're in Myrtle Beach, you might want to walk or ride Waccamaw Regional Transportation Authority's Lymo, (843) 488–0865. Lymo has more than 80 vehicles, including streetcars and buses, and offers service seven days a week, 364 days a year, with a fare of only $1.00. Lymo buses travel on 22 routes servicing the Coastal Carolina region, including Myrtle Beach, North Myrtle Beach, Surfside Beach, Conway, Loris, and Aynor. You'll find plenty of information on regular routes and schedules on the Lymo Web site at www. golymo.com.

History

20th-Century Myrtle Beach

Vacation Time

Even though the name Myrtle Beach has been around for less than 100 years, people have been enjoying the Grand Strand area for a few centuries, from the original Native American inhabitants to visiting dignitaries such as George Washington, to today's vacationers. Despite all the new development that obscures much of this history, you could say we're keeping up a historic seaside tradition by maintaining the Grand Strand as one of the East Coast's favorite getaways.

Long before Europeans landed on these shores, what is now U.S. Highway 17 and the section of it known as Kings Highway began as an Indian trail. It then evolved into a stagecoach route from Northern colonies (eventually states) to Charleston and Savannah. After his election, George Washington used the route and lodgings along the way (for more details about his journey, see the Close-up in this chapter). The Waccamaw and Winyah Indians were the area's first inhabitants and now lend their names to the rivers and bays here. The Indians called this land *Chicora*, which means the Land. The Horry County Museum in Conway (see the Attractions chapter for more details) has exhibits detailing their way of life. Additionally, an Indian burial mound is on Waites Island near Little River. In fact, Indian artifacts have been unearthed all along the Carolinas' coast.

As early as the 1520s, Europeans were attempting to settle this area, but it wasn't until the 1700s that things got exciting. Even before the American Revolution, pirates made good use of the bays and inlets of the Grand Strand. To this day locals relish stories about Blackbeard marauding local shippers and rumors that Captain Kidd buried treasure somewhere around Murrells Inlet. Edgar Allen Poe's novella *The Gold Bug* is a fantastic account of good old South Carolinian treasure hunting.

Georgetown is the state's third oldest port city. The city was planned by English colonists in 1730 and quickly became the center of America's colonial rice empire. *A Woman Rice Planter* is a fascinating personal account by Elizabeth Allston Pringle of her struggles to maintain her rice plantation after the Civil War ended and changed the plantation system irrevocably. The colonial spirit of Georgetown is preserved in many still-standing plantations; Hopsewee Plantation is the birthplace of Thomas Lynch Jr., a signer of the Declaration of Independence.

Pawleys Island, just north of Georgetown, is the original vacation spot for this area and one of the first resorts in the United States. A half-mile wide and 4-miles long, the island is abundant with oleander and oak trees pressed in between the old summer cottages. Pringle wrote of Pawleys Island, "To me it has always been intoxicating, that first view each year of the waves rolling, rolling, and the smell of the sea, and the brilliant blue expanse."

Also on the south end of the Grand Strand, Murrells Inlet is the oldest fishing village in the state. It is home to anglers, writers, poets, legends, and ghost stories. The area's history, much like a Southern romantic novel, recounts stories of pirates patrolling the seaside, aristocratic plantation owners accumulating immense wealth, the daughter of a U.S. vice president being forced to walk the plank of a pirate ship, phantom lighthouses steering ships from storms, and cemetery-walking ghosts searching for lost lovers. The Spanish moss laden oak trees do nothing but encourage these stories.

The story of Alice Belin Flagg is probably the most romantically tragic. Alice was caught in the traditional dilemma of the upper-class belle in love with a beau her family did not approve of. Her beau presented her with an engagement ring, but since she couldn't wear it on her finger, she wore it on a ribbon around her neck, where it was eventually discovered by her brother, who ripped it off and threw it into the creek on their plantation. Of course Alice pined away for the ring of her forbidden beau and died for want of true love.

Until the 1900s the beaches north of Murrells Inlet were practically uninhabited because of geographical inaccessibility and the poor economy. In what is now Restaurant Row at the north end of Myrtle Beach, a salt-making operation with more than 30 buildings was destroyed during the Civil War. The area later became the first campground in the area, mostly for people from Conway, and is still used as a campground today.

Alice's resting place is well tended. PHOTO: LISA TOMER RENTZ

20th-Century Myrtle Beach

The creation of Myrtle Beach as we know it began during the first part of the 20th century when F. A. Burroughs bought some timberland several miles inland from the South Carolina coast. In a story that rings with as much irony as buying Manhattan Island for beads and trinkets,

the owners of the timberland would only agree to sell if Burroughs would agree also to buy the "worthless" coastal land as part of the same deal. So Burroughs was stuck with that property, too. Confounded at the worthlessness of the area, called Long Bay, Burroughs sought to find a way to add value to the sandy strip.

Meanwhile, the towns of Cherry Grove and Windy Hill had been well-established. In an effort to find funding to develop the beach area into a resort to outclass Pawleys Island, Burroughs contacted a New York stockbroker named S. G. Chapin. To help with the effort, Burroughs' wife gave the area a more attractive name: Myrtle Beach, for the rows of myrtle trees growing along the coastline. Chapin was at first interested, but his wife was so adamant about not wanting to live in the wilderness that he was prepared to reject the idea outright. But after meeting, the two men became such good friends that they decided to go forward with the project. Thus in 1912 Myrtle Beach Farms Inc.—and the future of the Grand Strand—was born.

Although the area's first motel, Seaside Inn, was constructed in 1901 (under the direction of F. A.'s son, F. G. Burroughs), the rich and famous were not flocking to the beach. In fact, except for members of the Burroughs or Chapin extended families, there were very few visitors; Burroughs did convince some relatives to buy lots from him (at $25 each) to build resort cottages.

Following the Pawleys Island lead, the two entrepreneurs coaxed a wealthy textile magnate to build a resort playground hotel for the rich and famous. This 1925 venture, which included Myrtle Beach's first golf course, fizzled with the stock market crash of 1929. The result was the luxurious Ocean Forest Hotel, featuring

George Washington Tours the Grand Strand

Just as millions of people do every year now, George Washington toured the Grand Strand in 1791. Two years after he was elected president, George Washington wanted to visit the new states "to become better acquainted with their principal characters and internal circumstances as well as to be more accessible to numbers of well-informed persons who might give useful information and advice on political subjects." He also wished "to acquire knowledge of the face of the country, the growth and agriculture thereof; and the temper and disposition of the inhabitants toward the new government."

As you read Washington's comments, note that many of the family names he mentions are still in use today: Mrs. Horry (Horry County), Vereen (Vereen Marina and Vereen Park), Pawley (Pawleys Island). Also, we've preserved the president's spelling for historical flavor.

Washington followed the same road we take almost every day; in fact the section of U.S. Highway 17 that runs through Myrtle Beach is known as Kings Highway in his honor (the former colonists weren't quite comfortable with the new title of president). While he toured the coast, he saw the condition of the people at all levels of society, staying at public houses when possible and paying for his accommodations when allowed. When William Washington of South Carolina offered him use of a Charleston town house, President Washington declined. "I cannot," he wrote, "without involving myself in inconsistency; as I have determined to pursue the same plan in my Southern as I did in my Eastern visit, which was not to incommode any private family by taking up my quarters with them during my journey. It leaves me unencumbered by engagements, and by uniform adherence to it, I shall avoid giving umbrage to any, by declining all such invitations."

Even though it's the same road, the Carolina coast was much different for Washington: " . . . the country from Wilmington through which the road passes . . . is pine barrens with very few inhabitants . . . a perfect sameness seems to run through all the rest of the Country. On [the rivers] especially the swamps and low lands on the rivers, the soil is very rich; and productive when reclaimed. . . . " Obviously this president did not need to travel with a motorcade.

His accommodations were equally as rural. "Excepting the Towns (and some Gentlemens Seats along the Road from Charleston to Savanna) there is not with in view of the whole road I travelled from Petersburgh to this place, a single house which has anythh. [sic] of an elegant appearance— They are altogether of Wood and chiefly of logs— some indd. [sic] have brick chimneys but generally the chimneys are of split sticks filled with dirt. . . . The accommodations on the whole Road (except in the Towns and even there, as I was prepared for I had no opportunity of Judging, lodgings having been provided for me in them at my own expence) we found extremely indifferent the houses being small and badly provided either for man or horse; though extra exertions when it became known I was coming, wch. was generally the case, were made to receive me."

Washington found his constituents to be prospering. "The people however appear to have abundant means to live well the grounds where they are settled yielding grain in abundance and the natural herbage a multitude of mean with little or no labr. to provide food for the support of their stock. . . . The manner of the people, as far as my observations, and means of information extended, were orderly and Civil. and they appeared to be happy, contented and satisfied with the genl. [sic.] government under which they were placed."

Washington's first stop in South Carolina was at James Cochran's house, which stood in what is now the town of Little River near the intersection of Minneola Avenue and U.S. 17. Of course most of the places where Washington stopped at are now gone, but a few in the South Strand do remain; keep reading to find out where.

"April 27 . . . lodged at Mr. Vareens 14 miles more and two miles short of the long bay. To his house we were directed as a Tavern, but the proprietor of it either did not keep one, or would not acknowledge it. We were therefore entertained (& very kindly) without being able to make compensation."

The house of Jeremiah Vereen Sr. stood near the intersection of what is now U.S. 17 and Lake Arrowhead Road in Restaurant Row. The Vereens kept a public house for many years—possibly the progenitor of all the restaurants to follow?

"April 28, Mr. Vareen piloted us across the Swash (which at high water is impassable, & at times, by the shifting of the Sands is dangerous) onto the long Beach of the Ocean; and it being at a proper time of the tide we passed along it with ease and celerity to the place of quitting it which is estimated at 16 miles. . . . "

This swash referred to by Washington is probably Singleton's Swash, which enters the ocean just north of Myrtle Beach at the Dunes Golf and Beach Club.

"April 28 . . . Five Miles farther we got dinner & fed our horses at a Mr. Pauleys a private house, no public one being on the road. . . . "

Five miles past Singleton's Swash, Washington stopped at George Pawley's house. Pawley was also a government official; he had been in the First and Second Provincial Congresses (1775, 1775–1776) and in the First General Assembly (1776). He served as justice of the peace in 1765 and 1774 and as a colonel in the militia around 1775.

"April 28 . . . being on the Road, & kindly invited by a Doctor Flagg to his house, we lodged there; it being about 10 miles from Pauleys & 33 from Vareens."

Dr. Henry Collins Flagg (1746–1801) married Rachel Moore Allston, the widow of William Allston of Brookgreen Plantation on Waccamaw Neck, in 1784. The site of the house in which Washington stayed is now occupied by the Alligator Pool fountain at Brookgreen Gardens.

"April 29 . . . We left Dr. Flagg's about 6 oclock and arrived at Captn. Wm. Alstons' on the Waggamaw [sic.] to Breakfast."

Clifton Plantation, the home of William Alston (1756–1839), stood on the banks of the Waccamaw River on Waccamaw Neck. He and his new wife, Mary Motte, entertained Washington for breakfast at Clifton Plantation.

Now part of Arcadia Plantation, Clifton then "looked like fairyland" to Washington. "His house which is large, new, and elegantly furnished, stands on a sand hill, high for the Country, with his Rice fields below; the contrast of which with the lands back of it . . . is scarcely to be conceived."

"April 30 . . . Crossed the Waggamaw to Georgetown by descending the River three miles. At this place we were recd. under a Salute of Cannon, & by a Company of Infantry handsomely uniformed. I dined with the Citizens in public and in the afternoon, was introduced to upwards of 50 ladies who had assembled (at a Tea party) on the occasion." This is a party we would have loved to attended.

"Seven captains of vessels, dressed in round hats trimmed with gold lace, blue coats, white jackets . . . in an elegant painted boat" rowed George Washington across the river to Georgetown. Thirteen rounds of fire, one for each state of the Union, saluted his arrival, and he was escorted to his lodgings, reportedly the house of Benjamin Allston on Front Street. Locals now maintain that this is the same Adam-style brick house with a hipped roof that stands on a raised basement and faces the Sampit River at 1019 Front Street in Georgetown.

"May 1 . . . Left Georgetown about 6 Oclock, and crossing the Santee Creek [Sampit River] at the Town and the Santee River 12 miles from it . . . we breakfasted and dined at Mrs. Horry's about 15 Miles from Georgetown. . . . "

Another historic site you can visit, Hampton Plantation, was the home of Daniel Horry II. The original house was a 11/2-story central-hall structure. After 1757 Daniel Horry enlarged the house to its present size, and the wide portico and pediment were added to the front of the house around 1790. Called Hampton by 1769, it was a working rice plantation. Harriott Pickney Horry and her mother, Eliza Lucas Pickney, greeted Washington in 1791 when he stopped at Hampton for breakfast. The ladies "were arrayed in sashes and bandeaux painted with the general's portrait and mottoes of welcome."

Hampton Plantation State Historic Site is open to the public; see the Parks and Recreation chapter for more details.

From there Washington continued this inaugural journey to Charleston and Savannah. The South Carolina Department of Archives and History in Columbia has a more detailed record of this momentous journey; while you're in the Grand Strand, however, you can take the time to enjoy the same splendors of the coast that George Washington did.

chandeliers and an enormous ballroom in a classic high-rise (for the time) Old World hotel. The Ocean Forest ultimately was demolished in 1974.

The corporation continued to operate small hotels and cottages, rent and sell land, and develop beachfront attractions until the 1954 destruction wrought by Hurricane Hazel, and the dream to attract the rich and famous went on a back shelf in favor of survival . . . a survival that was supported by becoming an inexpensive beach for working-class families.

Vacation Time

From 1954 through the 1980s, a rebuilt Myrtle Beach—with a new boardwalk and modernized pavilion replacing the 1909 bathhouses and 1912 amusements building—remained a small summer beach resort for a few hundred thousand blue-collar families from North and South Carolina. Myrtle Beach was a minor destination dotted with small mom-and-pop hotels,

amusement parks, and minor regional attractions. Myrtle Beach had indeed grown into a modest and pleasant resort.

Hurricane Hugo hit in 1989, but again the Grand Strand rebounded. Building and rebuilding has become more than a hobby around here, and dozens of ambitious projects are always under way. The number of golf courses has reached more than 115. Barefoot Landing, formerly Village of the Barefoot Traders, expanded over a scenic marsh and set the precedent for a new, natural Myrtle Beach as opposed to the harsh neon that glowed in the 1980s. Broadway at the Beach opened in 1995 and successfully combines both glitzy and charming features for an all-day experience. This growth has anchored the Strand even more solidly as a major tourist destination and has been accompanied by many smaller and just-as-worthwhile establishments opening up throughout the Grand Strand area.

Currently, roughly fourteen million visitors relax here annually. People still come to get away from their busy, land-

Bikers and shaggers and classic cars have been crowding the Ocean Drive section of North Myrtle Beach in the spring for more than 50 years. PHOTO: LISA TOMER RENTZ

locked lives just as generations before have. Though we now have all the modern conveniences (some days you just can't do without air-conditioning) and distrac-tions (using up a roll of quarters at the ar-cade can be so satisfying), we're still here for the same reason: those rolling, rolling waves.

Accommodations

Considering that the Grand Strand offers literally thousands of accommodations for visitors, we have tried to narrow the scope to those establishments that consistently get positive reviews from the public. That's not to say that all others are dank tenements, but the numbers are far too vast to bring all the players into this arena. Lodging is in such demand along the Grand Strand that new facilities are being built as fast as you can turn these pages, and smaller mom-and-pop hotels are abundant here. Some locals have quipped that the construction crane should be designated the official bird of the Grand Strand.

It's safe to say that 95 percent of the hotels, motels, and condominiums on the Grand Strand line both sides of Ocean Boulevard, the road that parallels the Atlantic Ocean from North Myrtle Beach to Surfside Beach and becomes Waccamaw Drive in Garden City. Don't be confused if you're riding along, in awe of the hundreds of lodging marquees, and the road suddenly jogs west to U.S. Highway 17 Business. A couple of miles of private property separate North Myrtle Beach from Myrtle Beach, and you'll find several campgrounds between Myrtle Beach and the end of the South Strand.

A Room with a View

Properties closest to the beach are considered oceanfront. Properties with an ocean-view refer to rooms that have a view of the ocean but do not directly face it (on the side of the building) or, in some cases, rooms not on the east side of Ocean Boulevard. Rooms with a balcony or walkway are referred to as rooms with a side-view. You might also run across terms such as poolside or streetside that denote a room's location within the property. Be sure to ask specific questions about the location of your room when confirming your reservation.

About Pets

Those of you who travel with your pets might find it difficult to rent a room.

The city of Myrtle Beach passed an ordinance that prohibits animals of any kind in the downtown area from March 1 through September 30. It seems there was a problem with folks bringing their pets and other exotic animals (boa constrictors, ferrets, iguanas) down to the heavily populated Pavilion area, causing quite a stir with other pedestrians. The law was passed to mitigate any potential accidents or incidents caused by the animals.

Regarding Reservations

Like most resort areas, be prepared to make a deposit when calling in your reservation. It is required by the majority of properties and will be credited to your bill. Generally, a deposit equals a day's rent. To avoid hassles, use credit cards, cash, or traveler's checks to pay for everything; most local banks will not cash out-of-town personal checks unless you have an account with them or enough picture identification to satisfy the FBI on a manhunt. Vital reservation information includes the time you plan to arrive, the number in your party, the length of your stay, and the date you plan to depart.

Although rooms are plentiful, the Strand's population swells to almost four times its year-round size in the heat of summer, and all of these people need a place to lay their weary heads. Think twice about driving to the beach and "finding" a room, especially in the middle of the night. The tourism season blooms like the flowers each spring and peaks like the hot noonday sun each summer. As the autumn leaves fall, so do lodging rates; and in wintertime, snowbirds flock to the beach for cheap, cheap rates. In the 1960s and 1970s, most businesses rolled up the sidewalk from Labor Day until Easter. That is a practice of the past. As the Grand Strand is quickly becoming a year-round resort, the majority of properties remain open throughout the year.

Hotels and Motels

These accommodations are listed according to location, beginning on the North Strand and ranging southward through Myrtle Beach and the South Strand. In accordance with the Americans With Disabilities Act, all of these properties should be wheelchair-accessible; establishments must comply to stay in business. Keep in mind when making reservations that most accommodations offer at least a 10 percent discount if you're staying a week or longer. Most also offer senior citizen, travel club, and group discounts as well. Always ask about any special rates or entitlements.

On any given evening, there are approximately 60,000 rooms available on the Grand Strand—ranging from hotels, motels, and condos to time-share units. But even with so much capacity, there's apparently still room for more growth in the market. Annual occupancy rates are still on the rise and new accommodations continue to climb skyward.

Unless otherwise indicated all accommodations listed in this chapter accept at least Visa and MasterCard as methods of payment. Inquire about alternative options when you make your reservation.

Please note that we have also indicated establishments that provide baby-sitters or referrals for such services.

Have a pleasant and comfortable stay.

Price Code

The dollar-sign key used with each listing is based on the average room rate for two people (at least two double beds) per night in the middle of July, when hotel and motel rates are at their highest. This average rate was determined by taking into account all the types of lodging available at each property. Weekends and holidays always command a higher room rate.

$	$68 to $93
$$	$94 to $120
$$$	$121 to $145
$$$$	$146 to $171
$$$$$	$172 and up

North Strand

Blockade Runner Motor Inn $
1910 North Ocean Boulevard,
North Myrtle Beach
(843) 249–3561
www.blockaderunner-sc.com

On the oceanfront in the popular Ocean Drive section of North Myrtle Beach, the Blockade Runner offers 72 two-bed units, including efficiencies, all overlooking the ocean. In addition to an oceanfront pool and kiddie pool, guests can also enjoy the Jacuzzi and a delicious meal in the on-premises restaurant. The restaurant is open from 6:00 A.M. to 2:30 P.M. every day. Golf specials are offered from Labor Day through June 1.

Buccaneer Motel $
401 South Ocean Boulevard,
North Myrtle Beach
(843) 249–1466, (800) 548–7552

Ahoy mates, you've landed at the Buccaneer Motel, a very affordable place for families looking for one-room efficiencies or two-room apartments on the beach. If the ocean isn't for you, then splash around in the pool or in the hot tub. The Buccaneer has 37 newly remodeled rooms, and kids age twelve and younger stay free.

Helms Vista Family Motel and Apartments $
300 North Ocean Boulevard,
North Myrtle Beach
(843) 249–2521, (800) 968–8986
www.helmsvista.com

This small, friendly-looking oceanfront property offers 77 rooms, suites, and

Marsh, ocean, river, and beautiful vistas abound. You may be surprised at the diversity of the South Carolina Lowcountry. PHOTO: COURTESY OF MYRTLE BEACH AREA CHAMBER OF COMMERCE

apartments to guests looking for an affordable place to lay their heads. Each room has a refrigerator. Special package deals include golf, live entertainment, deep-sea fishing, and dinner cruises. In addition to a kiddie pool, the motel has two regular-size pools and a hot tub. The Helms Vista is within walking distance of North Myrtle Beach's finest restaurants and dance clubs.

Lake Shore Motel $
1443 Highway 17, Little River
(843) 249–1653, (800) 500–8508

The Lake Shore Motel has 20 spacious rooms featuring double and king-size beds. Each room is equipped with a refrigerator and cable TV. Championship golf, deep-sea fishing, excellent restaurants, and the beautiful beaches of the Grand Strand are all just minutes away. After enjoying the activities and attrac-

tions, you can relax by the motel pool or try the fishing on the lake.

Ocean Creek Plantation Resort & Conference Center $$$$$
10600 North Kings Highway,
North Myrtle Beach
(843) 272–7724, (800) 845–0353
www.oceancreek.com

Ocean Creek Plantation is one of the grandest resorts along the beach. The luxurious accommodations (435 in all) include studios and one-, two-, and three-bedroom condominiums in six separate complexes. The resort's oceanfront beach club features a large outdoor pool, sundecks, and a poolside bar. In 1996 the resort's beach club added a kiddie pool, playground, and volleyball court.

Guests can enjoy fine dining at the Four Seasons restaurant if they don't want to leave the property. Supervised activities for the kids are available in summer months, freeing parents for a little private vacation time. The resort also features seven on-site lighted tennis courts and extends guest privileges at a majority of area golf courses. Ocean Creek staff consider the finest details whether hosting a family of four or a conference for hundreds.

San-A-Bel Resort $$$$
1709 South Ocean Boulevard,
North Myrtle Beach
(843) 272–2079, (800) 458–9945

San-A-Bel offers 97 two-bedroom, two-bath condominiums. Each unit has a full kitchen with microwave and dishwasher as well as a washer and dryer adjoining the kitchen area. The beautiful indoor heated pool features expansive skylights and glass walls for unobstructed views of the ocean. Outside, a large wooden sundeck surrounds the whirlpool—a relaxing haven after a workout in the fitness room.

Sea Trail Resort & Golf Links $$$
211 Clubhouse Road, Sunset Beach, NC
(910) 287–1157, (888) 229–5747
www.seatrail.com

Not many resorts in the coastal region can offer three golf courses in their backyards. Sea Trail offers this and much more. The resort, midway between Myrtle Beach and Wilmington, North Carolina, welcomes guests looking for exclusive living. You can rent any one of the 324 villas, either with one, two, three, or four bedrooms. Each is complete with two full bathrooms, a fully equipped kitchen, living and dining areas, and a balcony overlooking the fairways.

Sea Trail is a perfect venue for biking, jogging, and nature walks. In 2002 Sea Trail opened the Museum of Coastal Carolina Ingram Planetarium, a 90-seat theater with a 40-foot projection dome. The Village Activity Center provides swimming pools, a sauna, whirlpool spas, a fitness room, and lighted tennis courts. A year-round activities director coordinates events for adults and children alike. Sea Trail keeps an updated list of reliable baby-sitters in the area, which the staff can refer you to.

Sea Trail has 70,000-plus square feet of meeting and function space, making it the largest conference facility on the North Carolina coast.

This off-the-beaten-path getaway spans more than 2,000 acres and offers two restaurants. Golf packages and an on-site golf school are also available.

The Seaside Inn $$
2301 South Ocean Boulevard, North Myrtle Beach
(843) 272–5166, (800) 433–5710
www.seasideinnmb.com

The Seaside Inn provides about 56 units; half are oceanfront. The rooms are clean and modest but provide all the comforts of home: microwaves, refrigerators, card tables, and remote-control TVs. Some Seaside units have sleeper sofas as well. Golf and entertainment packages are available, and there's a bonus for group leaders. The group leader who brings 10 players gets free lodging; one who brings along 20 players also receives a free golf package. By the way, there are about 25 golf courses within a 15-minute drive. Other features include a pool and hot tub, both of which are covered for comfortable use during the cooler temperatures of winter. The Seaside Inn is close to Barefoot Landing and also offers show packages at various theaters throughout town.

Myrtle Beach

Anderson Inn $
2600 North Ocean Boulevard, Myrtle Beach
(843) 448–1535, (800) 437–7376
www.andersoninn.com

You'll enjoy a stay at the Anderson Inn, a family-owned and -operated property. On the oceanfront it houses 112 units ranging from efficiency rooms to suites and singles. Rooms with fully equipped kitchens are available. The children will be amazed at the custom-built kiddie pool—the largest of its kind in the area. Other features include two more oceanfront pools, an indoor heated pool, an indoor Jacuzzi, and an exercise room, too.

Anderson Inn is in the center of Myrtle Beach, close to grocery stores, malls, enter-

Whether you stay in a cozy oceanside inn or a fancy downtown hotel, you can always expect a hearty dose of Southern hospitality. PHOTO: COURTESY OF BRANDON ADVERTISING

tainment, and restaurants. If you'd rather not venture out, don't worry: You won't go hungry with the Magnolia Cafe on the premises. The staff at the Anderson Inn also coordinates golf packages.

Atlantic Paradise Inn $
1401 South Ocean Boulevard, Myrtle Beach
(843) 444-0346, (800) 992-0269
www.atlanticparadise.com

Nothing fancy, but the 74 two-room apartments and efficiencies of Atlantic Paradise offer your family an affordable

vacation at the beach. Amenities include an oceanfront pool with deck, a kiddie pool, and an indoor whirlpool. Golf and country-music packages are available.

Beach Colony Resort $$$
5308 North Ocean Boulevard, Myrtle Beach
(843) 449-4010, (800) 222-2141
www.beachcolony.com

This resort has everything you'll need for a great vacation. Beach Colony is home to 218 vacation units that include oceanfront suites, two-, three-, and four-bedroom condominiums, and oceanview studios. Guests may dine in the restaurant or relax in the lounge. For water other than the ocean, the resort has a kiddie pool, two outdoor pools, an indoor pool, and indoor and outdoor whirlpools for winding down. An exercise room, saunas, and a racquetball center offer you options for working up a sweat. The Carolina Room at Beach Colony can accommodate up to 180 people for meeting or event purposes, and the Azalea Room can take in up to 60 guests. The resort also has a multilevel, covered parking garage.

In summer 1995 Beach Colony opened another tower that features 77 two-bedroom, oceanview condominiums. While they were at it, they added an outdoor Lazy River water ride and an arcade.

This resort is home to Fusco's, a wonderful Italian restaurant that serves one of the area's only Sunday brunch buffets. The folks at Beach Colony can refer guests to reputable baby-sitters.

Best Inn and Suites $$$$$
703 South Ocean Boulevard, Myrtle Beach
(843) 626–3610, (800) 255–5954
www.hotels.bestinn.com

This oceanfront hotel has a great location within a short walking distance to the Family Kingdom Amusement Park area, stores, bars, and restaurants. With 122 units in all, Best Inn and Suites offers sideview rooms and efficiencies, two-room suites, oceanfront accommodations that include efficiencies, and three-room penthouses.

There's an indoor pool, kiddie pool, and whirlpool, an oceanfront sundeck, a social area, and video game room. Golf and entertainment packages are available.

Best Western Grand Strand Inn and Suites
$$
1804 South Ocean Boulevard, Myrtle Beach
(843) 448–1461, (800) 433–1461
www.grandstrandmotel.com

This Best Western is located across the boulevard from the ocean and is a property that mainly caters to families and couples. Grand Strand staff takes pride in the cleanliness and value of their property.

Ninety-six units are available, ranging from single rooms to one-, two-, three-, and four-bedroom efficiencies, on up to luxury penthouse suites. There's even a three-bedroom, fully equipped cottage, which can be perfect lodging for an extended family vacation.

A large sundeck beckons guests to partake of the renowned Carolina sunshine—take a quick dive into the swimming pool for instant cool-offs. Just ask the front desk and they will be happy to arrange a scuba, golf, or entertainment package for you. Laundry facilities are available.

Breakers Resort Hotel & North Tower $$$$
2700 North Ocean Boulevard, Myrtle Beach
(843) 444–4444, (800) 952–4507
www.breakers.com

Staying at the Breakers has been a family tradition for generations; now the Breakers has an adjoining North Tower to accommodate even more vacationing families and golfers in brand-new two- and three-bedroom abodes. This property boasts more than 470 units based on more than 20 room plans. Typical rooms feature two beds facing the ocean, or you can choose from two- or three-room suites with fully equipped kitchens. Honeymoon, golf, and family packages are house specialties. During the summer season kids can take part in various

Insiders' Tip

After unpacking your bags in the room, it's always a good idea to discuss an emergency evacuation and meeting plan with the family in the event of fire, earthquake, or other disaster. Make sure the kids know where the emergency exits are located.

planned activities while their parents enjoy oceanfront dining or drinks in the Top-of-the-Green Lounge. This resort also sports one indoor and three outdoor swimming pools.

Near downtown Myrtle Beach, the Breakers is accessible to numerous shops, restaurants, and attractions. Ample parking is available, and that's hard to come by at most uptown places. The front desk can assist families with a baby-sitting referral service. Wheelchair-accessible facilities are provided in the main tower only.

Cadillac Court $$
2202 North Ocean Boulevard, Myrtle Beach
(843) 448–5143, (800) 525–1371
www.cadillaccourt.com

Choose from an array of units at the Cadillac (82 in total), including one- and two-bedroom efficiencies, two-room suites, and three- or four-bedroom apartments. A small cafe on the premises opens at 9:00 A.M. for breakfast and stays open until the last appetite of the night is satisfied. Amenities include an outdoor oceanfront pool, a kiddie pool, and a rooftop pool and Jacuzzi. The exercise room is open to all guests, and a game of shuffleboard can be scared up across the street.

Captain's Quarters Resort $$$
901 South Ocean Boulevard, Myrtle Beach
(843) 448–1404, (800) 843–3561

Although the Captain's Quarters Resort has been around for many years, the management continues to keep up with the times by expanding and renovating the property when needed. (Many newer hotels should look this good on their opening day!) There are 373 units: efficiency apartments, one-bedroom and two-room suites. The family can splash about in one of 11 pools and whirlpools. The resort's recreation center features an extra-large arcade, so bring lots of quarters. The on-site Captain's Restaurant serves breakfast, lunch (until 1:00 P.M.), or dinner. Guests also have access to laundry facilities. Golf privileges are offered at more than 70 championship courses in the area, so pack your clubs. The staff of Captain's Quarters will happily refer families to trusted baby-sitters.

Insiders' Tip

During the winter months, traffic on Ocean Boulevard is especially light, making it a pleasant option to Kings Highway.

Caravelle Resort Hotel & Villas $$$
6900 North Ocean Boulevard, Myrtle Beach
(843) 918–8000, (800) 785–4460
www.thecaravelle.com

To accommodate the ever-increasing demand for places to stay, the Caravelle added the Villas tower more than 10 years ago. The main hotel offers about 300 units, and the tower has 56 efficiencies. The two-room oceanfront executive suites feature kitchens and queen-size beds. Efficiencies include full kitchens with microwaves and queen- or king-size beds. In June 1997 Caravelle opened a second tower with 170 oceanview deluxe suites and oceanfront rooms and efficiencies.

Amenities featured between the buildings include several pools, a game room, an exercise room, and a restaurant. Adults and children love the Lazy River pool, where you grab an oversized inner tube and glide along the course of the ride. Now the complex has two kid-friendly Lazy Rivers and a kiddie pool. Golf and entertainment packages are available.

Carolina Winds $$$
200 76th Avenue North, Myrtle Beach
(843) 449–2477, (800) 523–4027
www.carolinawinds.com

Carolina Winds is known for its fine condominiums and guest suites—147 units in all. This oceanfront property is away from the hustle and bustle of downtown and features everything you'll need for a luxurious visit. Guests can take a dip in the 120-foot-long oceanfront pool and wind down in the Lazy River. An on-site sauna is available for visitors. Jacuzzis and hot tubs are added attractions, as are golf packages. If guests require baby-sitting services, the staff has a list of referrals.

Most of the area's accommodations boast plenty of amenities for fun away from the ocean. PHOTO: COURTESY OF BRANDON ADVERTISING

Compass Cove Ocean Resort $$$
2311 South Ocean Boulevard, Myrtle Beach
(843) 448–8373, (800) 331–0934
www.compasscove.com

Newly renovated and conveniently located near the center of Myrtle Beach, the famous Compass Cove Oceanfront Resort has been entertaining Grand Strand visitors for generations. With more than 530 luxurious units including one-, two-, and three-bedroom condominiums and 720 feet of oceanfront beach, Compass Cove is one of the area's largest resort hotels and offers a wide array of guest-pleasing amenities. Highlighting these amenities are 21 pool features, including 6 indoor and outdoor pools, 3 indoor and outdoor Lazy Rivers, Jacuzzi hot tubs, and kiddie pools—truly a water wonderland! A variety of golf, entertainment, and family packages are available.

Coral Beach Resort $$$$
1105 South Ocean Boulevard, Myrtle Beach
(843) 448–8421, (800) 843–2684
www.coral-beach.com

With 301 units and plenty of amenities, Coral Beach is definitely one of the trendiest and largest resorts on the beach. Accommodations include standard rooms, efficiencies, and two-room suites.

Coral Beach is one of the only resorts on the beach that houses an arcade, complete with a bowling alley. Children are entertained with supervised activities offered from June through August. Other amenities include in-room safes, complete kitchens in all efficiencies and suites, a steam room, saunas, and three whirlpools.

Did we say pools? How about two outdoor heated pools, kiddie pools, a Lazy River ride, and a pool bar. In addition to a full-service restaurant, guests may enjoy cocktails and entertainment in Mac-Divot's Clubhouse lounge.

Court Capri $$
2610 North Ocean Boulevard, Myrtle Beach
(843) 448–6119, (800) 533–1338
www.courtcapri.com

If for no other reason, we had to include this motel since it's the only one along the Grand Strand with a rooftop heart-shaped whirlpool and sundeck! Needless to say, Court Capri offers honeymoon packages. Rooms and one- or two-bedroom efficiencies can be booked as well as extensive golf packages. The Capri also offers guests an indoor pool, indoor whirlpool, Jacuzzi, kiddie pool, exercise facilities, and a full-service restaurant.

Crown Reef Resort $$$$
2913 South Ocean Boulevard, Myrtle Beach
(843) 626–8077, (800) 405–7333
www.crownreef.com

All 514 units in this beautiful motel are oceanfront, with balconies overlooking 125 feet of beach and the Atlantic. Efficiencies, rooms, deluxe suites, and Jacuzzi suites are for let. The property offers 21 pools and whirlpools, convention facilities, a fitness center, a game room, 575 feet of Lazy River (the largest on the beach), Jacuzzis, hot tubs, three full-service restaurants, and an express restaurant. During the summer there are lots of activities for kids—fitness walks, arts and crafts, face painting, seashell searches—keeping the younger set busy so grown-ups can lounge by the pool or indulge in an afternoon nap. Entertainment packages can be booked from this resort.

Days Inn Grand Strand $
806 South Ocean Boulevard, Myrtle Beach
(843) 448–8261, (800) 448–8261
www.myrtlebeachmotels.com

This modest property could be perfect for a family looking for bargains. Only 18 blocks to the Pavilion area, the Oasis rents 58 double rooms and efficiencies. It's across the street from the ocean and offers guests an outdoor pool, 27-channel televisions, and a free continental breakfast.

Dayton House $$$
2400 North Ocean Boulevard, Myrtle Beach
(843) 448–2441, (800) 258–7963
www.daytonhouse.com

For more than 30 years, the Thomas family has been rolling out the red carpet for families, senior citizens, and vacationing couples. In the last decade, four new buildings have been added to the property—now offering 327 units, including 96 two-room oceanfront suites. Amenities include a large outdoor spa, an oceanfront lawn and sunning area, a Lazy River, indoor and outdoor pools and whirlpools, an exercise room, and golf packages at more than 90 courses.

Driftwood On The Oceanfront $$
1600 North Ocean Boulevard, Myrtle Beach
(843) 448–1544, (800) 942–3456
www.driftwoodlodge.com

All of the 90 accommodations at Driftwood have refrigerators, microwave ovens, and remote-control TVs, whether you're staying in a room or efficiency unit. Just 6 blocks from the downtown Pavilion area, this hotel offers an on-site game room, a fitness room, and two outdoor pools.

Fairfield Inn Myrtle Beach-Briarcliffe $$
10231 North Kings Highway, Myrtle Beach
(843) 361–8000, (800) 369–8033

At Fairfield Inn you can always count on a comfortable room and friendly service. The hotel has 86 rooms, all with remote-controlled TVs, free local calls, and data-port-accessible phones. Cribs and in-room safes are also available. Amenities include an indoor heated pool with heated spa, outdoor sunning deck, a complimentary deluxe continental breakfast with 24-hour coffee and tea, laundry valet, and self-service laundry facilities. The Fairfield Inn is located just a short drive from area golf courses, beaches, attractions, and restaurants.

Firebird Motor Inn $$
2007 South Ocean Boulevard, Myrtle Beach
(843) 448–7032, (800) 852–7032
www.firebirdinn.com

exercise room, video-game room, and an independently leased bar and grill. Comforts of home include laundry facilities and spacious rooms. Golf and entertainment packages are available.

Four Seasons Beach Resort $$
5801 North Ocean Boulevard, Myrtle Beach
(843) 449–6441, (800) 277–7562

In the Cabana section, the Four Seasons Beach Resort offers 74 single and double rooms and fully equipped condominiums. Winter rates are outrageously low ($400 to $610 per month) for the caliber of accommodations and amenities offered here; it's an especially appealing lodging option for many senior citizens. The Four Seasons offers its guests exercise and steam rooms and an expansive outdoor pool.

The resort is just across the street from the beach and offers an unobstructed view of beachfront cabanas.

Hampton Inn $$$
4709 North Kings Highway, Myrtle Beach
(843) 449–5231, (800) 833–1360
www.mbhampton.com

The Hampton Inn is a family-oriented hotel with 150 units where children stay free with parents. A couple of blocks from the ocean, the Hampton Inn is somewhat of a landmark around these parts and is a favorite of local seniors. Guests may start the day with a free continental breakfast, and then you're on your own to explore the area. This Hampton Inn also houses a huge indoor swimming pool and a fitness room.

Hampton Inn Northwood $$$$
620 75th Avenue North, Myrtle Beach
(843) 497–0077, (800) 543–4286
www.mbhampton.com

This recent addition to Myrtle Beach's Hampton Inn lineup opened in August 1995. Like its sister on North Kings Highway, the Northwood is within walking distance of the beach and serves guests a complimentary deluxe continental breakfast. Among its 122 rooms are 21 two-room suites, four with Jacuzzis. Guests can enjoy a pool, exercise room, and sauna here.

The Firebird Motor Inn specializes in two-bedroom apartments for families. Single rooms and efficiencies are also available on the oceanfront, poolside, or along the sideview. Children will love the Lazy River, the video-game room and supervised summer activities. You can even fire up a grill in the cookout area.

Just south of the busy downtown area, the Firebird is still close to restaurants and attractions. Inquire about golf and entertainment packages.

Forest Dunes Resort $$$
5511 North Ocean Boulevard, Myrtle Beach
(843) 449–0864, (800) 845–7787
www.forestdunes.com

This resort, across the boulevard from the beach in the Cabana section, houses 110 oceanfront or oceanview units, which are one-bedroom and three-bedroom condominiums. Once you've unpacked, take advantage of the wide sandy beach in front of this resort, or float along the Lazy River. (The Lazy River is enclosed during the winter months, so it's always available to guests.) Other features include indoor and outdoor pools, a kiddie pool, whirlpool,

Holiday Inn Downtown Oceanfront $$$$
415 South Ocean Boulevard, Myrtle Beach
(843) 448–4481, (800) 845–0313
www.sixcontinentshotels.com
Located right in the middle of all the action, this oceanfront Holiday Inn hosts one of the liveliest, continuous pool-bar parties—it lasts all season. There are 306 rooms, and all oceanfront units boast private balconies to watch either the poolside happenings or the ocean. Amenities include a second bar in the lobby, indoor and outdoor pools, a sauna, a Jacuzzi, a video-game room, an exercise room, a full-service restaurant, and a gift shop.

Fall of 1997 finally brought the completion of a yearlong, $5 million renovation of this property. All of the guest rooms were gutted, redesigned, and given new carpet, paint, draperies, and furniture. A larger lobby now sports its own bar—the very popular Port O'Call lounge.

Holiday Inn Express $
9551 U.S. Highway 17 (Restaurant Row area), Myrtle Beach
(843) 449–5348, (800) 222–5783
www.sixcontinentshotels.com
Guests receive a free continental breakfast each morning. You'll find 85 rooms plus five Jacuzzi suites and an outdoor heated pool. Special packages include golf, entertainment, romance, Christmas, and New Year's options. Room rates are considered low during peak season but are relatively high during the winter months, as the hotel aims for consistent pricing rather than extreme fluctuations from one season to another. This hotel is 1.5 miles from the beach.

Holiday Inn South Beach $$$
803 South Ocean Boulevard, Myrtle Beach
(843) 913–5800, (800) 845–1112
With nine oceanfront pools and both an indoor and outdoor Lazy River ride, you would think all you'd have to do is splish and splash all day. But there's much more to do at this resort near the heart of downtown Myrtle Beach. The property boasts 1½ acres of oceanfront lawn and lounging.

There are 360 units in all, with 28 different room types to choose from, and all accommodations feature in-room voice mail for messages.

Relax in the lounge, pick up the sundries you left at home at the convenience store, or work out in the exercise room. Golf and entertainment packages are available, and a continental breakfast is served.

Jonathan Harbour $$
2611 South Ocean Boulevard, Myrtle Beach
(843) 448–1948, (800) 448–1948
www.jhoceanfront.com
Two- and three-room efficiency units with fully equipped kitchens and laundry facilities are what you'll find here. Enjoy recreation or relaxation in the indoor or outdoor pool, one of two whirlpools, the kiddie pool, an exercise room, sauna, or steam room. Guests have ample parking facilities across the street.

Kingston Plantation $$$$$
9800 Queensway Boulevard, Myrtle Beach
(843) 449–0006, (800) EMBASSY
Kingston Plantation is a multimillion-dollar resort with more than 700 hotel rooms (including 255 oceanview suites), condominiums, town homes, and villas set in a richly designed atmosphere. The grounds span 145 oceanfront acres east of Restaurant Row. The resort features conference centers, several pool decks, a year-round bar and seasonal pool bar, on-premise restaurant, and lush foliage. A visit here isn't complete if you don't take advantage of the $4 million Sport and Health Club that includes racquetball courts, aerobics classes, state-of-the-art tennis courts, cardiovascular and weight-training machines, and massage services. With an on-site golf department, arranging a round is easy here.

A renovation project changed this former Raddison hotel into the Embassy Suites, so the 20-story property is now under new ownership. Art deco furnishings have redecorated all of the suites, and Caribbean accents have been added to the exterior. The price code listed for Kingston

Plantation reflects Embassy Suites rates only. Other units are privately owned and rented separately.

This is more than a place to store your luggage; it's a vacation destination and group-meeting attraction—an exceptional choice as evidenced by two years of Gold Key Awards.

La Quinta Inn & Suites $$
1561 21st Avenue North, Myrtle Beach
(843) 916–8801, (800) 687–6667

If you're not particular about staying near the ocean, then you might try this proto-type La Quinta. The fresh design is one of the chain's first hotels to feature two-room suites and extended-stay facilities.

Across the street from Broadway at the Beach, this 128-room hotel treats guests to a continental breakfast every morning and accepts small pets. Amenities include an outdoor pool, exercise room, telephones with computer dataports, refrigerators, microwave ovens, and coffeemakers.

Each room sports a 25-inch television and Super Nintendo games.

Landmark Resort Hotel $$$
1501 South Ocean Boulevard, Myrtle Beach
(843) 448–9441, (800) 876–0010
www.landmarkresort.com

Everything you need for a great vacation is right here at this oceanfront property. This accommodation includes 327 single and double rooms as well as penthouse suites. In 1996 the Landmark completed construction of a new tower of one-room suites, bringing the total room count to 570. This hotel is the only Grand Strand property to have a covered pedestrian bridge across Ocean Boulevard that links its accommodations with the parking lot across the road. Completed in 1997, the walkway cost an estimated $750,000, while the parking facility was part of a $40 million expansion.

Entertainment includes an English-style pub and dining in the Gazebo restau-

With everything from basic rooms to well-equipped efficiencies and elegantly appointed beach houses, the accommodations available in Myrtle Beach are varied and plentiful. PHOTO: COURTESY OF MYRTLE BEACH AREA CHAMBER OF COMMERCE

rant. Families can play in the video-game room, relax in the sauna, or splash about in the indoor pool complex that includes Jacuzzis. The Landmark also specializes in hosting group tours and conferences. Golf packages are available. As of summer 1997 The Landmark added two 300-foot Lazy Rivers and full laundry facilities.

Meridian Plaza Resort $$$
2310 North Ocean Boulevard, Myrtle Beach
(843) 626–4734, (800) 323–3011
www.meridianplaza.com

The Meridian Plaza is a tall, sleek building that rents out 90 ultramodern one-bedroom suites, each of which has a fully equipped kitchen and two televisions. Parking in the downtown area is normally crowded; however, the Plaza provides spaces for its guests in the five-level garage. Amenities include indoor and outdoor pools and whirlpools, an exercise room, and video arcade. Special golf packages are available from September through May.

Ocean Dunes Resort & Villas $$$$
201 75th Avenue North, Myrtle Beach
(843) 449–7441, (800) 845–0635
www.sandsresort.com

The twin towers of this huge resort provide 400 rooms, suites, one-, two-, and three-bedroom villas, plus three-bedroom oceanfront penthouses. On-site features include oceanfront pools with bars, indoor pools and whirlpools, a steam room, saunas, massage therapy, weight room, game room, gift shop, and convenience store. But wait, there's much more. Entertainment options feature restaurants, a lounge, and a Lazy River.

During the summer, supervised programs are offered for children, and kids get a free T-shirt and identification bracelet. The Ocean Dunes staff can also refer you to reputable baby-sitters. Children younger than 18 also stay free in the same room with an adult. Golf, entertainment, and specialty packages are available. Courtesy airport pickup is provided.

Ocean Forest Villa Resort $$$$$
5601 North Ocean Boulevard, Myrtle Beach
(843) 449–9661, (800) 845–0347

All of the Forest's 243, two-bedroom villas face oceanfront, oceanview, or poolside. Each villa is conveniently designed to house two full baths, an equipped kitchen, a living room, dining room, and balcony.

This is a vacation place with children in mind. On-premise are two outdoor pools and two heated whirlpools. On top of that, special programs for kids and baby-sitting services run from Memorial Day through Labor Day.

Golf packages at 100-plus area courses can be arranged, plus entertainment tours. Privileges to an off-premise fitness center and tennis courts can be had for the asking. Ocean Forest provides airport shuttle transportation.

Ocean Reef Resort Hotel $$$$$
7100 North Ocean Boulevard, Myrtle Beach
(843) 449–4441, (800) 542–0048

The motif might be called "Come to the island, mon," but the beach is definitely Myrtle. All 204 units here face the ocean, and each has a private balcony with a view of the Grand Strand. All of the rooms have been renovated and upgraded with new decor and furniture. Near the northern end of a Myrtle Beach residential section, the Ocean Reef exudes a sense of exclusivity. The resort features an oceanfront swimming pool, sundeck whirlpool, exercise room, oceanfront restaurant, lounge, and a game room. You'll find another swimming pool and whirlpool indoors. Banquet and meeting facilities are large enough to accommodate 400 people. Golf packages and referrals to bonded baby-sitters are coordinated through the staff.

The Palace Resort $$$
1605 South Ocean Boulevard, Myrtle Beach
(843) 448–4300, (800) 334–1397
www.palaceresort.com

The Palace condominiums are fit for kings and queens. You'll feel like royalty in any of the 298 suites at this plush resort that towers over the ocean. Featured amenities include Jacuzzis, hot tubs, enclosed pools, a sauna, and a steam room. Although many of the condominiums are privately owned, there are numerous units available for weekly rentals. The Palace only rents to couples and families.

Patricia Grand Resort Hotels $$$
2710 North Ocean Boulevard, Myrtle Beach
6804 North Ocean Boulevard, Myrtle Beach
(843) 448-8453, (800) 255-4763,
(888) 255-4763
www.patricia.com

From the moment you step into the plush setting of the Patricia Grand, you'll know you're someplace special. The 501 luxurious accommodations include double rooms, efficiencies, and executive suites designed to pamper those with the most discriminating tastes. The oceanfront restaurant and lounge are relaxing retreats after you've had enough of the pool, whirlpool, Lazy River, or sauna. When it's time for more active pursuits, arrange a golf outing through the front desk. Hotel staff are happy to arrange golf and entertainment packages as well as group tour and travel excursions. The Patricia Grand's central location means shopping malls, attractions, and restaurants are within easy reach.

Poindexter Family Resort $$$
1702 North Ocean Boulevard, Myrtle Beach
(843) 448-8327, (800) 248-0003
www.poindexter-resort.com

This resort obviously caters to families. The Poindexter, set on 300 yards of white, sandy beachfront, is walking distance to the Pavilion area. Oceanview and oceanfront rooms and efficiencies are available. Poindexter offers guests the use of 10 pools (both indoor and outdoor), whirlpools, and a gigantic kiddie pool. There is an on-site restaurant for all meals, a meeting room, and exercise facilities.

Special package plans run the gamut from golf and amusement park to honeymoon and entertainment. Supervised children's activities are planned every day during summer.

Riptide Beach Club $$
2806 North Ocean Boulevard, Myrtle Beach
(843) 448-1486

The Riptide offers 80 one- and two-bedroom condos, most of which are rented out with permission of the owners. All have sleeper sofas or a set of twin or bunk beds for plenty of places to rest weary heads. Amenities include two pools, hot tubs, and an exercise facility. During the summer there are activities planned for the entire family including wine and cheese get-togethers, craft workshops, and trips to a water park.

Sandcastle Resorts $$$
Sandcastle at the Pavilion,
1802 North Ocean Boulevard, Myrtle Beach
(843) 448-7101,
(800) 626-1550 (reservations only)
Sandcastle South Beach,
2207 South Ocean Boulevard, Myrtle Beach
(843) 448-4316
www.sandcastleresorts.com

The Sandcastle people run two properties in Myrtle Beach, both of which offer 240 accommodations. Sandcastle at the Pavilion is within 9 blocks of the action-packed Myrtle Beach Pavilion area. Here guests can choose from oceanfront and oceanview rooms, suites, and efficiencies, many of which have separate sleeping and living quarters.

Amenities abound with a winding river, oceanfront pool, kiddie pool, plus another swimming pool, and whirlpool inside. There is also an on-premise cafe.

Sandcastle South Beach was brand-new in 1998. All of its units are oceanfront. Here you'll find rooms, suites, and efficiencies offering two queen-size beds. This newer Sandcastle has all the amenities of its northern cousin, but has added Jacuzzis, a lounge, and a gift shop. Both locations arrange an extensive array of golf packages.

Sands Beach Club All-Suite Resort $$$$$
9400 Shore Drive, Myrtle Beach
(843) 449-1531, (800) 845-6999
www.sandsresorts.com

This centrally located resort is on a point of land at the end of Shore Drive, overlooking both the Atlantic Ocean and the Dunes Club marsh. It's in the middle of everything, yet secluded. With 125 units, Sands Beach Club gives guests the option of a two-bedroom oceanfront suite or a one-bedroom unit with views of the ocean and marsh. Regardless of the number of bedrooms, each Sands suite is spacious and includes a separate living room, dining room, and full kitchen.

Topper's Restaurant and Topper's Lounge, on the premises, are totally encased in glass to take advantage of the spectacular seascape. A gourmet pizza shop, game room, and mini-convenience store are also on-site. Meetings for up to 200 people can be arranged by the staff.

For recreation, Sands Beach Club offers a sports deck with hoops and nets for impromptu basketball and volleyball matches. Here you'll also find two lighted tennis courts, indoor and outdoor pools, and whirlpools for guests. Supervised programs for the kids and a child-care service for toddlers are available from Memorial Day through Labor Day. A roster of specialty packages includes golf, entertainment, and honeymoon options. Sands also offers a free shuttle service from Myrtle Beach International Airport.

Sand Dunes Resort Hotel $$$$$
201 74th Avenue North, Myrtle Beach
(843) 449–3313, (800) 845–1011
www.sandsresorts.com

Once you've checked into the Sand Dunes, you'll have to leave the hotel only to sightsee. The 400 accommodations here range from double rooms and efficiencies to two-bedroom executive suites and oceanfront penthouses.

Overlooking the Atlantic Ocean is the hotel's steakhouse, The Flying Machine, and a sports lounge called Team Spirits. For a quick bite, there's a sidewalk pizza shop, ice-cream parlor, and beach bar and cafe.

This is an arena of activity with indoor and outdoor pools, a fitness facility, a Lazy River, and Bogey's Back Alley game room and entertainment center. From Memorial Day through Labor Day, the hotel coordinates programs for children and offers baby-sitting services. The Sand

Insiders' Tip
Whether it's golf, the Bluegrass Festival, fabulous Christmas shows at area theaters, shopping, or just escaping one's family, the Grand Strand has become a popular destination for the Thanksgiving weekend. Make those reservations early!

Dunes also treats its guests to courtesy airport pickup. Golf and entertainment packages can be arranged at any time.

Sands Ocean Club Resort $$$$$
9550 Shore Drive (near Restaurant Row), Myrtle Beach
(843) 449–6461, (800) 845–2202
www.sandsresorts.com

Treat yourself to a one-, two-, or three-bedroom suite or efficiency along the oceanfront at the Sands Ocean Club Resort. This upscale facility offers numerous on-site amenities, including several pools, lounges, Ocean Annie's Beach Bar, restaurants (including a delicatessen), gift and golf shops, an exercise room, and golf privileges at more than 100 area courses. During summer months, children's programs and a toddler service are available to guests. Kids will be happy to know that a Lazy River flows at the Sands Ocean Club Resort. Courtesy airport transportation is always available to the guests of Sands.

Sea Dip Motel $$
2608 North Ocean Boulevard, Myrtle Beach
(843) 626–3591, (800) 334–1467
www.seadip.com

Sea Dip is a small but friendly establishment that specializes in family vacations. Reservation options include single rooms, efficiency apartments, two-room suites, and efficiency suites with three double beds. Sea Dip offers guests two oceanfront pools, two whirlpools, a sundeck, a kiddie pool, a Lazy River, and laundry facilities. The ever-smiling staff is always happy to arrange golf, entertainment, honeymoon, or motor-coach packages. This motel is about a 12-block walk from the Pavilion and amusement areas.

Sea Mist Resort $$
1200 South Ocean Boulevard, Myrtle Beach
(843) 448–1551, (800) SEAMIST
www.seamist.com

The Sea Mist is a complete world within itself, sprawling along both sides of Ocean Boulevard. The resort houses more than 823 rooms, efficiencies, suites, townhouses, and bungalows for families and tour groups. As if that weren't enough to choose from, the Sea Mist turned some of its units into Jacuzzi suites. And if you stay six paid nights at standard rates, the seventh night is free.

This expansive complex features eleven pools and a large on-site water park with an inner-tube slide, an activity pool, and a Lazy River that stretches more than 500 feet. And that's not all. Guests can putter around on the resort's miniature golf course, work out in the health club, or dine in one of several restaurants. The kids really seem to go for the ice-cream parlor, doughnut shop, and video arcade. Organized activities focus on keeping the kids occupied. Adults enjoy golf privileges and the glorious Carolina sunshine.

The Sea Mist is smack-dab in the middle of downtown Myrtle Beach, and parking and traffic can be hectic. But once you've parked the car, you won't have to leave until it's time to pack up and go home; just about anything you'll need can be found in the resort complex.

Sheraton Four Points Resort $$$
2701 South Ocean Boulevard, Myrtle Beach
(843) 448–2518, (877) 553–3967
www.sheratonresort.com

The Sheraton continues its tradition of quality service at its Myrtle Beach Resort. More than 200 rooms overlook the ocean, including family suites and efficiencies.

Indoor and outdoor pools complete with sundecks, snack bars, and soft sea breezes mean relaxation galore. PHOTO: COURTESY OF MYRTLE BEACH AREA CHAMBER OF COMMERCE

During the 1996 off-season, the Sheraton spent $1 million on room and lobby renovations.

Geared more to the adults, Kokomo's oceanfront bar and restaurant attracts guests from the pool deck during the summer and provides fun for everyone. Other amenities include an exercise room and sauna. Golf and entertainment packages are available.

Super 8 Motel $
1100 South Ocean Boulevard, Myrtle Beach
(843) 448–8414, (800) 448–7577
www.super8.com

Across the street from the ocean, you'll find this humble motel that offers 41 one-room efficiencies with refrigerators and three two-bedroom units. An outdoor pool, picnic area, and shuffleboard are available to guests. Golf packages can also be arranged by the staff.

Wyndham Myrtle Beach Resort $$$$$
10000 Beach Club Drive, Myrtle Beach
(843) 449–5000
www.wyndham.com/resorts

Get ready for a one-stop vacation experience at the Wyndham, which offers 374 oceanview guest rooms and 11 full suites. Each has a private balcony, refrigerator, coffeemaker, and in-room safe.

The hotel is set on the 18-hole Arcadian Shores championship golf course, and guests are privy to reduced greens and cart fees at this course. You'll also find four on-site lighted tennis courts exclusively for guests. Tennis clinics and lessons are available for a fee. Other recreational options include volleyball, a fully equipped fitness room and, when you've had enough exercise, a resident masseuse.

The Wyndham is home to an oceanfront restaurant that serves breakfast, lunch, and dinner daily as well as Beachcomber Bob's, a small seasonal cafe that whips up sandwiches, finger foods, and pizza.

Wyndham's popular pool deck usually pays tribute to beach music, with live bands playing favorite shagging and dance tunes from 1:00 to 5:00 P.M. daily all summer.

The Yachtsman Resort Hotel $$$$
1400 North Ocean Boulevard, Myrtle Beach
(843) 448–1441, (800) 868–8886
www.yachtsmanhotel.com

The Yachtsman's twin towers house more than 142 all-suite units in the very heart of the downtown area. Exclusive packages cater to golfers, honeymooners, and tour groups. One of the closest attractions to the resort is Pier 14, a restaurant that extends over the ocean.

The studio and one-bedroom suites feature whirlpool baths big enough for two people and fully equipped kitchens. Inside you'll find one pool; outside are two pools, Jacuzzis, hot tubs, a miniature golf course, and shuffleboard. The Yachtsman was voted one of South Carolina's favorite getaways by *The State* newspaper, and it was a finalist for *Sun News*'s Best Hotel on the Strand.

South Strand

Barnacle Inn $
115 South Waccamaw Drive,
Garden City Beach
(843) 651–2828, (800) 272–1222
www.barnacleinn.com

From September through March a small deposit makes families with small pets welcome. Even students, who are often hard-pressed to find accommodations if visiting without adults, are welcome if they are willing to pay a deposit. Barnacle Inn is just steps from Garden City Beach and has thirty modest but comfortable units for a simple, affordable vacation. Guests can access an on-site swimming pool and laundry facilities. Winter rentals are a specialty. Entertainment packages can be arranged by management.

Days Inn Surfside Pier Resort $$$
15 South Ocean Boulevard, Surfside Beach
(843) 238–4444, (800) 533–7599
www.daysinnsurfside.com

The Days Inn Surfside Pier offers the same affordable rates as most area Days Inns. This hotel overlooks the Surfside Pier (hence the name), which was restored after sustaining severe damage during a

1995 storm. This area tends to be more crowded than others on the South Strand because of the pier. Guests enjoy sampling the restaurant's home-style cuisine and sipping their favorite beverages at Scotty's Beach Bar on the property's oceanfront. All 158 units offer a sideview of Surfside Beach. There's an outdoor heated pool and a Jacuzzi, too.

Litchfield Beach & Golf Resort $$$$$
U.S. Highway 17 South, Litchfield Beach
(843) 237–3000, (800) 845–1897
www.litchfieldbeach.com

There is no other resort in the historic Lowcountry that compares to Litchfield Beach & Golf. Set amid 4,500 acres of marshlands and oceanfront property, the complex features an array of accommodations including villas, condominiums, and cottages. The grounds are enhanced with avenues of century-old oaks, flowering gardens, and uncrowded beaches. Although the resort is about 15 minutes from Myrtle Beach, there is no hint of either neon or a hectic pace.

Ranked one of the top-ten tennis vacation destinations in the country by *Tennis* magazine, Litchfield's 12 on-site courts attract tennis lovers from far and wide. Three signature golf courses grace this resort: River Club, Willbrook Plantation, and Litchfield Country Club. Guests are exempt from golfing surcharges. A comprehensive summer children's program appeals to many families looking for accommodations a cut above those at traditional resorts. In addition to the spa, indoor and outdoor pools, and racquetball courts, the resort offers a sauna, beauty salon, and the ever-popular restaurant and lounge known as Webster's.

Royal Garden Resort $$$$$
1210 North Waccamaw Drive,
Garden City Beach
(843) 651–1929, (800) 446–4010
www.sea-breeze-realty.com

In the midst of the weather-worn beach houses and cottages of Garden City Beach is the Royal Garden Resort, with more than 206 condominium units and suites. The oceanfront property features golf

packages. Enjoy Royal Garden's indoor and outdoor pools, a Jacuzzi, sauna, game room, and gift shop. Restaurants and attractions are within walking distance, and there's a seasonal snack bar, too.

Water's Edge Resort $$$$$
1012 North Waccamaw Drive,
Garden City Beach
(843) 651–0002, (800) 255–5554
www.watersedgeresort.com

With 135 spacious condominiums boasting one-, two-, and three-bedrooms, this resort is larger than its neighbor, the Royal Garden Resort, but offers the same features, including pools, Jacuzzis, and an oceanfront lounge and deck with a perfect view of the beach. Golf, entertainment, and honeymoon packages are offered. Supervised activities for the kids are available during the summer months.

Other Featured Accommodations

The Atlantica $$$
1702 North Ocean Boulevard, Myrtle Beach
(843) 448–8327, (800) 248–0003
www.atlantica-resort.com

The Atlantica is located minutes from the Pavilion and offers anything your heart desires in condominiums ranging from one-bedroom efficiencies to a two-floor apartment with three separate sleeping rooms and a rooftop sundeck. All units have private, beachfront balconies and contemporary decor.

The property offers indoor and outdoor pools and spas. The staff will gladly arrange entertainment and golf packages with your reservations or upon arrival in slower seasons.

Days Inn Beachfront $$
1403 South Ocean Boulevard, Myrtle Beach
(843) 448–1636, (800) 826–2779
www.myrtlebeachmotels.com

If you're looking for an affordable, convenient stay for the family, Days Inn is just the ticket. This oceanfront inn rents 54 sideview and oceanfront efficiencies, double and king-size rooms. All have private oceanfront balconies.

Another beautiful day along the Grand Strand. PHOTO: COURTESY OF BRANDON ADVERTISING

The property offers a swimming pool and kiddie pool. It's located about 11 blocks from the popular Family Kingdom Amusement Park, and 1 mile south of the Pavilion area.

Entertainment and golf packages are available with reservations.

Myrtle Beach Resort $$
5905 U.S. Highway 17 South,
Myrtle Beach
(800) 803–7303
www.chicorabeachholiday.com

Myrtle Beach Resort is an all-in-one vacation destination, sprawling along more than 33 acres of oceanfront. Condominium and villa-style accommodations can be found here, ranging from studios to one- and two-bedroom units.

Here you'll discover a recreational wonderland that offers 6 swimming pools (2 indoors), 4 whirlpools, 3 saunas, basketball, shuffleboard, and tennis courts.

The resort also sports arcade games and a kiddie playground. Twenty-four-hour security keeps all of Myrtle Beach Resort's guests safe and sound.

Staff are always happy to arrange great golf packages for visitors. On average a week's stay in mid-July will cost $800.

Ocean Lodge $$
604 North Ocean Boulevard, Myrtle Beach
(843) 448–6770, (800) 757–1580
www.myrtlebeachmotels.com

Ocean Lodge is only a short walk to the Pavilion area, centrally located and oceanfront. It is a smaller property with 27 oceanfront, sideview, and poolside double rooms with full kitchens. Ocean Lodge also rents out two apartments that can accommodate up to six people.

Laundry facilities are available to guests, and the staff can arrange golf packages.

Pan American Resort $$$
5300 North Ocean Boulevard, Myrtle Beach
(843) 449–7411, (800) 845–4501
www.panamericanresort.com

Pan American Resort's features and amenities include indoor/outdoor pools, on-site tennis courts, Lazy River, and exercise facility. The rooms are spacious and well-decorated and the staff is friendly and helpful. Golf packages can be arranged upon request.

RV and Camping Facilities

Myrtle Beach-area campgrounds offer more than 9,000 individual campsites with all the comforts of home for a perfect family vacation. Each campground offers basic services plus a variety of recreational activities.

Summer is the area's most popular camping season; most children are out of school, and families can plan their vacations together. However, camping is quickly becoming a year-round activity along the Grand Strand, so don't roll into town during October through March and expect to find accommodations easily. The fall and winter seasons attract many campers due to the mild climate and off-season rates. All of the campgrounds are within walking distance of grocery stores, restaurants, and attractions.

North Strand

Barefoot RV Resort
U.S. Highway 17 and 48th Avenue South,
North Myrtle Beach
(843) 272–1790, (800) 272–1790
www.barefootcampingresort.com

Barefoot RV Resort offers 250 recreational vehicle campsites for a less crowded camping adventure on the oceanfront. Although smaller than most campgrounds in the Myrtle Beach area, the Barefoot RV Resort still offers all the comforts of the larger campgrounds, including utility hookups, bathhouses, laundry facilities, and a convenience store. The resort boasts a clubhouse complete with a game room, whirlpool, fitness center, and indoor pool. Outside you'll

find another swimming pool, a kiddie pool, and a Lazy River.

The Park Model rentals are equipped for up to six people, with two bedrooms and a sofa sleeper. Bring your own sheets, pillow cases, washcloths, and towels.

Depending on site location, the summer daily rate ranges from $30 to $42.

Myrtle Beach

Apache Family Campground
9700 Kings Road, Myrtle Beach
(843) 449–7323, (800) 553–1749
www.apachefamilycampground.com

You can select from 277 rental sites from the total inventory of more than 700 spacious campsites (the remainder are annual rentals or permanently booked) nestled beneath towering pines and oaks at Apache Family Campground.

All sites have sewage hookups (except for the handful close to the ocean), free cable TV, and picnic tables. Amenities include a large swimming pool, laundry facilities, and a fully stocked trading post. Apache Campground is home to the longest and widest fishing pier in the Southeast—Apache Pier (see the Fishing chapter)—complete with a restaurant and seasonal live entertainment.

Depending on site location, the summer daily rate is about $37.

KOA Kampground
613 5th Avenue South, Myrtle Beach
(843) 448–3421, (800) 255–7614
www.myrtlebeachkoa.com

Nestled in this densely wooded area, campers at the KOA might have trouble believing that the heart of Myrtle Beach is just 700 yards away.

More than 500 campsites are available in this 60-acre complex that offers log cabin–style rentals—called Kamping Kabins—in addition to its large, shaded tent sites. Free cable TV is included with utility hookups, and KOA provides bathhouses with showers. You and the family can splash about in the two pools or rent a bike for recreation. Other amenities include a convenience store with gas station, game room, and Laundromat.

Depending on site location and hookups, the summer daily rate ranges from $29 to $45. Kabins run from $48 to $59.

Myrtle Beach State Park
4401 South Kings Highway, Myrtle Beach
(843) 238–5325
www.discoversouthcarolina.com

The Myrtle Beach State Park is just 3 miles south of downtown Myrtle Beach and is one of the most popular public beaches in the area. It was the first state park opened to the public in South Carolina; it's also the site of the first campground and fishing pier on the Grand Strand.

The park offers 350 campsites, picnic areas with shelters, a swimming pool, nature trails, playground equipment, a park store, and snack bar. Campsites are rented on a first-come, first-serve basis. Only 100 sites are available each year for advance reservation. Each site has water and electrical hookups and is convenient to hot showers and rest rooms.

The summer daily rate is $23.00 per site, $24.00 for reserved spots, and there is an additional $2.00-per-person (age 16 and older) admission charge to enter the park.

Myrtle Beach Travel Park
10108 Kings Road, Myrtle Beach
(843) 449–3714, (800) 255–3568

Only 10 miles north of downtown Myrtle Beach, the Travel Park offers more than 1,100 campsites in a variety of locations: oceanfront, wooded, or lakeside, all complete with utility hookups. Furnished villas and 35-foot travel trailers are also available for rent. Campers can enjoy a variety of swimming activities, rent paddleboats, or fish for freshwater game from surrounding lakes.

The summer daily rate starts at $46.

South Strand

Huntington Beach State Park
U.S. Highway 17 South, Murrells Inlet
(843) 237–4440
www.discoversouthcarolina.com

Huntington State Park is a nature lover's dream come true. About 3 miles south of Murrells Inlet, the diverse natural environment of the South Carolina coast awaits at the freshwater lagoon, salt marsh, and nature trail. The view of the beach from Huntington Beach State Park is one of the most breathtaking you'll find along the Grand Strand. The park is also the site of the historic castle Atalaya, the former winter home and studio of American sculptress Anna Hyatt Huntington.

Park facilities include about 135 campsites, 53 of which can be reserved in advance; the rest are rented on a first-come, first-serve basis. There are picnic areas with shelters, a boardwalk, a park store, and nature programs directed by park staff. Each site has water and electrical hookups, and hot showers and rest rooms are nearby. Sewage hookups are available at about 22 sites. The summer daily rate, from April through October, is $23 to $25; from November through March, $19 to $21.

Lakewood Camping Resort
5901 U.S. Highway 17 South, Surfside Beach
(843) 238–5161, (800) 258–8309
www.lakewoodcampground.com

Lakewood, the 2000/2001 National RV Park of the Year, is among the largest oceanfront campgrounds in the South Strand area, with more than 1,900 campsites complete with utility hookups. It is also home of *High Steppin' Country*, a musical and variety show featuring professionally trained talent, local to the community. Each summer from June to August the entertainers perform three nights a week before packed houses, singing and dancing country favorites mixed with a few contemporary numbers.

The three-acre recreation complex provides a variety of activities, including an 18-hole miniature golf course. Four freshwater lakes are stocked with fish just begging for a hook. When it's time to cool down, kids of all ages will love rushing into the Olympic-size pool from the sliding board built into a tropical rock formation. Campers can also enjoy a heated pool and a Jacuzzi.

Beach Villa rentals are available in addition to camper storage and annual leases. Depending on site location, the summer daily rate ranges from $36 to $41.

Ocean Lakes Family Campground
**6001 South Kings Highway, Surfside Beach
(843) 238–1451, (800) 722–1451
www.oceanlakes.com**

Like many Grand Strand campgrounds, Ocean Lakes is a world within itself, providing campers with everything from convenient shopping, meeting rooms, and laundry facilities to a chapel, a book-exchange library, a post office, and telephones. Daily programs for children are available during the summer months.

Ocean Lakes is the largest campground facility on the east coast. Of nearly 3,500 sites, less than 1,000 are transient sites. Ocean Lakes offers 250 rental units (ideal headquarters for an affordable vacation), and the remaining sites are permanently leased.

From 1997 through 1999, Ocean Lakes was awarded the National RV Park of the Year award by the National Association of RV Parks and Campgrounds. In addition to a beachfront location, Ocean Lakes boasts an indoor pool and an observation deck that enables a breathtaking view of the Atlantic.

Depending on site location, the summer daily rate ranges from $43.50 to $45.50.

PirateLand Family Campground
**5401 U.S. Highway 17 South, Surfside Beach
(843) 238–5155, (800) 443–CAMP
www.pirateland.com**

Set among 140 acres of stately oak trees, private lagoons, and oceanfront property, PirateLand is a real treasure. More than 25 years of business has garnered PirateLand several generations of family vacationers whose visits turn into neighborhood block parties. Each of the 1,400 ocean-front and lakeside campsites is fully equipped with a picnic table and hookups for utilities and free cable TV. Trailer storage space is also available. Keep in mind that you don't have to be a camper to enjoy the surroundings at PirateLand. The campground also offers fully furnished, two- and three-bedroom Lakeview Villas for weekly and monthly rental.

Campground amenities include a heated indoor pool and spa, an Olympic-size outdoor pool, playgrounds, tennis courts, a miniature golf course, and an arcade. The staff organizes activities including beach volleyball, deep-sea fishing, golf, Bible school, arts and crafts, and neighborhood cookouts. The campground's general store is stocked with practically everything you can imagine or forgot to pack. There is also a coin-operated laundry facility for campers' convenience.

Depending on site location, the summer daily rate ranges from $44 to $46.

Vacation Rentals

North Strand
Myrtle Beach
South Strand

Want to take the whole gang, be it family or friends, on a little extended vacation? You may want to consider renting a large condominium or beach house. The kids, young and old, can be entertained by the sand and surf. The grown-ups looking for true rest and relaxation can pull a chair and a glass of lemonade on to the deck for a little wave watching and snoozing. These accommodations combine the comfort, convenience, and semiprivacy of home with the carefree existence of vacation. These short-term rentals have their own kitchens but some have restaurants on-site for the evening when you just don't feel like cooking. Others are equipped with laundry facilities.

The vacation rental option is great for large parties and events (such as family reunions) and often more affordable than resort hotels once the cost is divided. The option of bringing and preparing your own food helps the cost factor, as well as catering to the all-day snackers of all sizes!

The hard part of vacation rentals is finding one. Group accommodations tend to be rather elusive, since most are under the thumb of rental management companies or realestate firms. Still, you can expect a wide variety of design, decor, and amenities. It's wise to try to book a group accommodation well in advance of your stay, again depending greatly on during which season you plan to visit. Have a good idea of the amenities you'd like to have, whether you're looking for a cabin without phones or the full suite with recreation center and Jacuzzi or maybe your needs are more along the lines of a playpen and crib. We've uncovered a few that might be worth looking into.

North Strand

Century 21 Thomas
625 Sea Mountain Highway,
North Myrtle Beach
(843) 249–2100, (800) 249–2100
www.century21thomas.com

Strictly serving the North Myrtle Beach and Little River areas, this company maintains more than 400 units, condos, houses, and oceanfront or channel homes, and has been honored with Century 21's prestigious Centurion Award for the past five years. One- to seven-bedroom accommodations can be rented, and as many as 20 people can stay in one of the larger homes. Ninety-five percent of the condos offer pools, and all of the homes are oceanfront or second row from the Atlantic. Staff can arrange golf and entertainment packages for guests. Prices start at $505 per week for a one-bedroom

unit and range all the way up to $4,290 for a six-bedroom oceanfront beach house.

Shore Crest Vacation Villas
4709 South Ocean Boulevard (Windy Hill section), North Myrtle Beach
(843) 361–3600, (800) 456–0009
www.bluegreenonline.com

Beautifully decorated and outfitted, Shore Crest Villas offer one- and two-bedroom condo units with full kitchens, two baths each, and extra sofa beds. The one-bedroom villa accommodates four people easily; the two-bedroom can sleep six guests. The property sports an indoor pool and Jacuzzi, exercise room, and video-game arcade.

On the oceanfront is another pool, a Jacuzzi, and a Lazy River. A week's stay at Shore Crest in the middle of July costs approximately $715.

Opt for a creekside rental and enjoy the joys of crabbing and fishing from your own private dock.

PHOTO: COURTESY OF *LOWCOUNTRY COMPANION*

Myrtle Beach

Barefoot Vacations
3405 North Kings Highway, Myrtle Beach
(843) 626–7457, (800) 845–0837
www.barefootvacationsinc.com

Spanning the length of the sunny Grand Strand, Barefoot manages 100-plus properties, including one-room sun suites, one-bedroom condos, cottages, and apartment complexes. Barefoot Vacations' staff members are experienced coordinators of family reunions and large-scale affairs. All properties have swimming pools available to guests and some include a clubhouse for events. The staff can also arrange dining, show, and golf packages. The weekly cost of a Barefoot Vacations property in mid-July is $750 to $2,400.

Beach Vacations
357 Lake Arrowhead Road, Myrtle Beach
(843) 449–2400, (800) 449–4005

The staff of Beach Vacations promises to accommodate any size group, anywhere along the Strand. This company has a large inventory of one-, two-, and three-bedroom units, condos, cottages, and golf-course villas. All of the properties have access to swimming pools, and golf packages can be arranged. Peak season prices start at $600 per week and range to $1,500.

Booe Realty
7728 North Kings Highway, Myrtle Beach
(843) 449–4477, (800) 845–0647
www.booerealty.com

Booe's inventory of 225 rental properties consists of condominiums and town homes that sleep four to eight persons and beach houses that accommodate 9 to 21 guests. Except the condos, no other units include swimming pools. But keep in mind that most beach houses are oceanfront or just across the street from the blue Atlantic. In mid-July condos and town houses start at $545 per week, and oceanfront beach houses range from $1,495 to $4,000 weekly. Booe specializes in winter rentals and golf packages.

Chicora Beach Holiday
603 Briarwood Drive, Myrtle Beach
(843) 272–7070, (800) 845–0833
www.chicorabeachholiday.com

All along the Grand Strand, Chicora manages hundreds of vacation villas, condos, and cottages. Studios, efficiencies, and up to four-bedroom accommodations are available, most of which are within comfortable walking distance to the beach or offer an on-site pool. Chicora also arranges golf, tennis, and entertainment packages for guests. During peak season, rentals run anywhere from $675 to $1,065 a week. A four-bedroom, three-bath oceanfront villa costs about $2,545 for a week's stay.

LITUS* To Let
1551 21st Avenue North, Suite 24,
Myrtle Beach
(843) 448–9000, (800) 365–4887
www.litustolet.com

A state-of-the-art reservation and customer-service center at LITUS* can put you in touch with a huge inventory of rentals all over the Grand Strand, from efficiencies to luxurious oceanfront homes suitable for 25 people. Prices range from $50 per night to $6,000 for a week's stay. The staff encourages potential guests to call their customer-service center at any time, since last-minute cancellations often provide visitors with the perfect place at big savings.

The Noble Company
1211 48th Avenue North, Myrtle Beach
(843) 449–6625, (800) 358–6625
www.thenoblecompany.com

Since 1980 The Noble Company has arranged vacation packages for families in some of the nicest condominium properties in North Myrtle Beach and Myrtle Beach. One- to four-bedroom condos can be rented along with a limited number of large beach homes. Garnering a select group of vacation properties over the years, Noble prefers to rent to families, married couples, and singles older than 25. No house parties are permitted in any of the company's rental units, so look elsewhere if you want to have a beer bash. Prices in mid-July range from $625 a week for a two-bedroom, two-bath unit across the street from the ocean to $1,375 a week for a four-bedroom, three-bath oceanfront condo.

Oceanfront Vacation Rentals, Inc.
1551 21st Avenue North, Suite 12,
Myrtle Beach
(843) 626–2072, (800) 247–5459

Oceanfront Vacation Rentals represents more than 100 properties throughout Myrtle Beach, including one-, two-, and three-bedroom condominiums with fully equipped kitchens boasting microwaves, color cable TVs, VCRs, and laundry facilities. Most properties are only minutes from shopping, swimming, amusement parks, world-class family music shows, and other attractions. Prices range from $600 for one-, two-, and three-bedroom condos that overlook the salt marsh and golf course, are a short walk to the beach, and have indoor and outdoor pools, to $7,800 for a sprawling oceanfront home with eight bedrooms, seven baths, a pool and Jacuzzi, a large oceanfront porch, a fireplace, and a large back porch overlooking the ocean.

Sloan Realty and Management and Endless Summer Vacations
9600 Highway 17 North, Myrtle Beach
(843) 448–0835, (800) 476–1760

Approximately 200 units, efficiencies, cottages, and penthouse suites are available for rent through this company. Some of the properties are large enough to accommodate 10 people under one roof. All include access to swimming pools. Summer rentals began at $575 per week for an efficiency, $1,975 a week for a fancy penthouse suite.

Insiders' Tip
As you're reserving your vacation rental, be sure to ask if bed linens and towels are provided or if you need to bring your own.

South Strand

Dunes Beach Vacations
128 Atlantic Avenue, Garden City Beach
(843) 651–2116, (800) 845–8191
www.dunesbeachvacations.com

All up and down Surfside Beach and Garden City Beach, along canals, inlets, and channels, Dunes Realty manages a large inventory of condominiums, cottages, and beach houses. This company rents almost exclusively to family groups. The smallest accommodation starts at $500 a week in mid-July, and a seven-bedroom beach house will cost $4,900. Dunes Beach Vacations does not accept credit cards.

Garden City Realty Inc.
608 Atlantic Avenue, Garden City Beach
(843) 651–2121, (800) 395–5930
www.gardencityrealty.com

Staying in its own neighborhood, this company handles about 300 rental properties in the Garden City Beach and Surfside Beach areas. Garden City Realty offers one-, two-, and three-bedroom condos, homes, and oceanfront beach houses. Most units sport pools and some offer hot tubs. In mid-July a three-bedroom condo starts at $1,100 per week; a six-bedroom oceanfront home, $5,000.

Golf Colony Resort
1841 Colony Drive, Surfside Beach
(843) 650–6363, (800) 654–6522

Golf Colony offers 11 colonies of three to five buildings each. Each has its own pool, Jacuzzi, and barbecue area.

Set on the 1,500-acre Deer Track Golf Resort (see the Golf chapter), the colony offers guests 470 condos that range from studios to one- and two-bedroom accommodations. All have fully equipped

Highrise hotels are by no means your only option for vacation accommodations. Local rental agencies offer a wealth of alternatives that range from expansive beach houses to cozy cottages. PHOTO: COURTESY OF
MYRTLE BEACH AREA CHAMBER OF COMMERCE

kitchens and washers and dryers. The resort is just 1.5 miles from the ocean.

In July weekly rates run from $511 to $721; nightly stays are $75 to $105. There is a three-night minimum, six-person maximum for all reservations and a one-time cleaning charge of $55 to $80. Separate golf packages to stay at Golf Colony and play the 36 holes at Deer Track can be arranged by calling (800) 624-6886.

Pawleys Island Realty Company
88 North Causeway, Pawleys Island
(843) 237-4257, (800) 937-7352
www.pawleysislandvacations.com

With properties concentrated in the Pawleys Island and Litchfield Beach areas, this family-owned company offers all sizes of cottages in a variety of price ranges. On the average, Pawleys Island Realty handles accommodations for groups of about eight people but does not accept credit cards.

Plantation Resort
1250 U.S. Highway 17 North, Surfside Beach
(843) 238-3556, (800) 845-5039
www.plantation-resort.com

Although a little ways from the beach, this resort is nestled among the 36 championship fairways of Deer Track Golf Course (see the Golf chapter). Three-bedroom villas are available with three bathrooms, towels and linens, fully equipped kitchens, and washer and dryer. Staying here entitles you to free summertime shuttle service to and from the beach and

Insiders' Tip
Sunscreen is important year-round. When packing for your trip, don't forget the SPF.

access to a 70,000-square-foot health and swim club. The $1 million club includes a heated pool, sauna, steam rooms, weights, and aerobics. The staff can arrange golf and entertainment packages. Mid-July rates run $120 to $180 per night, with discounts applied to reservations of at least seven nights.

Surfside Realty
213 South Ocean Boulevard, Surfside Beach
(843) 238-3435, (800) 833-8231
www.surfsiderealty.com

If you're looking at Surfside Beach or Garden City Beach as your vacation destination, this company maintains more than 400 apartments, condos, duplexes, cottages, and houses. This company has been arranging vacations since 1962 and has a strict policy of booking families only. Golf packages can also be arranged through Surfside Realty.

During the summer a one-bedroom apartment rents for $430 per week, and a house with a pool runs about $2,800. Special off-season discounts apply from post Labor Day in September through May.

Bed-and-Breakfast Inns

Myrtle Beach
South Strand
Beyond the Strand

Besides the burgeoning number of hotel and motel suites springing up all over the Grand Strand, bed-and-breakfast establishments have also been making their mark. Most likely due to the incredible amount of competition from other accommodations from Little River through Garden City Beach, you'll find the majority of bed-and-breakfast inns have put down roots south of Murrells Inlet and especially in Georgetown.

It's not surprising that Georgetown should become the region's hub of bed-and-breakfast lodging, since the area is home to its fair share of sprawling, historic homes that lend themselves perfectly to the concept. Georgetown is a woman with a past—fascinating and mysterious—and is known as the "Ghost Capitol of the South." Founded in 1729, by 1840 Georgetown was not only an ideal port for shipping vessels, but also produced more than half of all the rice grown in the United States.

As the rice plantations flourished, so did the townspeople and antebellum life. Culling incredible wealth in a relatively short period of time—from 1840 through the 1850s—well-appointed homes began to line the oak-shaded tunnels of streets in town. Gracious plantations entertained and farmed along the shores of Winyah Bay, the Waccamaw, Black, and Pee Dee Rivers.

Georgetonians have worked hard to preserve their heritage, and their town remains a lovely step back in time with an intact historic district, preserved homes, and original churches and storefronts. Today historic tour companies run a brisk business by boat, by tram, or by horse-drawn carriage.

Each of the bed-and-breakfast inns we have listed in this chapter has a distinct personality that seems to have evolved from the property itself and its proprietors. The owners also operate their bed-and-breakfasts, taking great pride in what they consider to be their labor of love.

Price Code

This price code indicates the average one night rate for two people during peak season.

$ . . . .$70 to $95
$$ . . . .$96 to $120
$$$ . . . .$121 to $145
$$$$ . . . .$146 and up

Myrtle Beach

The Brustman House **$$**
400 25th Avenue South, Myrtle Beach
(843) 448–7699, (800) 448–7699
www.brustmanhouse.com

Although the Brustman House's architecture is Colonial, its decor is Scandinavian.

This bed-and-breakfast inn has three guest rooms with white onyx oval whirlpool tubs for two. One suite has a separate entrance and cooking facilities to accommodate a group or family. The house is 300 yards from the beach, situated on two quiet acres in the heart of Myrtle Beach.

Wendell C. Brustman, who holds a Ph.D. in clinical psychology, created the breakfast recipes that include a stack of 10-grain pancakes, French toast made with gourmet bread, and vegetarian delights. Guests are served high tea from 4:00 to 6:00 P.M. daily, consisting of sweets, wine, and gourmet coffee and tea. Fresh roses from the carefully tended gardens adorn the rooms, and hand-picked herbs lend flavor and aroma to wonderful recipes. The Brustman caters to honeymooners and romantic anniversary celebrations.

Sea Island, An Inn on the Beach $$$
6000 North Ocean Boulevard, Myrtle Beach
(843) 449–6406, (888) 748–1060

Sea Island looks like a regular oceanfront hotel from the outside, but inside its ambience and food plan made us consider it a bed-and-breakfast inn. Its 113 oceanfront units range from full rooms to efficiencies to deluxe accommodations with Colonial decor. Guests may partake of a full breakfast and a five-course dinner in the quaint dining room. Chefs change the menu daily to keep palates pleasantly surprised, never bored.

Sea Island offers two outdoor swimming pools and two kiddie pools. The staff has a list of preferred baby-sitters that they are happy to share with guests.

Serendipity Inn $$
407 71st Avenue North, Myrtle Beach
(843) 449–5268, (800) 762–3229

A short, 300-yard walk from the beach, Serendipity is completely enclosed by dense foliage and a wraparound wall. This decades-old property was built to offer guests separate entrances and baths.

Fifteen appointed rooms are available; a few noted as King suites with three rooms. Visitors are treated to a private pool and hot tub in the central courtyard, shuffleboard, table tennis, and bicycles.

Insiders' Tip
Many bed-and-breakfasts do not allow pets, but if you call ahead your host or hostess may be able to recommend a boarding facility for your pet.

Breakfast is served fresh every morning. The menu changes daily but always includes a large fruit tray and steaming baked goods.

Owners Kay and Phil Mullins are happy to coordinate and cater special events, such as family reunions, gatherings, and weddings. They can also make provisions for baby-sitting services on an as-needed basis. Smoking is permitted outside in the courtyard only.

South Strand

1790 House Bed and Breakfast $$$
630 Highmarket Street, Georgetown
(843) 546–4821, (800) 890–7432
www.1790house.com

If you're looking for sumptuous accommodations where antiques and atmosphere abound, head to the 1790 House Bed and Breakfast Inn, where the motto is "let us pamper you." This B&B is a meticulously restored 212-year-old West Indies colonial plantation–style inn located in the heart of Georgetown's National Register Historic District. The house features a wraparound veranda, lovely gardens, six luxurious rooms furnished with private baths, and sitting areas. Shops, restaurants, museums, tour opportunities, and numerous historically significant homes and attractions are within easy walking distance. Innkeepers Denise and Bill Heurich Gower offer the delicious tradition of "taking tea." High Teas and Deluxe Teas are served by reservation only. Prices include a delectable gourmet breakfast and evening refreshments. Be sure to ask Captain Bob about the "Cruise and snooze" private yachting excursions. Unexpected extras include fresh flowers, complimentary concierge service, nightcaps, luxury bath robes, late arrival supper baskets, and more. The 1790 House has been rated "excellent" by the American Bed and Breakfast Association and awarded three stars by Mobil. Games and Ping-Pong are available to guests. Smoking is permitted on the veranda and patio only.

Antiques and atmosphere abound at the 1790 House in Georgetown. The house is post Revolutionary War, and the sheer dimensions of its West Indies style command attention. PHOTO: COURTESY OF THE 1790 HOUSE BED AND BREAKFAST

Alexandra's Inn $$
620 Prince Street, Georgetown
(843) 527–0233, (888) 557–0233

Surrounded by manicured gardens, flower beds, and scented magnolia trees, Alexandra's Inn was built in 1880 as an overflow for guests of the Winyah Inn (now the Masonic Lodge). The main house was dramatically restored. Special detail was given to enhancing the gracious home's original pine floors, moldings, 11-foot ceilings, and fireplaces that come with every room.

Because the home resembles Tara from *Gone With The Wind*, each bedroom is named after a character in the famous story and decorated with that person in mind. Here you'll find Scarlett's, Bonnie's, Ashley's, Melanie's, and Rhett's rooms. Each room has cable TV and telephone as well as a private bath with shower, tub, or Jacuzzi. The main-house rooms are designed for two people only; young children cannot be obliged.

Standing poolside the carriage house is a private accommodation with two bedrooms, a large bath, living room, dining room, and full kitchen. Decorated in light, breezy colors, it is a favorite for families or the business traveler looking for longer stays.

A gourmet breakfast is served every day for guests staying in the main house. The front porch hosts a full army of rockers. Innkeepers Vit and Diane welcome small weddings or other special events. They can even coordinate and/or cater functions for you.

DuPre House Bed & Breakfast Inn $$
921 Prince Street, Georgetown
(843) 546–0298, (877) 519–9499
www.duprehouse.com

The charming atmosphere, enchanting artwork throughout, warm hospitality, and historical significance of DuPre House has earned this bed-and-breakfast inn a three diamond rating by the American Automobile Association.

Records of the house date from 1734 when Elisha Screven first laid plans for her dream home on town lot 53 in Georgetown. The home changed ownership several times, the last surviving chronicle showing that Susannah Gignilliat lived there and filed a claim in 1776 for reimbursement for supplies given to American troops during the American Revolution. The inn is named after Susannah's mother, Mary Magdalen DuPre. Unfortunately all other documents of ownership for the next 60 years were destroyed by Sherman's Advance during the Civil War.

Now in the hands of Richard and Judy Barnett, DuPre House has been extensively altered over the course of the 20th century, but its second-floor wall overhang on the northwestern facade remains a rare example of an old building technique, uncommon to the southeastern states.

Each of DuPre's five rooms boast queen-size poster beds and private baths. Three of the suites include fireplaces. A full breakfast is served every morning to guests that includes a private roast coffee, blended especially for the DuPre House. Afternoon and evening refreshments are also served. Without leaving the grounds of the inn, you can take a refreshing dip in the pool or bubble away in the hot tub.

DuPre House accepts bookings for weddings, receptions, small meetings, and family gatherings. Business travelers and children are accepted. Smoking is allowed outside only.

Harbor House Inn $$
15 Cannon Street, Georgetown
(843) 546–6532, (877) 511–0101
www.harborhousebb.com

Harbor House Inn (circa 1765) is located directly on Georgetown's working waterfront. It is, in fact, Georgetown's only historic, waterfront B&B. Sailors say its distinctive red roof is visible 3 miles out across the bay. Harbor House has welcomed seafarers from across the globe for more than two centuries. The imposing 3-story Georgian house is listed on the National Register of Historic Places, gracing the banks of the Sampit River from a bluff amid magnolia trees, camellias, and venerable live oaks. Harbor House is within walking distance to main-street stores, restaurants, and the Historic District of Georgetown.

The house is accompanied by another monument of South Carolina history—The Red Store. This circa 1740 shipping warehouse formerly stored silks, indigo, and imported wines. From shaded rockers on the inn's porch, visitors can view sailing ships and the blue waters of Winyah Bay—a view that has remained unchanged for centuries.

Innkeeper Meg Tarbox runs the immaculately restored house, keeping the original heart pine floors gleaming and dust off family antiques, eight fireplaces, and oriental carpets. Meg is a Georgetown native with an intimate knowledge of her area.

The inn offers four beautifully appointed rooms with private baths. In addition to the popular porch rockers, guests can share the joggling board, piano, bicycles, games, and books. Smoking is permitted on the open-air porches.

Litchfield Plantation $$$$
Kings River Road, Pawleys Island
(843) 237–9121, (800) 869–1410
www.litchfieldplantation.com

At the end of a quarter-mile avenue lined with live oaks draped in Spanish moss, you'll find the stately Litchfield Plantation Manor House (c. 1750). The home overlooks fields where Carolina long-grain rice flourished in the early 1800s.

The inn tariff includes lodging in one of the four gracious rooms, a daily continental breakfast, use of the private heated pool and cabana, a private beach club at Pawleys Island , on-site tennis courts, and access to the award-winning, on-premise Carriage House Club Restaurant. The Plantation boasts additional suites and villas for a total of thirty-eight rooms and suites to accommodate couples, families, and small groups. Nonsmoking rooms are available.

Litchfield Plantation is a member of the prestigious society for Small Luxury Hotels of the World.

Mansfield Plantation $$
1776 Mansfield Road, Georgetown
(843) 546–6961, (800) 355–3223
www.mansfieldplantation.com

A national historic landmark on the site of many archaeological digs, Mansfield is an authentic antebellum plantation of the Old South, offering bed-and-breakfast stays and historical tours. Especially for Civil War buffs, the plantation offers the retracing of the footsteps of Dr. Francis S. Parker, a signer of the South Carolina Ordinance of Secession, who planted rice here from 1842 to 1862. Parker was forced to leave his beloved Mansfield in April 1862 when Federal gunboats crossed into Winyah Bay and raided plantations along the Black River. The Mansfield innkeepers, Sally and Jim Cahalan, are astute historians who love to share this history with their guests.

Situated on 900 idyllic acres of pine forest, rice fields, and dikes, Mansfield retains the original plantation house, avenues of 220 live oaks draped with Spanish moss, more than 100 blooming camellia bushes, the antebellum slave village, chapel, school house, winnowing tower, and parts of the rice threshing mill. The unspoiled environment plays host to alligators, beavers, fox, deer, otters, and birds, including an occasional bald eagle.

Eight charming and comfortably outfitted rooms in historic guest houses, featuring hand-carved woodwork and mantelpieces, are for let. Private baths and air-conditioning keep each room comfortable. A full breakfast is served every morning in the elegant dining room of the plantation house.

Mansfield Plantation was featured in the April 1997 issue of *Charleston Magazine*

Beautiful views and salt-borne breezes make the porch of any area bed-and-breakfast an enviable place to be.   PHOTO: COURTESY OF THE CYPRESS INN

as one of the "Ten Great Romantic Getaways" and received the coveted 5-Paw rating from Pets Welcome travel guide. Needless to say, family pets are welcome here.

This site is also home to the Mansfield Duck Hunting Club, and guests have the opportunity to fish for bream and bass or play golf on the adjacent 18-hole Wedgefield Plantation course. Weekend getaway packages are also offered at the plantation. Smoking is permitted outside on the grounds.

Sea View Inn $, no credit cards
414 Myrtle Avenue, Pawleys Island
(843) 237-4253
www.seaviewinn.net

This place is a Pawleys Island tradition. Sea View's 20 rooms overlook the ocean and the salt marshes of the inlet. As bed-and-breakfast inns go, this is among the most rustic. For more than 40 years, families have dined on authentic Lowcountry cuisine and have relaxed in the privacy of the traditional wraparound porch. This is the ideal vacation destination for anyone who wants to get away from it all and have it all at the same time.

For a week in April, the Sea View hosts a Wellness Week where guests participate in a myriad of activities that include a daily massage, readings by psychics and astrologists, creative writing instruction, yoga, meditation, and healing touch. They dine on food prepared by chefs who specialize in nutritional healing. At other times of the year, Sea View is the home of a weeklong artists' workshop and a nature program.

In addition to your swimsuit, shorts, and T-shirts, the other things you'll need are a good book and a fishing pole. Your stay includes three meals daily. From Memorial Day through Labor Day, Saturday to Saturday reservations are required. During other times of the year, a two-night minimum stay is required. Children age three and younger are not allowed. Smoking is not permitted in the living or dining rooms.

Insiders' Tip
The owners of local bed-and-breakfasts usually know a lot about local history, activities, and events. Be sure to spend some time talking with your hosts.

The Shaw House Bed-and-Breakfast $
613 Cypress Court, Georgetown
(843) 546-9663

Mary and Joe Shaw operate this refuge that overlooks Willowbank Marsh, considered by many to be a bird watcher's paradise. Getting to the Shaw House requires a jog through town, since it's set off the beaten paths of Georgetown, yet within walking distance of its historical district, shops, and restaurants.

Three spacious rooms can be rented here, all furnished in antiques and offering a king- or queen-size Rice bed. Bicycles, games, and an extensive library are extended to guests. Nightly turn down and chocolates are mainstay luxuries at the Shaw House.

A Southern home-cooked breakfast is served each morning that includes fresh baked bread and pots of rich coffee. Many guests of Shaw House have written that Mary is the ultimate hostess and personification of Southern hospitality.

Smoking is permitted on the outside porches.

Beyond the Strand

The Cypress Inn $$
16 Elm Street, Conway
(843) 248-8199, (800) 575-5307
www.acypressinn.com

Just 12 miles from the heart of Myrtle Beach in the charming town of Conway, this AAA Four Diamond Bed & Breakfast

Overlooking a marina in Conway's charming riverfront, just 15 miles from Myrtle Beach, the Cypress Inn offers luxury accommodations and personal service. PHOTO: COURTESY OF THE CYPRESS INN

offers a welcome change of pace. Overlooking the Waccamaw River, it boasts twelve guest rooms, each with its own personality. The Carolina Room offers a king-size mahogany four-poster bed, fireplace, and a two-person Jacuzzi with a 12-inch French showerhead above. The Miss Marple Room, featuring Country English decor, is home to more than sixty Agatha Christie novels. Other amenities found in the rooms are plush bathrobes, luxurious bed linens, herbal soaps and shampoos, and comfortable beds.

The business traveler will find the amenities and comfort of a luxury hotel—in-room desk, telephone with dataport, TV/VCR, private baths, fax and copier on-site—along with the personal service a bed-and-breakfast provides.

Each morning, breakfast is served in the sunny breakfast room. Wonderful, specially blended coffee, teas, homemade breads and muffins, fruit, and a hot entree are presented to the guests. Some guest favorites include Sweet Potato Pancakes, Cypress Eggs, and Peachy French Toast.

The inn is ideally located on Conway's Riverwalk. Guests can spend a leisurely afternoon rocking on the porch, renting a boat and cruising the Waccamaw River, biking around town, or playing tennis just across the street.

The Cypress Inn serves an English Afternoon Tea the second and fourth Sunday each month. Teatime at the Inn is a time to relax and let the gentility of a bygone era sweep over you. Although the menu varies each week, some of the items served include scones, tea sandwiches, sweets, and baked savories. There are two seatings at 2:00 and 3:00 P.M., and the cost is $12 per person. Reservations are required.

Restaurants

North Strand
Myrtle Beach
South Strand

We all work hard to have a good time, strolling the beach in that soft sand, fighting the waves, spiking volleyballs, spotting and picking up all those pesky shells, stretching out on beach towels and working on a tan. Whatever you do here on the Grand Strand, you're going to work up an appetite whether you like it or not.

Nearly 1,600 restaurants accommodate our various palates. If you want to try every one of them on your next visit, plan on staying and eating three square meals a day for one year, five months. With this many restaurants from which to choose, this chapter can't begin to do justice to all the area's offerings. So we've opted to highlight a handful of favourites-mostly individually owned restaurants unique to the Strand. Of course there are lots of good places we don't have room to cover, so our best advice for you is to explore!

One caveat: You might have to look a little harder to find a selection of exotic ethnic cuisine. Grand Strand restaurants have easy access to fresh seafood and therefore rightly emphasize the fresh catch and local nettings; you'll definitely find more family-style seafood buffets here than any single genre, followed closely by pancake houses. But as Myrtle Beach grows, so do our tastes, and restaurant owners are branching out into Thai, Fusion, Australian, and Mediterranean, establishing some of the finest restaurants in America right in our biscuit-and-country-ham kind of town.

And the number is growing almost weekly. The village of Murrells Inlet, on the South Strand, is billed as the "seafood capital of South Carolina" with its several dozen restaurants; the town of Calabash, North Carolina (on the North Strand), is credited with inventing Southern-fried seafood; and the stretch of U.S. Highway 17 between Myrtle Beach and North Myrtle Beach has been dubbed "Restaurant Row" because of its historical concentration of eateries. The opening of Broadway at the Beach and downtown Myrtle Beach establishments' efforts to be competitive have brought even more restaurants into the mix.

What to wear? What to wear! Yes, you can dine in long dresses and dark suits in some of the Strand's establishments; but you also can wear shorts and even bathing suits in others. From candlelight elegance to beer bashes in flip-flops, it's all here.

Don't think even for a minute that the phenomenal number of restaurants or the incredible choices of cuisine are Johnny-come-lately ventures for tourism's sake. The dining heritage of the Grand Strand goes back two hundred years and is deeply entwined with the ghost stories, pirate adventures, and folklore of this historic strip.

Hushpuppies, the deep-fried and seasoned dollops of cornmeal-fish breading served with most Southern seafood dishes, are delivered as baskets of delicious little Ping-Pong-ball-size treats. The tasty morsels were invented more than 150 years ago, when it was fashionable for families to let dogs sleep under the table while they were eating. It was at one particular Murrells Inlet plantation that the cook decided to do something about the dogs that weren't sleeping as much as they were begging for treats from the table—especially when the meal was full of the aroma of fresh-cooked fish. This cook decided to take some leftover breading, add a little sugar, and make some quick-fried dough balls to set in baskets on the table. The idea was that when the dogs began begging, diners would toss a couple of dough balls under the table to "hush" the puppies. Of course it wasn't long before the humans at the table took a taste, and soon the dog pacifiers were "hushing" people, too.

Over the years many seafood restaurants nationwide have offered hushpuppies, but it is only in Murrells Inlet that the original sweet-flavored treats retain that unique plantation recipe. The cook at one Inlet restaurant today claims that his hushpuppy recipe was handed down through eight generations. Even restaurants along the North Strand are often baffled by the South Strand flavor that seemingly no one has been able to duplicate; most Calabash-style restaurants serve hushpuppies with onions in place of the sugar-sweet flavor.

"Calabash" is a word you'll see a lot when you go cruising for restaurants along the Strand. Calabash is a little fishing village in North Carolina, just across the state line, where Myrtle Beach vacationers since the 1930s have driven the 25 or so miles north on U.S. Highway 17 to enjoy the delicious fresh seafood meals. But in the past 10 or so years more than half the seafood buffet restaurants in Myrtle Beach have incorporated the word "Calabash" into the menus or signs describing their seafood. It has come to refer to the style of cooking that made tourists flock to the town: oily seafood dipped in a light cornmeal batter, deep fried and smothered with seasoned butter, then delivered to your table golden brown and piping hot.

Also in the Grand Strand's gastronomic mix are plenty of regionally and nationally known restaurants whose quality you can always count on: Cracker Barrel, Shoney's, Quincy's, Red Lobster, The Olive Garden, Pizza Hut, Fuddrucker's, T.G.I. Friday's . . . the list is nearly endless. And we haven't even considered the fast-food regulars, all of which are present here.

Please note that many Grand Strand restaurants don't accept reservations, and long lines are common at the more laid-back walk-in places. The best bet here is to call before going or just drop in and see. As Insiders, one thing we have learned is that half the fun of eating at the beach is the adventure of finding a new favorite.

Price Code

The following key indicates the price range for a dinner for two, excluding cocktails, tax, and tip. Lunch fares usually run a third to a half less than the dinner prices. All prices, of course, depend on what you choose as an entree, so this key uses the price of an average meal (based on both the restaurant's response to our questions as well as our own computation from menu entrees).

Unless we note otherwise, all restaurants in this chapter accept at least Visa and MasterCard as methods of payment.

$ . . . . .Less than $20
$$ . . . .$21 to $35
$$$ . . . .$36 to $50
$$$$ . . . .$51 and more

North Strand

Benito's Brick Oven Pizza $$
1596 U.S. Highway 17 South, North Myrtle Beach
(843) 272-1414
Benito's New York–style pizzeria and pasteria offers a variety of traditional Italian specialties. The hand-tossed pizza is prepared with homemade care in an authentic wood-fired brick oven and is among the Strand's finest. Many of Benito's pizza selections are inspired by locations from around the world. From the Tropical Tahiti Island special to tempting choices that hint at locales from Barcelona to Mexico, there are a wealth of choices for every palate. Benito's offers more than 20 toppings—from artichoke hearts to chunks of fresh pineapple. Although the undisputed specialty is pizza, fresh salads and a handful of pasta dishes round out the menu.

The Brentwood Restaurant $$
4269 Luck Street, Little River
(843) 249-2601
www.webs4you.com/brentwoodrestaurant
The Brentwood is a feast for all your senses. The first floor of this remodeled Victorian-style restaurant, built in 1910, is reserved for dining. Upstairs there is a European "salon" where guests can retire after dinner for dessert and drinks, in-

cluding espresso and cappuccino. It's also the perfect place to relax and leisurely enjoy a bottle of wine with cheese. Toss in a game of backgammon, and you've got the makings of a splendid interlude.

The food is, quite simply, excellent. Prior to opening The Brentwood, chef and owner Bill Stublick worked at two of the North Strand's best-loved restaurants: The Parson's Table and Oak Harbour Inn. Those in the know realize the value of those credentials. In addition to home-made desserts, the gourmet menu includes fresh veal, rack of lamb, fresh local seafood (the soft-shell crabs are extraordinary!), beef, pork, and duck. Entrees include fresh-baked bread, a crisp salad, your choice of rice pilaf or Chantilly potatoes, and a guaranteed-tasty vegetable of the day. There is also a delicious vegetarian menu available.

The Brentwood is open for dinner Monday through Saturday. Seatings begin at 5:00 P.M., and reservations are suggested but not required.

Damon's Grill $$$
Barefoot Landing, 4810 Highway 17 South, North Myrtle Beach
(843) 272–5107
www.damons.com

One sample is all it takes to understand why Damon's is best known for its award-winning ribs. Even so, those who prefer something lighter or with less mess will be more than satisfied with a menu that also offers excellent grilled steaks, numerous chicken selections, fresh seafood, and giant salads. Whatever you order, do not miss the opportunity for a side of onion rings. A thick, amazingly tender stack of the sweetest kind always arrives hot and golden. Damon's has mastered the art.

Those in search of a lighter meal should opt for the Honey-Lime Salad. Chicken is scattered atop tossed greens and tomatoes, but what makes this salad a real standout is the fruit—loads of mandarin orange slices as well as fresh pineapple and strawberries. The honey-lime dressing is unique and uniquely delicious. All the desserts are worthwhile, but the Triple Chocolate Truffle Cake is sure to bring you back for more.

Guests can choose between the restaurant's quiet and understated dining room or a high-energy clubhouse atmosphere that showcases DTV—a proprietary state-of-the-art, multiscreen entertainment system that delivers sports, network programming, and interactive games.

Greg Norman's Australian Grille $$$
Barefoot Landing, 4930 Highway 17 South, North Myrtle Beach
(843) 361–0000
www.shark.com/gwse

This exceedingly popular restaurant's namesake is the same Greg "the Shark" Norman of golfing fame who designed the Norman Course, which you can view from your table at his Australian Grille.

The flavors and seafood-heavy selection of the Australian Grille perfectly complement a stay on the Carolina coast, and the lively, aboriginal decor of the Grille

Insiders' Tip
During June, July, and August, Brookgreen Gardens offers the most soothing dinners available on the Grand Strand. Open until 9:30 P.M. Tuesday through Friday, Brookgreen offers a gourmet summer supper amidst their spectacular, manicured gardens. Adult admission is $12.00 plus the cost of dinner. Additionally, the Terrace Cafe is open for lunch and dinner. Call Brookgreen at (843) 235-6000 for more information or visit www.brookgreen.org.

goes well with our own Lowcountry stylings. The menu is amazing: pan-fried lobster dumplings, Tasmanian sea mussels, miso and cane sugar–marinated sea bass, habanero-rubbed tenderloin, yellow fin tuna, and all sorts of Australian-inspired nightly specials. Tables are hard to get, and reservations are recommended. The Shark Pub is just as spacious and elegant as the dining rooms and includes a few TVs for sporting events (hmm, wonder which ones). It has its own satisfying menu: fried calamari tossed in a sweet-and-sour chili glaze, Queensland cut fries, and famous pizza baked in an authentic wood-burning oven.

Jaspers Cafe $$
310 McCorsley Avenue, Little River
(843) 663–2233

Jaspers Cafe is a fairly new addition in the Little River area. Owners Shirley Jobmann and John Mazzucca have created a rustic and comfortably casual atmosphere that is perfect for families. Many support the claim that Jasper's serves the best burgers on the beach. Other entrees include everything from steak and seafood to pasta. Prices are extremely reasonable, particularly for the midday meal. Jaspers Cafe is open for lunch and dinner Monday through Saturday but is closed on Sunday.

Joe's Bar & Grill $$$
810 Conway Avenue, North Myrtle Beach
(843) 272–4666
www.dinejoes.com

Owner and chef Joey Arakas wanted to give the Grand Strand a restaurant that would make diners feel as though they never left the comforts of their own homes. Fine dining in a rather rustic atmosphere is what has kept Joe's one of the busiest establishments in town for more than a decade.

Joe's is not the place to go if you have a craving for something fried: There is no such thing on this menu. The cuisine is

Many area restaurants offer live entertainment—making dinner and dancing a delightful option.
PHOTO: COURTESY OF LITCHFIELD BEACH & GOLF RESORT

definitely continental, including steak, seafood, veal, and poultry dishes. All marinades, sauces, soups, and dressings are made fresh daily. For seafood lovers, be sure to try the char-grilled swordfish with a jalapeño-lime cream sauce or the teriyaki tuna bites. Joe's is open for dinner only.

The Parson's Table $$$$
Highway 17 North, Little River
(843) 249-3702
www.parsonstable.com

Ed Murray Jr., executive chef and owner, brings more than two decades of culinary experience to the Parson's Table. He was recently selected one of the Best Chefs in America—one of only eighty chefs in the country to attain the designation. As such, he joins illustrious company that includes Wolfgang Puck, Alice Waters, Jeremiah Tower, Lydia Shire, Louis Osteen, Jean-Louis Paladin, and Elizabeth B. Terry. With credentials like these, you can rest assured you will enjoy a truly world-class meal.

Mouth-watering entrees run the gamut from prime rib and tender filet mignon, to veal, pork, lamb, roast duckling, and plenty of fresh seafood. This writer's favorite are the Little River Crabcakes. Lightly sautéed and served with a distinctive dill mustard sauce, this crab cake stands out in a region where almost everyone has a favorite crab cake recipe. Sautéed in lemon butter, the Little River Shrimp and Scallops, featuring fresh local shrimp and tender scallops, boasts an unexpected southern touch—chopped pecans. It's a different twist you won't soon forget.

A longtime favorite of locals and returning visitors, the Parson's Table is ranked among the "Top 50 Best Overall Restaurants" in the United States by the Academy Awards of the Restaurant Industry. It was recently ranked number one in *Historic Restaurants of South Carolina Mobil Travel Guide* and received a coveted Silver Spoon award from the Gourmet Diners Club of America. If you're looking for elegance and a sure bet, this is your winner.

Sante Fe Station $$
1101 U.S. Highway 17,
North Myrtle Beach
(843) 249-3463

The single most distinctive thing about Sante Fe Station is the menu. It's bound to remind you of a metropolitan area phone book . . . it's enormous!

Sante Fe Station is fun—very youthful in atmosphere but not at all trendy. This restaurant has a great bar; have the bartender whip you up a fabulous specialty drink. There are 18 items on the appetizer menu alone! (Skip the reading: Order Oysters Rockefeller or Blackened Filet Tips.) Entrees run the gamut, from healthy salads and fresh seafood to fat sandwiches, steaks, burgers, chicken, and ribs. There's a kid's menu, too. For dessert the Key lime pie will soothe your sunburn. Better still, order a pitcher of Long Island iced tea and forget your worries. Sante Fe Station is open seven days a week for dinner only.

T-Bonz Gill & Grill $$
Barefoot Landing, 4732 U.S. Highway 17,
North Myrtle Beach
(843) 272-7111
U.S. Highway 17 Bypass and 21st Avenue
North, Myrtle Beach
(843) 946-7111
www.tbonz.com

T-Bonz' big ole menu and spacious (if noisy) interior is fun, fun, fun. Hearty portions of beef, grilled chicken, vegetarian entrees, seafood, and more are standard fare. For the Southern born 'n' bred, we think you'll be particularly fond of the shrimp-and-grits specialty—a creamier dish of the snowy stuff has never been created to our knowledge. We sometimes choose T-Bonz just because the folks there are so environmentally conscious. They recycle all their glass and cardboard and avoid the use of plastic foam. The atmosphere is casual, the price is affordable, and kids are welcome.

Open from 11:00 A.M. until late night, T-Bonz also offers light lunches and an after-hours social scene. Stop in at either location.

Theme Restaurants

A glass-cased, cyborg Arnold Schwartzenegger, armed and dangerous, watches you. Captain America's suit stands at the ready. A huge pyramid covered with mysterious hieroglyphics rises out of a palm tree–studded parking lot. A $50,000, vintage chopper gleams with chrome. The Chevrolet that Jeff Gordon drove to win the Winston Cup Championship is parked out front. One of the country's largest collections of Folk or "Outsider" art by artists in the rural South fills walls with shoes, bottle caps, license plates, and memorials to artisans. Bullwinkle pulls a rabbit out of his hat.

Myrtle Beach restaurants have all this and more.

So many restaurants compete for our attention that every single one strives for that niche that will make you crave its own specialized menu. But quite a few restaurants are getting a little more aggressive than hanging wacky antiques on the walls or letting you draw on the paper tablecloths with crayons. From outlandish architecture to glass-encased collections to celebrity owners, quite a few restaurants along the Grand Strand are rewriting the recipe for a fun, new-experience-filled, and bedazzling dining experience.

House of Blues, Hard Rock Cafe, NASCAR Cafe, Caddyshack, Planet Hollywood, the Dixie Stampede, and Bullwinkle's are the best examples of this new restaurant trend. They're also the most popular, so they are easy to recognize and find but, then again, parking might not be. They put on an elaborate show, though, and work hard for their money.

House of Blues in Barefoot Landing, North Myrtle Beach, is visible from U.S. Highway 17, but you might mistake it for a massive barn that someone forgot to tear down. Don't keep on driving—the House of Blues means to present this elegantly shabby image, and once you're a little closer you will not only agree with their decision, you will be entranced. The 43,000-square-foot structure looks like it is one of the originals in Myrtle Beach, but it has been open just a few years. To achieve this effect, the House of Blues went around the country buying not only the art and artifacts that fill the place, but also actually used and worn architectural and construction material, then carefully pieced it all together into the 700 capacity restaurant, outdoor "Sugar Shack" deck, and 1,800 capacity concert hall that stands today.

The grand opening of the House of Blues was the biggest yet of all the splashes these restaurants put on, and we had the opportunity to attend. Instead of the formal, roped off runway of stars and the many celebrity investors, the House of Blues hosted a casual affair where we all enjoyed the courtyards and patios together. Dan Aykroyd, James Belushi, and John Goodman rode right in on their loud Harleys; Cheech Marin brought all his kids; Alice Cooper showed up, as did quite a few bands and other musicians, including James Brown.

Inside and out the House of Blues is covered with more than 5,000 original paintings and sculptures by more than 60 self-taught creators. The art is almost primitive and rough but at the same time inspirational and full of expression. New favorites will inspire every time you visit. The deep porches and covered walkways serve as an openair gallery; there's even plenty of wicker to rest on in the spacious Charleston-influenced courtyard shaded by live oak trees. You don't have to spend any money for this cultural experience; just walk through the welcoming, 11-foot wrought-iron gates.

However, don't expect to get off without spending a few pennies. The restaurant, with its Southern pit-cooking smells and ceiling embossed with portraits of blues legends, will draw you in. Every time we go, much as we try to order something else, we can't stay away from the Mississippi Cat Bites and the mashed sweet potatoes. Of course there's a lot more, from the Blues Brothers Salad to jambalaya to the smoked double-cut pork chops.

But even more irresistible is the House of Blues' Sunday gospel brunch. Every Sunday morning gospel groups from around the South perform at the House of Blues concert hall. It is an invigorating, soul-stirring experience. The elaborate banquet of grits, biscuits, roast beef, shrimp and rice, sausage, and delicious bread pudding almost gets in the way of all the napkin waving, foot stomping, and hallelujah-ing. By the end of the performance, your tummy is full, your spirit renewed, and half the audience members are up on stage singing their hearts out. As you can imagine, kids love it.

For more information on the musical talent that appears at the House of Blues, see the KICKS! entertainment section of every Friday's *Sun News*.

Hard Rock Cafe at Broadway at the Beach is probably the most recognized and picturesque; at any sunny moment, the sphinxes that guard the Hard Rock entrances are a favorite snapshot point. This international Pharaoh of restaurants occupies a huge pyramid surrounded by palm trees along the U.S. Highway 17 Bypass. It's hard to miss; at night it is lit up with spotlights, and around the clock it blares good old rock 'n' roll. The Hard Rock Cafe in Myrtle Beach—with its pyramid shape—is the only Hard Rock Cafe in the world built in this distinctive shape. The spectacular lighted fountain that graces its entrance is also one of a kind. When you enter the structure, you're a floor above the dining room—from this vantage point you get a bird's-eye view of everyone else's meals and the cafe's collection of historic rock memorabilia.

The interior is covered with a stone finish, more hieroglyphics, and mementos of rock and roll. The walls vibrate with echoes from the guitars of Hank Williams Jr., The Who, Joe Walsh, the Allman Brothers, Black Crowes, Black Sabbath, Pearl Jam, Guns and Roses, Jimi Hendrix, Bob Dylan, and Jerry Garcia. These instruments were once in the hands of legends, and now they're out in the open to enjoy as you dine. A

Hard Rock Cafe in Myrtle Beach rocks like an Egyptian. PHOTO: LISA TOMER RENTZ

myriad of displays fill every nook, even at the phone booth and in the rest rooms: Nancy Sinatra's made-for-walkin' boots, gold lamé shorts from Rocky of the *Rocky Horror Picture Show,* Brian Jones' fur coat, and countless gold and platinum records from the likes of Buddy Holly, Nirvana, the Osmonds, and the Beatles.

Of course the menu can't be outdone by the elaborate interior, and you have your choice of almost 50 items. The Hard Rock, with its "Love All, Serve All" philosophy, has cooked up a selection for every lifestyle, from the Hard Rock Natural Veggie Burger to the Hickory Chicken 'N Ribs Combo. If you're just old fashioned, you can top it all off with a thick, cold milk shake or malt.

Just south of Hard Rock on the Bypass is the NASCAR Cafe festooned in checkered flags. NASCAR has definitely transcended the restaurant category by adding a 20-acre racetrack—please see the Attractions chapter for more details. The designers couldn't even stop thinking about the track when they designed the restaurant; upon entry to the building you have to look both ways to cross Bill France Boulevard, which is busy with people checking out the displays and playing the many interactive video games. The boulevard is a walk through NASCAR history; Mr. France, whose life-size wax figure starts off the course, founded NASCAR in 1948. Huge sections of wall are dedicated to the icons of the racing world: Richard Petty, Dave Marcis, Dale Earnhardt, Chad Little, even Speed Racer. Throughout the restaurant 13 race cars are suspended from the ceiling, providing you with a novel, not to mention sloweddown, look at the machines.

Inside the circle of Bill France Boulevard is the NASCAR Cafe proper. Booths form another circular track around a massive bar that is crowned with David Pearson's Mercury Purolator, which won the 1976 Daytona Championship. Even the wait staff is groomed for speed; everyone wears a sleek red jumpsuit for ease of movement and a headset for quick communication; all the sooner to zip out platefuls of Thunder Road Burgers, Longtrack Chili Dogs, Bill France Pork Chops, or a chocolate fudge tire.

For more theme-time fun, back in Celebrity Square at Broadway at the Beach is Caddyshack. Murray Brothers Caddyshack is one of the more recent additions to Broadway at the Beach. The restaurant is designed to look and feel like a country club gone awry. Comedian Bill Murray and his five brothers—actors Brian, Joel, and John and businessmen Andy and Ed—encourage guests to "Eat, Drink and Be Murray." The concept is accredited to Andy Murray, longtime chef and restaurateur, and co-founder Mac Haskell. Here the brothers' love of golf runs headlong into their side-splitting sense of irreverence. The Caddyshack name recalls the brothers' teenage years, when all of them worked as caddies and in other golf-related jobs to earn tuition for Catholic school. And it is of course the name of one of Bill Murray's hit movies, which was co-written by Brian Doyle-Murray.

The 8,500-square-foot restaurant opens onto a 3,000-square-foot deck that overlooks Broadway at the Beach's lake. Nearly 300 guests can be accommodated easily. The "Bunker Bar," featuring specialty drinks and televisions aplenty to cover multiple sporting events, seats a few additional dozens. Looper's Lounge, which doubles as a billiards room, provides a spacious area to accommodate large groups. And "The Shed" sells Murray Brothers merchandise, including T-shirts, hats, glasses, golf attire, and miscellaneous golf gadgets.

The restaurant's interior highlights the brothers, the sport of caddying, and that classic Murray trait—humor. More importantly for hungry patrons, the restaurant features a full-service, continental menu that includes everything from wings and peel 'n' eat shrimp to oversize salads, all sorts of sandwiches and signature clubs, as well as steaks, barbecue, fresh seafood, chicken, ribs, and pasta. Murray Brothers Caddyshack is open seven days a week for lunch and dinner.

Planet Hollywood sits just across 25th Avenue from Broadway at the Beach. A meal here will leave you feeling like you've broken bread with your favorite luminaries. The building itself is a blue and green planet, and the cement foundation is imprinted with the handprints and signatures of Bruce Willis, Demi Moore, Sylvester Stallone, Arnold Schwartzenegger, Melanie Griffith, Don Johnson, Jean Claude Van Damme, and others. The wait at Planet Hollywood begins right here since most visitors love to compare their own hands with those of the stars.

Inside Planet Hollywood is a panorama of blockbuster movie hits. Throughout all the display cases, between booths, around pillars, and covering an entire two-story wall is a collage of superstar faces a la the Sgt. Pepper's Lonely Hearts Club Band album cover. George Clooney looks mischievous, Elvis croons, Melanie hugs Don, Demi looks captivating in an evening gown as does Bruce in his muscle T, Mel Gibson and Wesley Snipes compete for a toughness award and, for some reason, Antonio Banderas is bowling but still manages to look smooth as can be.

In unmistakable Hollywood kitsch, animal print is the upholstery of choice, lending a stylish appeal to the fun restaurant. So settle in and unfold the 4-foot-long menu. Start off with a cocktail—a Ghost or a Cliffhanger or, if you're brave, The Terminator (catch that pattern?). As an appetizer we recommend the Chicken Crunch,

Planet Hollywood's outlandish architecture causes you to wonder what awaits you inside.
PHOTO: COURTESY OF PLANET HOLLYWOOD

which is tender chicken strips coated with CAP'N CRUNCH™ cereal and served with creole mustard. For the main course the menu offers a fusion of West Coast, Italian, and Asian.

Bullwinkle's Family Food and Fun is also on 25th Avenue, within easy sight of Planet Hollywood. The Bullwinkle's building keeps pace with the architectural precedent set by its colorful neighbors. Cartoonishly klondike, the restaurant is a split-log lodge straight out of Frostbite Falls. Inside, children have the opportunity to play in a towering soft play structure, while Bullwinkle the Moose ("Guess I didn't know my own strength") and Rocky the Flying Squirrel ("Again? That trick never works") are as animated as ever. The play structure has slides, wobbling walkways, and a clubhouse, among many other tricks and turns for young'uns to explore. Since there is no size or age limit, parents are encouraged to accompany their mini-mounties through this rollicking obstacle course. Fortunately, after all that hard play, you won't need Mr. Peabody's Way Back Machine to find and enjoy Rocky's Remarkable burgers, Dudley's Done Right Pizza, or some yummy Klondike Fried Chicken.

Music City Grille (formerly The Alabama Grille) is located on Highway 17 Bypass, across from Broadway at the Beach. The Grille promises as much entertainment as its original namesake, the Alabama Theatre at Barefoot Landing. The menu is suitably hearty, and special "Alabama's favorites" are marked with a musical note: bacon and cheese skins, ultimate club sandwich, southern fried chicken salad, smokehouse burger, the Alabama savory sirloin, and smoky mountain chicken. The Grille's specialty dessert is a down-home cheesecake with a luscious swirl of sweet potato. Randy, Teddy, Jeff, and Mark, who make up the supergroup Alabama, got their start right here in Myrtle Beach in the '70s. Since then they have sold more records than the Beatles, a figure built on over 40 No. 1 hits. So, in one day, you can experience their beginnings at the Bowery (near the Pavilion) have dinner amongst all their pictures, guitars, signatures, carefully framed outfits, sheet music, and favorite meals, and see them live at their theater. Though the memorabilia posted around the restaurant (and the items in the gift store, and many of the videos played in the video walls) do concentrate on Alabama, there is a unifying country theme, bringing in the biggest country hits of the moment.

A bit farther north, where Highway 17 Business and Bypass meet, Dolly Parton's Dixie Stampede has proved itself one of the Grand Strand's most spectacular dinner shows. With nearly three dozen horses, dozens of talented cast members, and cozy seating for a thousand situated around a 35,000-square-foot arena, Dixie Stampede is a Dolly Parton creation. A one-price ticket includes the show, a satisfying four-course feast, and entertainment in the nonalcoholic saloon prior to the show.

Tony's Italian Restaurant $$
1407 Old Highway 17 North,
North Myrtle Beach
(843) 249–1314

Tony's is the oldest Italian restaurant along the Grand Strand and has been owned and operated by the Springs family since opening its doors in 1953. The recipes for Tony's dishes have been handed down from generation to genera-tion, and the kitchen never compromises its homemade quality. Nothing on your plate at Tony's is prepackaged or frozen; even the herbs are fresh-picked from the restaurant's very own garden.

Our perfect Tony's dining experience starts with the Clams Posillipo (steamed clams draped with marinara sauce) as an appetizer followed by the Terri Lynn Veal Scallopini featuring fresh mushrooms and artichoke hearts in a brown brandy sauce.

For dessert we heartily recommend the chocolate Godiva cake, a wicked seven-layer cake laced with Godiva liquor. Tony's is open Monday through Saturday for dinner.

White Point Cafe $
3303 U.S. Highway 17 South,
North Myrtle Beach
(843) 272–6732

White Point Cafe has successfully combined the big Calabash-style seafood-house flavor with the atmosphere of the keep-it-a-secret neighborhood restaurant.

The menu offers all your favorite seafood—she-crab soup, oysters, shrimp, flounder, and scallops—in plate-filling combinations topped off with, what else, some of the Grand Strand's best hush-puppies. Occasionally we stop in just for a hushpuppy fix, lunch or dinner.

Myrtle Beach

U.S. Highway 17 Business is known as Kings Highway throughout Myrtle Beach. The Kings Highway address is used for establishments listed in this section.

Akel's House of Pancakes $
6409 North Kings Highway, Myrtle Beach
(843) 449–4815

For local color, don't miss Akel's; it's a Myrtle Beach landmark. In an area known for its stellar lineup of pancake houses, Akel's rates right up top. Whether for the food, the service, or the all-night hours, we're not sure. The atmosphere is friendly and surprisingly familiar. Gossip, laughter, and local news travels from one table to another; a meal here is as good as reading the local paper!

Open 10:00 P.M. to 2:00 P.M., Akel's is everybody's favorite way to wrap up a night on the town. Needless to say, it's a great way to start your morning, too. Come watch the locals in their element! While breakfast fare is the house specialty, Akel's offers lots of sandwiches, salads, and burgers, too.

Angelo's Steak & Pasta $
2011 South Kings Highway, Myrtle Beach
(843) 626–2800

Angelo's is the home of the all-you-can-eat Italian buffet that includes lasagna, chicken cacciatore, pizza, spaghetti, stuffed shells, tortellini Alfredo, stuffed ravioli, and Italian sausage. Every meal at this restaurant is accompanied with a big bowl of crisp salad served family-style and wonderful garlic rolls.

A full-service menu is available as well, and Angelo's claims to serve "the greatest steaks in the universe." If you're like us, you'll spend a good amount of time mulling over whether to head for the buffet or try a sirloin . . . Both are mouth-watering.

Angelo's opens for dinner at 4:00 P.M. every day of the week. The Italian buffet closes at 8:30 P.M.

The Bistro $$$
5101 North Kings Highway, Myrtle Beach
(843) 449–0465

The Bistro is a very quaint restaurant that serves sumptuous continental cuisine and extraordinary desserts. Indoors, about 40 people can enjoy the friendly atmosphere. If the weather cooperates, about 16 additional guests can dine on the porch. Specialties include veal, steaks, chicken, and pasta dishes.

The Bistro is open for lunch and dinner, and it's the perfect choice for a romantic interlude. Dinner is served from 5:00 P.M. at this longtime locals' favorite. They are closed on Sunday and Monday.

Cagney's Old Place $$$
Restaurant Row, 9911 U.S. Highway 17 North,
Myrtle Beach
(843) 449–3824

For nearly two decades, Cagney's Old Place has been a favorite local dining and dancing spot—and tourists have discovered our secret. There's ambiance aplenty and great food, too. Many of the antiques that enliven Cagney's decor came from the Ocean Forest Hotel, a fabulous ocean-front accommodation that was demolished in 1974.

Cagney's specialty has always been prime rib, but everything is perfectly delicious. A children's menu is also available. *Southern Living,* a magazine reputed for its high standards, recommends this classic.

Only dinner is served at Cagney's.

Carolina Roadhouse $$
4700 North Kings Highway, Myrtle Beach
(843) 497–9911
www.californiadreamings.com

Brought to you by Jerry Greenbaum, who created wildly successful restaurants in other cities—California Dreaming, Frank ManZetti's, and Joey D's, to name a few—Carolina Roadhouse is another "home run."

Like her sister restaurants, Carolina Roadhouse displays unusually beautiful architecture and interior design. Soaring ceilings, arched windows, skillfully positioned mirrors, and an abundance of recessed lighting establish a mood that is intimate without a hint of stuffiness. The sweet, spicy scent of cedar abounds, as does a medley of exquisite smells from the wide-open kitchen.

The service is outstanding; so is the food. From tender barbecue chicken to melt-in-your-mouth ribs, steaks, and seafood, the portions and variety are impressive. Salads, sporting an incomparable hot bacon and honey-mustard dressing, are enormous and otherworldly. A plain ole croissant takes on a new dimension served hot, dripping with warm honey. Seafood gumbo, brimming with okra, shrimp, and crawfish, is anything but ordinary. And vacating the premises without sampling a bowl of baked potato soup would be an absolute injustice. For dessert, try the Key lime pie. It tastes "straight from the grove."

Open daily for lunch and dinner (same menu), Carolina Roadhouse is one of the most happening restaurants in Myrtle Beach, so don't miss out. Dress is casual, and reservations are accepted. Go quickly.

Chestnut Hill $$$
Restaurant Row, 9922 U.S. Highway 17, Myrtle Beach
(843) 449–3984
www.chestnuthilldining.com

In an area saturated with fine-dining options, Chestnut Hill distinguishes itself. Smack-dab in the heart of Restaurant Row, Chestnut Hill sits beneath age-old oaks and overlooks a small, quiet lake. Its location is worlds removed from the resort hustle-bustle and sets the stage for a dining experience that's out of the ordinary.

From the pasta sauces to the cheesecakes, absolutely everything is made from scratch, and 80 percent of the fresh seafood served here was caught on Chestnut Hill's own boat—just hours before. The menu is filled with gourmet dishes, and the service is friendly and accommodating.

Owners Chris and Greg Lee have several extremely popular restaurants along the Strand, and they know more than a thing or two about feeding hungry people.

Dinner is served every evening. Chestnut Hill serves an outstanding Sunday brunch.

Collectors Cafe and Gallery $$$$
7726 North Kings Highway, Myrtle Beach
(843) 449–9370

Everybody has their own concept of a great restaurant. Some enjoy the casual, comfortable, and unpretentious. Some like the blue-blood feeling they derive from the attentive service in an elegant restaurant. Still others prefer the intimacy of a neighborhood bar or coffeehouse. Amazingly, Collectors Cafe has managed to fuse all three environments, and we can't imagine anyone who wouldn't be satisfied spending an evening here.

In the dining room, columns and high ceilings exude elegance and original paintings depict Lowcountry seascapes as well as Parisian cityscapes. Beyond the dining room, a grill room with oversize canvases and hand-tiled, bar-height tables allow you to watch Collectors' chefs chop and sizzle. In the coffeehouse room you can relax and feel a little bohemian while surrounded by more original art that includes not only hanging canvases but artwork on every surface, table, wall, and chair.

Surrounding patrons with all this art, Collectors Cafe serves up a feast for the senses as well as for the appetite. (By the way, most of the art is available to add to your own collection. Please refer to the Arts and Culture chapter for the Close-up on one of the artists, Thomas Davis.)

The restaurant bills itself as serving Mediterranean cuisine. Appetizers include a filet of beef carpaccio with extra virgin olive oil, spicy mustard, balsamic vinegar, and Parmesan cheese. A favorite entree is pan-sauteed crab cakes with crisp, grilled asparagus. The roasted garlic turnip puree is pleasantly different—and delicious. Of course, there are also pasta and salad selections as well as veal and lots of fresh seafood.

After dinner take time to enjoy the homemade tiramisu, or for that matter any of the desserts; you can walk an extra mile or two on the beach tomorrow.

As a gallery, Collectors Cafe opens at noon, Monday through Saturday. The restaurant is open for dinner only and reservations are highly recommended.

Dagwoods $
400 11th Avenue North, Myrtle Beach
(843) 448–0100
www.dagwoodsdeli.com

Since the 1940s, the term "Dagwood" has referred to a multidecker sandwich stuffed with anything and everything. That pretty much describes the fare here.

It takes two big hands to handle the monstrous subs at Dagwoods. There's not a lot of ambience—Dagwoods is a frat hangout at its best—but with sandwiches and prices like these, who cares?

Baskets of homemade bread (baked fresh daily) and an authentic deli case greet you at the door—reminiscent of a New York delicatessen. Choose from a variety of hot and cold sandwiches that showcase a mile-high stack of meats and cheeses. You can feast on burgers and Philly cheese steaks, too. At lunchtime, local business folk frequent the place, so it's gotta be good.

Dagwoods is open for lunch and dinner. (Suggestion: Come for lunch and eat the other half of your sub for dinner.)

Dirty Don's Oyster Bar & Grill $$
408 21st Avenue North, Myrtle Beach
(843) 448–4881

Dirty Don's is small in size but big on character. Serving lunch and dinner, Dirty Don's features oyster shooters, clams on the half shell, a variety of sandwiches, and a tasty seafood chowder. The catfish fingers are fab, especially with a margarita. Bigger appetites are fond of the juicy steaks and king-size shrimp dinners.

Dirty Don's is the perfect place to spend an afternoon out of the sun . . . noshing on appetizers and drinking tall cool ones.

Fiesta Del Burro Loco $$
960 Jason Boulevard (U.S. Highway 17 Bypass and 10th Avenue North), Myrtle Beach
(843) 626–1756
www.californiadreamings.com

Fiesta Del Burro Loco is one of the newer restaurants on the Strand, but you'd never know it by looking. The exterior of the building was created to look authentically old and straight from Mexico; its visual appeal alone is a draw.

Once inside you won't be disappointed. The interior is eclectic and every bit as extraordinary as the exterior. At the door you'll be greeted by a three-sided, 45-foot-tall mural of a bullfight.

Other murals are scattered throughout. A billboard collage covers the ceiling. There's an upside-down velvet Elvis mural above the bar. And the whole place is filled with authentic artifacts . . . so filled, you'll discover something new each and every time you visit.

And you must visit. Burro Loco manages to assault your senses in a most delightful way. The smell of fajitas sizzling on a mesquite grill will make your mouth water, as will the pizzas cooking in the wood-burning oven. Once you've tasted Burro Loco's handcrafted margaritas (the limes are squeezed by hand) and their made-from-scratch tortillas, your taste buds will be hooked.

Fiesta Del Burro Loco is open for dinner every day. Reservations are not required, but call-ahead seating is available. Don't miss the fajitas, a house specialty, or the hand-pitted, stuffed jalapeños.

Flamingo Seafood Grill $$$
7100 North Kings Highway, Myrtle Beach
(843) 449-5388

Insiders' Tip

One easy way to pack a picnic is to stop by the Grecian Corner in the Galleria Shopping Center in Restaurant Row. There's not much sitting room, but the menu covers all the Greek favorites, such as gyros and souvlaki, and they serve pizza too. Call ahead, (843) 449-9234.

Flamingo Grill's art-deco decor—black lacquer accented with pink and blue neon—sets the pace for a trendy evening of dining. Owned by the same folks of Cagney's fame (see this chapter's previous entry), this restaurant has become quite popular.

The menu includes lots of fresh seafood prepared in a variety of ways. The grilled fish with Cajun spices is especially tasty. Other entrees include pasta (the Pasta Flamingo is delish), chicken, prime rib, and steak. As an appetizer, the filet mignon chunks are outstanding. Save room for dessert; the Outrageous Derby Pie is . . . well . . . outrageous. A children's menu is also available.

Flamingo Grill serves dinner only.

Joe's Crab Shack $$
1219 Celebrity Circle, Broadway at the Beach
(843) 626-4490
www.joescrabshack.com

It's a tacky-looking shack of a restaurant. The interior feels like a Gulf Coast fishing camp and the menu serves up scads of crabs—cooked in a myriad of ways. As a whole the Joe's experience is classic, cool, and comfortable. You can pound a few crabs on the patio or slip inside for a newspaper-covered table. Either way, cool beverages enhance the experience. The menu is enormous—not just crabs—and includes plenty of appetizers, sandwiches, salads, steaks, and more.

Obviously Joe's specialty is crab and variety is offered year-round. Steamed, barbecued, or garlic style, expect whatever's in season—Alaskan King Crab, Dungeness Crab, Alaskan Snow Crab, and Blue Crab. Joe also offers "Rug Rat" and Group menus.

For kick-backed and casual, Joe's can't be beat.

Liberty Steakhouse and Brewery $$
Broadway at the Beach,
U.S. Highway 17 Bypass, Myrtle Beach
(843) 626-4677
www.tbonz.com

The idea of combining a restaurant and microbrewery is hot these days, and Liberty Steakhouse is doing well sustaining

Broadway at the Beach has a plethora of shops and restaurants in a breezy, bright setting. PHOTO: LISA TOMER RENTZ

the craze. Here guests enjoy beer that's made fresh every single day. On special holidays, such as Oktoberfest and St. Patrick's Day, seasonal brews are all the rage. Everyone who comes gets the opportunity to observe the working brewery staffed by expert brewmeisters. In itself, the beer-making lesson is worth the stop. The pleasant surprise is that the food is wonderful, too.

The menu includes hearty and delicious standard fare in whopping portions: specialty cuts of beef, original-recipe burgers, and unique appetizers and entrees such as buffalo shrimp.

Liberty is open for lunch and dinner.

The Library $$$$
1212 North Kings Highway, Myrtle Beach
(843) 448–9242

The Library is one of the most elegant restaurants in the entire South—recipient of guests' kudos as well as prestigious professional accolades. Offering consummate European cuisine and superior service, this restaurant has been quietly collecting fans since 1974. In a *Sun News* survey, locals voted The Library the "most romantic" dining spot on the Strand—with so many restaurants, that's a real coup! The menu includes veal, seafood, duck, beef, and chicken . . . first class all the way. The name comes from the literary decor, of course; the walls are lined with cases of literature that accentuate the leisurely and almost genteel atmosphere. Open for dinner only.

New York Prime $$$$
405 28th Avenue North, Myrtle Beach
(843) 448–8081
www.newyorkprime.com

New York Prime is one of the area's finest restaurants. Owners Ed Cribb and Jerry

Greenbaum first envisioned the restaurant when they returned from a trip to New York, where they ate at Peter Luger's, The Palm, Spark's and Smith and Wollensky. Reminiscing, they wondered if a real New York–style steak house would make it on the Grand Strand. In researching the concept, Ed and Jerry traveled around to see what America's best steak houses have in common. They discovered that people will pay more for quality, but the food must be truly exemplary.

Concept confirmed, they went to Nebraska, where they established a unique supply chain, purchasing only from two slaughterhouses that ship according to Ed's and Jerry's incredibly stringent specifications. Upon receipt, they age their meat for 28 to 35 days, then trim it of excess fat.

The cooking completes the technique. No spices and no tenderizers disguise inferior meat. Cuts are extra thick, and ceramic broilers cook at 1,700 degrees.

The same attention to detail in supply and preparation goes into every morsel of food at New York Prime. Expect the freshest fish, giant lobsters shipped direct and kept live (never frozen), fresh Idaho potatoes, sweet Vidalia onions, and tomatoes straight from sunny California. An extensive wine cellar will complement your dining experience.

The prices are steep, but the experience is extraordinary, and the quality entirely justifies the prices. Open for dinner nightly.

Nick's on Sixty-First $$$
503 61st Avenue, Myrtle Beach
(843) 449–1716

As attentive owners greet you, prepare to launch an incredible culinary experience. A spectacular menu is comprised of certified prime steaks, lamb, veal, duck, pasta, always-fresh fish, and other creative surprises.

This is one of few restaurants on the Strand that's adopted the tradition of tapas. They're perfect with a few glasses from the extensive wine list. Tapas-size portions also allow patrons to save room for dessert. The pastry chef, John Nye, has

won awards for his Roasted Pear with champagne-vanilla sauce. The Flowing Chocolate Soufflé has earned quite a following as well.

Nick's is open for lunch and dinner Monday through Saturday. Since savvy locals have made this one of the area's most popular restaurants, reservations are strongly suggested.

River City Cafe $
404 21st Avenue North, Myrtle Beach
(843) 448–1990
U.S. Highway 17 Business, Murrells Inlet
(843) 651–1004
www.rivercitycafe.com

River City Cafe is the best hamburger joint on the beach for reasons only a bona fide hamburger connoisseur would appreciate. First, it's the perfect setting: a wood-frame building that resembles an old beach house. Inside you'll find worn wooden floors, benches, and chairs. Car tags, bumper stickers, and party paraphernalia adorn the ceiling and walls.

Outside at the Murrells Inlet location, you'll find a wraparound porch with swings and a sunny deck peppered with big picnic tables. Inside not a single table or chair matches. Expect a crackling fire to be burning in winter, and the music is great.

At both locations, customers serve themselves from the big bin of dry-roasted peanuts and throw the empty shells on the floor—just oozes class, huh? But this all leads to the best part: huge, 100-percent pure-beef burgers topped with a variety of fixin's, such as thick slabs of cheese, jalapeños, lettuce, tomatoes, grilled onions, bacon . . . the works!

These burgers require two hands to manage, and although they can be a little messy, they're worth several napkins. Don't forget the homemade jumbo onion rings. River City also serves a variety of other sandwiches and hot dogs. It's been said that only an ice-cold longneck bottle of beer truly complements River City Cafe's burgers. We think Jimmy Buffett's *Cheeseburger in Paradise* was inspired by this savory spot. Open for lunch and dinner daily.

Rossi's $$$
The Galleria, 9600 U.S. Highway 17 North, Myrtle Beach
(843) 449–0481

Rossi's bills itself as "everything a restaurant ought to be," and we have to agree. A bevy of delights awaits your arrival: overly generous servings of veal, homemade pasta, fresh seafood, and Black Angus beef; fine wines; a cozy dining room featuring weathered brick, stained glass and chandeliers; a piano bar; live entertainment; and desserts that'll make you do the two-step.

Rossi's is open daily for dinner only.

Sam Snead's Tavern $$
Restaurant Row, U.S. Highway 17 North, Myrtle Beach
(843) 497–0580
www.samsneadstavern.com

In the heart of Restaurant Row, Sam Snead's Tavern offers a delicious retreat from the workaday blues—or from vacation overdrive. Not small but marvelously cozy, Sam Snead's serves up memorable food in a memorable atmosphere.

The experience begins when the dark, sweet smell of burning oak assaults you. Fascinating golf memorabilia from Sam Snead's renowned PGA career is richly displayed on every available surface. Soft lights spill shadows in corners and polished wood abounds. The result is casual elegance that is both fun and affordable.

As for the food, there's a lot of it—and it's remarkably good. A great many choices feature flavors fresh from the aromatic wood-burning oven. Don't miss the Deep-Fried Wontons: delicate pastries filled with a smoky puree of chicken and peppers. The ribs—hand-rubbed, oak-smoked, and served with homemade Jim Beam barbecue sauce—are a must-try item, too. Desserts are wicked and well worth the mischief; save room or you'll be disappointed.

Skip lunch; you can enjoy only dinner here.

Sea Captain's House $$$
3002 North Ocean Boulevard, Myrtle Beach
(843) 448–8082
www.seacaptains.com

Back around 1930, the Sea Captain's House was a traditional family beach cottage. Converted to an oceanfront restaurant in 1962, it has remained a family-owned and -operated business to this day.

If you enjoy understated elegance, delicious food, and a panoramic view of the ocean, Sea Captain's House is sure to please. Specials range from grilled salmon fillets with roasted garlic sauce to baked breast of chicken topped with Cajun-spiced shrimp. The kitchen staff is known for its culinary talents, particularly with seafood and Southern recipes.

Visit this lovely Myrtle Beach landmark—another personal favorite—for breakfast, lunch, or dinner.

Sea Island, An Inn on the Beach $$$$
6000 North Ocean Boulevard, Myrtle Beach
(843) 449-6406
www.seaislandinn.com

The dining room at the Sea Island Inn is irrefutably one of the best-kept secrets in Myrtle Beach. Because this establishment caters first and foremost to its in-house guests, Sea Island doesn't do a lot of advertising to an outside market. But on a limited basis, the restaurant is open to the public. Lucky us.

This full-service restaurant serves fine continental cuisine for breakfast and dinner with a beautiful ocean view. Dinner is a special treat—you'll need to dress up (men must wear coats). The chef always prepares a five-course meal; you get to choose between five mouth-watering entrees. Seafood is an option, and you'll find enough chicken, beef, and veal alternatives to make your decision a tough one. Everything is fresh, never frozen. The service is impeccable, the atmosphere is intimate, and reservations are required.

Thoroughbreds $$$$
Restaurant Row, U.S. Highway 17 North,
Myrtle Beach
(843) 497-2636
www.thoroughbredsrest.com

A favorite among locals and tourists, Thoroughbreds' popularity has grown by leaps and bounds since it opened in 1988. When the restaurant became unable to accommodate nightly reservations as well as the community's requests for public and private functions, owner and operator Scott Harrelson made the decision to overhaul. Not someone to do anything in a small way, Harrelson spent in excess of $500,000-and it shows. The new Thoroughbreds, featuring five beautifully appointed dining rooms and a captivating veranda, offers an unparalleled celebration of food, spirits, music, and art.

Arguably, this is the most elegant restaurant on the Strand. The wait staff is meticulously trained and very professional, harp music often is highlighted, and candlelight abounds. The menu combines gourmet seafood and continental cuisine. Caesar salads are prepared table side. In our opinion the certified Angus beef is best, but you'll also enjoy chicken, veal, pork, and even duck.

Thoroughbreds boasts a selection of more than 350 wines and is the recipient of several recent Wine Spectator awards.

Lest you be fooled into thinking Thoroughbreds is too ritzy for your average vacation meal, think again. Yes it's elegant, and you do need to dress up a bit, but the atmosphere is cozy, the staff is friendly and accommodating, and children are welcome. We think you'll be glad you donned your finery. This is one of our personal favorites.

Only dinner is served, and reservations are suggested.

Tony Roma's—A Place For Ribs $$
Broadway at the Beach, U.S. Highway 17
Bypass, Myrtle Beach
(843) 448-RIBS
www.tonyromas.com

It's been said that Tony Roma's offers the best ribs in America, and we believe the rumor. Conservative Republicans should choose the original baby backs. If you're a bit more adventurous, consider one of the other four flavors: Carolina Honeys are basted with a sauce made with real honey and molasses; Blue Ridge Smokies boast a hint of molasses laced with burning wood; Tony Roma's Red Hots feature a nearly electric sauce created from five types of peppers; and Bountiful Beef Ribs are big, juicy, and smoky to the bone.

Tony Roma's also serves sensational salads, grilled specialities, a few seafood selections, chicken, and steak. As for appetizers, don't pass up the fried jalapeños stuffed with cheese. With an ice-cold brew in hand, life doesn't get any better than this.

We'd like to point out from personal experience that the staff at Tony Roma's is exceptionally friendly. Obviously they've realized that service makes the difference in a town filled with dining choices.

Villa Mare $$
7819 North Kings Highway (behind Bank of
America), Myrtle Beach
(843) 449-8654

Outdoor decks are among the area's most cherished spots for kicking back to relax, enjoy great food and entertainment, and sip tropical cocktails. PHOTO: COURTESY OF THE MYRTLE BEACH AREA CHAMBER OF COMMERCE

This Italian restaurant is an indisputable locals' favorite. Its simple, unassuming location in a strip mall around the corner from a grocery store is deceiving—this place has class. But, for all its class, it's not a bit pretentious. Clothing is casual; "come as you are, just come hungry," says owner Fred Fusco in a lilting Italian accent.

You'll find everything you'd expect on an Italian menu including calzones and plenty of pastas, and the prices are pleasantly surprising. You can order veal, chicken parmigiana, shrimp piccata, and fettuccine Alfredo and other pasta dishes, all made to order; absolutely everything is good. Plus everyone is friendly, and the atmosphere is light.

We think Villa Mare is a must for anyone who appreciates fine Italian cuisine. Seating is limited, so call ahead for reservations. Villa Mare is open for dinner only Monday through Saturday; it's closed Sundays.

Vintage House Café $$$
**1210 North Kings Highway, Myrtle Beach
(843) 626–3918**

Vintage House Cafe is a gem of a restaurant in the heart of Myrtle Beach. This oasis in the midst of all the hustle and bustle is quite literally a locals' favorite. The atmosphere is cozy and unassuming, and the food is prepared with a flair that always surprises.

Plain ole salads rise to new heights thanks to Vintage House dressings such as raspberry vinaigrette and the splendid fresh herb. The grilled chicken and spinach salad, dressed in toasted pecans and Gorgonzola cheese, is a popular choice. At least one made-from-scratch soup is offered daily. Gourmet sandwiches, quiche, and a host of specials round out a lunch menu that keeps business folks coming back.

The dinner menu is equally impressive. Consider these options: Corn and Black Bean Eggrolls with a Cajun gumbo sauce; and local grouper dusted with Japanese bread crumbs, pan sautéed and topped with sun-dried tomatoes and fresh basil cream. Desserts change daily; all are diet-busting and wonderful.

The Vintage House Cafe is closed Sundays. Lunch is served Monday through Saturday; dinner, Tuesday through Saturday.

South Strand

Bovine's $$$
U.S. Highway 17 Business (on the water-front), Murrells Inlet
(843) 651-2888
www.bovineswoodfired.com

If ever a restaurant was fun, Bovine's is the place: expansive windows overlooking Lowcountry marsh, cozy lighting spilling shadows in every corner, exquisite smells drifting from a wood-burning oven, and the low hum of happy patrons.

Bovine's decor is a tribute to the wonders of the West. Cowhide-covered seats, dark wood, and the mounted head of a gargantuan bull reinforce the theme. The bar scene, separate from the main dining area, spotlights an awesome horseshoe-shaped bar as well as electronic darts, a couple of mounted TVs, and bistro tables scattered about. Comfy booths offer a ringside view of swaying spartina grass and the faraway, blooming lights of Garden City. Feels a little like the summertime hangouts of lost youth—only the patrons are seasoned and a bit more mellow. This is a great place for a beer and an individual-size, gourmet honey-crust pizza from the wood-burning oven. A see-and-be-seen crowd always gathers after work.

As for the food, Bovine's recipe for success features a few ingredients unique to the area. Nearly every selection on the titillating menu boasts a Southwestern slant. A great many choices come from the red-hot, marvelously aromatic, igloo-shaped oven. The variety is quite impressive, including tender char-grilled chicken, melt-in-your-mouth steaks, seafood, and pasta dishes.

Desserts are sinful but worth the mischief. The classic pecan pie is second only to the chocolate walnut brownie.

Bovine's serves dinner only, and reservations are suggested.

Calypso Beach Bar & Grill $$
Oceanfront in Litchfield Inn, Litchfield Beach
(843) 235-5545

This upbeat island-inspired eatery offers what few can—an open-air bar with a spectacular view of sea and surf. Almost as informal as the bar & grill, the upstairs dining room also overlooks the ocean and serves up breathtaking views. As for the menu, the Blue Crab Dip rates up there with Mom's pot roast and potatoes. Standard quesadillas are transformed to extraordinary by the unexpected addition of a spicy Jamaican jerk sauce. And there's plenty more to choose from, including sandwiches, salads, and soups and classic selections from pasta, seafood, and chicken to baby back ribs and steak. One of several house specialties is the Whole Catch of the Day—this chef's selection is actually served whole. The "Sunset Menu" is especially popular. Call ahead for current details. Calypso's is generally open from 6:00 until 10:00 P.M.—sometimes later, if the bar's hoppin'. There's a kids' menu, too—so don't hesitate to bring the little ones!

The Captain's Restaurant $$
3655 U.S. Highway 17 Business,
Murrells Inlet
(843) 651-2416

If you've got a hankerin' for that blue-blood feeling, head straight for The Captain's Restaurant. This beautiful old dining establishment has been in business for more than a quarter century. Only extraordinary restaurants last that long on the Grand Strand.

Good ole Southern cooks Mattie and Ernestine have been laboring in the kitchen since The Captain's Restaurant first opened its doors, and they prepare seafood simply, classically, and complemented by from-scratch accompaniments. Everything is a treat for the palate, but if you love crab, don't pass up the jumbo lump crabmeat dish. Big tender chunks of fresh crabmeat straight from the docks of McClellanville (south of Georgetown) are pan-broiled with a little butter, then served with drawn butter for dipping. It's simple . . . and simply unbeatable. Our second choice is scallops. The Captain serves a hearty plate of the oversize deep-sea kind everyone loves but can never seem to find.

In addition to seafood, the dinner menu includes country ham, beef, and chicken entrees. And nearly everything on the regular menu is also on the seniors' menu, featuring smaller portions and prices—a real hit with older folks. The desserts are to-die-for.

His salads are known far and wide. The shrimp salad with capers is light and unusual. The Neptune salad, a longtime favorite, features shrimp, crabmeat, and lobster. The avocado salad showcases crabmeat, the sweetest shrimp we connoisseurs have ever discovered, and a tarragon-laced remoulade sauce.

This quaint Cape Cod structure overhung with centuries-old oaks is steeped in history and beauty. All the bricks, columns, beams, mahogany wainscoting, pine floors, and the tabby fireplace are original and authentic. Many of the architectural elements were salvaged from the ruins of Charleston's historic buildings.

In June, July, and August The Captain's Restaurant is open seven days a week for lunch and dinner. The rest of the year the Captain takes Monday off. Reservations are not necessary.

The Charleston Cafe $$$
815 Surfside Drive, Surfside Beach
(843) 238-2200

Surfside Beach welcomed The Charleston Cafe with appropriate if inauspicious fanfare: Six hours after opening, Hurricane Hugo swept ashore and left the restaurant without power or water for 10 days. In years since, The Charleston Cafe has developed a fine reputation for romantic meals in an intimate setting; attentive, personable service; and creative, attractively presented food.

Specializing in certified Angus beef, local seafood, and veal and chicken dishes,

The Charleston Cafe also offers a "light eaters" menu with smaller portions of well-liked items. The dessert menu is daunting, and servers parade the choices in front of you. Who can resist?! The Charleston Cafe also features a large list of wines by the glass.

Dinner is served daily, and reservations are strongly suggested.

Conch Cafe $$$
1482 North Waccamaw Drive,
Garden City Beach
(843) 651-6556

Dining at the Conch Cafe is like inviting 100 or so good friends to your beach house for grilled tuna, baked scallops, conch fritters, tenderloin, teriyaki chicken and shrimp, mussels in garlic butter, and a mess of backfin crab cakes. Throw in a Happy Hour, and it's not a shabby way to host a party, right?

Did we mention the covered outdoor deck overlooking the ocean? It's great for stargazing and drinking concoctions with tropical-sounding names.

Lunch and dinner are served daily. Come early and stay late.

From seafood to salad, buffets offer something for everyone. PHOTO: BILL SCROGGINS

Drunken Jack's Restaurant & Lounge $$$
U.S. Highway 17 Business (on the water-front), Murrells Inlet
(843) 651–2044
www.drunkenjacks.com

As legend has it, Drunken Jack was a black-hearted pirate who patrolled Murrells Inlet incessantly, seeking treasure until his alcohol led him to a watery grave. His namesake, a time-tested restaurant and lounge, is a preferred waterfront dining establishment in the Murrells Inlet area. Take time to have cocktails in the lounge and watch the fishing boats come in. Live musical entertainment is another treat.

Seafood and steaks are the house specialties, including filet mignon, frog legs

(a true Southern delicacy), and Robinson Crusoe Special Seafood Coquille. Low-country specialties abound. A children's menu is offered, too.

Drunken Jack's serves dinner only.

Flo's Place & Cajun Restaurant & Raw Bar $$
3797 U.S. Highway 17 Business,
Murrells Inlet
(843) 651–7222
www.flosplace.com

Hats off to owner Flo Triska—literally! For years she and husband Ralph have been running this upbeat Cajun-style restaurant, and people show their gratitude by donating their chapeaus of all shapes and sizes to the area's largest hat display—right in the restaurant. This wood-framed eatery is set on the creek in Murrells Inlet and features Cajun and Creole food that'll make you think you're in steamy New Orleans. In the spirit of Mardi Gras, the clientele has been known to form a conga line through the indoor/outdoor dining room to "eat, drink and be merry."

An all-time favorite menu item is the Dunkin' Pot, a large cast-iron kettle filled with jumbo spiced shrimp, clams, mussels, oysters, corn on the cob, red potatoes, and crawfish. (If you don't know how to eat crawfish, Flo will come by and demonstrate. It's really elementary: Snap off the tail and suck the head first; then peel the tail shell away, revealing the plump meat, and pop it in your mouth.) Another time-tested favorite is the Henry the Eighth rib eye: a 20-ounce, aptly named wonder. Authentic po'boy sandwiches, served on grilled French bread, are marvelous.

There are several sensational appetizers, two of which incorporate alligator meat. The smoked alligator ribs are prepared in a honey-mustard dressing and cooked on the grill. The alligator stew contains more than 24 ingredients!

All the food here is made from scratch. Quench your thirst with a Pitcher of Watermelons, a fruity punch with a kick of rum and vodka. "Good food, great time" says it all.

Flo's Place is open for lunch and dinner seven days a week.

Frank's Restaurant & Bar $$$
U.S. Highway 17 South, Pawleys Island
(843) 237–1581
www.franksandoutback.com

Frank's Restaurant & Bar, or just plain Frank's as locals call it, opened in 1988 and has been growing ever since. Today many locals consider Frank's the best restaurant on the entire length of the Grand Strand. It's no wonder. The chef's creations feature an array of different influences, including Southwestern, French, Oriental, and Thai.

Frank's menu changes weekly, and the selections are guaranteed to tempt the strongest dieter's resolve. A large selection of appetizers are great for combining. The entrees are diverse—classic to cutting edge.

Vintage wines and homemade desserts round out a culinary experience worthy of many return visits.

Naturally, fresh seafood is a specialty at Frank's. Selections include a delicious sautéed cornmeal-and-black-pepper-encrusted snapper entree. But seafood is only a beginning. Free-range chicken and veal are featured often, along with crispy duck and roasted lamb.

Frank's serves only dinner Monday through Saturday from 6:00 to 10:00 P.M.

Gulfstream Cafe $$$
1536 South Waccamaw Drive,
Garden City Beach
(843) 651–8808
www.californiadreamings.com

The two-story Gulfstream Cafe sits high above the marsh and overlooks Murrells Inlet. Sunsets are spectacular and romantic. (Try to talk your host into giving you a table with a view.) Although dress is casual, the menu is upscale, and reservations are recommended.

Insiders' Tip

North Myrtle Beach is home to the first Jackaroo Australian Steakhouse, a new branch of the infamous Hooter's chain. Jackaroo, at 1211 U.S. Highway 17 North, North Myrtle Beach, is a more family-oriented restaurant, featuring such Australian flavors as the Aussie Bloom (a whole, colossal onion deep fried), coconut prawns, John Hops Chops, and the Great Barrier Reef Fish of the Day. For more information call (843) 280-9800.

Appetizers range from lumpmeat crab cakes to oysters on the half shell. A popular appetizer is the Gulfstream sampler: stuffed shrimp, bacon-wrapped scallops, oysters Rockefeller, linguine with a delicate clam sauce, and blackened fish. (Hope you're hungry!)

Our number one entree is Gulfstream's Salmon Portobello—perfectly broiled salmon topped with tender sautéed Portobello mushrooms.

We've eaten at Gulfstream many times and have never had a bad night. Sounds impossible, but it's true. An early-bird menu, served from 4:00 to 5:30 P.M., is a secret well-kept by locals. A children's menu is also available. Gulfstream Cafe is open for dinner only.

Kyoto Japanese Steak House $$
U.S. Highway 17 South, Murrells Inlet
(843) 651–4616
Restaurant Row, U.S. Highway 17 North,
Myrtle Beach
(843) 449–9294

Kyoto's brings the beloved Japanese tradition of hibachi cooking right to your table. The chef, usually an authentic personality from the Orient, wows diners with tricks of his trade-knife juggling and flipping tiny shrimp tails from a spatula to a small bowl high atop his chef's hat. All entrees are served with salad (the ginger-root house dressing is the way to go) and a delicate onion soup.

The main course of chicken, beef, or seafood and a variety of vegetables are diced and cooked right before your eyes. It's so satisfying, you'll literally have to push yourself away from the table.

A trip to either Kyoto's is best enjoyed with a group and is a great way to celebrate a birthday, anniversary, or other special occasion. Try the sushi bar, if you dare, and spring for a glass of sweet plum wine.

Kyoto's serves dinner only, and reservations are strongly suggested; the lines can be murderous. But after all, good things are worth waiting for.

Oliver's Lodge $$$
4204 Highway 17 Business, Murrells Inlet
(843) 651–2963

Oliver's rustic and weathered appearance is a welcoming landmark to everyone that knows and loves Murrells Inlet. Serving fresh, local seafood since 1910, it's the oldest restaurant in the inlet and the panoramic view (reason enough for a visit) is breathtaking.

Dinner at Oliver's feels a lot like visiting the home of a much-loved family member who happens to be an extraordinary cook. In Southern style, the decor is understated and unpretentious. Don Edwards, Oliver's owner, will likely greet you at the door. Best of all he's passed on his penchant for fine, friendly service to his staff, so you can expect to feel pampered throughout the evening.

Appetizers include homemade chowders, delicately seasoned crab cakes, crisp-fried calamari, oysters on the half shell, and stuffed mushrooms. Fresh seafood takes center stage and can be served grilled, broiled, fried, or blackened. The broiled lobster tails are always tender and sweet. Steaming oyster and clam pots (in season) and Alaskan Snow Crab legs are ever popular choices, too. Roasted prime rib, New York Strip steaks, barbecue ribs, and at least three other specials are offered nightly. There's also a "light fare" menu featuring seafood platters, grilled quail or

Insiders' Tip

One of the Strand's smartest secrets is the "early-bird special." Before the dinner rush begins, many restaurants offer reduced dinner and drink prices. This tip is especially helpful for families who can eat early, eat cheaper, and get back to the beach or hotel pool before turning in for the night.

chicken, and fried flounder—as well as children's selections.

Oliver's serves dinner on Thursday through Saturday during the off-season, and daily during the summer, from 5:00 P.M. until the folks stop coming.

Tyler's Cove $$$
727 Wachesaw Road, Murrells Inlet
(843) 651-5135
www.tylerscove.com

Tyler's Cove Restaurant occupies the original farmhouse of the nineteenth-century Eason plantation. The house was built in 1887 and has been renovated by Tyler's Cove owners, Terri Rostafinski and Don DeBenedetto. The traditional Lowcountry cuisine served at Tyler's Cove is a unique combination of French, English, and African recipes and ingredients perfected among plantation owners and slaves along the South Carolina coast. Tempting appetizers include Oysters Moscow—oysters topped with horseradish sauce; red and black caviar; triple cheese onion soup; and baked brie turnovers with Amaretto butter and almonds. The menu runs the gamut from Cajun fried chicken salad with honey-jalapeño dressing (a lunchtime favorite) to such elegant evening indulgences as seafood strudel and applejack pork medallions. Entrees are accompanied by a fresh salad, seasonal vegetables, a starch, and a loaf of the most delicious wheat and honey bread. Tyler's Cove, open daily for lunch and dinner, also has an extensive wine list and delicious homemade desserts.

Nightlife

Like the song says, "There's no use in sitting alone in your room; come to the cabaret." With the happening nightlife this area has to offer, there is no need to entertain your own company and absolutely no excuse for lamenting that there is nothing to do. When the sun sinks below the horizon, the lights come up around the Grand Strand, alive with the buzz of animated conversation, laughter, and the beat of various musical genres. Locals who can "hang" with the best of them all night long and rested vacationers congregate until the wee hours of the morning in too many nightspots to mention. Besides the places included in this chapter, many restaurants double as late-night spots, and most resort hotels provide lounges with live entertainment. And around almost every corner along the Strand you'll find a little bar or pool hall where the clientele is usually neighborhood locals.

Nightlife really picks up during the spring and summer months, so consult the Friday "kicks!" section of the *Sun News* for the most up-to-date profile on the entertainment scene.

Now let's get into some of the rules and regulations about partying so you can avoid any possible trouble or surprises.

Rules and Regulations for Nightlife

IDs, If You Please

The legal drinking age in South Carolina is 21, and that is a strict order around here. Some clubs allow underage patrons to enter with a clearly marked hand stamp—they can purchase only soft drinks at the bar. You'll find that Grand Strand club bouncers are fastidious ID checkers, so make sure you have some form of photo identification.

Make It a Double

South Carolina is still a minibottle state when it comes to serving alcohol. You won't see a shot glass used by a bartender in these parts! Each minibottle contains nearly two ounces of liquor, so you're getting a double compared to most free-pour bars. If you prefer mixed drinks containing more than one liquor, such as Long Island iced teas or fuzzy navels, keep in mind that you must pay for each separate liquor that is opened and poured. More than one unsuspecting cocktail imbiber has nearly fainted when presented with the tab at the end of the evening!

Drinking and Driving

Local patrol officers show no mercy to drunken motorists, and if you're picked up for driving while impaired, you will spend the night in jail before facing charges. Remember: No excuse is a good excuse where drinking and driving is concerned, so use your head—and stay out of the slammer.

Dancing the Night Away

North Strand

Ducks & Ducks Too
229 Main Street, North Myrtle Beach
(843) 249–3858
www.ducksatoceandrive.com

When you come to Myrtle Beach, shagging is a must. Consequently, Ducks & Ducks Too is "a must," too. If you are shy about trying this quintessentially Strand dance, just drop in to watch—with a cold drink and classic shag tunes, the experience makes for a relaxing end to any day.

Hall of Famer Judy Duke offers professional shag lessons on Thursdays at 7:00 P.M. In June, July, and August, lessons—presented by nine-time National Shag Champions Jackie McGee & Charlie—are often offered free of charge.

If a shag-inspired special event is being held during the year, odds are good Ducks will be involved. Currently popular events hosted here include the Dewey Kennedy Mixed Doubles Contest, a popular New Year's Eve Party, the Bunk Leach Mixed Doubles Dance Contest, and the Harry Driver Golf Classic.

During summer Ducks is open Wednesday through Saturday. In the slower winter months, you will still find them open Thursday through Saturday. If you like shagging, we suggest you call ahead or visit the Web site so you won't miss a sleeper special event.

Spanish Galleon
100 Main Street, North Myrtle Beach
(843) 249–1047

The Galleon has been a favorite Grand Strand dance club for years. This place houses several dance floors under one roof to appeal to a variety of musical interests, including beach music and high-energy dance music. Live beach music bands entertain Galleon customers throughout the year, and an oceanfront grill keeps everyone from going hungry. Although you can wear T-shirts and shorts, most people tend to turn a night at the Galleon into a fashion show.

Recently renovated and bigger and better than ever before. Spanish Galleon is traditionally open nightly in the summer and several nights a week in the winter from 8:00 P.M. 'til . . . Call ahead for specific hours and admission prices.

Stool Pigeons
Barefoot Landing, North Myrtle Beach
(843) 272–4123
www.stoolpigeonspub.com

Word has it Stool Pigeons Pub features the largest selection of draft beers on the entire Grand Strand. While this boast could likely be argued, the deck is undeniably a very cool place to kick back with a beverage—if you can resist the temptation to shoot some pool inside with friends. This is a place well-known for excellent live entertainment. In fact the place is rightfully billed as "the coolest perch on the Strand." Relaxed fun reigns supreme.

Myrtle Beach

2001 VIP Entertainment
920 Lake Arrowhead Road, Myrtle Beach
(843) 449–9434, (877) 662–0016
www.2001nightclub.com

2001 is an upscale entertainment complex—and one of the longest-running nightlife success stories in a fickle resort community. Two separate nightclubs and a private lounge guarantee a variety of club atmospheres. Whether you feel like

Insiders' Tip
If you're going out on the town, be sure to carry along some form of picture identification with you. Most establishments check all patrons to ensure they're of legal drinking age; their liquor license depends on it.

dancing or kicking back in a quieter spot, 2001 is ideal.

DJs deliver high-energy progressive and Top-40 tunes in the Echelon Dance Club. The sound system is high tech. Combined with art deco touches, intelligent lighting, and a simulated laser centerpiece, a visit here will make you feel like dancing even if you didn't expect to.

In the very next room, discover Razzies Beach Club. In the warm embrace of Razzies, folks shimmy a bit slower—but only a little—to beach music, oldies, and the softer side of Top-40 hits. 2001's own Show Band performs nightly. Carribays Island Bar easily meets a standard set by larger clubs by offering a Key West setting for relaxing, sampling the tunes of guest musicians, and enjoying private party functions thrown by the local set.

Bars are interspersed throughout 2001, and professionally trained bartenders can whip up specialty cocktails as well as a few shooters even the seasoned club devotee cannot name. Valet parking adds a touch of class and convenience. With a nod to the area's laid-back resort setting, casual wear passes muster at 2001. Nonetheless, leave your hats in the car and don something besides a tank.

The club is open year-round Monday through Saturday from 8:00 P.M. until well beyond midnight. Last call is at 2:00 A.M. on Saturdays. In winter the Club often closes on Sunday and Monday. Locals are admitted free, but a cover charge applies to all others, and the exact price is contingent upon special nights and the entertainment being featured. Expect to pay an admission that ranges from $6.00 to $10.00.

The Attic
812 North Ocean Boulevard, Myrtle Beach
(843) 448-6456

Above the Myrtle Beach Pavilion, The Attic is the area's only under-21 nightclub. It's well-supervised, and no alcoholic beverages are sold—just soft drinks. For decades teenagers have danced at The Attic to live bands and their favorite Top-40 hits during their summer vacations.

The Attic is usually open 7:00 P.M. to midnight, March through October. Call

ahead for late-breaking details. Admission is $8.00 per person.

Beach Wagon
906 South Kings Highway, Myrtle Beach
(843) 448-5918

Country music fans have come here for more than 18 years for live concerts and all-night two-steppin'. The club itself is a large, long dance hall with little neon but big rootin' tootin' fun. Names such as Marty Stuart, John Anderson, Sweethearts of the Rodeo, Aaron Tippin and McBride & The Ride all played the Beach Wagon just before their careers took off. It just goes to show, the performers you see at this club today might be the country-music stars of tomorrow.

House band Silver plays Tuesday through Saturday nights from 9:00 P.M. to 2:00 A.M. Ladies are admitted free Monday through Thursday and on Sunday evenings from 7:00 to 9:00 P.M. Locals get in for free on Wednesday nights and are invited to take the microphone or join the band to show off their own talent. Free dance lessons are taught every Sunday, Monday, and Tuesday night from 7:00 to 9:00 P.M. For everyone else a cover charge of $3.00 each applies Sunday through Thursday, and a $5.00 door fee applies on Friday and Saturday nights.

Beach Wagon is open every night of the week from 7:00 P.M. to 2:00 A.M., except during the winter when it operates Tuesday through Saturday only.

Dead Dog Saloon
404 26th Avenue North, Myrtle Beach
(843) 626-6890
4079 Highway 17 Business, Murrells Inlet
(843) 651-0664
www.deaddogsaloons.com

Dead Dog Saloon has two locations. The Myrtle Beach location established the eatery (and bar's) claim to fame, but the Murrells Inlet boasts the best view—marsh to ocean—from a deck that easily rates among the best the Strand has to offer.

You can enjoy live bands in Myrtle Beach from Wednesday through Sunday. The Inlet location hosts live entertainment from Tuesday through Sunday, plus karaoke on Thursday evenings. Both locations have a better-than-basic menu for seafarers and landlubbers. Golfers and bikers and jaded locals all seem to gravitate to the Dead Dog. The atmosphere is fun and there's no cover charge. Both locations are open for lunch and dinner.

Club Boca
Celebrity Square
Broadway at the Beach, Myrtle Beach
(843) 444–3500
www.celebrationsnitelife.com

Redesigned and redefined as recently as 2002, Club Boca could accurately be described as "a party come to life." DJs serve a steamy, steady stream of mainstream and Latin dance tunes. The result feels like Miami and Vegas colliding in Myrtle Beach.

Dual YAG lasers and a brightly hued kinetic light system make this the place to see and be seen. You must be 21 years of age; this place is in vogue and completely hot, but Thursday night is "College Night"—meaning that you are in luck if you are age 18 or older. Club Boca is open until 2:00 A.M. on weekdays and Saturdays and until 4:00 A.M. on Fridays.

If you're young—or just want to feel like it—make haste to Club Boca.

Froggy Bottomz
Broadway at the Beach, Myrtle Beach
(843) 444–3500
www.celebrationsnitelife.com

Here's a one-stop nightclub for diverse live entertainment, current Top-40 tunes, favorite oldies, Latin beats, and plenty that falls somewhere in between. If you can't decide where you want to go and what you want to listen to, count on Froggy Bottomz as a sure bet. The club's in-house band, Illuzions, knows all the chart busters. If you're age 21 or older, you're welcome. Thursday night is College night—meaning that if you're age 18, for this one night a week, you're cleared for entry. Froggy Bottomz is open until 4:00 A.M. on Fridays and 2:00 A.M. on Saturdays.

An assortment of venues makes Celebrity Square, located at Broadway at the Beach, a one-stop opportunity for nightlife aficionados. PHOTO: COURTESY OF MYRTLE BEACH CHAMBER OF COMMERCE

Malibu's Surf Bar
Celebrity Square,
Broadway at the Beach, Myrtle Beach
(843) 444-3500
www.celebrationsnitelife.com

High-energy Top-40 music keeps the crowd gyrating on a dance floor that has a giant shark as its backdrop. This place is usually packed on weekends when tourists and locals wander in from a day at the beach or dinner at Broadway at the Beach.

Call ahead for prices and the frequently changing schedule. Regular admission for patrons is $10.

Mother Fletcher's
Eighth Avenue North and Ocean Boulevard,
Myrtle Beach
(843) 448-2545

A girl could make a living just entering the contests held at Mother Fletcher's. Each night, between the sets of pumping dance tunes, girls compete in such events as the wet T-shirt contest, the skirt-flirt contest, and the legs contest, cajoled by testosterone-induced howling and clapping. Wednesday night, Ladies Night, offers an especially wild night. The other breathtaking view at Mother Fletcher's is from the double oceanfront deck. The club is open daily in the summer from 8:00 P.M. until 2:00 A.M. Cover charge is $8.00 per person.

Original Shucker's Raw Bar
Broadway at the Beach, Myrtle Beach
(843) 626-9535
www.shuckers.net

Happy hour sports discounted drink prices that make this an excellent end-of-the-day option no matter what mood you are in. The late-night menu rates among the best around. Play pool or cutting-edge video games, watch the establishment's live entertainment, or simply abandon yourself to the simple pleasures of an absolutely excellent outdoor patio. You'll find lots of locals here.

Revolutions Retro Dance Club
Celebrity Square,
Broadway at the Beach, Myrtle Beach
(843) 444-8032

For sure-fire fun, head to Revolutions. This locals' favorite has been voted Myrtle Beach's No. 1 nightclub by *Sun News* readers for four years in a row. Featuring songs from the '60s, '70s, and '80s, Revolutions has become a surprising dance-hall hit around here. Music making alternates between DJs and bands, with performers dressed in bell bottoms, wedgies, and Afro wigs. This is a happening place on weekends. Don't be afraid to don your white jacket and medallions. Get ready to bump the night away to a K.C. and the Sunshine Band tune; say "groovy" all you want. Revolutions is open seven nights a week from 9:00 P.M., April through October. It's open only Wednesday through Saturday the rest of the year. A $5.00 cover charge is always the case on weekends; $7.00 when a live band is playing. The cover charge also entitles you to admission at Crocodile Rocks—the home of dueling pianos—across the Square.

Studebaker's
2000 North Kings Highway, Myrtle Beach
(843) 448-9747
www.studebakersclub.com

A nonstop dance party unfolds every night at Studebaker's, and at least a couple-decades' worth of patrons would be willing to attest to the fact. This establishment delivers neon and nostalgia—a high-spirited combination that smacks of high-school proms—with all the stuff you loved and nothing you would opt to forget.

Studebaker's is a no-risk option for after-hours fun. From Motown to old school to the Retro craze that's sweeping current culture, Studebaker's can be counted on for a party. If you're age 80, zany DJs and shapely Studebopper dancers will make you feel 18.

Studebaker's is open from 8:00 P.M. until 2:00 A.M. every night in summer. Hours are abbreviated in the off-season; call ahead. Locals are admitted free year-long, which is a great reason to make this a regular hangout. The cover charge for others ranges from $5.00 to $10.00 depending on season and entertainment.

The area's abundance of theme restaurants allows lots of choices for great food and great entertainment—no matter what your interests are! PHOTO: COURTESY OF NASCAR CAFE

South Strand

Creek Ratz
4065 Highway 17 Business, Murrells Inlet
(843) 357-2891
www.creekratz.com

One of Murrells Inlet's newest offerings, Creek Ratz has quickly become a favorite of both locals and tourists. Owned by the son of a longtime local, success is not surprising. Why? Rustic, nautical appeal. Spectacular views. Good food. Friendly service. Interesting clientele. With a reasonably priced menu, a full raw bar, happy hour, live entertainment, and plenty of TVs on which to watch your favorite sporting events, reasons continue to accumulate. Enjoy shagging—on the edge of one of America's most beautiful

creeks—on Sunday afternoons. Happy hour runs from 4:00 to 7:00 P.M. Creek Ratz is open 11:00 A.M. to 11:00 P.M. and is very family friendly.

Hot Fish Club Gazebo
4911 Highway 17 Business, Murrells Inlet
(843) 357-9175
www.hotfishclub.com

The original "Hot and Hot Fish Club" was founded near the end of the eighteenth century and might have been Murrells Inlet's first dining establishment. Out back behind the restaurant, the Gazebo—overlooking an undeniably spectacular view of the Inlet, offers the South Strand's best view for live nightly entertainment from Wednesday through Sunday. The food is better than average. To start try the Key West Crabcake and Jack Jennie's Blackened Shrimp. There is also a Raw Bar and several tempting sandwich selections. Locals patronize this bar. There are many reasons. Discover them for yourself.

Bands on the Beach

The Myrtle Beach band scene is better than ever. The expanding diversity and increasing number of bands has given the area a wonderful musical texture that includes everything from modern rock and punk to blues, jazz, and big band. Renewed attention to "southern rock," in the wake of the phenomenal success of Hootie and the Blowfish, Edwin McCain, and others, has created an exciting environment for record companies and music promoters to recruit and develop up-and-coming talent. As a result you will find music to satisfy every taste.

For rock 'n' roll aficionados, the guitar-driven "heavy" sound dominates the scene among several bands playing original mush and hoping to take the next big step toward a major label recording deal and regional prominence. Echo 7 has emerged as the leader among the heavy rock bands for their outstanding musicianship, smart lyrics, and strong stage presence. Two lead vocalists who complement the hard rock hooks with haunting melodies round out the band's unique sound. Remember the Echo 7 name, as they are poised for mainstream success. Other heavy rock bands regularly heard in local clubs include Grill, Haven, Flick It, Bleen, and Confliction, all of whom put on a great show.

For sophisticated tastes, two bands have filled the niche for "Jam" bands quite well. After 20 years the Mullets (the fish, not the haircut!) have become local heroes to listeners and club owners. The Mullets pack 'em in every show. A combination of blues and Grateful Dead–type rock 'n' roll, they have established onstage antics that have been known to include tequila shots for everyone in the crowd! The Mullets are truly a Myrtle Beach tradition. Another popular "Jam" band is McDowell Shortcut, currently playing and touring in support of their second CD. From Neil Young to Velvet Under Ground, they serve up a fabulous blend of classics and original material with memorable style. Also check out up-and-comer Rollo!

If what you crave is the punch and power of bar bands that do their original stuff along with more familiar covers of popular rock, there's Walona and the Tim Clark Band. Both provide straight-on rock 'n' roll from classics to modern fare with enough original material to keep it interesting.

For eclectic tastes check out the very theatrical and crunchy punk blast of the Independents. Self-described punk-meets-ska-meets-surf-meets-the-Ramones, with a touch of Elvis, be sure to catch this up-and-coming group. The most popular and probably the most hyperactive bands on the scene are the indie rock groups. The Envelopes and The Typewriters are at the forefront with their beach-boy-esque tempos and melodies. They can often be found playing the same venue on the same night as some members perform with both bands.

If it's jazz and blues you're after, there are two local "Big Bands" that keep snowbirds and local retirees glidin' and boppin' across the dance floor. The first is Swingtime, a Myrtle Beach Big Band that showcases well-seasoned musicians and attracts a crowd anywhere and every time they play. Similarly, the popular Andrew Thielan Big Band has established themselves as a mainstay at the beach's many festivals and special events. This fantastic ensemble is made up of an all-star cast of musicians and vocalists from across the Carolinas. Its music ranges from the golden era of the Big Bands to the new standards of today. Everything from Glenn Miller to Harry Connick Jr., Disney tunes, Broadway standards, and light rock makes their sound appealing for all ages. Other veteran jazz players in town are Dan Ramsey, Chris Connely, and the longtime duo Jazz Etc.

As for the Blues, gritty, down-home, delta-style blues is always a favorite. Here, an even more popular derivation is the Chicago Barrel–house style that has become a local shag dance favorite. Seek out the Smokehouse Brown Blues Band to be shuckin' and jivin' into the wee hours, Cheyenne, or Silver, the house band for the popular Beach Wagon for the last 25 years. Their vast experience and unbelievable repertoire of songs has made them age like fine wine.

For the latest information on bands and schedules, check out the kicks! section of the *Sun News* on Fridays, or call Jeff Roberts at Sounds Familiar, the Strand's best-known, time-tested music store, at (843) 448–6408.

Sports Bars

Sometimes you just wanna hang out somewhere, have a brew, watch a game, and play a few rounds of pool or darts. If that's how you're feeling, we have a sports-bar lineup here that should satisfy. While

House of Blues is "party central" for great live bands. Add fabulous food and decor that features some of the nation's finest folk art and you've got an unbeatable recipe for success. PHOTO: COURTESY OF MYRTLE BEACH CHAMBER OF COMMERCE

a number of places in town hail themselves as sports bars (apparently it's quite fashionable to do so), we have come up with some guidelines to ensure the full "sports-bar experience."

By our criteria, a bar was only given mention in this section if it had at least four televisions locked on sporting events and at least two games to play. There's never a cover charge at area sports bars, unless a major boxing event is to be aired. Then you'll have to consult the media to find out which places will be showing the fight and what the admission cost will be.

North Strand

Mulligan's Sports Pub
1500 U.S. Highway 17 South,
North Myrtle Beach
(843) 249–9700, (843) 361–2999

Mulligan's relocated late in 1997 and changed its ambiance to a more upscale sports bar and steak house. The inside is impressive, with a decor of muted greens, rich woods, and brass. More than 40 televisions broadcast sports all the time. Games have been moved into a separate room where you can shoot pool or play shuffleboard.

This sports pub is open every day of the week from 11:30 A.M. to 2:00 A.M. A full dinner menu is served from opening to 11:00 P.M. every day and includes steaks, chops, and pastas. Monday night is Prime Time evening, when Mulligan's offers all you can eat Prime Rib for $10.95.

Oscar's
4101 U.S. Highway 17 North,
North Myrtle Beach
(843) 272–0707

This sports bar is a continuous arena of action, with 100 TVs and an array of games including trivia, pinball machines, a virtual-reality race car game, and the latest rage, Goldentee.

You're likely to work up an appetite, so it's a good thing Oscar's now offers a full menu until 1:00 A.M.

Oscar's is open from 11:30 A.M. to 2:00 A.M. Monday through Saturday and noon to 2:00 A.M. on Sunday.

Myrtle Beach

Broadway Louie's Grill
Broadway at the Beach, Myrtle Beach
(843) 444–3500, (843) 445–6885
www.celebrationsnitelife.com

Broadway Louie's Sports, Games & Grill is great fun for one or more of the entire family. The joint boasts 12,000 square feet, including interactive video games, more than four dozen large screen TVs, the Karaoke Big Show, and extremely comfortable couches in a sports bar that's legendary—if only locally. Enjoy family-friendly competition with the latest and greatest in video arcade and skill games, featuring Star Wars Trilogy, Jurassic Park's Lost World, Rapid Rivers, Daytona 2, and lots more.

Those in the know know this is one of the best—if not the best—local place for New York–style pizza. Louie's Grill serves it hand-tossed and fresh from the oven. Extraordinary subs and appetizers round out the menu. The trivia game that's all the nation's rage is available right at your table. You can also rack 'em up for pool. Doors open at noon every day and all ages are admitted.

Droopy's
5201 North Kings Highway, Myrtle Beach
(843) 449–2620

Droopy's stays open as late as business dictates Monday through Friday and until 2:00 A.M. on Saturday and Sunday. More than 14 TVs are scattered throughout along with two pool tables, lots of video games, and Foosball, too.

Basic appetizers and sandwiches are available from the kitchen, but Droopy's also offers excellent daily specials.

Doors open at 4:00 P.M. Monday through Friday. Droopy's opens earlier when the NFL season game schedule dictates.

Foster's Cafe & Bar
6307-A North Kings Highway, Myrtle Beach
(843) 449–7945

Foster's offers more than half a dozen televisions, darts, a pool table, and a satisfying menu. While this place is very small, its rough-hewn wood decor exudes a certain coziness, and locals love its off-the-beaten-path allure.

Foster's is open Monday through Friday from 11:00 A.M. until 4:00 A.M. and Saturday and Sunday from 11:00 A.M. to 2:00 A.M. The kitchen closes at 2:00 A.M. on weeknights and at 1:00 A.M. Saturday and Sunday.

Jimmagan's Pub Sports Bar
6003 North Kings Highway, Myrtle Beach
(843) 497-5450

Jimmagan's Pub, with 35 TVs locked on sporting events, pool tables, and electronic darts is a small corner location that's cozy and down-home. Jimmagan's guarantees you can see every Sunday NFL game during football season. It is a favorite of motorcycle enthusiasts and has an additional location in Murrells Inlet, south on Business 17.

The menu is limited to sandwiches, burgers, and finger foods; wings are always 25 cents. Jimmagan's is open seven days a week—11:30 A.M. to 4:00 A.M. weekdays; 11:00 A.M. to 2:00 A.M. on weekends.

Magoo's Sports and Spirits
905 Oak Street, Myrtle Beach
(843) 946-6683

Magoo's is one of the only dart bars to have sprouted up along the Grand Strand. View one of 12 televisions; head to the back room, chalk up a cue stick and shoot some pool. Electronic and steel tip darts are at the front end of the bar.

Under the category of "fine food," Magoo's menu ranges from fabulous burgers to juicy steaks. Their wings have been voted "Best on the Beach" for three years in a row. Wings for 15 cents and half-price appetizers are the special on Sunday and Monday. Take it from us, it's absolutely delicious!

Magoo's is open Monday through Friday from 4:00 P.M. until the last sports fan leaves and Saturday and Sunday until 2:00 A.M. During football season, doors open earlier.

Marvin's
918 North Ocean Boulevard, Myrtle Beach
(843) 448-4926

Insiders' Tip
We know that lines to use rest rooms at nightclubs and amusements can be lengthy and, depending on the number of beers you've taken in, sometimes agonizing. Be forewarned: The only other offense that local police enforce as strongly as drunk driving is urinating in public. If caught you will be arrested, fined, and taken to jail.

Marvin's has been around since 1975, evolving from a taco stand into a sports bar complete with pool tables. Besides a vast collection of NASCAR memorabilia that owner Marvin McHone has collected over the years, this sports bar is oceanfront with 80 feet of windows showing off the Atlantic.

The menu is basic bar fare: fried foods and appetizers, chicken wings, pizza, nachos, burgers, dogs, and sandwiches. Marvin's operates from 10:00 A.M. until at least 2:00 A.M., seven days a week for most of the year. Hours are 11:00 A.M. to 1:00 A.M. daily in January and February.

Murphy's Law Sports Bar
405 South Kings Highway, Myrtle Beach
(843) 448-6021

Patrons of Murphy's Law enjoy two pool tables—positioned in the middle of the tables and chairs—electronic darts, and golf as well as 25 television sets. Murphy's sells draft beer during happy hour for $1.00 a glass.

The sandwiches at Murphy's are popular fare and monstrous in their proportions. The "50-yard" steak sandwich will stuff you; the "100-yard" version requires a friend to help you. Raw bar selections include oysters, clams, steamed shrimp, and crab legs. Chicken wings are a hit here, too. Try them.

Murphy's Law is open seven days a week from 11:00 A.M. to 2:00 A.M. It is closed for two weeks during the Christmas holiday season.

Shamrock's Restaurant & Sports Bar
2510 North Kings Highway, Myrtle Beach
(843) 448–2532

Shamrock's Restaurant and Sports Bar has 20 beers on tap and 20 ounce pints guarantee no one goes thirsty. Miller's Highlife comes at the very reasonable price of $6.00 per pitcher all the time! This club is also noted for a late-night Munchie Special. From 9:00 P.M. to 1:00 A.M. from Monday through Friday, everything on the well-loved Munchie Menu is half price. Popular choices include buffalo wings and chili skins, mouthwatering nachos, and other fried favorites. The menu also offers soups, salads, sandwiches, and specialty plates. Shamrock's is open Monday through Saturday from 11:30 P.M. until 2:00 A.M. and on Sundays from noonish until 2:00 A.M.

South Strand

Beach Club at Fenway
118 South Ocean Boulevard, Surfside Beach
(843) 828–1111

This upstairs sports bar on the boulevard blasts sports (especially any NFL game that New England is playing) from one large-screen television and seven smaller tubes scattered throughout the bar area. Fenway subscribes to Direct TV and carries all NFL games as well as, of course, Red Sox games and other events. Pool tables and arcade-type games round out the sports theme, albeit in cramped quarters.

With the use of partitions, the dining room at Fenway is excluded from the bar area and serves up a full menu. This sports bar quickly made a name for itself when it comes to baby back ribs that locals swear are "practically liquid." Lunch and dinner can be ordered from any room at Fenway Park and food ranges from steaks to chicken, pasta, soups, and finger foods.

Fenway's bar is open daily from 11:00 A.M. until after 2:00 A.M. On Saturday the bar closes at 2:00 A.M.

Sundown Restaurant & Sports Pub
810 Surfside Drive, Surfside Beach
(843) 238–1240

Sundown offers its patrons eight televisions for viewing games, three pool tables, electronic darts, pinball, and golf machines.

A full menu is available, but the staff says that appetizers and sandwiches are the usual order. A free breakfast is served every Saturday morning, whenever the cook gets to fixing the plates. You have to be there when breakfast is ready, or you're out of luck.

It's open all week, 24 hours a day. Sundown closes on Sundays from 2:00 to 10:00 A.M.

Karaoke

We've included karaoke houses in this chapter in case you get an overwhelming urge to put to the test all of those singing lessons your mother made you take. Actually karaoke has become serious entertainment business. The places we've included feature some tone-deaf singers who can't seem to focus on the words to the song, but you'll be amazed at the majority of everyday Joes and Janes with incredible singing talent.

Karaoke seems to have developed a veritable cult following. Picture this: Someone gets up on stage with the microphone to belt out his or her selected tune and is met with the same audience reaction as if he or she had just blown away a panel of Broadway casting directors at a walk-on audition. The best karaoke performers pick just the right time to perform and, when finished, are met with tears, hugs, and the inimitable Hollywood-style alternate cheek kissing. Hey, it's a lot of fun—and, who knows, there may be an incredible crooner hidden in those vocal chords of yours!

OK, now it's criteria time. There are a number of local clubs and restaurants that offer karaoke at one time or another.

But for our purposes, an establishment must offer this form of entertainment at least two nights per week to qualify for mention.

Myrtle Beach

Bummz on the Beach
2002 North Ocean Boulevard, Myrtle Beach
(843) 916–9111
www.bummz.com

Bummz has been riding high as the only beachfront garden cafe in Myrtle Beach for more than a couple of years. They pride themselves on atmosphere, and rightfully so. From the finely crafted Georgia pine interior to the expansive beach patio, Bummz offers an unforgettable experience for every beach night, regardless of particulars.

Bummz delivers live music on a nightly basis (seasonal) and offers a full menu with excellent specials. Check out Tequila Tuesday and karaoke on Wednesday and Saturday evenings from 9:30 P.M. until 1:00 A.M.

Warren's Restaurant & Lounge
1108 Third Avenue South, Myrtle Beach
(843) 448–3110

Warren's Restaurant & Lounge is about as local-yokel as it gets with karaoke in full swing every night from 8:30 P.M. to 2:00 A.M. This is a serious singing venue that showcases a mind-boggling number of terrific singers regularly. On Friday, Saturday, and Sunday, Warren's has added a full dinner menu that includes steaks and prime rib.

Taking in a Movie

The Grand Strand strip is sprinkled with class-act movie houses. All are comfortable, clean, climate-controlled, and heady with the smell of fresh-made popcorn. What you won't find in this area's cinemas is an assortment of foreign or fine-arts movies. Every once in a while one pops up but not very often. This is an area where movie-going audiences eat up blockbuster hits, thrillers, adventures, love stories, and

Insiders' Tip

South Carolina is the only state that still serves liquor by the mini-bottle. Whenever you order a cocktail here, you're getting 1.7 ounces of alcohol compared to a national average of one ounce per drink. Pace yourself!

comedies. To find out what's playing where, always consult the Friday edition of the *Sun News* for its "kicks!" entertainment section. You will find descriptions of current films, what theaters are showing them, box office figures, and a theater-finder map.

As we speak, Grand Strand moviegoers enjoy selection, amenities, and a range of prices. Film buffs have 39 first-run screens to choose from or have the option of waiting a few weeks after a big Hollywood release to catch it at one of the area's 24 discount houses. Viewing times vary from one cinema to the next, so it's best to call ahead for that specific information.

North Strand

Carmike Briarcliffe Cinema
Colonial Mall, 10177 North Kings Highway,
North Myrtle Beach
(843) 272–1777
www.carmike.com

A Carmike Cinema, Briarcliffe Cinema is one of only two movie houses along the Grand Strand housed in a shopping mall. It's a successful marriage as Colonial Mall recently cited that 85 percent of moviegoers visit the theater after a shopping spree. All matinees before 5:30 P.M. are $5.00 a seat, every day. After that, adults ages 12 to 59 will pay $7.50 to see a show; children ages 3 to 11 pay $4.50 all the time, and seniors 60 years or older will pay $5.00 per ticket.

Myrtle Beach

Broadway Cinema 16
Broadway at the Beach, Myrtle Beach
(843) 445-1616

Another Carmike Cinema, Broadway is the largest cineplex of its kind in South Carolina and sits amid the hustle and bustle of a shopping and entertainment complex. Eight of the "plexes" here are auditoriums that guarantee unsurpassed viewing and sound quality. All matinee seats are sold for $5.00 per person. Regular prices are $7.50 for adults and $4.50 for children ages 11 and younger and those 59 years of age or older.

Dunes Cinema Eight
44th Avenue North and Kings Highway, Myrtle Beach
(843) 449-7733
www.carmike.com

If you don't mind waiting a bit for the second run of a new release, seeing a show at the Dunes Cinema Eight, the Strand's third Carmike Cinema, is sure to be the best bang for your buck. Recently renovated to include two auditoriums plus a George Lucas (yes, of the *Star Wars* fame) sound system, you can see any movie playing at any time for just $2.50. The manager of this cinema described its audio system as "near perfect."

IMAX Discovery Theater
Broadway at the Beach, Myrtle Beach
(843) 448-IMAX
www.myrtlebeachimax.com

At IMAX you not only watch a movie, you experience it. The screen is an incredible 6-stories tall, and a 6-track digital sound system surrounds you. Located at Broadway at the Beach, the Grand Strand's IMAX is one of more than 200 IMAX theaters operating in 25 countries. IMAX thrusts its guests into the action in a way no ordinary movie can. Featuring images that fill peripheral vision and 12,000 watts of sound so intense participants swear they can feel it, IMAX movies are absolutely unmatched at the art of transporting their audience to another place and time.

Join all those gone before and discover the world's greatest theater experience. IMAX features a variety of wholesome, family-friendly movies at the top of every hour. Movies vary seasonally, so there's always something to please everyone. The IMAX Cafe offers a wonderful selection of treats to enjoy during your movie experience. And afterward, do leave time for browsing among unique gifts and educational toys in the gift shop.

Adults pay $7.25 for a ticket. The cost for children ages 3 to 12 and those age 65 or older is $6.25. Children younger than age three are admitted free of charge. Group and school rates are also offered.

Insiders' Tip

Recent surveys indicate that the typical American household spends an annual average of $2,116 on food away from home. That works out to a figure that approaches $850 per person every year. At $1,190, husband-and-wife households record the highest average per-capita expenditures. Add offspring to the equation and the figure drops to $741 per person.

South Strand

Inlet Square (Regal Cinemas)
Inlet Square Mall, Murrells Inlet
(843) 651–5500

At Inlet Square you can enjoy 12 screens equipped with Digital Theater Sound (DTS). Admission for adults is $7.50. Those 60 years of age or older and kids ages 3 to 11 can buy tickets for $4.75. All matinees before 6:00 P.M. are $5.25 a seat. Combo specials usually apply here, giving a price break on popcorn, drinks, and candy.

Cigar-Friendly Haunts

No amount of official health warnings or nose-holding whining has put a dent in the current demand for good cigars. As managing editor of *Cigar Aficionado*, Gordon Mott, said, "A cigar helps create an environment where sociability and relaxation are promoted."

Thousands of golfing enthusiasts who come to play on Grand Strand courses every year feel not fully equipped for the day without stuffing a few fine cigars in with their clubs. As a matter of fact, there's now a cigar on the market called "The 18 Hole Special" that is big enough to last a full round of golf.

It's only fitting that the Grand Strand should have a cigar-friendly atmosphere; this area has always been home to tobacco farming. Whether you want to enjoy a puff after dinner or while sipping on a good single-malt Scotch, the following establishments (many of which you can read more about in the Restaurants chapter) invite you to light up to your heart's content.

North Strand

Mad Boar Restaurant & Brewhouse
Barefoot Landing, North Myrtle Beach
(843) 272–7000

Mad Boar Brewhouse allows you to smoke a cigar anywhere in the bar and lounge. A Don Tomas will cost about $6.00, but Macanudos are modestly priced at $8.00 each. The Mad Boar stocks

three small-batch bourbons and two single-malt Scotches at the bar.

Dick's Last Resort
Barefoot Landing, North Myrtle Beach
(843) 272–7794

Dick's encourages cigar puffing, albeit preferably in the bar area. In true Dick's style, a spokesperson declared, "There's something wrong with a person who can't enjoy the smell of a good cigar."

The Brentwood Restaurant
4269 Luck Avenue, Little River
(843) 249–2601

The Brentwood accommodates cigars in two upstairs parlor rooms plus a bar. Smokes range from $8.00 to $15.00 apiece, including the heavy Padron. Brentwood stocks a full complement of sherry, cognac, and scotch; specialty coffees, desserts, and appetizers can be ordered at the Brentwood—not to mention savory full-course meals.

Myrtle Beach

Blarney Stone's Pub & Cigar Bar
Celebrity Square, Broadway at the Beach, Myrtle Beach
(843) 626–6644
www.fantasticclubs.com

This is Myrtle Beach's only authentic Irish pub. As such, the joint focuses on pint beer and ales from the British Isles. On the mezzanine level, an upscale cigar and martini bar features more than 50 varieties of martinis, nearly three dozen wines and champagnes, and almost as many cigar selections. In season Blarney Stone features nightly entertainment from Thursday through Saturday. As it should be, St. Patrick's Day is celebrated on the 17th of each month. Happy hour runs from 4:00 until 7:00 P.M. On weeknights Blarney Stone's is open from 4:00 P.M. until 1:00 A.M. On weekend evenings, hours are 4:00 P.M. until 2:00 A.M.

Collectors Cafe and Gallery
7726 North Kings Highway, Myrtle Beach
(843) 449–9370

Collectors Cafe normally carries more upscale brands including Davidoff. At Collectors you can savor a cigar in the bar and lounge areas, where they also shake or stir a list of martinis—even chocolate flavored. The art on display is an added benefit.

Liberty Steakhouse and Brewery
Broadway at the Beach, Myrtle Beach
(843) 626-4677

This establishment has been cigar friendly since it opened in November 1995. Liberty brews its own beer, and a manager there claims that people who tend to drink more flavorful beverages are more likely to enjoy a cigar with drinks.

Rossi's Italian Restaurant
9600 North Kings Highway, Myrtle Beach
(843) 449-0481

Puff away in the lounge and piano bar sections of Rossi's, where cigars start at $4.00 and range up to a $17.00 Porlorranaga and $25.00 Cohiba. Rossi's pours vintage port wines and four single-malt scotches.

Thoroughbreds Restaurant
9706 North Kings Highway, Myrtle Beach
(843) 497-2636

Thoroughbreds Restaurant allows patrons to light up in the outdoor courtyard or in the bar after 11:00 P.M. It is known for mixing a mean martini and also stocks a good selection of fine cognacs.

South Strand

Frank's Restaurant & Bar
10435 Ocean Highway, Pawleys Island
(843) 237-3030

Frank's tries to keep about 10 fine cigars on hand at all times for patrons, which can be smoked in the bar or outdoor dining area. A cigar at Frank's will run you $5.00 to $35.00.

Adult Entertainment

The Grand Strand region has its fair share of adult entertainment establishments, even though area authorities and courts seem to be constantly debating club locations and what constitutes the appropriate amount of nakedness displayed therein. A recent court battle determined that bare butts must stay outside of 6 inches from a patron's face to be within the law. However, no details were given as to how this would be enforced or whether or not it posed a health risk.

We won't list the clubs here, because all you have to do is consult the Yellow Pages or ask almost anyone—after a wink and a nod, you'll be set in the right direction. Besides, isn't half the fun just getting there? Sort of like a fleshy version of a treasure hunt? There is even one club that showcases only male dancers who strut their stuff in cages . . . things that make you go "hmmmm."

Shopping

Major Malls and
Outlets

Distinctive Shopping
Stops

Bookstores

From the warehouse-sized to the quaint and oh-so-small . . . from grab-bag dollar stores to exclusive designer clothiers, the Grand Strand is a resort destination for bargain-hunters as well as quality seekers. It is true that many people come here for no other reason than the shopping—seemingly oblivious to sunshine, theaters, golf courses, and the beach.

Belk, JCPenney, Sears, and Peebles department stores all have multiple locations here. Almost every major clothing, department, and dry-goods store has an outlet here (the Saks store is actually part of the Off 5th chain of Saks outlets). You'll find some of the largest booth-rental flea markets in the South. Antiques stores appear in every section of the beach. And some of the very best shopping opportunities can be found in the small, privately owned stores and shops.

It goes without saying that this chapter can't even begin to detail every shop, every store, or even every shopping center that comprise this 60-mile-long shopping spree. Even locals are overwhelmed by the variety; thus, we tend to migrate to the geographic part of the Strand where we live.

If you are a seasoned shopper, born to shop, then you already know as many secrets as we do for finding the best stores; at best, we can make a road map for you and highlight some of the more interesting concentrations of shops. Keep your eyes open; 'round every curve in the crowded highway there's yet another clutch of shops to browse and burrow through.

As for the basics, we've already mentioned Belk department store, which can be found at any one of three area malls. Other notable department stores with a presence on the Strand include JCPenney, Sears, and Peebles. Several discount "chain" stores pepper the Strand, including Wal-Mart, Kmart, and Target.

The larger supermarket chains include Food Lion, Bi-Lo, Kroger, and Winn-Dixie; most are open 24 hours a day (except Sunday nights). Both Kroger and Winn-Dixie are continually opening new "superstores" with almost as much general merchandise as groceries, deli items, and flowers.

It's impossible to take an overview of shopping without mentioning the plethora of T-shirt and souvenir stores along the Grand Strand. Stores such as Eagles, Pacific, and Wings sparkle with bright lights and seemingly every-other-block locations. They specialize in swimsuits, suntan products, sun shades, beach chairs, rafts, umbrellas, souvenir items, beach toys, T-shirts, and summer sportswear of the most casual sort. And believe it or not, in many of these stores you can actually negotiate with the sales staff for the very best prices.

Although seasonal hours are frequently abbreviated, many places are open seven days a week; if you shop between 1:00 and 6:00 P.M., you should find anything you're looking for.

North Strand

Barefoot Landing
U.S. Highway 17 North, North Myrtle Beach
(843) 272–8349
www.bflanding.com

Barefoot Landing bills itself as "the East Coast's most exciting waterfront shopping, dining and entertainment destination center." While the truth of such marketing hype is disputed by other shopping areas, the fact is that Barefoot Landing plays host to an estimated 7 million visitors every year. Its restaurants, shops, and attractions have been featured in magazines, newspapers, and television clips throughout the nation. *Southern Living,* the *Wall Street Journal, USA Today, Barron's Investment, Forbes,* and *Country America* are just a few of the biggest media names that have come to know and love Barefoot Landing.

Built around a 27-acre freshwater lake, fronted by U.S. Highway 17 North and bordered in back by the Intracoastal Waterway, Barefoot has more than 1,200 feet of floating dock on the waterway as well as miles of rocking-chair-peppered boardwalks and bridges. This development, a rare marriage between commerce and preservation, prides itself on environmental sensitivity. While strolling among the more than 100 specialty and factory-direct shops, 13 waterfront restaurants, and an array of attractions, you can enjoy sea gulls swooping over the lakes, alligators swimming stealthily, and all manner of water birds, including swans, geese, blue herons, snowy egrets, ducks, and pelicans; you can even feed the fish (fish-food-filled gumball machines abound) from many of the boardwalks.

Barefoot Landing's eclectic villages of shops and restaurants are housed in quaint, cedar-shake buildings with bright green awnings. Specialty stores feature resort wear, jewelry, designer fashions, Western wear and accessories, handmade gifts, and unusual collectibles.

The Boardwalk Shops, Carousel Court, and the Barefoot Factory Stores and Dockside Village are separated by floating bridges and are accessible by walkways that are well worth a stroll even if you don't buy a thing. But don't think there will be no temptation—stores like Conley's House of Magic, River Street Sweets, Klig's Kites, Bearfoot Dolls & Bears, and Black Market Mineral will mesmerize you with choices of baubles and toys to take home. H2O Plus is your skincare fitness center. Kandlestix, Surf & Sand Beach Shoppe, Myrtle Beach T-Shirt, and the Sunglass Hut make for a lot of bags to carry home. You could even re-do your wardrobe at Chico's, the Geoffrey Beene and Izod Factory Stores, and Bass Shoes. There are a dozen factory outlet stores that sell fine apparel and designer merchandise at 20- to 50-percent savings. With this irresistible combination of atmosphere and savings, you could redecorate your life.

This breezy complex is also the home of Alligator Adventure (see the Attractions and Kidstuff chapters), the Alabama Theatre (see the Entertainment chapter) and the House of Blues (see the Restaurants and Entertainment chapters). Throughout the year, Barefoot Landing also hosts

Insiders' Tip

The Myrtle Beach Convention Center is host to a few shopping extravaganzas throughout the year. The Carolina Women's Show has endless tables of accessories and fashions, J. Crew recently held an open house and, of course, the perennial Gun and Knife Show makes the circuit. Contact the convention center at (843) 918-1225 to find out what events are going on while you're in town.

such events as car shows and chili and rib cookoffs for charities. On top of this bounty, Barefoot is expanding—actually more than quadrupling in size, making it the Grand Strand's largest project-in-progress. Four golf courses, a swing bridge, a Main Street area with more shops, a convention center, acres and acres of horseback riding, and even homesites will complete Barefoot Landing. See the Real Estate and Golf chapters for more details.

Colonial Mall
U.S. Highway 17 North (north of Restaurant Row), North Myrtle Beach
(843) 272–4040
www.colonialmallmyrtlebeach.com

Like all the area's malls, Colonial is a one-level facility. Since opening in 1986, it has been anchored by Belk, Kmart, and a state-of-the-art cinema. Belk has recently doubled in size, replacing an earlier outlet store and actually building a few hundred additional square feet. Other Colonial stores that are recognizable from their position in malls nationwide include Lane Bryant, The Limited, Express, Lerner's, Structure, Victoria's Secret, and Waldenbooks.

Colonial is the largest of the area malls and offers an average-size food court, including Chick-fil-A, Taco Bell, Great Steak and Fry, and Ruby Tuesdays.

Myrtle Beach

Broadway at the Beach
U.S. Highway 17 North Bypass at 21st Avenue North, Myrtle Beach
(843) 444–3200
www.broadatthebeach.com

Broadway at the Beach is the centerpiece of the Burroughs & Chapin Company's

Located in the heart of the Grand Strand, Broadway at the Beach offers shopping galore as well as theaters, restaurants, and an assortment of attractions. It's a daylong destination well suited for the entire family. PHOTO: COURTESY OF MYRTLE BEACH AREA CHAMBER OF COMMERCE

plan for the future of Myrtle Beach. The complex already features more than 100 shops, a live-entertainment theater, a multiscreen IMAX theater, dozens of restaurants including the Hard Rock Café, and a nightclub street titled Celebrity Square that features well-known musical acts and signed handprints in cement from more than 30 celebrities such as Donna Summers, Johnny Mathis, Barry Manilow, and Wayne Newton.

Trying to provide an entertainment venue, a restaurant district, a complex of high-energy nightclubs, and a quaint shopping village (complete with the Disney technique of ¾-scale building) seemingly would be an unobtainable mixture of tasks, but Burroughs & Chapin is pulling it off well. And despite the initial failure and closure of 30 or more stores, the crowds keep coming—and new merchants keep opening.

Do more people visit Broadway at the Beach for the shopping and the restaurants, or is it the huge attractions like Ripley's Aquarium (see the Attractions chapter) and activities like the Fourth of July and Halloween parties that the management throws? Fortunately no one has to choose and there is enough to draw everyone, from the right jeans at the Gap to collectibles from Sports Heroes. The shopping is divided into three districts:

Caribbean Village, Charleston Boardwalk, and New England Village. With a range of stores from Perfumania and Autographs Plus to Hammock Hut and Noah and Friends, Broadway is a specialty store extravaganza, so be sure to bring your birthday and Christmas present list along.

In addition to the shopping, Broadway at the Beach has a fine selection of restaurants that in addition to the popular seafood theme, also have specialty themes such as Harley-Davidson motorcycles, sports and rock stars, movie memorabilia, and race cars. These restaurants also have some of the most popular gift shops around. (Check out the Restaurants chapter for details on the food.)

Myrtle Beach Factory Stores
4635 Factory Stores Boulevard (west of the Intracoastal Waterway), Myrtle Beach
(843) 236–5100
www.shopmyrtlebeach.com

One visit to Myrtle Beach Factory Stores will give you a vivid understanding of exactly why "shopping" comes in a strong second—just behind "beaches"—when folks explain why they choose the Myrtle Beach area for their vacations. Best of all, every purchase will net you a savings of 20 to 70 percent off original retail prices!

With nearly half-a-million square feet, this outlet center is among the top-twenty largest outlet projects in the country. Conveniently located on Highway 501, the main corridor leading into Myrtle Beach, a pleasantly designed "village" of shops now boasts more than 100 brand-name outlets. The names are well-known: Banana Republic, Perry Ellis, Britches, Casual Corner, GAP, Brooks Brothers, NIKE, Polo/Ralph Lauren, and more. In fact Myrtle Beach Factory Stores lists more than 50 percent of the nation's 22 largest outlet retail chains as tenants.

Myrtle Square Mall
2501 North Kings Highway, Myrtle Beach
(843) 448–2513
www.myrtlebeachtrips.com/msquare

With more than 90 stores and attractions, Myrtle Square is the oldest and most centrally located mall in Myrtle Beach proper. Anchored by Sears, Peebles, and Belk, it of-

Insiders' Tip
It's Christmas year-round in quite a few shops in the area. Fantastic decorations are always available at such stores as the Christmas Mouse at Barefoot Landing, the Christmas Elegance village in Myrtle Beach, and St. Nick Nack's in Calabash, North Carolina.

Shopping runs a close second to beaches as the area's most lauded attraction. PHOTO: COURTESY OF MYRTLE BEACH AREA CHAMBER OF COMMERCE

fers a nice combination of specialty shops, apparel stores, food, electronics, books, health products, music, and more. This mall originally opened in the late 1970s as part of the Burroughs & Chapin Company's plan to dominate the local tourism market. (Burroughs & Chapin owns the Pavilion Amusement Park, Broadway at the Beach, and more than 100,000 acres of Grand Strand real estate.)

Some of the better-known mall-esque stores include Fye Music, where you can listen to music before you buy it; Things Remembered, for collectibles and gifts; and Radio Shack, for home electronics. Interestingly enough, with the opening of so many new shopping areas, there has been a fairly large turnover of smaller stores in the mall. Vacant stores are rare, however, because so many businesses covet this prized commercial space.

Myrtle Square boasts the area's only indoor carousel, with 20 high-steppin' horses, tigers, giraffes, spinning lights, and old-fashioned music. It also claims to have the world's largest clock (though this is only a claim)—a 60-foot-diameter timepiece that combines centuries-old pendulum technology, 1960s graphics, and special time-triggered fountains—in the mall's center court.

Tanger Outlets
Highway 17 intersection with Veterans Highway, 10785 Kings Road, Myrtle Beach
(866) 838–9830, (843) 449–0491
www.tangeroutlet.com

The Tanger Outlets represent the latest,

greatest shopping addition to the Myrtle Beach area. The 43-acre complex is located where Veterans Highway meets Highway 17 near Colonial Mall. At a cost that approaches $50 million, the 400,000-square-foot retail complex offers roughly 60 outlet and specialty stores, including Tommy Hilfiger, Nautica, Liz Claiborne, and the area's first Old Navy. Visitors enjoy a pedestrian-friendly design that features landscaped courtyards and a diverse food court.

Tanger Outlet Center is a joint venture between Tanger Properties Limited Partnership and Rosen-Warren Myrtle Beach LLC. Rosen Associates Development Inc. has developed retail properties throughout the country and is active in multifamily developments.

Tanger Factory Outlet Centers Inc., based in Greensboro, North Carolina, essentially founded the concept of factory outlet shopping centers nearly two decades ago. Today the Company owns 29 outlet parks in 20 states—representing more than 1,100 brand-name outlet stores.

Waccamaw Factory Shoppes
3200 Pottery Drive, Myrtle Beach
(843) 236–6152, (800) 444–VALU
www.waccamawfactoryshoppes.com

Waccamaw Factory Shoppes is the only outlet shopping destination in Myrtle Beach where you can have as much fun in the sun as in the rain. Located on Highway 501 on the Intracoastal Waterway, the outlets are only 3 miles from downtown Myrtle Beach. Enjoy bargain hunting in the enclosed, climate-controlled malls. Stores include Liz Claiborne, QVC Outlet, Easy Spirit, Burlington Brands, Dress Barn, Samsonite, and Kasper—among many others. There is also a food court with selections that range from salads to hamburgers to pizza and assorted foreign fare. Waccamaw Factory Shoppes has two on-site ATMs and free wheelchairs on request. The Factory Shoppes are open Monday through Saturday from 9:00 A.M. to 9:00 P.M. and Sunday from 10:00 A.M. to 6:00 P.M. Off-season hours are often abbreviated. Call ahead to be sure.

South Strand

The Hammock Shops
U.S. Highway 17, Pawleys Island
(843) 237–8448
www.thehammockshops.com

Once you've been to The Hammock Shops, you'll understand what many of the other outdoor shopping complexes on the Strand are attempting to imitate. Just to see it is an experience; we even considered including it in the Attractions chapter, but its function as a shopping destination cements its place here.

In 1889 John Joshua Ward, a young riverboat captain who shipped supplies up and down the Waccamaw River from Pawleys Island to Georgetown and Charleston, created the first Pawleys Island hammock. In an attempt to find relief from the scratchy straw mattresses then used on river barges, he first tried working with canvas, then knotted string; but both were as uncomfortable as the straw. What finally evolved was a hammock of soft cotton rope—woven, rather than knotted, and held open by use of a curved "spreader bar." The new design allowed air to circulate, making the hammock far cooler and more comfortable than the scratchy straw beds. And the spreader bar lent a gentle curve, keeping the soft weave from collapsing inward.

This concept behind the famous Pawleys Island hammock spawned a design faithfully retained for more than 100 years. Ward taught the intricacies of the pattern to his brother-in-law, A. H. "Cap't Doc" Lachicotte, and soon the Lachicottes and Wards were busy making hammocks for family members and friends. In the late 1930s, "Doc" set up a small shop on U.S. Highway 17 to sell the hammocks to travelers. And that modest business became the nucleus around which today's famed Hammock Shops at Pawleys Island sprang up. The Lachicottes remain one of the most prominent families on the South Strand and head a real-estate conglomerate on Pawleys Island.

"Quaint" might be an overused adjective, but it is truly appropriate when applied to The Hammock Shops. This clutch of retail establishments is the kind of

Located in Pawleys Island on the Strand's south end, The Hammock Shops is not-to-be-missed for unusual boutiques, fine dining, a rich sense of history—and the finest handmade hammocks in all the world. PHOTO: COURTESY OF MYRTLE BEACH AREA CHAMBER OF COMMERCE

place you can return to again and again, finding something new and unique each time. Two dozen shops, many offering the work of Carolina artists and craftspeople, are now clustered beneath moss-draped trees on the edge of a beautiful salt marsh. Some occupy historic Lowcountry buildings that include an original post office and schoolhouse. The newer shops are careful not to compromise the mood of the original architecture; they feature old beams, used timber, and ballast brick. Clearly this complex is a welcome complement to the razzle and dazzle of Myrtle Beach.

But this little complex features much more than beautiful nature scenes and great hammocks. You also will find

Want to Cook like a Southerner—Instantly?

Biscuits, grits, and pork rinds: the foods that come to mind when someone mentions Southern cooking. And once you've been to Myrtle Beach, Calabash moves up to the top of that list. But there are some other dishes to be explored; delicious items that most visitors haven't heard of, or that restaurants won't serve because they're tired of explaining, for example, what a Lowcountry boil is.

Fortunately, quite a few gourmet shops exist along the Grand Strand, and they all rightfully place an emphasis on the down-home, wholesome flavors that abound in this region. Better still, the stores carry instant mixes so you can carry these home to relish your vacation memories for the rest of the year and maybe even share the tidbits with friends.

The Barefoot General Store, at Barefoot Landing of course, emphasizes the good old days with a penny candy counter, a roasted-nut corner, and a soda counter dispensing glass-bottled 6.5 ounce Coca-Colas. Amidst all the merchandise, vintage bottles and tins, speckled enamelware, and antique hand tools, the Barefoot General Store also has a few aisles of savory concoctions to take home. The Carolina Kitchen line is there, featuring a luscious Creamy Vidalia Dressing. The Bubba's brand, which you'll see all over, is a whole line of marinades, salsas, and seafood seasonings out of Charleston.

The peanut, also known as the goober pea, is one of the most revered foods of the South and manifests here in many forms, from boiled to buttered. Around the turn of the twentieth century, the South's cotton crop was nearly destroyed by the boll weevil. This is when the legendary George Washington Carver saved the day by convincing farmers to plant the legume for its many uses. Today boiled peanuts can be found at every roadside stand, and a few lucky cities have the Peanut Shop.

Also in Barefoot Landing, the Peanut Shop successfully re-creates the old-time mercantile. The shop carries its own line of nuts and soup mixes, and it showcases some of the finest delicacies around, all smartly packaged for you to take home. The *New Southern Cookbook* was spotted on their shelves, right along with jars of Carolina Swamp Stuff. These jars are accented with twine and hand-scrawled labels that recollect roadside stands hidden deep in the swamps of this state, where few people make their way. Pine Tar is a spicy salad dressing and marinade, Seaweed Splash is a tasty pesto dressing. A Fiery Sweet Peach Salsa, labeled with the claim that it "tastes like a hot Southern night" is available. Try out the mix for Vidalia Onion Cheese Biscuits, or a few of the blends from Gullah Gourmet: Grandputter's Fried Oysters, Lobster Pasta with Slap Yaself Silly Cream Sauce, Hush Dem Puppies. Mixes

Peanuts are a popular Southern food.
PHOTO: COURTESY OF A & I PRODUCTION

like these are even more irresistible because of the packaging; along with the amusing descriptions, the mixes come in cotton bags with vintage illustrations and usually a tie of ribbon or twine. A similar brand, Southern Ease (the name says it all), entices you with Shrimp and Grits and She Crab Soup.

While in the south end, stop by the Carolina Gourmet at the Hammock Shops. Carolina Gourmet also carries its own line of canned goods, ranging from peach preserves (from Carolina peaches, of course) to Vidalia Onion Summer Tomato Dressing to Muscadine and Scuppernong preserves. Benne wafers, which abound in nearly every gourmet shop from here to Savannah, are plentiful. Benne seeds are also known as sesame seeds, but this particular recipe hails from a slave tradition of carrying benne seeds for good luck. The crispy and rich wafers come in a range of flavors from cheese to sweet. Carolina Gourmet's specialty is gift baskets, which they pack with expertise and ship anywhere.

gourmet foods at The Carolina Gourmet, wildlife prints at The Audubon Shopping Gallery, hand-crafted jewelry and contemporary clothing at Three Feathers Gallery, toys and gifts for the "child in all of us" at Hollipops, and a host of other distinctive and unusual items. If you want a genuine taste of local color without the neon, glitter, and paved parking lots with numbered rows, then you must visit The Hammock Shops. Springtime visits offer the extraordinary beauty of blooming azaleas, dogwoods, and tulip trees. Around Christmas the trees sparkle with tiny white lights, and all the stores don holiday finery, making the holiday season a particularly enjoyable time to visit.

Inlet Square Mall
U.S. Highways 17 Business and Bypass,
Murrells Inlet
(843) 651-3499
www.inletsquaremall.com
Anchored by Belk, Kmart and JCPenney, Inlet Square offers most of what you'd expect from a typical midsize mall: apparel shops, a bookstore, electronics, jewelry, shoes, a cinema and more. The Body Shop is a familiar name apreciated by tourists and locals.

The Food Court at Inlet Square offers Chick-fil-A, a fast-food staple of almost every mall in America. Corrado's Pizza and the Flaming Wok make a mean egg roll.

The mall is managed by General Growth Properties. Marketing manager Sandy Jeffcoat is a master at organizing popular special events and promotions. Whether it's free Saturday morning movies for kids at the theaters, the most elaborate Christmas centerpiece on the Strand, or live elephants and a real circus, promotions at Inlet Square Mall provide vacationers special diversions that they likely couldn't find at malls back home.

Distinctive Shopping Stops

North Strand

The Town of Calabash
Calabash is one of those sleepy little towns that is just now beginning to awake to the alarm of Myrtle Beach's growth. Even though it's in North Carolina, Calabash can't escape progress; it's only 15 minutes across the border from North Myrtle Beach. A series of small shops has sprung up, creating an atmosphere akin to Barefoot Landing or The Hammock Shops (see previous entries), featuring antiques, flowers, fashions, and curiosities. This is also

where all the Calabash-style restaurants you see in North Myrtle Beach and Myrtle Beach get their cue from, so you might want to stay and try out the originals like the Docksider, Ella's and Captain Nance's. Most of the restaurants are waterfront with scenic views.

Calabash Nautical Gifts
9973 Beach Drive, Calabash, NC
(910) 579–2611
www.callahansgifts.com

Aside from the seashell roadside stands that clustered around the restaurants of Calabash, the Nautical Gift Shop was one of the first stores in the area and it has been growing every year for the past 25 years. The long arm of this L-shaped store has a fudge counter, a clothing section, weather vanes, and a whole review of items from a $1.00 harmonica to $3,500 brass and leather telescopes.

St. Nick Nack's completes the other arm of the L, and probably has the most, if not the best, selection of Christmas decorations around. The displays of St. Nick Nack's are breathtaking. Glass ornaments from teeny to colossal surround you, oversized reindeer vault down from the ceiling, thick garlands trim everything, and Christmas trees are tucked in every corner. There is also a Halloween and an Easter room.

The Pea Landing Mercantile Country, Home, and Garden section was recently added. Expect to see a plethora of nature-inspired selections from frogs to windchimes.

Calabash Low Country Stores
8550 Beach Drive, Calabash, NC
No central phone

The facade of this grouping of boutiques is a successful blend of colorful Charlestonian and the laid-back Hammock Shops (see previous entry in this chapter). The yellow, blue, pink, and brick shops include Low Country Quilting, Periwinkle's Coffee Shop, and Darcie's Delicious Delights, a delightful little parlor serving up your favorite flavors of ice cream.

Ragpatch Row
10195-3 Beach Drive, Calabash, NC
No central phone

Nestled against a backdrop of live oaks, this row of shops gets its name from Victoria's Ragpatch, a fashion standby for many locals. Victoria's is heavily stocked with everything from casual wear to evening gowns to perfumes. The whole store drips with style and creative displays. The Mole Hole is next door, one of five in this successful chain that is the epitome of a gift store; you will be delighted at every turn.

Just across the way is one of the cutest post offices we've ever seen; the little cottage has scalloped trim and an old-fashioned life-preserver ring for a sign. Across the pathway from the post office is the Art Plus Gallery, featuring quite a few pieces of pottery amongst all the paintings and prints. Tucked behind all of this is Caffe Latte, a casual restaurant whose menu includes homemade soups and the popular fried shrimp platter.

The Town of Little River

Little River looks like the rest of Myrtle Beach as you drive through on U.S. Highway 17. However, its distinction lies in its waterfront: Little River has a working coastline. Instead of children building sand castles, when you see the ocean from Little River, you will find shrimp boats pulling up to dock, happy fishermen back from the Gulf Stream, and well-fed pelicans roosting on the piers. Instead of lifeguards, the fresh seafood restaurants (with inlet views) await you. The waterfront of Little River is canopied by resplendent live oak and Spanish moss, creating a setting that looks as good as the local hush puppies taste. To find the waterfront, and the heart of Little River, turn at Mineola Avenue from U.S. Highway 17.

Toby's World Gifts
1530 Highway 17, Little River
(843) 249–2174
www.tobysworldgifts.com

Toby's World Gifts is a special store where Southern hospitality and Old World charm collide in positive fashion to deliver a unique shopping experience. Located on Highway 17 in Little River, this historic circa-1912, two-level building is filled to the brim with gift items, collectibles, home accents, gourmet food, and more. While listening to the genuine old player piano, you can browse through the store enjoying both the unique inventory and the unusual antiques that are used to display it. The building's historic atmosphere is captivating.

North Myrtle Beach

Main Street
Ocean Drive Section, North Myrtle Beach
No central phone

Shag shops and ice cream are shops that sum up this small town–style Main Street. Ocean Drive is quintessential North Myrtle Beach and sets the mold for a summertime, seaside community. The mom and pop shops here make for great window shopping and browsing; they also serve to break up the shag clubs that line Main Street. Windows are filled with shag record albums, bathing suits, hand-painted rocking chairs, and historic O.D. (as Ocean Drive is referred to by the locals) memorabilia. If you claim to be a Myrtle Beach fan, you don't want to miss the place where it all started.

Cameron Diego
9652 North Kings Highway (at the Galleria),
North Myrtle Beach
(843) 692–0220

This is one of those boutiques that make you sigh with relief that finally you've found a place that combines style and comfort. You could happily find your entire traveling and entertaining wardrobe behind these stained-glass doors. With all the accent pieces also available, this breezy flair could run over into your home, too. Owned and managed by local Frankie Jones, this boutique shows off the best of Myrtle Beach's casual style.

Myrtle Beach

Christmas Elegance
4301 North Kings Highway, Myrtle Beach
(843) 626–3100

Christmas decorations in the middle of July? No, really. The complex features seven stores in a natural setting. This wonderland features a seemingly endless variety of holiday decorations in addition to items such as music boxes, collector-quality dolls, electric trains—even a cutlery shop. Other stores carry yard ornaments, fine handmade jewelry, candles, and cards. While most of the shops carry lots of Christmas merchandise, you'll find gifts for all occasions.

The Galleria
9600 U.S. Highway 17 and
Lake Arrowhead Road (Restaurant Row),
Myrtle Beach
(843) 449–7576

If you're looking for convenience, The Galleria is a place to keep in mind. Its location in central and visible Restaurant Row makes it easy to find, and the stores there thrive by providing you with the essentials—as well as the conveniences—you might need on your vacation. The Kroger grocery stores dominates the highway front and offers everything from produce to a full pharmacy to beach chairs. From Kroger a long line of storefronts ensue: Smoothie King, Jerry's Ice Cream Shop, Heavenly Hams, and Fudge Nut. You can also drop off your dry cleaning at Sunny Cleaners, get your hair done at McQuaigs, send a fax from Mail Boxes Etc., and pick up breakfast at Manhattan Bagels. At New Life Natural Foods you can get your vitamins in pill form, or fresh squeezed out of your choice of fresh fruits.

Gay Dolphin
Ocean Boulevard at Ninth Avenue North,
Myrtle Beach
(843) 448–6550
www.gaydolphin.com

No chapter on Grand Strand shopping worth its salt could overlook Gay Dol-

Beach vendors boast many colorful selections. PHOTO: LISA TOMER RENTZ

phin, a world-famous shopping attraction and Myrtle Beach institution for more than five decades. Even if you're not interested in shopping, you'll be wowed by an inventory of more than 60,000 items, ranging from postcards to collectibles. You've got to see this place to believe it.

This gift shop actually has "coves," small shops within the larger store, extending from the boulevard to the oceanfront. Collector's Cove features Hummel figurines, clowns, gnomes, bells, and more. More than 50 coves include merchandise such as stuffed animals, souvenirs, golf memorabilia, shark's teeth, nautical items, toys, swimwear, ceramics, and shells.

We can remember shopping here with family in the early 1960s, and when we visited them recently we noticed that little had changed. Definitely check out the shark's-teeth cove!

Hidden Village Shops
9902 U.S. Highway 17 North
(Restaurant Row area), Myrtle Beach
No central phone

On the east side of U.S. Highway 17, look for this interesting strip of specialty stores. Diva's has recently expanded to take up two full storefronts, offering colorful clothing and gifts. The Wild Bird Marketplace has also found a niche at the Hidden Village. If you can turn your gaze from the colorful facades of Hidden Village, immediately across U.S. Highway 17 is the busy and useful Corning Revere Outlet, which, we have noticed, is constantly being restocked.

King's Highway
Kings Highway at 79th Avenue North,
Myrtle Beach
No central phone

Two impressive shopping centers face each other across King's Highway (also called U.S. Highway 17), forming a busy intersection. On the inland side is Northwood, where a brand-new and extensive SteinMart offers clothes for everyone. A Food Lion Grocery Store, a GNC (in case you need some protein powder), and the soothing Michael and Company Salon and Spa also occupy Northwood, as does the Atlanta Bread Company, serving a medley of sandwiches on their own fresh baked breads. A Bank of America and Blockbuster form the outparcels. Across King's Highway, at the Professional Plaza, the Jolly Roger is a time-tested Myrtle Beach favorite, and features fine home furnishings. The Wacky Rabbit is a whimsical gift shop featuring bunnies and samples of chocolate fudge. At the tail end of this same shopping center, at the corner of 77th Avenue, is Studio 77, a colorful and contemporary gift shop, while at the opposite end of the parking lot, back at 79th Avenue, a produce stand sets up during the summertime under a big umbrella, offering some of the best local watermelon around.

A few worthwhile shops radiate south on Highway 17 from these two centers.

One block down at 75th Avenue North, on the same side of U.S. 17, is Joan Crosby's. This women's-wear store is a 40-plus-year-old Myrtle Beach institution and is a particularly nice find for older women seeking traditional clothing styles in sizes that leave Kate Moss out in the cold. Again on your left, 2 blocks south at 73rd Avenue North, is Country Vogue. This elegant shop features scads of popular, high-quality apparel from Lanz, Liz Sport, Liz Claiborne, and J. H. Collectibles. Styles lean toward classic more than trendy, and Country Vogue has a good selection of petite sizes, too. The clothing here is top-quality—the kind of stuff you wear around your country club buddies who recognize designer names.

Rainbow Harbor
Kings Highway at 49th Avenue North,
Myrtle Beach
(843) 449–7476

This group of retail options is clearly designed for people who cherish the finer things in life. At the Gaye Sanders Fisher Gallery, you can browse an extensive collection of exquisite watercolors, Gaye's specialty. She appreciates—and takes advantage of—the medium's natural transparency. Her work focuses on the Lowcountry's wealth of natural resources and beautiful architecture. The real treat at Rainbow Harbor is Diane Kirkpatrick

Ramsay's Femme Fatal. At first glance you might think that this is just a clothing and accessory store for large-size women. But after examining the inventory, you will see why women travel from surrounding states and even large cities such as Charlotte and Atlanta just to shop at Femme Fatal. Diane flies to New York twice a year to handpick the latest designer fashions in large sizes. Her attention to cutting-edge style and the most minute detail has led her to begin a catalog and consider opening other stores in several cities. Her store alone is worth the visit to Rainbow Harbor.

In 1996 The Melting Pot joined Rainbow Harbor as the only fondue restaurant along the Grand Strand. Dining tables are furnished with their own hot plates to keep oil, broth, cheese, or chocolate bubbling as you cook your food on skewers. Other specialty shops include Kitchen Capers, Foxy Lady's largest store on the beach, B. Graham Interiors, and R. Jordan Jewelers.

Insiders' Tip

Jammin' Leather, (843) 903-3603, www.jammin leather.com, has set up shop on U.S. Highway 501, just inland from Waccamaw Pottery. If you are vrooming in on your Harley (or just wish you were) stop and check out the merchandise, and all the other customers' impressive rides. If you're on the south end Myrtle Beach, stop at Myrtle Beach Harley Davidson in their new location, right on U.S. Highway 17 as you get to Surfside, or call them at (843) 651-5555.

South Strand

Antiquing in Murrells Inlet
U.S. Highways 17 Business and Bypass, Murrells Inlet

With a deep history, Murrells Inlet is a great find for antiques collectors. Both U.S. 17 Business and Bypass here are peppered with a number of antiques shops. This strip of the Grand Strand is less developed and more relaxed in atmosphere, brimming with history and full of Lowcountry color. The drive itself is pleasant and pretty. Begin at Wachesaw Row Antique Mall, just south of Inlet Square Mall on U.S. 17 Business, where you can pick up a brochure that will list all the antique shops. Here you'll find A & G Furniture, a 9,000-square-foot outlet of antiques, furniture, glassware, clocks, books, and a staggering amount of collectibles. Also in Murrells Inlet is Legacy Antique Mall, where you'll find estate jewelry, silver, and paintings.

The Island Shops
U.S. Highway 17, Pawleys Island
No central phone

Just south and across the highway from The Hammock Shops are The Island Shops. Nestled beneath gnarled, weathered oaks, these shops are filled with one-of-a-kind finds. A ribbon of wooden walkways and bridges amid a series of small ponds unites the different shops and boutiques. Be sure to pause and enjoy the antics of the friendly population of ducks. Happily splashing in and out of their Lowcountry "swimming hole," they graciously accept tasty tidbits from shoppers. And if the web-footed friends can't calm your shopping frenzy, cozy benches, oversize rockers, and well-placed hammocks surely will do the trick.

If you're curious about what you'll find, here's a few of the shopping selections: Locals "in-the-know" travel from miles around to visit The Cricket Shop. Featuring fine swimwear from leading designers, this fun shop also boasts sportswear and dresses.

If the kitchen is your favorite place, head to Pawleys Pantry for an absolutely unmatched selection of great gadgets and gourmet cookware. The Mole Hole is an infinitely intriguing little gift shop that's become a Pawleys Island landmark. There's no telling what delightful trinket you might discover. Lowcountry Jewelers, for example, offers one-of-a-kind charms of Lowcountry subjects.

Harrington Altman Ltd.
10729 Ocean Highway, Pawleys Island
(843) 237-2056

Just north of The Island Shops is Harrington Altman Ltd., an extraordinary gift shop on the west side of the highway (look for the big digital clock). The inventory here leans toward elegant—with more than a touch of "cozy" tossed in for spice. This shop features a rotating selection of tastefully striking furniture: coffee tables, sideboards, china cabinets, bookshelves, and dining tables. Many items are hand-painted and one of a kind. It also stocks a medley of what your mom might call "knickknacks" or "whatnots"—lovely collectible pieces of tabletop decor that could add a touch of whim or an element of class to an existing display. Harrington Altman showcases some art, flower arrangements, fancy pillows, lots of handmade heirlooms, and an impressive collection of upholstery fabrics.

Village Shops
2634 U.S. Highway 17 North, Pawleys Island
(843) 237-4886

Across the street from Harrington Altman, in the Village Shops, you'll find George Pawley Company Inc. Since 1990, owner Michael York has provided his customers with the finest in outdoor furnishings, decorative accessories, and practical pieces for the serious birder or gardener.

Check out the handmade items of heirloom quality: fountains, furniture, planters, statuary, weather vanes, mailboxes, and so much more. All those garden catalogs you covet in the spring come to life at George Pawleys. A growing reputation has prompted the store to expand and offer even more choices.

And ask Mike (or his mom) to tell you the history of George Pawley and why they chose that name for their store.

The natural beauty of Barefoot Landing, built around a 27-acre freshwater lake, enhances the unique shopping village. PHOTO: MICHAEL SLEAR, COURTESY OF BRANDON ADVERTISING

Bookstores

Out of all the attractions in Myrtle Beach, sitting in front of the ocean with your toes in the sand and a good book on your lap ranks in the top five, at least. Stroll down the beach and you will see quite a few people relaxing with their favorite classic or the latest best-seller. Most of these places even carry the Insiders' Guide series!

North Strand

The Bookstall
10497 U.S. Highway 17 North, North Myrtle Beach
(843) 272–2607

Sandwiched between Colonial Mall and Barefoot Landing, The Bookstall is a book lover's dream; it's an entire house covered with books and book shelves. Here you can buy, sell, or trade your books. We recently were shopping for a hard-to-find book and this was the place we found it. The selection includes comics, collectibles, and rare books.

Waldenbooks
4720 B Barefoot Landing,
North Myrtle Beach
(843) 361–8756
Myrtle Square Mall, Myrtle Beach
(843) 448–4534
www.waldenbooks.com

In addition to the usual lists of classics and best-sellers, Waldenbooks sets out quite a few tables of discount books, racks of magazines, and many regional newspapers.

Myrtle Beach

Barnes & Noble
1145 Seaboard Street, Myrtle Beach
(843) 444–4046
www.bn.com

One of America's oldest bookstores, Barnes and Noble's large freestanding building can be seen from the U.S. Highway 17 Bypass, just south of Broadway at the Beach. The store is a more than complete source of reading materials that include a tremendous selection of newspapers and magazines, software, and a Starbucks Cafe. Barnes & Noble also offers the occasional book signing by current authors, so be sure to stop by and pick up their flyer to fill in your idle or rainy-day time.

Book Warehouse
3278 Waccamaw Boulevard, Myrtle Beach
(843) 236–0800

Book Warehouse offers a tempting selection of literature and pulp at discount prices. Best-sellers are 20 percent off and the rest of the inventory is up to 50 percent less than usual.

Entertainment

It all started in 1986 with Calvin Gilmore's Carolina Opry, a family-style opry house in Surfside Beach. Locals clearly remember that the buzz around town was, "It'll never make it. . . . There are not enough people to support it year-round. . . . This Gilmore guy is crazy." But before long, shows were sold-out in advance as throngs of residents, bus tours, and visitors vied for tickets to see the countrified, musical/comedy production that was whispered to be "better than anything in Nashville or Branson." If you didn't have your tickets to the Christmas show by June, you were certainly out of luck.

Gilmore was crazy . . . crazy like a fox, that is. The former time-share salesman opened Carolina Opry only after conducting extensive marketing research that indicated the Myrtle Beach area was fertile ground for such grand entertainment. Regardless of most locals' patronage, estimates showed the opry house could survive on ticket sales from tourists and the ever-growing retirement community. The rest is a history lesson in success.

Gilmore and the Carolina Opry were the forerunners of an entertainment explosion that now includes Dolly Parton's Dixie Stampede, Alabama Theatre, Medieval Times, and Legends in Concert. And the list of entertainment options doesn't stop there. As you read on, you'll discover the full extent of live performances here. As a rule the variety shows are wholesome and entertaining for the entire family. Tickets are sold by reservation, so call ahead to secure seats. Keep in mind that prices are subject to change, we've listed what we knew at press time. Refreshments are sold before each show and during intermission. Few venues serve alcohol.

North Strand

Alabama Theatre
Barefoot Landing, U.S. Highway 17 North,
North Myrtle Beach
(843) 272–1111, (800) 342–BAMA
www.alabamatheatre.com

In 2002 the Alabama Theatre introduced an extraordinary show simply entitled *ONE*. The name is completely appropriate for this one-of-a-kind musical production guaranteed to astonish and delight any Myrtle Beach visitor.

After experiencing *ONE*, everything else will seem second. To describe *ONE* in detail presents a challenge because there is so much to experience within this two-hour show. From Country to Rock, from Broadway to Big Band, from Pop to Tap, and from Hollywood to Gospel, just about every musical genre is explored and in many different ways. Little wonder the theater was recognized as the Palmetto State's top-attended theater for four years in a row!

The theater also boasts a Celebrity Concert Series that has featured stars such as Patty Loveless, Diamond Rio, Kenny Chesney, Tim Conway, Don Knotts, Billy Ray Cyrus, Ricky Van Shelton, the Oak Ridge Boys, Jim Nabors, Charlie Pride, Sammy Kershaw, Roy Clark, Lou Rawls, and—of course, the theater's namesake, supergroup Alabama.

For value, the $79 season pass can't be beat. This pass entitles the holder not only admission to Alabama Theatre's house show, but also the customer's pick of one guest-artist performance, plus admission to the Christmas in Dixie Show.

Showmanship, eclectic music, lavish costumes, and dazzling special effects . . . Alabama Theatre has it all. You'll wonder why you didn't visit sooner.

ALABAMA THEATRE

NORTH MYRTLE BEACH, SC

Featuring the vision and skill of supergroup Alabama and Opryland USA, two of the biggest and best-respected names in entertainment, Alabama Theatre delivers a rich musical mix spiced with side-splitting comedy and dynamic dance numbers. PHOTO: COURTESY OF ALABAMA THEATRE

House of Blues
4640 U.S. Highway 17 South at Barefoot
Landing, North Myrtle Beach
(843) 272–3000
www.hob.com/venues/clubvenues/myrtle
beach

It was an exciting time for Grand Stranders when the House of Blues officially opened to the public with a gala ceremony that featured The Blues Brothers—Dan Aykroyd and John Goodman—and the Godfather of Soul himself, James Brown. Even South Carolina's then-governor, David Beasley, roared in on a Harley for the event.

The House of Blues now stands as the area's only true music hall, a massive space that can hold 2,200 people at one time. Sellout crowds have come to the House of Blues to see ZZ Top, Steve Winward, INXS,

K.C. and the Sunshine Band, Gregg Allman, Collective Soul, and The Wallflowers. Acts are booked year-round depending on artist availability. Each performance commands its own ticket price, but it's safe to say you'll pay $15 and up for admission to any of the shows. Except for low seating and scattered bar stools, the music hall is a stand-up, dancing venue.

In its trail-blazing style, the House of Blues also brought Gospel brunches to the Grand Strand with continuous seating between 9:00 A.M. and 2:00 P.M. on Sundays. The House is spiritually inspired by gospel choirs singing praises while the audience dines on a Southern-style all-you-can-eat buffet meal. Gospel show and buffet is $16.95 per adult and $8.50 for those 6 to 12 years of age; children 6 and younger need not pay.

For more on the House of Blues, which also has a restaurant, see the Close-up in the Restaurants chapter.

Myrtle Beach

Carolina Opry
North Kings Highway (at U.S. Highway 17 Bypass), Myrtle Beach
(843) 913–1400, (800) 843–6779
www.thecarolinaopry.com

Since 1986 when Calvin Gilmore opened The Carolina Opry and launched the entertainment industry in Myrtle Beach, the Grand Strand has taken its place among the nation's most popular centers for live entertainment. Taking in at least one show is an absolute must and The Carolina Opry, the area's original show, is one great choice. Need proof? *USA Today* called it "a big hit." *New York Post* said it was "a hot ticket." The *Saturday Evening Post* wrote, " . . . tourists can't beat the two-hour show at The Carolina Opry." And *Southern Living* magazine delivered this accolade: "Music, comedy and glitter . . . an entertainment phenomenon."

Offering something for everyone, this ultimate variety show is a mix of Nashville, Vegas, and Broadway and showcases stellar performances by world-class singers, musicians, comedians, and dancers. In this 2,200-seat show palace with premier sound and lighting systems and three giant screens, every guest sees every performer "up close and personal."

The Carolina Opry has remained the only show that has won every major South Carolina tourism award, including the Governor's Cup and Most Outstanding Attraction. Readers of the Myrtle Beach Knight-Ridder newspaper the *Sun News,* has voted this live music and comedy variety show the Best of the Beach year after year. These accolades only reinforce what people who see the show already know: The Carolina Opry entertains with America's

The Carolina Opry's elegant, 2,200-seat theater, reminiscent of an opulent Southern-style plantation mansion, is home to a show USA Today *referred to as "a big hit."* PHOTO: COURTESY OF CAROLINA OPRY

best-loved music and is widely acclaimed as Myrtle Beach's best show. Visit their Web site for show photos and videos, as well as to purchase tickets on-line.

Shows begin at 8:00 P.M. except during November and December when the curtain rises at 7:00 P.M. Ticket prices for the regular season are $30.95 for adults, $20.00 for students, and $15.00 for children. During the November and December holiday shows, tickets for adults are $35, and children are $20. Reservations for all shows are strongly recommended.

Comedy Cabana
9588 North Kings Highway, Myrtle Beach
(843) 449–HAHA
www.comedycabana.com

If you're in the mood for a good belly laugh, the Comedy Cabana is the only five-star comedy club on the Grand Strand. The cabana features three new professional comedians each week. The past year's lineup included Tim Wilson, Bobby Collins, Killer Baez, and James Gregory.

Comedy Cabana is divided into two rooms. The Good Humor Bar and Grill is open before and after shows for food and drink. A full menu is offered, including appetizers, sandwiches, pizza, steak, chicken, and pasta. Showtime is in another theater room where seating is intimate, cabaret style. Dinner is also served during the show. As is the norm with most comedy clubs, guests must buy at least two items during the evening. The cabana stocks a full bar plus a good selection of coffee drinks, nonalcoholic elixirs, soft drinks, and sparkling waters.

Doors open at 6:30 P.M. Performances are two hours long and begin at 8:00 P.M. Tuesday through Saturday during spring and fall, with an additional 10:15 P.M. show on Friday and Saturday. During the summer season you can enjoy comedy every night of the week. The cover charge is $15. Reservations are recommended.

Crocodile Rocks Dueling Pianos Saloon
1320 Celebrity Circle, Broadway at the Beach, Myrtle Beach
(843) 444–2096
www.fantasticclubs.com

Crocodile Rocks is a unique show that features nonstop dueling pianos. Two grand pianos face one another on stage and alternating players ensure high-energy tinkling of the ivories all night.

Usually packed on weekends, audiences are normally clapping and screaming with laughter at bawdy renditions of songs. Patrons are brought up on stage during the show to become the brunt of a joke or to participate in enacting the lyrics of a tune. The singer-musicians at Crocodile Rocks are incredibly talented. Requests (with a little cash) for songs are taken throughout the evening.

Use caution if escorting an ultraconservative relative or child; some of the skits could make even your drunken cousin blush. Admission to Crocodile Rocks is $5.00 per person and allows you entry into Revolutions Retro Dance Club across the square.

Dixie Stampede
North Kings Highway at U.S. Highway 17 Bypass, Myrtle Beach
(843) 497–9700, (800) 433–4401
www.dixiestampede.com

Dixie Stampede, a Dollywood Production, is a dinner attraction that combines country cookin' with a rodeo-style show for a rompin', stompin', finger-lickin' good time. And we're not just whistling Dixie about the finger-lickin' part: Don't expect silverware for your four-course dinner of creamy vegetable soup, whole roasted chicken, hickory-smoked pork, corn on the cob, herb-basted potato, homemade bread, dessert, and beverage.

The vocal talent—and costumes—will "wow" you all night long. PHOTO: COURTESY OF ALABAMA THEATRE

And just in case you're wondering, the soup is served in a drinking cup. Thankfully, you can wash your hands with warm, wet towels provided by the singing waiters and waitresses.

Before dinner everyone is corralled into the Dixie Belle Saloon (no alcohol served) for live musical entertainment, specialty drinks served in boot mugs, popcorn, and peanuts. Then the audience is seated in stadium fashion above the arena where the action is held. Country-music artist and icon Dolly Parton had a hand in developing this $5 million dinner attraction, so expect Southern belles, glitzy costumes that light up in the dark, cowboys who perform trick riding with some 32 trained horses, and audience participation that's downright neighborly. The show's theme is created from the romance of the Old South and the rivalry of the Civil War. Let's face it, a pig race between Ulysses S. Grunt and Robert E. Lean is pushing the cornball, but it sets the pace for a knee-slapping good time.

Dixie Stampede was responsible for bringing ostriches to the Grand Strand to step up the show's North-South conflict. Two riders, one in Union blue, the other in a Confederate uniform, jockey their big birds around the arena. These feathered racers are between 3 and 6 years old, already 7 feet tall and weigh in at about 350 pounds.

Tickets are $34.99 plus tax for adults and teens and $18.99 plus tax and gratuity for children ages 4 to 11; kids younger than 4 are admitted free. The theater seats about 1,000, but call ahead for reservations. Regular shows are held at 6:00 P.M. daily from March through May. Two shows, at 6:00 and 8:00 P.M., are performed nightly from June through August. You can catch one show per evening at 6:00 P.M. during September and October, and performances are scheduled for every Monday, Wednesday, Friday, and Saturday night at 6:00 P.M. in November and December.

The holiday *Christmas at Dixie* show is performed from mid-November up until New Year's Eve. The yuletide season finds the trick horse rider dressed as a toy soldier and the sassy girls bantering about who (the North or the South) celebrates Christmas with the most style. *Christmas at Dixie* costs adults $34.99 and children age 17 and younger $18.99.

Medieval Times Dinner & Tournament
(800) 436–4386, (843) 236–8080
www.medievaltimes.com

There's nothing on the Grand Strand quite like Medieval Times. This 60-mile stretch of vacation paradise offers plenty of great places to dine, but none features the awe-inspiring thunder of rare Andalusian stallions. There are theaters, more than a few, but not one has a more fantastic (and authentic!) story line. There are world-class performers, but none more committed to excellence. Dinner at Medieval Times is anything but a typical night on the town. Dinner at Medieval Times is a journey into the past . . . a journey into fun . . . and a unique vacation experience.

Medieval Times is family entertainment from the Middle Ages, when the lord of the castle would invite a thousand friends, neighbors, and foes to a feast and royal tournament. Guests should expect to eat without utensils and experience horsemanship, swordplay, falconry, sorcery, and romance created by the cast of 75 actors and 20 horses.

As a member of the royal audience, you'll boo and cheer as six Knights of the Realm compete to become Champion of the Evening. The champion knight is bestowed the pleasure of choosing his Queen of Love and Beauty from the audience and crowning her as such. For the 1996 season, Medieval Times added the Knight Club, where guests may adjourn after the show is over to dance the rest of the night away. A cash bar is available.

A young relative adamantly swears that Medieval Times is the best place to go out for an evening—that the entertainment and food are second to none!

Tickets are $37.95 plus tax for folks over the age of 12 and $20.95 plus tax for children age 12 and younger. Kids younger than age three are admitted free of charge. Prices do not include gratuity.

It's best to call ahead to secure reservations. (See the Kidstuff chapter for more information.)

As if outstanding vocals and dancing are not enough, the costuming showcased by many of the area's first-rate shows is also spectacular. PHOTO: COURTESY OF CAROLINA OPRY

World-class dancers move Myrtle Beach to the "Big League." PHOTO: COURTESY OF LESNIK HIMMELSBACH WILSON HEARL & HIRSCH

The Palace Theatre
Broadway at the Beach
1420 Celebrity Circle (off U.S. Highway 17 Bypass), Myrtle Beach
(843) 448–0588, (800) 905–4228
www.spiritofthedance.com

The Palace Theatre is located at the hugely popular shopping and entertainment complex known as Broadway at the Beach. Characterized by the style of theaters built in the 1950s, The Palace is easily one of the most elegant venues of its kind. Crowned with a striking cupola dome easily visible for miles, the theater makes a memorable first impression even before guests pass through the doors. In true antebellum style, the luxurious foyer showcases a winding staircase, enormous marble columns, and grandiose chandeliers. The 2700-seat auditorium is equally impressive. With a magnificent Austrian curtain measuring an awe-inspiring 30 by 75 feet and weighing more than 7,000 pounds, a state-of-the-art lighting and sound system, and a truly elegant seating arrangement, you are sure to enjoy the show—whatever it is.

In 2002, the international smash hit *Spirit of the Dance* took center stage. Irish in origin and bursting with raw energy, *Spirit* was a foot-stomping production featuring a spectacular blend of traditional culture that has thrilled audiences all over the world. To find out what's on tap, call ahead for reservations, show times, and pricing.

A wonderful and easy way to check out The Palace Theater's schedule is to visit their Web site. In addition to a current schedule, you'll find special offers, detailed show information, group sales information, and much more.

South Strand

Legends in Concert
301 U.S. Highway 17 South, Surfside Beach
(843) 238–7827, (800) 960–7469
www.legendsinconcert.com

Words alone cannot describe the music and magic of Legends in Concert. A live, on-stage recreation of performances from the world's best-loved entertainers, Leg-

Insiders' Tip

Book your tickets for special holiday shows at least six months in advance. By June of any given year, a waiting list for available seats is already being compiled at most of the area's entertainment venues.

ends showcases astounding impersonations of stars that include Tom Jones, Dolly Parton, The Blues Brothers, Elton John, Madonna, the inimitable Elvis, and more! Legends' stars deliver much more than uncanny resemblances to the stars they portray. Their acts are not lip-synched; this lineup of performers actually sing the memorable tunes you remember. Close your eyes and you'll swear Dolly is on stage. Elvis has mastered "the King's" legendary moves. And if it is at all possible, the Blues Brothers may actually bring even more vim and vigor to their act than the original Brothers did!

In addition to the Superstars' glittering recreations, this world-famous show showcases an accomplished lineup of singers and dancers, as well as the smooth sounds of the live Legends Orchestra. State-of-the-art sound, lighting, and multimedia special effects round out a spectacular full-stage production that's anything but ordinary. Legends in Concert has been awarded the titles "Show of the Year," "Entertainers of the Year," and "Show of Shows" by the International Press Association. The annual Christmas show is a particular delight.

Tickets are priced at $29.50 for adults and $14.50 for children ages 3 to 16.

Attractions

Amusement Parks

Water Parks

Nature Centers

Museums and Educational Activities

Historic Churches

The Grand Strand is an attraction; every aspect of a visit here involves one or more attractions. And if you try to hit them all ... well you might as well move here like us!

Of course in a broader sense, there are many attractions here beyond the beach, restaurants, theaters, shopping destinations, and golf courses. You'll also find amusement parks, water parks, nature centers, historic gardens, museums, zoos, racecar tracks, bumper boats, arcades, hundreds of miniature golf courses, driving ranges and par 3 courses (see the Golf chapter for details) ... more attractions than you can possibly imagine. If you have kids, or just want to feel like a kid, be sure to peruse the Kidstuff chapter; it's filled with neat stuff we don't list in this chapter. This chapter culminates with a special Historic Churches section featuring some architectural treasures.

Here are a few suggestions to get you started. In many instances prices and hours vary seasonally. We provide peak-season rates and times; call ahead during the off-season.

Amusement Parks

North Strand

Alligator Adventure
U.S. Highway 17 North,
North Myrtle Beach
(843) 361–0789
www.alligatoradventure.com

Alligator Adventure adjoins Barefoot Landing and is different from any other attraction along the Grand Strand. One of the largest facilities for reptile life in the world, the natural 20-acre setting of this unique facility is home to a variety of exotic birds, frogs, snakes, tortoises, and lizards as well as a huge collection of alligators and crocodiles.

Here are a few examples of the fascinating things you and your family will see: two rare, snow-white albino American alligators; giant Galapagos tortoises; West African dwarf crocodiles (they're often referred to as "ferocity in a 4-foot package"); a serpentarium that holds enormous pythons, boas, and anacondas (the largest species of snake on earth); beautiful but deadly king cobras (some more than 13 feet long); and hundreds of American alligators, from newly hatched to 13-foot-long adults that weigh nearly a half ton. In 2002 the world's largest crocodile visited Alligator Adventure from Thailand.

Alligator Adventure's 5,000 feet of boardwalk weave in and out of natural surroundings that emulate the beautiful wetland habitats to which these animals are accustomed. Thanks to unusual plants, colorful birds, rare species, giant snakes, and 'gators galore, photo opportunities abound 'round every bend in the boardwalk. To help visitors understand the wildlife of the wetlands, a rotating collection of exciting and informative exhibits is displayed throughout the park, and demonstrations are scheduled. For example, an on-site amphitheater with 700 seats hosts a "show" of sorts every hour. Often but not always these shows feature hands-on interaction with the audience. But don't waste time worrying about safety; Alligator Adventure is supervised by a safety-minded, world-renowned staff that's dedicated to protecting guests and animals alike.

Alligator Adventure is wheelchair accessible. The park is designed for self-guided tours; guests can wander the entire 20 acres or choose only the exhibits and demonstrations they find interesting.

During the summer, general admission for folks age 12 and older is $12.95; kids ages 4 through 11 get in for $8.95;

and little ones age 3 and younger get in free. Senior-citizen price is $10.95. Rates drop slightly during slower seasons.

Alligator Adventure is open year-round. Hours vary from season to season, but generally the park opens at 9:00 A.M. Closing time depends on the time of year, so please call ahead. Tickets are sold until an hour before closing. For more information on Alligator Adventure, see the Close-up in the Kidstuff chapter.

Barefoot Landing
U.S. Highway 17 North
(843) 272–8349, (800) 272–2320
www.bflanding.com

Barefoot Landing is a scenic attraction; the wood boutiques blend with the lake setting comfortably (see the Shopping chapter), and the Intracoastal Waterway as a backdrop makes Barefoot unique. Barefoot highlights this with firework displays all summer long, the *Barefoot Princess River Boat*, plenty of wildlife to ooh and ahh at, and Carousel Courtyard for the kids. Additionally Barefoot has gathered a superior selection of restaurants (see the Restaurant chapter for more information) that is an attraction in itself.

Myrtle Beach

Broadway at the Beach
21st to 29th Avenues South and Highway 17 Bypass
(843) 444–3200
www.broadwayatthebeach.com

Broadway at the Beach deserves mention in this chapter because it has gone way past the whole nine yards it takes to lure tourists to its facility. In addition to all the shopping, kidstuff, and restaurants (see the pertinent chapters for more details) Broadway also has some delightful attractions and activities—beyond the simple fact that there is already so much to do in one place. Broadway's attractions can be summed up in one word: spectacular. From Memorial Day to Labor Day there is a firework display every Tuesday. The lake in the center of it all isn't just for the ducks; you can take a water taxi or get yourself around in a paddleboat. There are even a few specially padded spots just for kids, including Carousel Park, so see the Kidstuff chapter for more details.

Family Kingdom
Third Avenue South and Ocean Boulevard, Myrtle Beach
(843) 626–3447
www.family-kingdom.com

We remember back in the 1960s when the Swamp Fox roller coaster was being built in a (then) newly paved marsh. It was planned to be the largest old-style wooden roller coaster (with a 62-foot drop) in the South. It wasn't until some years later that the South's largest Ferris wheel—nearly 100 feet in diameter—was added to the complex.

Owned today by the Sea Mist hotel, Family Kingdom is open to one and all. Kids of all ages love the miniature locomotive that tours the perimeter of the park. An antique carousel is also a favorite of those who might not be daring enough for the roller coaster or Ferris wheel. There is even an indoor arcade in the center of the park.

This home of family fun takes a great deal of pride in its reputation as a family-friendly park. Little kids are the focus here; in fact there's a special separate area called Kiddie Land that's just for toddlers and tots. In Kiddie Land you'll find lots of "small" rides for the small fry, including a miniature Ferris wheel and kid-size roller coaster.

If hunger strikes, enjoy pizza, hamburgers, ice cream, and lemonade. There are a number of ticket-pricing plans that

Insiders' Tip

Keep your eyes open for coupons because they are out there. In almost every lobby or information booth, you will be sure to find something that will save you either $2.00 or 10 percent.

vary depending on the time of year and the options taken; it is best to call ahead. In peak season, however, day passes are $18.50 per person; individual tickets are 54 cents each.

Family Kingdom is open from late March to late November. Operating hours vary, depending on the season. The peak-season hours are 4:00 P.M. to midnight Monday through Friday and 1:00 P.M. to midnight on weekends.

NASCAR SpeedPark
Highway 17 Bypass at Broadway at the Beach
(843) 918–8725
www.nascarspeedpark.com

NASCAR SpeedPark is one of the Strand's new attractions. It was the first SpeedPark in the world! You get to set the standards and the records for the 10 additional SpeedParks scheduled to open nationwide. The SpeedPark is designed to bridge the gap between go-kart family entertainment and the professional NASCAR stock-racing circuit. The 26-acre park is an authentic replica of the NASCAR experience: 151 downsized NASCAR race cars, 4,000

Goodyear Racing Eagle tires, 17 NASCAR show cars on display, a scoring system measuring the lap speed of each car with a 1/1000 of a second margin of error.

There are seven tracks to test your driving skills and courage. "The Qualifier" is specially designed for the younger driver; children at least 40 inches tall can take on this 220-foot track. For the "Young Champions" 725-foot track, add 8 inches to that minimum.

With the "Gatorade Family 500," things get serious; you must be at least 60 inches tall to compete with 24 other drivers. However, passengers of at least 48 inches are allowed on this 1,200-foot track featuring both a tunnel and a bridge. The "Slidewayz" track is an indoor, tough challenge for anyone more than 52 inches tall.

"The Intimidator" is so tough that it is named for NASCAR champion Dale "Intimidator" Earnhardt, and is for drivers at least 50 inches tall. "The Intimidator" features an 800-foot slick track and 12 open-wheeled cars in each race. "The Competitor" is considered high performance, which raises the height minimum to 64 inches. This is a chance to race half-

Area amusement parks offer rides to the young and young at heart. PHOTO: COURTESY OF MYRTLE BEACH AREA CHAMBER OF COMMERCE

scale NASCAR style cars side by side on a 36-foot wide, D-shaped oval with high-banked curves.

Finally, "Thunder Road" is the largest rack with the most realistic cars—just what you've been looking for. The half-mile twisting, turning road is also the fastest experience at the SpeedPark. The ⅝-scale NASCAR Winston Cup–style cars were custom-built for this wind-in-your-face experience. Anyone 16 years or older, with a valid state-issued driver's license and a height of at least 64 inches can race.

When you get too dizzy from racing around, the SpeedPark also offers the "Speed Dome," a state-of-the-art arcade, a souvenir shop, an indoor/outdoor restaurant, the NASCAR Challenge miniature

Coasters, Ferris wheels, and more make for a classic vacation experience at the Myrtle Beach Pavilion. PHOTO: COURTESY OF COTTON COMPANY

golf course, and free parking for you and 1,000 competitors. Racers, start your engines!

North Myrtle Beach Grand Prix
3900 U.S. Highway 17 South,
North Myrtle Beach
(843) 272–6010
www.mbgrandprix.com

We were at an amusement parks trade show in New Orleans when we were pleased to learn that the North Myrtle Beach Grand Prix was being pointed out as an example of excellence in park operation. And we have to agree with that assessment.

North Myrtle Beach Grand Prix offers a total of more than 50 acres of family entertainment. From kiddie rides to Formula 1 racecars, speed racers, and go-carts, Grand Prix is a must-see-every-visit destination on the itinerary for most of the Strand's experienced vacationers.

The impressive Grand Prix array of vehicles includes go-carts, mini Ferraris, Jeeps, and professional-style racecars that can be maneuvered on any one of numerous tracks for high-performance fun. A few of the most challenging tracks are accessible only to licensed drivers; however, you'll find plenty of racing excitement for all ages and abilities.

The park also offers a miniature golf course and water-race park with bumper boats. There is a complete Kiddie Park with rides that include Dinosaurs, a Car Carousel, and a merry-go-round.

We tested the Grand Prix out on a group of 13 little girls from Russia. After trying every track, every ride, and playing every game in the arcade, they wanted to start all over again. As one of the girls jumped out of a bumper boat, she gleefully shrieked, "This is best of America!"

Tickets range from $2.00 to $6.00 per ride. Parking is free of charge. All-you-can-ride armbands are $34.98 for children ages six and older. Other combo passes may be available. In summer the gates are open from 1:00 until about 11:00 P.M. or midnight. Hours vary during other seasons, so call ahead for details.

The Pavilion, located on Ocean Boulevard in the heart of Myrtle Beach, is surrounded by arcades and shops and special activities and attractions. PHOTO: COURTESY OF MYRTLE BEACH AREA CHAMBER OF COMMERCE

Pavilion Amusement Park
812 North Ocean Boulevard, Myrtle Beach
(843) 448-6456

The granddaddy of all Grand Strand attractions is the world-famous Myrtle Beach Pavilion Amusement Park. In the very heart of downtown Myrtle Beach, the Pavilion has been the area's number-one family attraction for more than four decades.

Covering 11 acres, the Pavilion offers 40 rides. Many of these rides have become annual favorites for return visitors. Lines never stop for the Hydro Surge, an 1,100-foot-long white-water experience that re-creates the excitement of rafting down a wild river in an eight-person raft. Another hair-raiser, the Typhoon Plunge, sends you plummeting down 40 feet of hairpin twists, fast turns, and heart-in-your-throat drops.

But there are more than get-your-clothes-wet rides here. The Atlantic Speedway Course, a 900-foot-long go-cart course, allows the young and the young-at-heart to test their driving skills on sharp turns and straightaways. There are two separate kiddie areas, one of which showcases the gentle beasts of a lovely, turn-of-the-twentieth-century merry-go-round. Food booths abound at every corner, tempting you with soft drinks, snow cones, hot dogs, corn dogs, ice cream, and cotton candy.

The Pavilion area includes the amusement park, a much-loved boardwalk along the ocean, a shopping area, and an alcohol-free, teenagers' dance club called The Attic (see the Nightlife chapter).

All-day passes are $23.95 for those ages 7 to 55. Children ages 3 to 6 and adults older than age 55 are $14.95. Children younger than age three get in free. Individual tickets cost $1.00, and each ride requires from two to five tickets. The Pavilion is open from early March through mid-October. The park is open only on weekends until April and then daily through mid-September; it's open on weekends in October. Peak-season hours are 1:00 to 11:00 P.M. Operating hours do vary, so please call ahead.

South Strand

Garden City Pavilion Arcade
103 Atlantic Avenue, Garden City Beach
(843) 651–2770

This attraction is one of those classic finds that really sets the Grand Strand apart as a unique vacation spot. In this relatively quiet section of the South Strand known as Garden City, you'll find the incongruously flashy Garden City Pavilion Arcade. Featuring the neon and clamor of more than 200 arcade games, this little gem feels exactly like the Myrtle Beach of 35 years ago. In fact, if you want to know what it was like to visit the Strand in the early 1960s, stop by here; though, we have to admit that the arcade games are a lot more high tech than we remember from those black-and-white television days.

Within walking distance are lots of carnival-type games and a batting cage as well as several souvenir shops. In addition, ice cream, snow cones, popcorn, and hot dog booths make a showing to appease both your appetite and your sweet tooth. Visit this little Garden City street—welcome to the real Grand Strand. Peak-season hours are 9:00 to 2:00 A.M. daily.

Insiders' Tip
Get the most out of a trip to one of our amusement parks: get an all-day pass, go early, and stay late. Day passes even allow you to leave the park and come back later.

Water Parks

All tourist areas seem to have a water park or parks. But like many things on the Grand Strand, we've outdone them all with a wild-and-wicked collection of water-park rides and slides. Food concessions are available at all parks, as are lockers and clean rest rooms. Get ready for some really serious water splashing.

Myrtle Beach

Myrtle Waves
3000 10th Avenue North
(off U.S. Highway 17 Bypass), Myrtle Beach
(843) 448–1026, (800) 524–WAVE
www.myrtlewaves.com

This 20-acre park of water slides and rides is the Strand's largest water park, with more than 30 rides and attractions. It is anchored by a 10-story Turbo Twisters, three completely enclosed dark tubes that send you spiraling through darkness at 50 feet per second! Myrtle Waves is staffed by certified lifeguards.

The just-for-kids Tad-pool, only 18 inches deep, includes a Little Dipper Slide and the Magic Mushroom water fountain. The Lazy River is a leisure soak-and-float pool. Then there are a host of water slides: Snake Mountain, Pipeline Plunge, and Ricochet Rapids. Of course there is a flume ride . . . in fact, Myrtle Waves has two body flumes. Finally, Myrtle Waves even has a wave pool; Ocean In Motion uses wave-making machines to create an effect that many amusement parks in other parts of the country use as their central attraction. In spring 1996 Myrtle Waves introduced Splash Zone, with a 256-foot Racin' River that swirls riders around at nearly 10 mph and the Bubble Bay leisure pool with bubbler jets.

Food concessions and a picnic area are available. Footwear, such as aqua booties or sandals, is suggested but not required. Admission is $21.95 for those ages 7 to 54. Kids ages 3 to 6 enter for $12.95, as do senior citizens; children under age 3 enter free.

The park is open weekends from April through May and throughout September,

Every kid knows a water park is the fast track to vacation paradise. PHOTO: COURTESY OF MYRTLE BEACH AREA CHAMBER OF COMMERCE

and daily from late May through August. Operating hours are 10:00 A.M. to 5:00 P.M., with extended hours until 6:00 P.M. during peak season.

South Strand

Wild Water & Race Theme Park
910 U.S. Highway 17 South, Surfside Beach
(843) 238–WILD

This popular park takes two of the Strand's most popular attractions—water parks and go-carts—and combines them into a daylong adventure.

This 16-acre park features a tremendous variety of water rides and slides. The Dark Hole is a fully enclosed tube ride filled with dramatic dips and twists. The 16-foot-wide Lazy River takes you through a rain forest and waterfalls and traverses the entire length of the park. You'll also find the Sidewinder and Serpentine body flumes. The 65-foot-high Free Fall Cliff Dive and the 65-foot-high Triple Dip Speed Slide remind you that these parks can be as exciting as they are massive.

Wild Water also offers a kids' park with a pool, a simulated shipwreck, slides, and more.

More than a water park, this park also features five racetracks. Since the tracks are age-scaled, everyone from toddlers to adults can participate. Bumper boats and an 18-hole miniature golf course round out the recreational opportunities.

An all-day Slide&Ride combo is $26.95 plus tax per adult. Children shorter than

> ### Insiders' Tip
> Avoid unnecessary accidents from pushing the boundaries of safety. Make sure that kids are regulation size and height for any amusement rides or go-carts.

48 inches and seniors age 55 and older enter for $14.98. Children younger than age 3 are admitted free. The park opens for the season in early May and closes in mid-September. Operating hours vary until after the Memorial Day weekend; then the park is open daily from 11:00 A.M. to 7:00 P.M.

Nature Centers
Myrtle Beach

Waccatee Zoological Farm
8500 Enterprise Road (in the Socastee Community), Myrtle Beach
(843) 650–8500
www.waccateezoo.com

For kids and animal lovers, this is a not-to-be-missed opportunity to view myriad unusual animals. This is a real off-the-beaten-path surprise! For more information please see the Kidstuff chapter.

South Strand

Brookgreen Gardens
U.S. Highway 17 South, Murrells Inlet
(843) 235–6000

One of North America's most renowned sculpture gardens is on the Strand. If you see no other natural beauty here, do visit Brookgreen. Less than 20 miles south of Myrtle Beach, you will find more than 550 classics of American sculpture showcased amid botanical wonders. In addition to its sculpture and plant collections, Brookgreen is also home to a 50-acre wildlife park that protects the habitats of indigenous animals.

The property that is today Brookgreen Gardens once flourished as four rice plantations. A designated National Historic Landmark, Brookgreen's history is awash in famous faces. "Swamp Fox" Francis Marion, the South's much-loved and legendary guerrilla leader, plied its waterways during the American Revolution. Washington Allston, celebrated painter of the Romantic period, was born on Brookgreen Plantation in 1779. In April 1791

Brookgreen Gardens, built on the grounds of four former plantations, is filled with plantings and sculpture. PHOTO: COURTESY OF BROOKGREEN GARDENS

George Washington enjoyed an overnight stay at Brookgreen. Theodosia Alston, daughter of Aaron Burr and wife of former South Carolina governor Joseph Alston, made her home at The Oaks Plantation, one of the four aforementioned rice plantations, until her tragic disappearance at sea in 1813. Carolina golden big-grain rice, which played a central role in the Old South's economy, was discovered and cultivated at Brookgreen. And Pulitzer Prize–winning author Julia Peterkin used the plantations as a backdrop for several of her novels published in the 1920s about the descendants of the slaves who worked this land.

It was through the extraordinary vision and generosity of railroad magnate Archer Milton Huntington and his wife, sculptress Anna Hyatt Huntington, that this magnificent site was dedicated to the preservation of nature and art. In 1930, when the Huntingtons purchased the four

colonial plantations that make up the Brookgreen property, their plan was to establish a winter home. But the beauty and history of the land quickly transformed their simple vision into something far more grand. In 1931 they organized a nonprofit institution with a dual mission: to preserve habitats for native plants and animals while providing an outdoor showcase for American figurative sculpture.

Under the directorship of only one curator from the day it opened until recently, Brookgreen became world-famous for its sculpture collection. In 1995 the original director retired, and a professional museum administrator from Williamsburg, Virginia, was brought in.

Brookgreen Gardens has maintained world renown to this day for its skillful integration of superb art with the complementary beauty of nature. What began with a small number of art works from the Huntington's personal collection as well as

Anna's own creations has grown into the world's largest and finest outdoor collection of American Figurative Sculpture. You'll find works from the country's premier Contemporary Figurative sculptors, such as Marshall Fredericks and Charles Parks, as well as many of the greatest sculptors in American history, including Augustus Saint-Gaudens and Carl Milles. And, with each passing year, the sculpture collection continues to grow in size and stature.

Brookgreen's botanical gardens feature more than 2,000 species and subspecies of plants. The collection includes moss-laden oaks, magnolias, and wildflowers as well as numerous naturalized and exotic species, including propagated azaleas and camellias. Beneath the stately oaks and nestled around murmuring fountains, the beautifully orchestrated plant collection provides a breathtaking backdrop for the diverse sculpture. The simple beauty of green foliage against cool, white marble or the visual excitement of brightly colored blooms in contrast with bronze exemplifies the cooperative interplay of the plant and sculpture collections. While each of the gardens has its special emphasis, all mesh into a delightful medley of landscapes and walkways.

Brookgreen is also home to a 50-acre wildlife trail that exhibits indigenous animals in their natural environment. The young and young-at-heart always enjoy the Cypress Aviary, Otter Pond, Alligator Swamp, Fox Glade, Raptor Aviary, and the White-tailed Deer Savannah.

Brookgreen Gardens is one of the Grand Strand's oldest and best-loved attractions. PHOTO: COURTESY OF BROOKGREEN GARDENS

Free walking tours (included in the admission price) are offered every day at Brookgreen Gardens. For an additional fee, tour guides are available. Light refreshments and lunchtime fare are available in the Terrace Cafe. Picnic areas are available. Brookgreen Gardens is completely accessible to handicapped individuals, and wheelchairs are provided.

The recently opened E. Craig Wall, Jr. Lowcountry Center has allowed Brookgreen to expand programs that seek to teach the distinctive nature and culture of the Lowcountry. The $4 million renovated center, once a maintenance facility and stables, now houses Learning Laboratories, an exhibition hall, auditorium, Information Desk, Courtyard Cafe, Program Shed, a cultural garden and courtyard with a rice-field trunk replica, and native plants. Wildlife sculpture completes the connection with nature.

Some of the programs hosted at the center include *Lowcountry: Change and Continuity,* which traces the changes and constants in Lowcountry land with unusual artifacts, interesting information, and Tom Blagden's glorious nature photography. *Digging Deeper* focuses on the people who lived in the Lowcountry before us. In *Meet the Animals,* trained interpreters show several native animals. The *Trekker* is a custom-made overland vehicle offering an hour of driving the back roads and trails through Brookgreen's vast nature preserve. You will see distinctive environments of the Lowcountry, a beautiful view of the Waccamaw River, and silent reminders of once-thriving rice plantations and the people who lived on them.

One of the most popular tours is the 50-minute exploration of the waterways around Brookgreen Gardens on the 48-foot pontoon boat, *The Springfield.* View the scenic cypress swamps, remains of irrigation systems, Spanish moss–covered trees, and abandoned rice fields.

Brookgreen Gardens is open daily year-round, 9:30 A.M. to 5:00 P.M. Hours are slightly abbreviated during winter months (call for details). Admission is $12 for adults age 19 and older, $10 for seniors 65 and older and students ages 13 to 18, and free for kids age 12 and younger.

Hobcaw Nature Center
U.S. Highway 17, south of Pawleys Island
(843) 546–4623

The Hobcaw Nature Center is part of Hobcaw Barony, the former home of stockbroker and 1940s powerbroker Bernard Baruch.

The Hobcaw Nature Center features displays and audiovisual programs on Hobcaw's history, local wildlife, coastal environments, and the teaching and research programs of the Baruch Institutes. If you want to get a real "feel" for the animals that call our area home, stop by the center and visit the saltwater touch tank and snake displays. Audiovisual programs are also shown daily. There are no walking trails or self-guided tours, and advanced reservations are required for guided tours and special programs.

Hobcaw Nature Center is open year-round, and admission is free. Operating hours are 10:00 A.M. to 5:00 P.M. Monday through Friday and 1:00 to 5:00 P.M. on Saturday. From April 1 throughout summer, it's open Saturdays only.

Museums and Educational Activities

Myrtle Beach

Carolina Safari Jeep Tours
(843) 497–5330

This unique attraction is brought to you by the team of Virgil Graham, photographer and naturalist, and Valerie Graham, nature and history writer, who guide passengers through the history and natural beauty of the Lowcountry. Covered Jeeps take you on a tour, complete with binoculars. Turn to the Kidstuff chapter to get all the details of this safari experience.

The Children's Museum of South Carolina
2501 North Kings Highway, Myrtle Beach
(843) 946–9469
www.cmsckids.org

A visit to this museum guarantees a fun-filled day for adults and children of any age, while sneaking in a little education.

Exhibits include "Discovery Lab" and "Bubble Play," among others; a hospital room was recently added so kids can experience the fun and science side of a hospital. See the Kidstuff chapter for information about hours and admission fees.

IMAX Discovery Theater
Broadway at the Beach,
1195 Celebrity Circle, Myrtle Beach
(843) 448–4629
www.myrtlebeachimax.com

With its six-story screen and state-of-the-art sound technology, this John Q. Hammons theater makes you feel involved in every picture. Harrison Ford narrates *Lost Worlds*, a scientific adventure from the Arctic to the equator. Weaving different worlds, the film provides insight into the diversity and puzzle of human survival. Please refer to the Kidstuff and Nightlife chapters for more information.

Ripley's Believe It or Not! Museum
901 North Ocean Boulevard, Myrtle Beach
(843) 448–2331
www.ripleys.com

Explorer and cartoonist Robert Ripley has put together a bizarre collection of human oddities, amazing artifacts, and displays of the unbelievable, including a two-headed calf, shrunken heads from Ecuador, and a man who could put three golf balls in his mouth and whistle at the same time. Check out the replica of Cleopatra's barge made entirely out of confectioner's sugar—the ship's detailing is incredibly "delicious." Take a self-guided tour of the more than 500 exhibits displayed throughout the two-story museum. By the way, don't let this building's "cracked" exterior fool you; though it looks as if an earthquake has wreaked havoc, it's just part of the decor.

Don't expect a museum in the traditional sense. This is more of an attraction than a museum; most displays are either reproductions or pure fantasy. But that doesn't take away any of the fun.

Tickets cost $8.95 for adults and $5.95 for children ages 6 to 12; children age 5 and younger are admitted free of charge. Ripley's is open year-round. Summer hours are 10:00 A.M. to 'round midnight; off-season hours vary, so call ahead for specifics.

Ripley's Aquarium
Broadway at the Beach, between 21st and 29th Avenues North, Myrtle Beach
(843) 916–0888
www.ripleysaquarium.com

Ripley's™ Aquarium is a $40 million, state-of-the-art, 87,000-square-foot aquarium experience. It is South Carolina's most visited attraction. Guests are entertained by some of the worlds' most beautiful, fascinating, and dangerous aquatic life. Visitors are surrounded by menacing 10-foot sharks as they travel through Dangerous Reef, a 750,000-gallon tank, on the world's longest (330-foot) moving glidepath.

Other spectacular features include Ray Bay, highlighting a variety of rays from multiple viewing levels, and Friendship Flats, where guests touch Atlantic and Southern Cow-Nose Rays and Bonnet-Head sharks. Rainbow Rock offers a stunning view of thousands of brilliantly colored Pacific fish from Hawaii, Australia, and the Indian Ocean through an acrylic window the size of two movie screens.

The freshwater Rio Amazon exhibit showcases piranha and other exotic species unique to the Amazon rain forest. A collection of delicate undersea life such as Pacific Giant Octopus, sea anemones, living corals, jellies, weedy sea dragons, sea horses, and pipefish are featured as art in The Living Gallery.

The Schooling Fish Tank, a 10-foot cylindrical exhibit, is home to a unique collection of beautiful lookdowns. Guests experience the thrill of holding horseshoe crabs at The Sea-For-Yourself Discovery Center, an interactive, multimedia playground and educational resource center that fascinates children and adults of all ages. Dive shows and marine-education classes are presented hourly.

Admission for adults age 12 and older is $14.95. Children ages 5 to 11 enjoy the fun for $8.95. Children ages 2 to 4 cost $2.95, and children under two years of age are free.

South Carolina Hall of Fame
Myrtle Beach Convention Center
21st Avenue North and Oak Street,
Myrtle Beach
(843) 918–1225
www.mbchamber.com

Regional history buffs will find the South Carolina Hall of Fame provides interesting insight into the growth of the state. Set as a display inside the Myrtle Beach Convention Center, this designated area honors native South Carolinians who achieved fame as well as people who were born elsewhere but made significant contributions to the Palmetto State. Portraits of each inductee are accompanied by a written biography.

Admission is free. The convention center is open 8:30 A.M. to 5:00 P.M. Monday through Friday yearlong.

South Strand

Hopsewee Plantation
U.S. Highway 17 South,
12 miles south of Georgetown
(843) 546–7891

Yes, this is South Carolina, and you can visit a Tara-like mansion here.

The house at Hopsewee Plantation, a National Historic Landmark, is an early Georgian-style mansion—a typical example of a Lowcountry rice plantation dwelling of the early eighteenth century. Although it was built nearly 40 years before the Revolutionary War, only five families have owned it. Surprisingly, it is not a publicly owned tourist attraction, but rather a privately owned plantation.

Built of black cypress, the history-steeped residence features four rooms opening into a wide central hall on each floor. In particular, note the charming attic rooms as well as the full brick cellar, lovely staircase, hand-carved molding in every room, and beautiful heart pine floors.

Hopsewee was the home of Thomas Lynch Sr. and Thomas Jr. Both men were distinguished political figures, and they were the only father and son who served in the Continental Congress. Unfortunately the elder Lynch suffered a stroke and could not sign the Declaration of Independence. A space remains on the document where his signature was supposed to appear.

Featuring a beautiful vista of the North Santee River, Hopsewee is open to

The South Carolina Hall of Fame is one of the Grand Strand's best-kept secrets. History buffs will love this free attraction. PHOTO: COURTESY OF MYRTLE BEACH AREA CHAMBER OF COMMERCE

the public 10:00 A.M. to 4:00 P.M. Tuesday through Friday from early March through early November. Other times are available by appointment. Frank and Raejean Beattie, the current owners of Hopsewee, will happily serve as tour guides.

Admission is $8.00 for adults and $5.00 for children ages 5 through 17.

Mansfield Plantation
SC Highway 701 North, Georgetown
(843) 546–6961, (800) 355–3223
www.mansfieldplantation.com

Mansfield really isn't a museum per se, but it sure is filled with history. To experience this rarity, a reservation is required, as are groups of 12 or more. This authentic antebellum plantation stands as a poignant reminder of the Old South. It was once owned by Dr. Francis and Mrs. Mary Parker; the gentleman was one of the signers of the Ordinance of Secession. Approximately 100 slaves once lived and worked at Mansfield. Today visitors can tour the former slave village and even the chapel. Visitors can also see the old rice fields, serene marshlands, and the only winnowing building (where rice chaff was separated from rice kernels) that still stands in these parts.

Three separate tours are offered. The first tour, which lasts about an hour and costs $6.00 per person, leads through the slave village and across the plantation landscape. If you opt for the second tour ($9.00 per person), you get not only the slave village tour but also a tour of the plantation house filled with mid-nineteenth-century American paintings and furnishings.

You'll also enjoy a tour of the residence's special features: double parlors, a grand dining room, beautifully carved woodwork, elaborate mantelpieces, and genuine antique furnishings. The third tour includes all of the above and is capped off with tea and sweets served in the dining room of the big house. The tea is poured from antique silver teapots into china cups, and the homemade sweets are created from nineteenth-century recipes adapted for twenty-first-century tastes. (Both the original recipes and the adapted versions are available to visitors.)

Mansfield is also a bed-and-breakfast.

Rice Museum
Front Street, Georgetown
(843) 546–7423
www.ricemuseum.com

The Rice Museum, in the beautifully renovated heart of Georgetown, offers a concise and fascinating overview of the society that flourished around rice cultivation. Old maps, dioramas, artifacts, and a 17-minute-long video give the visitor an intriguing glimpse into the past . . . into a history that literally changed the face of this country. A changing exhibit gallery provides revolving exhibits—contemporary as well as historic.

The building itself was erected as a two-story structure in 1842 and is known locally as the Town Clock because it has clock faces on all four sides of its bell tower and, presumably, can be seen from all directions. Originally a hardware store, this building has evolved from two to three stories over the past 150 years.

In 1878 a rear addition was added and the facade remodeled. In 1989 a renovation to the first floor earned the Rice Museum the coveted Superior Renovation Award, presented by the American Institute of Architects. And the evolution continues. Currently, renovations are under way on the second and third floors. When complete, the second floor will include a small theater, rice exhibits, and an area dedicated to African-American history. The actual frame of the Browns Ferry Vessel, a ship built in the early 1700s, will be displayed on the third floor.

Tickets are $5.00 for adults; students and children age 12 and younger are admitted free. The Rice Museum is open year-round Monday through Saturday from 10:00 A.M. to 4:30 P.M. and is closed on major holidays.

Beyond the Strand

Horry County Museum
438 Main Street, Conway
(843) 248–1282, (843) 626–1282
www.horrycountymuseum.org

This place is actually off the Strand, just west of Myrtle Beach. The name of the Horry County Museum is a bit misleading in that it showcases not only Horry County history, but also much of the surrounding area's history. You'll find a variety of informative displays, interesting artifacts, old photographs, life-size animal specimens, scale models, and memorabilia galore.

Originally a post office, the building stands on what was formerly the grounds of a historic home. Just outside the museum, the twisted arms of the stately old Wade Hampton oak tree welcomes visitors. A plaque on the oak commemorates the day in 1876 when Confederate general Wade Hampton brought his campaign for the governorship to Conway and addressed the residents from beneath the tree. Many years later, when construction of a railroad threatened the historic oak, a spirited local lady named Mary Beaty brandished a loaded shotgun and ordered workers, "Touch not a single bough." Her defiance inspired other residents to actively protect the town's magnificent live oaks.

Start your self-guided museum tour by ambling among display cases filled with wildlife specimens. One fascinating display—a favorite of visitors both young and old—features a black bear family. Papa bear, tipping the scale at 300 pounds, was actually hit by a car on U.S. Highway 501 many years ago. Papa represents an estimated population of 400 black bears that still call the less-developed areas of Horry County home.

Other exhibits feature birds of prey such as owls, hawks, ospreys, and herons as well as a 400-pound, 11-foot-long alligator. *Resources of the Land,* a three-dimensional exhibit, brims with photos and scale models of naval stores produced in the area in the 1700s. *Loggers and Locomotives* boasts nearly life-size images of loggers, wagons, and other lumber-related subjects. Antiquated logging equipment is also on display. It's truly fascinating to see how much life has changed.

For another surprise, be sure to peruse the exhibit on *Native Americans of the Coastal Plains.* Displays feature tools, arrowheads, and other artifacts, along with models that re-create the intricacies of the Indians' daily existence.

Admission is free, and the museum is open from 9:00 A.M. to 5:00 P.M. Monday through Saturday year-round. Special events and exhibitions are hosted throughout the year. Call ahead or check the Web site for details.

Historic Churches

Some fine examples of historic churches are still in operation, if you'd like either a soul-saving or a historic peek. See the Worship chapter for an overview of the Grand Strand's spiritual scene.

South Strand

Prince George Winyah Episcopal Church
Highmarket Street, Georgetown
(843) 546-4358
www.pgwinyah.org

Prince George Winyah is one of the town's most fascinating examples of historic meeting places. Its story begins in the early-18th century.

The Parish of Prince George, formed in 1721, was named for the man who eventually became King George II of England. The first sanctuary was situated in a bend on the Black River, roughly 12 miles north of the current Georgetown location. Due to the area's growth, the parish divided in

Insiders' Tip

Do you have the rainy-day blues? Kids driving you nuts in the hotel room with nothing to do? Take them to the discount movie theater in town listed in the Nightlife chapter. They can watch movies for hours for about $2.50 each.

A bevy of rides and slides await at area amusement and water parks. PHOTO: COURTESY OF MYRTLE BEACH AREA CHAMBER OF COMMERCE

1734. Since the original church fell within the boundaries of the newly established Prince Frederick's Parish, commissioners were appointed to build a new sanctuary for the Parish of Prince George. The first rector, sent by the English Society for the Propagation of the Gospel in Foreign Parts, held the initial service in Prince George on August 16, 1747.

The church building was ravaged by enemy troops in both the Revolutionary War and the War Between the States. In 1809, following the American Revolution, the existing gallery and chancel were added. The steeple that overlooks the shady streets of Georgetown was added in 1824.

The box pews still used today were a customary feature in colonial churches. Heating systems were nonexistent, so pew owners usually brought charcoal burners to their own "boxes" in winter. The design of the box pews helped to retain some of the heat lost to the beautiful building's high ceilings.

The stained-glass window that graces the back of the altar is English stained glass and was originally in St. Mary's Chapel at Hagley Plantation on the Waccamaw River. St. Mary's was a lovely little sanctuary built by Plowden C. J. Weston for his slaves. (Colonial churches did not have stained-glass windows.) The windows on either side of the church were installed early this century. Four of the original clear windows remain. Prince George is one of South Carolina's few original colonial church buildings still in use.

All Saints Episcopal Church
River Road, Pawleys Island
(843) 237-4223
www.allsaintspawleys.org

All Saints, in Pawleys Island, is a not-to-be-missed historic site. The church was established by an act of the Colonial Assembly of South Carolina on May 23, 1767, primarily because it was very difficult for worshipers to get from the Waccamaw Neck area to Georgetown for services at Prince George Winyah. The first chapel was built on land donated by George Pawley II. In 2002 the church celebrated its 235th anniversary.

After the War Between the States, All Saints came close to perishing due to a lack of funds. The church's only income came from the rental of a house built in 1854 as the rector's summer home. By 1876 the Rev. William Habersham Barnwell was hired at a salary of $700 a year. From that point All Saints began its journey down the road to recovery.

It is an understatement to say that the original All Saints is a lovely church. Overhung with enormous oaks, its historic setting is peaceful and genuinely captivating. The cemetery offers a fascinating history lesson in itself.

Beyond the Strand

Kingston Presbyterian Church
800 Third Avenue, Conway
(843) 248–4200

West of Myrtle Beach, the city of Conway boasts its own taste of history. Kingston Presbyterian is on the National Register of Historic Places and is designated as an American Presbyterian and Reformed Historical Site. No one knows exactly when Presbyterians started meeting in Conway, but local historians believe it was before 1754. The church was assigned its first preacher, the Rev. William Donaldson, in 1756.

One of the first churches on the site overlooking Kingston Lake was destroyed in 1798 in a storm (probably a hurricane) and wasn't rebuilt until the 1830s. In fact one local historian, Catherine Lewis, said Conway survived for about 40 years without any churches at all. However, Conwayites didn't neglect their worship during those years; they simply met in private homes and at a campground outside the town. In 1858 the present building was erected. Since then it has been extensively renovated.

The yard of Kingston Presbyterian Church is undoubtedly one of the most serene spots in the Grand Strand area. The lake, huge oaks, dogwoods, camellias, and azaleas add to the sense of history and beauty. A community burial ground that dates from the 1700s makes for a fascinating afternoon excursion.

First United Methodist Church
1001 Fifth Avenue, Conway
(843) 488–4251

Organized in 1828, First United Methodist is also on the National Register of Historic Places and on the Register of United Methodist Historic Sites. The original church, now home to the Hut Bible Class, was built in 1844 and was replaced by a Gothic building in 1898. The mission-style church, now a fellowship hall, was built in 1910. The present Georgian style sanctuary was built in 1961. Of special interest is the cemetery, with graves dating from the 1830s.

Water, water everywhere. There are several water parks to choose from; choose at least one.
PHOTO: COURTESY OF COTTON COMPANY

Kidstuff

Kidstuff. It's a trick word. If you cruise the "kids" attractions along the Grand Strand, you are going to discover that the term "kid" has very little to do with age and refers more to fun. While clearly there are scores of Grand Strand adventures that anywhere else in the world would be loved by kids only, here at the beach kidstuff fun overtakes everyone, regardless of age.

But step away from the ocean; the Strand offers outdoor playgrounds, water parks, arcades, adventures, candy makers, amusement parks, racetracks, adventure theaters (not recommended for some so-called "adults"), skating, splashing, oversize playpens and even a supervised overnight lockup inside a giant playground/mall. In fact, the only thing lacking here is time; there is just not enough in one vacation to hit all the kidstuff and the beach.

Be sure to scan the Watersports, Fishing, Attractions and Parks and Recreation chapters for rad stuff we didn't list or detail here because, like we said, it is all kidstuff!

North Strand

Alligator Adventure
U.S. Highway 17 North, North Myrtle Beach
(843) 361–0789
www.alligatoradventure.com

Alligator Adventure, an alligator park and reptile research institute that adjoins Barefoot Landing in North Myrtle Beach, is completely different from any attraction along the Grand Strand. It's a must-see for children.

Alligator Adventure is wheelchair-accessible. The park is designed for self-guided tours; guests can wander through the 20 acres or choose only the exhibits and demonstrations they find interesting.

Hours and rates are seasonal, so definitely call before you go. At press time, general admission for adults is $12.95. Children ages 4 to 11 get in for $8.95, seniors pay $10.95, and children age three and younger are free. Refer to the Attractions chapter for more details.

Barefoot Landing
U.S. Highway 17 North, North Myrtle Beach
(843) 272–8349

Despite the more grown-up venues of nightclubs, bars, and boutiques, Barefoot thoughtfully includes distractions for kids. You can start with the above-listed Alligator Adventure, then walk the planks over the lake to check out the enormous fish, take a ride on the carousel in Carousel Court and, finally, round off the whole afternoon at Johnny Rockets where the chirpy wait staff will serve you a sizzling burger and milk shake while singing and dancing to favorite, bouncy '50s tunes. Just don't step on their blue suede shoes. For more on Barefoot Landing, please see the Attractions chapter.

Peachtree Farms
NC Highway 57, Calabash
(910) 287–4790

Horseback beach and trail rides, carriage rides, and a horse-lover's adventure on a private island all highlight this attraction for kids of all ages.

Ride through hundreds of acres of fields and forests, over high rolling terrain, past salt marshes, and along miles and miles of uninhabited barrier island beaches. This family-fun adventure offers a genuine alternative to the glitter and ping of the high-tech arcades and all-inclusive amusement-park rides.

Reservations are highly recommended because prices and hours vary greatly.

Alligator Adventure is a great way to sneak a little education into your vacation. PHOTO: COURTESY OF MYRTLE BEACH AREA CHAMBER OF COMMERCE

One-hour trail rides begin at $35 per person, and you must be age nine or older.

Myrtle Beach

Butterfly Pavilion
Broadway at the Beach, Myrtle Beach
(843) 839–4446

Discover the world of entomology! Or, just get to know some bugs. The Butterfly Pavilion is a welcome addition to the beach's growing emphasis on nature. This creepy-crawly pavilion features native North American butterflies, and includes a Wild Encounters Theater, a lorikeet aviary, a gift shop, and a restaurant. Once within the magnificent butterfly pavilion, you will be surrounded by thousands of butterflies. The pavilion is a glass structure towering to a height of 40 feet, encompassing 9,000 square feet of lush landscape. Over 2,000 native North American butterflies and moths make their home in the carefully reproduced natural habitats. The Butterfly Pavilion is truly a pathway to discovery for kids: Enter the Nature Zone Discovery Center to be immediately transported to the mountainous jungles of Mexico, the winter home of thousands of Monarch butterflies. Step back in time into the Carboniferous Era to see giant dragonflies whose wing span is 2½ feet across. Enter the English beehive and come face-to-face with thousands of honeybees as they make their golden sweet concoction. Crawl into a giant ant mound alongside thousands of leaf-cutter ants. All this creepy-crawly information could actually come in handy someday in your future travels—or in your own back yard.

Broadway at the Beach
U.S. Highway 17 North Bypass at
21st Avenue North, Myrtle Beach
(843) 444-3200
www.broadwayatthebeach.com

Broadway successfully strives to cater to everyone's vacation dreams—and that includes kids. On-site, permanent attractions include the Interactive Fountain, the Carousel Park & Kiddie Rides section, Dragon's Lair Fantasy Golf, and, finally, an activity that will really wear anyone out, pedal boats to get around the whole Broadway lake by your very own leg power. Additionally, Broadway has street performers sparking laughter everywhere and hands-on dinosaur statues. For more on Broadway, see the Attractions chapter.

Build A Bear Workshop
Broadway at the Beach, Myrtle Beach
(843) 445-7675, (877) 789-2327
www.buildabear.com

"Choose me, stuff me, stitch me, fluff me, name me, dress me, take me home!" The Build A Bear Workshop is an activities-oriented, stuffed-animal store where cuddliness abounds. As quoted above, you choose your teddy bear from more than 30 forms: from the classic brown teddy ($18) to a 15-inch-long floppy bear ($18) to the sumptuous white Polar bear ($25). When we visited, a frog, a cow, and a few bunnies were also waiting for homes. The store is set up like a factory, which is where the stuffing and stitching and fluffing and naming come in. The end of the production line is at a wall full of clothes and accessories for your newfound friend (all at an extra charge). This is definitely the place for kids who like hands-on activities and handmade souvenirs.

Carolina Safari Jeep Tours
(843) 497-5330
www.carolinasafari.com

These tours are the first of their kind in the Lowcountry. Tour directors Virgil and Valerie Graham, who are a magazine photographer-naturalist and a nature and history writer, respectively, have a professional knowledge of the area so you can look forward to more than a few unique and beautiful sites. Each specially designed tour vehicle seats 10 to 14 passengers and a tour guide "safari-style," allowing for an extensive and personalized overview of area history and local ghost lore as well as tons of narrative information.

The itinerary includes natural coastal attractions, historic areas, old plantations, a barrier island, and an unexpected abundance of natural beauty; until you've seen the natural side of the Grand Strand, you're missing something extraordinary. You'll see Atalaya, an imposing Spanish-style castle; the lovely old homes of Pawleys Island, the oldest resort area in the United States; a maritime forest; mystery-shrouded marshes; historic grave sites; nesting bald eagles, and more.

Binoculars are provided, and you're welcome to bring cameras; you'll likely encounter lots of photo opportunities for the vacation scrapbook. Don't worry about inclement weather; the tour Jeeps have covers and heat and are winterized.

Insiders' Tip
Broadway at the Beach often has unannounced, free kids' activities. Check any of the sandwich-board directory signs there. Past freebies included a Hollywood dinosaur adventure and a petting session with live tigers.

Alligator Adventure

In the heart of North Myrtle Beach awaits a place inhabited by some of the most spectacular creatures on earth. Alligator Adventure, the world's largest reptile park, occupies more than 20 acres of wetland habitat. In this natural setting, a series of boardwalks connects numerous tastefully designed exhibits that serve as home to an array of nature's most impressive and unusual reptiles. A wide variety of waterfowl and other exotic birds abound in indoor sanctuaries that separate the main attractions.

Alligator Adventure is the proud home to more than 800 alligators ranging in size from 8-inch infants to 13-foot adults that weigh 500 to 600 pounds. In the main alligator exhibit pool, more than 300 large adults wait patiently while skilled lecturers explain the fascinating life history of these ancient creatures. The talks are climaxed with staff members feeding the large reptiles by hand.

Alligator Adventure is also home to dozens of rare and unusual reptiles. "Spot," the giant Alligator Snapping Turtle, lies motionless underwater with jaws agape, wiggling his pink wormlike tongue in hopes of attracting unsuspecting fish. This, the largest of the freshwater turtles, can weigh nearly 200 pounds. The odd Mata Mata Turtle, with its flattened leaflike head, also resides in the exhibit, as does the rare Pig Nosed Turtle, with flippers like a sea turtle. Many species of lizards can also be viewed, including the deadly Gila Monster, one of the world's only two venomous lizards, and the prehistoric-looking Rhinoceros Iguana. Additionally, many varied and colorful frogs and toads supply their own unique appeal.

The albino alligators at Alligator Adventure are part of a small group of true albinos known to exist. PHOTO: COURTESY OF BRANDON ADVERTISING

And then there are the snakes. This state-of-the-art facility is fully air-conditioned and houses an impressive assortment of the world's snakes. Species such as the giant Green Anaconda, the world's largest snake (can grow to more than 37 feet!) and the Reticulated Python (rivals the Anaconda in size and occasionally preys on deer) coil peacefully in spacious and artfully decorated cages. Many poisonous varieties are also on display, including the king cobra, which may reach 18 feet in length and is considered by some to be the most intelligent snake. Rattlesnakes, deadly African and Asian vipers, bizarre tree snakes from Madagascar, and lemon yellow Eyelash Vipers are but a few of the many specimens to be observed. This exhibit is considered by many to be one of the best reptile houses in any zoological park.

Crocodile Cove is a special area of the park dedicated to a wide variety of the world's crocodiles. More than 13 species are currently on exhibit and range from the fearsome Saltwater Crocodile, which can attain lengths of 20-plus feet and sometime preys on man, to the tiny West African Dwarf Crocodile, with large brown eyes and a bulldog-like appearance. The Cove's star attraction is Tommy, the False Gharial from Southeast Asia. This long-nosed crocodile is nearly 15 feet in length and weighs more than 1,000 pounds.

Carolina Safari will even pick you up at most area resorts.

Tours run seven days a week yearlong. Ask about tours to additional locations. Rates are $30 for adults and $15 for kids age 12 and younger. Coupons are available. Call for reservations.

The Children's Museum of South Carolina
2501 North Kings Highway, Myrtle Beach
(843) 946–9469
www.cmsckids.org

Adjacent to Myrtle Square Mall and next door to Office Depot, The Children's Museum features exhibits with good kid names: *Circuit Center, Bubble Mania, Fairway Physics, Fossil Hunt, the Magic School Bus,* and *Starlab.* Ideal for children of all ages, this place sneaks a little education into a fun-filled adventure, and the kids are none the wiser (yet all the more informed!).

The Children's Museum is open Tuesday through Saturday from 10:00 A.M. to 4:00 P.M. Admission is $4.00 for anyone age three and older. Annual Family Memberships are $60, and Annual Grandparents' Memberships run $45.

Dixie Stampede
North Kings Highway at U.S. Highway 17 By-pass, Myrtle Beach
(843) 497–9700
www.dixiestampede.com

It's always a fun addition to pencil in Dixie Stampede (see the Entertainment chapter) on your vacation agenda. Created by a league of talented planners, performers, and all-star dreamers, Dixie Stampede is brought to you by the Dollywood Theme Park Association and is the same famous show as the ones in Pigeon Forge, Tennessee, Branson, Missouri, and Orlando, Florida. For one all-inclusive admission ($34.99 plus tax for adults and $18.99 plus tax for children ages 4 to 11 at press time; prices might change mid-season, so please call ahead), this unique dinner attraction serves up heaps of Southern food, unlimited beverages, and as much rib-ticklin' horse-filled show as a body can stand. Even if they're too young to understand the context, kids will love the thrilling reenactment of the North/South rivalry, complete with prancing horses, handsome heroes, and fair maidens. The spectacular finale showcases no fewer than 15,000 sparkling lights. Little ones age three and younger can enjoy the fun for free if they sit on an adult's lap and share the grown-up's meal.

You can't just walk in like a traditional restaurant; there are specific show and dinner times, and generally there is only one sitting (two during peak season). You will need reservations because the place is always packed. (See the Entertainment chapter for specific prices and showtimes.)

IMAX Discovery Theater
Broadway at the Beach, Celebrity Circle, Myrtle Beach
(843) 448–IMAX, (800) 380–4629
www.myrtlebeachimax.com

More than 400 million people have viewed giant-screen productions in more than 100 permanent IMAX theaters around the world. This amazing high-

Kids of all ages love to frolic in the fountain at Broadway at the Beach. PHOTO: COURTESY OF MYRTLE BEACH AREA CHAMBER OF COMMERCE

tech filming and projection process puts you in the middle of movie action in a way no ordinary screen presentation can. At this theater you don't just watch a movie; you'll actually feel propelled into the scene as you view six-story-tall images and listen to digital surround sound. With titles such as *Alien Adventure, Lost Worlds,* and *Extreme Dive,* it should be quite a show.

There are shows every hour of every day, though operating hours vary from month to month. The theater is open 364 days every year (it's closed Thanksgiving Day), and prices are $6.25 for kids ages 3 through 12, $7.25 for teens and adults, and $6.25 for seniors. See the Attractions and Nightlife chapters for more details.

Medieval Times
Fantasy Harbour, 2904 Fantasy Way,
Myrtle Beach
(843) 236–8080, (800) 436–4386
www.medievaltimes.com

Imagine the year is A.D. 1093, and you are a noble guest of the Spanish kingdom's Royal Family. The lord of the castle has invited more than 1,000 of his friends, neighbors, and foes to enjoy the sport and splendor of a royal tournament. As you step back in time nearly a millennium, you will feast on a hearty four-course meal. You'll marvel as spirited stallions perform intricate equestrian drills, and you'll gaze in awe as fearless knights compete in daring tournament games, jousting matches, and sword fights. Sound intriguing? You bet it is!

In North America there are currently seven Medieval Times castles in locations from Florida to Ontario to California; all operate within the same program format, and all have been tremendously successful. A Spanish-owned company, the spectacle is based on an actual event in the family history of one of the company's founders. (You can guess which side is his family after you see the show.)

At Medieval Times (see the Entertainment chapter), the evening of quality family entertainment begins as you cross a drawbridge into the eleventh-century castle.

Once inside you are personally greeted by the Count and Countess of Perelada, who invite you to share in a sumptuous banquet while cheering for brave knights on horseback.

Festivities begin as trumpeters herald the guests into the Grand Ceremonial Arena. Gracious serfs and wenches scurry to fill glasses and attend to the count's honored guests, who feast on succulent roasted chicken, tasty spare ribs, and cas-

tle pastries. An awe-inspiring thunder of hooves fills the arena as the master of ceremonies leads a talented cast through a truly spectacular array of medieval pageantry. Sitting proudly astride colorfully attired Andalusian horses, the valiant knights of yore face their competitors in breathtaking and authentic tournament games, including the ring pierce, the flag toss, and the javelin throw.

The one-price admission includes the show, dinner, and two rounds of beverages (and adults can order alcohol). Sales tax and gratuity are extra. Adult and teen admission is $37.95. Children age 12 and younger get in for $20.95. Reservations are suggested.

Motion Master Moving Theater
917 North Ocean Boulevard, Myrtle Beach
(843) 448–2331
www.ripleys.com

As implied by its name, Motion Master is a theater that literally thrusts participants into film adventures, with seats that move in eight different directions. Seats are

Fun in the sun is still the leading attraction here. PHOTO: COURTESY OF MYRTLE BEACH AREA CHAMBER OF COMMERCE

motion-synchronized with the giant-screen action for realism that's heart-pounding, nonstop fun. Brought to you by the folks of Ripley's Believe It or Not! fame, you can be sure this pastime will keep your attention from start to finish. This adventure is really for kid-age kids who are able-bodied ...management describes the ride as "aggressive" and doesn't want anyone with any type of health condition to take any chances.

The cost is $6.95 for children and $9.95 for adults for two rides, with several discount packages available if you also go to the Ripley's museum up the street. Take note: Your little one must be 43 inches tall to climb aboard.

Hours are 10:00 A.M. until at least 10:00 P.M., depending on the volume of business ...sometimes until midnight during midsummer.

Ripley's Aquarium
**Broadway at the Beach, between 21st and 29th Avenues North, Myrtle Beach
(843) 916–0888, (800) 734–8888
www.ripleysaquarium.com**

This 87,000-square-foot aquarium, right in the middle of Broadway at the Beach, is a stunning fish-behind-glass exhibit.

Expect to tour on a moving pathway; get up-close and personal with sharks, eels, and stingrays; and experience the glorious beauty of a living coral garden.

Five major portions of the aquarium explore different sea habitats. Dangerous Reef is centered around a shipwreck

Blue crabs are fun to catch and delicious to eat on the South Carolina coast. PHOTO: LISA TOMER RENTZ

The Grand Strand area has been called the "Miniature Golf Capital of the World." PHOTO: COURTESY OF
COTTON COMPANY

swarming with large sharks, poisonous predators, Caribbean reef fish, and green moray eels. Rainbow Rock re-creates the Pacific Ocean to be home to more than 1,000 fish, which dazzles with a swimming kaleidoscope of colors. To take it all in, the aquarium is viewed through two movie-screen-size windows. The Living Gallery is also a Pacific environment. The inhabitants are unusual, even mythic, and include the Pacific giant octopus, jellyfish, and sea anemones. Rio Amazon highlights the threatening piranha. At the Sea-For-Yourself Discovery Center, the experience is "hands on" as you actually get to touch some of these creatures.

Ripley's Aquarium is open 365 days a year from 9:00 A.M. to 9:00 P.M. Admission is $14.95 for adults, $8.95 for ages 5 through 11. Children ages three and four are $2.95, and those two and younger are free.

Waccatee Zoological Farm
8500 Enterprise Road (in the Socastee Community), Myrtle Beach
(843) 650–8500

For kids and animal lovers, this is a not-to-be-missed opportunity to view a myriad of unusual animals including Bengal tigers. It's a real off-the-beaten-path surprise. Waccatee covers 500 acres that include pasture and woodlands for the zebras, buffalo, and deer. In the zoo itself you can see the traditional lions, tigers, bears, and monkeys—more than 100 species of animals. In the zoo the walk is about a mile long and makes for a casual, relaxed, educational afternoon.

Admission is $6.00 for those age 13 and older, $3.50 for kids ages 12 months to 12 years. Kids eleven months and younger are free. Hours are 10:00 A.M. to 6:00 P.M. every day, year-round, excluding holidays.

South Strand

Brookgreen Gardens
U.S. Highway 17 Bypass, Murrells Inlet
(843) 237–4218
www.brookgreen.org

This Grand Strand landmark melds nature and history in an incomparable way. An absolute must for families with kids (and without), Brookgreen Gardens is an unequalled picnic spot. See the Attractions chapter for full details.

Captain Dick's Saltwater Marsh Explorer Cruises
4123 U.S. Highway 17 Business, Murrells Inlet
(843) 651–3676
www.captdicks.com

Discover the amazing collection of plants, animals, birds, and marine life that makes up the best example in nature of a complete ecosystem. Not an artificial environment like a zoo or aquarium, this is the real thing. The captain's discovery tour is interactive. Various nets and dredges are employed to retrieve specimens from beneath the water. Specimens go into onboard touch tanks where they can be seen, observed, and, when appropriate, touched and held. All living specimens are returned to the water. There's also a fishing demonstration and a beach walk along a barrier island not accessible by car. Frequently, though not always, this adventure includes up-close encounters with bottle-nosed dolphins. All *Explorer* vessels are equipped with rest rooms and operate from late spring through early fall. Please call Captain Dick's Marina for current rates and schedules.

> **Insiders' Tip**
> In the open boardwalk area between Mad Boar and the General Store, Barefoot Landing in North Myrtle Beach has added a jungle gym for kids.

Annual Events

With all of the entertainment options available along the Grand Strand, you will probably be amazed at this lineup of annual events, festivals, tournaments, and shows. And you can well believe that even though there are 101 things for you to see and do here, these events are well received and attended. Myrtle Beach Convention Center hosts a number of annual events and, although we don't provide the center's address in respective listings, we won't leave you in the dark as to its whereabouts—Oak Street and 21st Avenue North in Myrtle Beach. Since plans can vary at any given time when coordinating such large programs, we cannot guarantee that dates, places, times, and prices won't change. Keep your eyes and ears tuned to the news for current information, or call the number listed to verify details.

Now let's get in the game and join in the fun!

January

North Strand

North Myrtle Beach Winter Run
Throughout North Myrtle Beach
(843) 280-5570

This event includes the 5K and 15K road races for the southeastern region. Sponsored by the North Myrtle Beach Recreation Department, this competition, which takes place each year on the last Saturday in January, attracts 400 to 500 entrants. Following the grueling race, an awards ceremony is held to recognize the top-five overall runners and the best in each age category—including those older than 60! Registration costs $12 to $15 and is open until the day of the race.

Myrtle Beach

Lifestyles Expo Myrtle Beach
Convention Center
(800) 62-SHOWS
www.mb-cc.com

Dedicated to our senior citizens, this late-January, two-day expo usually attracts more than 6,000 people each year. Continuous entertainment and speakers fill the agenda.

The two-day extravaganza marked its 17th consecutive year in 2003. Offerings include cooking demonstrations, blood-pressure screenings, and floral-design displays. Nearly 140 exhibitors are on hand and the entertainment—which is always commendable—is continuous throughout the two-day show. Previously featured acts

Insiders' Tip

If there's an annual event that particularly interests you, give the coordinators a call to see how you can be of assistance. Most annual events are put on by community volunteers and need lots of people to help run the project. What better way to gain free admission to your favorite event, get the scoop on the inner workings, and, most likely, meet a whole new group of friends?

have included the famous Dancin' Grannies, lots of big-band groups, the Myrtle Beach Barbershop Quartet, and many others.

The Lifestyles Expo is sponsored by Media Services Inc., a publishing and consumer show enterprise based in Charleston, South Carolina. The admission fee is $5.00 per person.

National Shag Dance Championships
To Be Announced, Myrtle Beach
(843) 497-7369
www.shagnationals.com

For enthusiasts of the shag, the vintage dance born and bred in the Carolinas, this is nothing short of stupendous! (For an in-depth look at this dance, refer to the related Close-up in the Nightlife chapter.)

The National Shag Dance Championships originated in March 1984 and cel-ebrated its 20th year during CanAm days in 2003. This competition, where shaggers dance for placement in four divisions—juniors, non-professional, professional, and masters—is often called the longest-running shag contest in the United States. The Nationals contest has won two Feather Awards as Best Swing Event in the USA. National winners have appeared on *Good Morning America, CBS This Morning, The Crook & Chase Show, The Gatlin Brothers Show,* and *From Nashville to Broadway* in Myrtle Beach. They have also performed exhibitions at the Charlotte Hornets games, the Beach Ball Classic, the P.G.A. annual banquet, the Cammy, and more.

The 2003 contest was held at the Attic at the Myrtle Beach Pavilion. Preliminaries were held January 24 and 25, 2003; finals were held March 6, 7, and 8. The contest is sponsored by Myrtle Square Mall. As of

Annual shag competitions are among the area's favorite pastimes. Here a couple competes in the National Shag Dance Competition. PHOTO: COURTESY OF THE MYRTLE BEACH AREA CHAMBER OF COMMERCE

this writing, lots of locations and events for 2004 remain to be announced. For late-breaking details, please visit the championships' Web site.

February

Myrtle Beach

Horry County Museum Quilt Gala
Ocean Lakes Family Campground
(843) 248–1542, (843) 626–1542
www.horrycountymuseum.org/gala2.htm

The year 2003 marked the ninth annual Horry County Museum Quilt Gala. At this popular event, held at the Ocean Lakes Family Campground on the south end of Myrtle Beach, guests enjoy browsing hundreds of quilting entries from South Carolina and the East Coast in categories that include wall hangings, wearables, bed quilts, and more! Hourly demonstrations on quilting techniques and applications are especially popular. Lots of vendors provide supplies and answer questions. There are also door prizes and raffles. Dates vary. Call ahead for details.

South Carolina Hall of Fame
Induction Ceremony
Myrtle Beach Convention Center
(843) 626–7444
www.mb-cc.com

Two notable South Carolinians are inducted into this hall of fame each year, representing a gallant procession of statesmen, scientists, artists, soldiers, and teachers. Inductees include President Andrew Jackson, jazz legend Dizzy Gillespie, painter Jasper Johns, Gen. William C. Westmoreland, author Elizabeth Boatwright Coker, and more than 30 others. The South Carolina flag that was taken to the moon by NASA astronaut Charles M. Duke Jr. is also on display.

In 2002 former South Carolina governor John C. West and James L. Coker, the foremost South Carolina philanthropist of his generation, were inducted.

Previous recipients include Bobby Richardson, who joined the New York Yankees at the age of 19 and played more than

The South Carolina Hall of Fame, located inside the Myrtle Beach Convention Center, pays homage to famous South Carolinians. PHOTO: COURTESY OF MYRTLE BEACH AREA CHAMBER OF COMMERCE

1,400 games while the Yankees were winning American League pennants. Named the Most Valuable Player in the 1960 World Series (still the only player from a losing team to be so named), Bobby holds numerous World Series records, including runs-batted-in in a game, runs-batted-in in a series, and hits in a series. He also holds the record for having played in 30 consecutive World Series games.

Joseph Cardinal Bernadin was ordained to the priesthood in 1952 and served 14 years in the Diocese of Charleston before being named a papal chamberlain in 1959 and a domestic prelate in 1962 by Pope John XXIII. He was appointed Auxiliary Bishop of Atlanta by Pope Paul VI, which made him the youngest bishop in the country. In 1982 Archbishop Bernadin was appointed by Pope John Paul II as Archbishop of Chicago and was elevated to the Sacred College of Cardinals in early 1983. He died in 1996.

In 1980 Charles F. Bolden, Jr. was selected as an astronaut candidate by NASA, qualified as a shuttle pilot in 1981, and subsequently flew four missions logging more than 690 hours in space. In 1986 he helped deploy the SARCOM KU satellite; in 1990 he piloted the shuttle *Discovery*, which launched the Hubble telescope. In 1992 he commanded the shuttle *Atlantis* on NASA's Mission to Planet Earth; and in 1994 commanded STA-60, the first joint US/Russian mission. After leaving NASA, he was promoted to major general and assumed duties as Deputy Commander, United States Forces, Japan.

The hall is open from 8:30 A.M. to 5:00 P.M. Monday through Friday, and admission is free.

Grand Strand Boat Show and Sale
Myrtle Beach Convention Center
(843) 238–0485
www.mb-cc.com

This mid-January/early-February show attracts up to 10,000 boating enthusiasts and more than 90 exhibitors displaying motor boats, fishing equipment, pontoon boats, sailboats, one-person kayaks, watersports gear including scuba-diving equipment and a host of accessories. Safety instruction is offered, and the U.S. Coast Guard is represented. Recent seminars have included Flounder Fishing, Live Bait Fishing and Speckled Trout and Drum Fishing. Admission is $5.50 for adults; children younger than age 16 are admitted free of charge.

Myrtle Beach Stamp Show
Holiday Inn West (next to Waccamaw Pottery)
101 Outlet Boulevard, Myrtle Beach
(843) 347–0087

Children receive a free pack of stamps and an album to begin their stamp-collecting careers at this mid-February event. Ten dealers participate from the Southeastern region and display goods from beginner status to advanced. The United States Postal Service is on hand to sell current stamps. Collections are appraised free of charge. About 600 philatelists and other enthusiasts join the fun every year.

Home Show
Myrtle Beach Convention Center
(843) 347–7311
www.mb-cc.com

This annual event held in late February or early March is literally 100,000 square feet of displays concerning home building, design, and decorating. Sponsored by the Horry-Georgetown Home Builders Association, a recent show offered designer furniture, floor covering, wallpaper, window treatments, whirlpool tubs, doors, stained glass, and mirror ideas.

For the yard and garden, plants, flowers, shrubs, trees, pools, spas, and statuary exhibits were on hand. The three-day event featured a list of seminars and workshops that ranged from learning to make garden stepping stones using recycled materials to orchid care to the Plant Doctor Booth, where participants could take a sick plant for care.

A one-day ticket for adults is $5.00. A three-day ticket can be purchased for $8.00, and children under the age of 14 are admitted free.

March
North Strand

Saint Patrick's Day Parade and Celebration
Main Street and Ocean Boulevard,
North Myrtle Beach
(843) 361–0038
www.stpatnmb.com

Not only do most of the area's nightclubs and restaurants host themed parties for this much-lauded party weekend, the North Myrtle Beach Parade and town square party has become the biggest thing to hit the North Strand since that shimmy-in-your-shoes state dance known as the shag.

A Saturday parade kicks off this mid-March event (look up St. Patrick's Day on your calendar and plan accordingly). The parade begins at 9:30 A.M. at the Surfwood Shopping Center (look for Lowe's) and continues down Main Street. There are dozens of bands, floats, and beauty queens, as well as Irish musicians, cloggers, and more. Plenty of food and entertainment, kids activities, and a fine display of arts and crafts make this the ideal family outing. After the parade an all-day "Irish Publick Square" commences. Best of all, admission is free of charge!

Myrtle Beach

Annual Canadian-American Days Festival
Throughout Horry County
(843) 626–7444, ext. 7239
www.myrtlebeachinfo.com

The Canadian-American Days Festival is the Myrtle Beach area's premier kickoff to the spring season. The 2000 event attracted more than 100,000 Canadian and American visitors who came to see the sporting events, concerts, parade, and other special activities. The festival, which celebrated its 42nd year in 2003, has been chosen as one of the region's top-20 events during March for the past 14 years by the Southeast Tourism Society.

Can-Am, which happens in the middle of the month, traditionally coincides with Ontario's school holiday, so many families attend.

The festival includes a wide variety of indoor and outdoor activities, with a ever-growing lineup of new events each year. Highlights of the 2003 festival included the National Shag Dancing Finals, a deep-sea fishing tournament, an antique car show, celebrity look-a-like contests, an International Kitefest, Can-Am Little Olympics, and the Can-Am Cup youth soccer tournament.

During this much-anticipated week, local radio stations feature Canadian news and weather broadcasts. For more information call or visit their Web site.

The Canadian-American Days Festival attracts tens of thousands of Canadians and American visitors for mid-March sporting events, concerts, a parade, and other special activities. PHOTO: COURTESY OF MYRTLE BEACH AREA CHAMBER OF COMMERCE

Annual Doll Show & Sale
Myrtle Beach Convention Center
(843) 248-5643
www.geocities.com/myrtlebeachdollshow

You'll find doll dealers from 15 states and more than 200 tables of goods at this show, which is usually held the first weekend in March. Items include antique dolls, collectibles, modern artists' dolls, accessories, doll-making supplies, miniature furniture, replacement parts, and molds. Special exhibits and demonstrations are scheduled, and a raffle is held to raise money for a number of area charities. Tickets for adults are $4.00. Children ages 6 to 12 can enter for a minimal fee of $1.00.

April

North Strand

S.O.S. Spring Safari
Throughout North Myrtle Beach
(888) SOS-3113
www.myrtlebeachinfo.com

This is the world's largest spring break for mature adults. More than 15,000 shaggers, members of the Society of Stranders, and lovers of the beach gather in North

Myrtle Beach in mid-April for an annual rite of spring. Ten full days and nights of beach music and activities are all part of this riotous ritual. There's a parade along Main Street in North Myrtle Beach. At one point during the 1996 festivities, 3,000 of the crowd danced in unison, completely unconcerned about traffic. Admission to the dance clubs (Ducks and Ducks Too, 229 Main Street; Fat Harold's Beach Club, 212 Main Street; and Spanish Galleon, 100 Main Street) is free for card-holding S.O.S. members. The S.O.S. card costs $35 for individuals and $70 for a husband and wife team.

Myrtle Beach

Grand Strand Fishing Rodeo
April 1 through October 31
(843) 626-7444
www.myrtlebeachinfo.com

The Grand Strand Fishing Rodeo, sponsored by the Myrtle Beach Area Chamber of Commerce, was created roughly fifty years ago in an effort to enhance recreational fishing along the Grand Strand. It has succeeded admirably. The seven-month-long tournament awards more than $10,000 in cash and merchandise to recreational fishermen entering qualified catches from April 1 to October 31.

The event includes four divisions: pier, surf and inlet, deep-sea catches, and tag and release. The tag-and-release program has been instituted to award special certificates for marlin, sailfish, swordfish, and tarpon to fishermen submitting documentation of their participation. Entrants receive an official Grand Strand Fishing Rodeo decal. An official shoulder patch is awarded to anglers entering the three heaviest fish of each species in each division for that month. Additionally, Fish-of-the-Month awards consisting of various donated prizes are given to the anglers entering the four heaviest fish out of all eligible entries for the month's designated species.

Entry forms are available at any one of the official weigh stations: Cherry Grove Pier, Apache Pier, 2nd Avenue Pier, Springmaid Beach Pier, Myrtle Beach State Park,

> ### Insiders' Tip
> If you're hungry and planning to attend an annual event that features food, be sure to go early! Organizers can never be absolutely sure of attendance numbers, and food vendors often miscalculate the crowd. More than once we've found ourselves at a festival in late afternoon with nothing to eat.

Pier at Garden City, Marlin Quay Marina, Capt. Dick's Marina, and Surfside Pier.

For additional information regarding locations, rules, regulations, and other details, please contact the Myrtle Beach Area Chamber of Commerce at the number given above.

Annual Spring Games Kite Flying Contest
Broadway at the Beach, between 21st and 29th Avenues North, Myrtle Beach
(843) 448–7881

This is a great mid-April event for veteran kite flyers and novices alike. Professional flyers will take to the breezes for stunt and single-line flying for a points-only competition. Professor Kite will be on hand to give out free kites to participating children and to give demonstrations and lessons.

Look to the empty fields around Broadway at the Beach for this event, which is usually held on a Saturday and Sunday. Admission is free. A donation can be given that benefits a local charity.

South Strand

Annual Georgetown Plantation Tours
Throughout Georgetown
(843) 545–8291

Sponsored by the women of Prince George Winyah Parish, one of the oldest and most beautiful churches in Georgetown, this much-loved annual event is more than 50 years old! The tour, usually held early in late March or early April, allows an up-close look at a wide variety of plantations and Colonial town houses. Most of the homes are privately owned and are graciously "loaned" to this worthy cause once each year. Many are listed on the National Register of Historic Places. A different selection of homes is featured each day.

A one-day ticket for Friday or Saturday costs $30. A two-day ticket costs $50. Histories and maps are provided with the tickets. Tickets are sold at the Prince George Winyah Parish Hall on Highmarket Street in Georgetown on each day of the event. Visitors must arrange their own transportation. At each location trained

hostesses are available to answer questions. Box lunches will be available at the Parish Hall and may be reserved in advance. Call ahead for information on advance purchase of tickets.

May

North Strand

Blue Crab Festival
On the waterfront, Little River
(843) 249–6604
www.littleriverchamber.com

Every year about 30,000 people flock to the waterfront streets of this historic fishing village to attend the Blue Crab Festival. Held late in May, this much-loved festival features more than 150 arts-and-crafts booths with everything from paintings to brass and copper sculptures, wearable art, jewelry, wood carvings, and children's goods. Food booths boast yummies including steamed crabs, grilled tenderloin, and pizza. The children's area includes a petting zoo, pony rides, face painting, and puppets. Entertainment promises widespread appeal; enjoy a variety of live musical performances including jazz, country, bluegrass, and gospel. Admission is $4.00. Children five years of age and younger enter free.

Myrtle Beach

The Carolina Harley-Davidson Dealers Association and
Harley-Davidson Motor Company Spring Rally
Throughout the Grand Strand
(843) 651–5555

As a Grand Strand Insider, you can always tell when "bike week" is fast approaching. Makeshift trading posts (mostly hocking metal and leather goods) spring up all along U.S. Highway 501, the roads begin to rumble and roar, tattoos cease to seem out of the ordinary, and bar owners are smiling ear to ear as they stock up on beer. Rated as one of the top-five motorcycle events in the nation—and the oldest dealer-sponsored motorcycle event in the country—the 2000 rally marked its 60th year on the Grand Strand.

An estimated 200,000 cyclists roar into town for four days in mid-May. A race is usually held on the Friday of the event at the Myrtle Beach Speedway.

Blessing of the Inlet
Highway 17 Business, Murrells Inlet
(843) 651–5099
www.gbgm-umc.org/belin/blessing/

After a half dozen years, Murrells Inlet's Blessing of the Inlet Festival continues to grow and receive regional and statewide support and recognition. An estimated crowd of 7000-plus joined the latest celebration on the first weekend in May. Held throughout the fishing village that's known for its delectable seafood, the day-long event is full of activities and games for the children, arts and crafts for adults,

entertainment galore, and lots of delicious local specialties. There is something for everyone and every age at this family-flavored festival. In years past, children's activities have included mural painting, face painting, a climbing wall, candy art, and the ever-popular "Dunking Tank." There is no admission or parking charge, and the event is held rain or shine.

June

Annual Sun Fun Festival
Throughout the Grand Strand
(843) 626–7444
www.myrtlebeachinfo.com

The Myrtle Beach area's well-known Sun Fun Festival celebrated its 50th birthday in 2001. This fun-filled four-day festival kicks off the summer season along South Carolina's Grand Strand with a host of

Big floats and bathing beauties are the order of the day for the eagerly anticipated Sun Fun parade.
PHOTO: COURTESY OF MYRTLE BEACH AREA CHAMBER OF COMMERCE

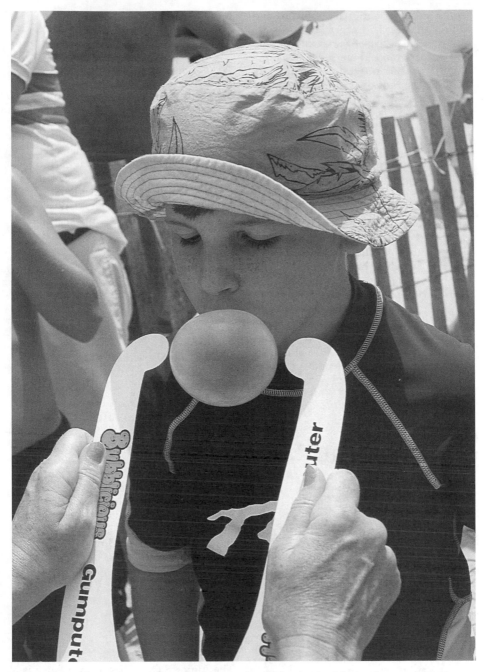

A bubblegum blowing contest is but one of dozens of activities organized during the annual Sun Fun Festival. PHOTO: COURTESY OF MYRTLE BEACH AREA CHAMBER OF COMMERCE

events featuring national celebrities and fun for all ages. The largest annual event of its kind in either of the Carolinas, Sun Fun attracts more than 300,000 visitors of all ages and interests. The dazzling sights and sounds of a typical summer vacation combine with dozens and dozens of exciting festival events—from celebrity concerts to high-flying air shows—making Sun Fun a tradition with thousands of teenagers and families alike.

During Sun Fun, visitors participate in such beachfront activities as beauty contests, sandcastle-building competitions, watermelon eating and bubblegum blowing contests, beach games and volleyball games galore. A huge kick-off parade always features some favorite big-name celebrity, as well as high-school and military bands, pageant queens, and all manner of roving entertainment.

Extensive event listings are available at all chamber offices and on www.myrtle beachlive.com. Follow the link to the Myrtle Beach Area Chamber of Commerce; you will find the full calendar of events under "Chamber Festivals."

Insiders' Tip

During the hotter months of May, June, July, and August, it would be prudent planning to attend an outdoor annual event in the morning. Especially if you have children in tow, the heat of the day coupled with the gathering of hundreds of people can turn your pleasant outing into a nightmare.

South Strand

Harborwalk Festival
Downtown Georgetown
(843) 546–1511

The annual Harborwalk Festival celebrates the historic city of Georgetown—South Carolina's third oldest. Festivities are held every year during the last full weekend in June. This summer street festival offers live music on stages throughout the downtown area, food, games, and arts and crafts. The festival is enhanced by its beautiful downtown location—close to the Harborwalk, the Kaminski Museum, and all sorts of historical sites. It runs from 10:00 A.M. to midnight.

July

North Strand

Fourth of July Fireworks Display
Various Locations
(843) 281–2662

Fireworks let loose on the north end of the strand at 9:00 P.M. from just south of the runway at Grand Strand Airport. Since the airport is adjacent to Barefoot Landing, the complex offers some parking at the Alligator Adventure entrance. Besides Barefoot Landing as a vantage point to watch the show, try a spot anywhere along U.S. Highway 17 North from 33rd Avenue South in North Myrtle Beach to Barefoot Landing.

Myrtle Beach

Junior S.O.S. Shag Party
Various Locations
(888) SOS–3113
www.shagdance.com

The Junior S.O.S. Shag Dance Party is a weekend for young folks under the age of 21. All the fun takes place in the Ocean Drive area of North Myrtle Beach. For one weekend only in mid-July, several of the adult shag clubs open their doors and hearts to the juniors to support them and help create a safe and fun event. Around 400 juniors attend this annual event with more than 20 Free Junior Dance Workshops, a Junior Mixed-Doubles Contest, a Juniors-Only Dance Party, a volleyball tournament, and other beach activities. Call for exact dates and details.

Fourth of July Fireworks Displays
Various Myrtle Beach Locations
(843) 444–3200, (843) 626–8480

The only venue in the Myrtle Beach area that shoots off fireworks on Independence Day is Broadway at the Beach.

Broadway at the Beach usually begins its display at 10:00 P.M. and includes a light and music fountain show.

On the following evening, Second Avenue Pier (second phone number) holds its Beach Bang with a 25-minute fireworks display that can be seen along the beach and in the downtown area.

South Strand

Murrells Inlet Fourth of July Boat Parade
Murrells Inlet
(843) 651–0900
www.july4thboatparade.com

For 20 or so years, more than 100 boats have gussied up for the Fourth of July and entertained multitudes who watch from and picnic on the shores. From 14-foot fishing boats to 40-foot yachts, participating watercraft start the aquatic caravan at high tide at the jetties of Garden City Beach and proceed to Murrells Inlet. Public points of view to watch the flotilla are Captain Dick's Marina, the Marshwalk, the Belin United Methodist Church, and the Murrells Inlet boat landing, all on U.S. Highway 17 Business in Murrells Inlet. Launch time is 3:00 P.M. Trophies are awarded to the "best-dressed" docks and boats. This event keeps growing because it is so much fun.

Fourth of July Fireworks Displays
Various South Strand Locations
(843) 651–5850

The Murrells Inlet Fireworks Display blasts off at 10:00 P.M. and can easily be seen from just about anywhere in Murrells Inlet and Garden City Beach. Best viewing points cited are the Belin Memorial United Methodist Church parking lot, Captain Dick's Marina, the Marshwalk, and the public boat landing in Murrells Inlet.

Another south-end display begins at 9:00 P.M. as the city of Georgetown puts on its firecracker show. The display is visible all along the Harborwalk in Georgetown on Front Street.

August

Myrtle Beach

Annual DuPont World Amateur Handicap Championship
Various Grand Strand golf courses
(800) 833–8798
www.worldamateur.com

Generally held at the end of August, the DuPont World Amateur Handicap Championship is the world's largest amateur golf tournament. With nearly 5,000 participants, 10 major sponsors, 60-plus exhibitors, and more than $400,000 in prizes, there's nothing amateur about the fun at this eagerly anticipated annual event. It's a week most people never forget, leading many to make the annual trek an opportunity to visit with old friends—and make new ones.

Now nearing its 20th year, the World Amateur has firmly established itself as the premier and largest amateur golf championship in the world. The competition, which began with 680 golfers in 1984, has attracted more than 45,000 golfers of all ages and abilities. Last year's event drew 5,000 participants from 49 states and 20 foreign countries.

Appropriately referred to as The Everyman Open, neither skill level, age, height, weight, nor gender affects an individual's ability to participate in the event. Thanks to the golf handicap system absolutely anyone and everyone can compete. Over the years players with handicaps ranging from 3 to 35 have been crowned World Champions in this four-day, 72-hole event.

South Strand

The Pawleys Island Festival of Music and Art
Various South Strand Locations
(843) 237-4774
www.pawleysislandfestivalofmusic.org

The hugely successful Pawleys Island Festival of Music and Art usually opens in early September and runs for four weeks. Now in its twelfth year, each new season brings a new theme and a veritable plethora of music and art performances at venues throughout the South Strand all the way to the historic port of Georgetown. There are far too many events to list separately and the schedule changes dramatically from one year to another, but if you are the "artsy" type rest assured you will not want to miss this. Call ahead for specifics.

September

North Strand

S.O.S. Fall Migration
Various locations in North Myrtle Beach
(888) SOS-3113
www.shagdance.com

The Society of Stranders calls its thousands of active members to return to North Myrtle Beach in mid-September for one last big party before winter sets in. Days and nights are filled with activities, shagging, and sight-seeing. Eight clubs around the Ocean Drive section pitch in to make sure that every evening resounds with nonstop beach music.

Myrtle Beach

South Carolina's Largest Garage Sale
Myrtle Beach Pavilion Parking Garage,
Kings Highway and Ninth Avenue North,
Myrtle Beach
(843) 918-1242

For one Saturday in mid-September, the Pavilion's parking garage is filled with the hubbub of hagglers hawking wares. Hundreds of booths set up on every parking

The fun begins on Sunday when participating golfers pick up registration information and a gift bag at the Myrtle Beach Convention Center. The next four days are filled with spirited competition, score viewing, long-drive contests, putting equipment demos, lots of food and drink, and—if you're lucky—bragging rights, too.

Craftsmen's Summer
Arts & Crafts Festival
Myrtle Beach Convention Center
(336) 274-5550

Collectors and unique gift-givers alike are surrounded by a smorgasbord of authentic, handcrafted items at this arts and crafts show in early August. More than 250 exhibitors from 20 states bring in original designs that include pottery, wood, fine art, toys, jewelry, baskets, stained glass, leather, tin, weaving, sculpture, musical instruments, and furniture.

Prices are $5.50 for adults and $1.00 for children 6 to 12 years of age. Please call in advance for specifics on group rates.

level feature household goods, clothing, toiletries, sporting goods, furniture, toys, food, and just plain junk. The sale runs from 8:00 A.M. to 1:00 P.M., and admission is free.

Italian Festival
Chapin Park, Kings Highway at 16th Avenue North, Myrtle Beach
(843) 650–3466
www.sonsofitalylodge.com

This mid-September festival is nearly ten years old and continues to grow. It's a day of food, music, and arts and crafts—Italian-style. The Sons of Italy and area restaurants that specialize in Italian cuisine bring in the goodies that range from New York–style pizza to pastas. Musical entertainment usually features the smooth sound of the Big Band era, while strolling accordionists provided a little taste of Italy. The event runs from 10:00 A.M. to 6:00 P.M. in the park, and admission is free.

South Atlantic Shrine Parade
Along Ocean Boulevard, Myrtle Beach
(843) 448–5797

This four-hour procession in late September features Shrine Temple representatives from six states: West Virginia, Virginia, North and South Carolina, Tennessee, and Kentucky. Expect to see a proliferation of wacky go-carts, clowns, and floats traveling along Ocean Boulevard from Sixth Avenue South to 11th Avenue North in Myrtle Beach. The parade usually starts at 9:30 A.M.

Those little motorized units competed in the parking lot of Waccamaw Pottery; title challenges for the legion-of-honor band, Highlander Concert and Chanters were held at the Myrtle Beach Convention Center; and the clown units out-mugged one another at a meet at the Sea Mist Resort.

The event usually brings approximately 4,000 Shrine families to the area. The South Atlantic Shrine Association supports 22 Shriners hospitals and 3 burn institutes.

South Strand

Annual Atalaya Arts and Crafts Festival
Huntington Beach State Park,
U.S. Highway 17 South, Murrells Inlet
(803) 734–0156, (843) 237–4440

For the Atalaya Arts and Crafts Festival, one of the largest art shows in the Southeast, the food-and-fun-with-a-view formula has proved successful for more than 25 years. Scheduled in mid- to late September at Huntington Beach State Park, this festival has earned a reputation for attracting some of the region's—even the nation's—finest artisans. Because the show is juried—meaning participating artisans are screened for merit and appropriateness—you can be assured the maze of artwork is top-of-the-line in quality. It is, in fact, quite an honor to be accepted as an exhibitor. Consequently the festival has become a not-to-be-missed pilgrimage for knowledgeable art collectors and plain-ol' admirers.

Not only does the Atalaya Arts and Crafts Festival give you an opportunity to peruse the wares of talented artists and craftsmen, it offers you a delicious taste of authentic history. Atalaya (pronounced At-a-lie-a not At-a-lay-a), after which the festival is named, is a majestic Moorish-inspired structure located in the park. Construction was launched on Atalaya in 1931. Archer and Anna Hyatt Huntington, new owners of a vast track of land that included four Colonial plantations, orchestrated plans for the castle that was to be their winter home. Mr. Huntington was a scholar of Spanish history and culture, so it is not surprising his new home was fashioned after the eighth-century Moorish fortresses along the Mediterranean coast of Spain. Mrs. Huntington was a brilliant sculptress, and her creative influence can also be detected in Atalaya.

This year, as always, the breezy courtyard and rooms of this beautiful old building will serve as a breathtaking and mystical backdrop for the eclectic works of more than 100 artists and craftsmen. There will be lots of area food vendors

Atalaya (pronounced At-a-lie-a not At-a-lay-a), after which the Atalaya Arts and Crafts Festival is named, is a majestic Moorish-inspired structure located in Huntington Beach State Park. PHOTO: COURTESY OF MYRTLE BEACH AREA CHAMBER OF COMMERCE

offering delicious Lowcountry cuisine. (With the exception of special tours, Atalaya is typically closed to the public. So, just seeing the interior of the old castle is reason enough to attend!)

October

North Strand

Farm Heritage Day
Indigo Farms, Little River
(843) 399–6902, (910) 287–6794

Farm Heritage Day is on the first Saturday in October at Indigo Farms in Little River, 4.5 miles off S.C. 9, at the North Carolina state line. The event features informational presentations on traditional farming methods and culture, as well as farmer games, history talks, and the popular "NASPIG" races. Lots of event specifics change from one year to another, so do take the time to call ahead to find out about everything on tap for this year.

Indigo Farms also hosts Pumpkin Day on the third Saturday in October. Enjoy nighttime hayrides and an on-site bakery,

ice-cream parlor, and florist. Additional products and services include school tours of farms and animals in spring and fall with hayrides. Farm-fresh, homegrown fruit and vegetables and pick-your-own strawberries (in season) are reason enough to visit anytime.

Trick or Treating
Various North Strand Locations
(843) 272–8349, (843) 272–4040,
(843) 280–5570

If you're looking for tried-and-true trick-or-treating opportunities for kids on Halloween night, one option is to take the little gremlins to Barefoot Landing. Kids can trick-or-treat through the stores from 5:00 to 7:00 P.M.

Colonial Mall, located at 10177 North Kings Highway, (843) 272–4040, hosts a Boo Bash on All Saints' Hallow night with a costume contest at 6:00 P.M. and trick or treating throughout the mall at 7:00 P.M.

The annual Halloween Carnival is held at the North Myrtle Beach Recreation Center on Possum Trot Road, from 6:30 to 8:30 P.M. The carnival typically features lots of games for the kids, a haunted house, and a costume contest. Call (843) 280–5570.

Myrtle Beach

"Merrily Myrtle," A Holiday Celebration
(843) 626–7444
www.mbchamber.com

Enjoy Merrily Myrtle—A Holiday Celebration by the sea in the Myrtle Beach area from October through January. The holiday season shines as the entire beach comes to life with beautiful, holiday decorations. The inviting sights and sounds of the Myrtle Beach area ensure a warm welcome to visitors. All sorts of special events comprise the celebration, from Thanksgiving and Christmas services to concerts, parades, children's events, arts and crafts exhibits, festivals, sporting activities, and a slew of New Year's Eve extravaganzas. There is something on the agenda to dazzle both young and old.

Oktoberfest
Baseball stadium at the former
Myrtle Beach Air Force Base, Myrtle Beach
(843) 918–1242

Beer and bratwurst are the favorites at this early October celebration of the harvest season. Authentic oom-pah music is played and arts and crafts are on display. Visitors show up to consume German brown bread, sauerkraut, and sausages in addition to the usual festival fare of hamburgers, pizza, and funnel cakes. Some hot-selling items that you are likely to find are homemade dolls, clothing, and Christmas and Halloween decorations.

Oktoberfest admission is $2.00 for adults age 21 and older and $1.00 for those under the age of 21; kids age 6 and younger are admitted free.

Ride-A-Thon
29th Avenue South to 45th Avenue North,
Myrtle Beach
(843) 626–3939
www.horsebackbeachride.com

Hundreds of horses trot along the Grand Strand shoreline for this annual event that raises money to fight heart disease and stroke. Nearly 1,500 riders raise in excess of $100,000.

Each adult participant contributes a minimum of $105 and teenage and child riders must kick in at least $55. After the 20-mile hike on horseback, entrants are treated to a barbecue lunch, awards ceremony, and a raffle. The horses are led along the beach by a police escort and the public is invited to watch from the sidelines.

Trick or Treating
Various Myrtle Beach Locations
(843) 448–2513, (843) 444–3200
www.myrtlesquaremall.com
www.broadwayatthebeach.com

For trick or treating, the Scare Fair held at Myrtle Square Mall, 2501 North Kings Highway, is always a good bet. Free Halloween bags are given out in the Food Court and children can beg candy from stores from 5:00 to 7:00 P.M. Games and prizes, entertainment, and caricature drawing are all part of the Scare Fair.

Broadway at the Beach, (843) 444–3200, also invites kids to come trick-or-treat with them from 5:00 to 7:00 P.M. Free bags are given to children at the visitor center and an adult costume contest is held at 10:00 P.M.

South Strand

Surfside Beach Family Festival
One block off Surfside Drive, Surfside Beach
(843) 913–6339

What started out as a little ole family picnic in 1985 has now grown into a full-fledged festival attended by more than 10,000 people each year! It's a daylong affair in early October, with plenty of food and arts and crafts for sale plus information booths if you need directions. Even during a downpour in 1999, an estimated 9,000 people came out to enjoy homespun crafts, games, and performers under a covered bandstand.

Several bands perform, and more than 90 vendors offer everything from hot dogs to rides on an oversized stuffed panda and tiger. This event always coordinates lots of games for children. There is no admission fee.

Pawleys Island Tour of Homes
(843) 237–8454

The Pawleys Island Tour of Homes, scheduled for mid-October, benefits the Georgetown Chapter of Habitat for Humanity. The eight-year-old-tour is comprised of a dozen or more Pawleys Island beach homes—ranging from nineteenth-century summer cottages to contemporary year-round residences. Unusual artifacts, windswept landscaping, and porches perched on the edge of the Atlantic combine to make this house tour uniquely enjoyable. Tickets can be ordered in advance; call for prices and details. Even the locals come, so don't miss this.

Annual Wooden Boat Exhibit and Challenge
Front Street (on the waterfront), Georgetown
(843) 545-0015

Here's an exciting twist to the usual boat shows and races: You make your own boat from scratch before sailing! At the Annual Wooden Boat Exhibit and Challenge, two-person teams are given a four-hour time limit in which to construct a functioning 12-foot rowing dory. Each team starts off with the same raw materials and equipment, marine-quality plywood, nails, and oar locks.

The overall competition takes into account speed, quality, and the results of a short relay race in the dory to Goat Island and back. After being awed by the pace of building, onlookers usually get a real kick out of watching the rowers trying to steer the rudderless, awkward boats in a straight line.

The event also includes all the trappings of maritime life: displays of handmade oars, intricate models of shrimp boats, pillows decorated with nautical themes, knot-tying demonstrations, and simmering pots of spicy, delicious gumbo.

There is no admission fee to the exhibit; spectators are allowed to watch from outside the working tents of the competing teams.

Trick or Treating
Various South Strand Locations
(843) 651-6990, (843) 546-6317

Trick or Treat at Inlet Square Mall in Murrells Inlet allows children to collect candies from store to store from 6:00 to 8:00 P.M. on Halloween night. The mall

also hosts a costume contest at Center Court at 6:30 P.M. For more information call (843) 651-6990.

The Georgetown County United Way and the Downtown Business Association work together to assist kids in their trick-or-treating ventures along downtown Front Street in Georgetown. Call (843) 546-6317.

November

North Strand

Intracoastal Christmas Regatta
Little River to North Myrtle Beach
(843) 280-6354

On the Saturday after Thanksgiving, dozens of vessels get decked out for the holidays. Beginning at 5:00 P.M., boats launch from Little River Inlet and travel down the waterway for an estimated 7:00 P.M. arrival at Dock Holiday's Marina at 13th Avenue North in North Myrtle Beach. Viewing sites encompass the restaurants along the Little River waterfront, the Riverboat Restaurant at North Myrtle Beach Marina, the Blue Marlin Yacht and Fishing Club at Anchor Marina, and Marker 350 at Harbourgate Marina. (See the Boating chapter for extensive information on each of these marinas.)

The regatta benefits local children's charities and spurs an annual toy collection for needy kids. Participating boaters pay a $25 entry fee or donate new, unwrapped toys. The event offers a $1,000 grand prize.

Myrtle Beach

Taste of the Town
Myrtle Beach Convention Center
(843) 448-6062

If you would like to sample foods from a variety of Grand Strand restaurants, make sure you do not miss this early November event. More than 30 restaurants participate each year, serving up the best they have to offer. Taste of the Town has become so popular that it has taken over three rooms of the convention center. Attendance has risen to more than 7,000 people.

The competitive part of the show is watched closely by residents and other restaurants. While the event is always good-natured, a positive showing can mean an increase in business for the coming year; for smaller restaurants that must close to send their staff to Taste of the Town, winning or placing is everything. In fact, some popular mainstay establishments had to bow out because of the tremendous amount of work involved to participate in Taste of the Town. To give you an idea of the pace, one restaurant served 2,000 portions of food by 8:00 P.M.

Awards are bestowed for the best overall food, the best entree, the best dessert, and the People's Choice.

This event is a fund-raising project for St. Andrews Catholic School. Taste of the Town is held from 4:00 to 9:30 P.M. Admission is $4.00 for adults; children age 14 and younger are admitted free with a paying adult. Food tickets cost $1.00 each, and most food items cost from one to three tickets.

ACBL Sectional Bridge Tournament
Sites to be announced
(843) 449-2194

This tournament in early November draws 1,200 duplicate bridge players to compete for three days. Eighty tables are set up per day, and entrants pay a nominal fee to compete. A championship match of the Myrtle Beach Bridge Association is played during Can-Am Days in mid-March (see previous entry in the "March" section).

Cammy Awards
Various Locations
(843) 272-1111, (800) 342-2262
www.cammy.org

The celebration of the Cammy Awards (Carolina's Magic Music Years) began in 1995 as an exciting party for performers and fans of Carolina Beach Music. Fourteen bands entertained at the first awards show held in Salisbury, North Carolina.

In 1998 the Cammys moved to North Myrtle Beach and the Cammy Weekend was born.

During this fun-filled weekend in November, entertainers perform at various beach clubs on Friday and Saturday nights. A "Band Fair" is held prior to the awards show on Sunday afternoon, and The Hayes Jewelers VIP Party, held after the awards event, has become a beloved tradition. The show honors winners in various categories and honors the memory of the pioneers who originated this music and helped make it great.

Annual Dickens Christmas Show & Festival
Myrtle Beach Convention Center
(843) 448-9483
www.dickenschristmasshow.com

You know that Christmas is just around the corner when the Dickens Show gears up at the convention center in mid-November. And what a charming way to get in the holiday spirit. Grand Stranders spend hours decorating the trees and wreaths on display, and the adornments are a sight to behold. The beautifully trimmed tannenbaums and handsome wreaths are usually auctioned off by the end of the festival, and hundreds of holiday gifts and ornaments are available for show and sale. Money collected from the silent auction of the Festival of Trees, decorated by area businesses, benefits Citizens Against Spouse Abuse. The Myrtle Beach Kiwanis are the charity of choice for the proceeds from the Festival of Wreaths. In 1996 a Festival of Holiday Tables (featuring centerpieces) was added; proceeds were donated to Habitat for Humanity of Horry County.

The 2002 admission price to the show and festival was $7.00 a head for adults, $3.00 for children ages 2 to 12; a multiple-day pass was $9.00, and children younger than age 2 were admitted for free.

Enjoy an authentic Victorian Tea in an elaborate period setting where you will dine at tables bedecked in red plaid and gold and white centered by traditional English topiaries as period-clad wait staff attend to your every need. The highlight of, the tea is the one-man-show of "Dickens'

A Christmas Carol" performed by Howard Burnham. Mr. Burnham's riveting portrayal of Ebenezer Scrooge is sure to delight both young and old.

Annual South Carolina State Bluegrass Festival
Myrtle Beach Convention Center
(706) 864-7203

This festival is touted as "the Palmetto state's oldest, largest and best bluegrass event."

Drawing fans from throughout the eastern United States and Canada, promoters are proud to say that the late November festival will always be a "who's who" of traditional bluegrass performers. The festival has played host to such performers as the Grand Ole Opry's Osborne Brothers, the Lewis Family, Doyle Lawson & Quicksilver, Jim & Jesse and the Virginia Boys, IIIrd Tyme Out, Ralph Stanley & the Clinch Mtn. Boys, Raymond Fairchild, the Bass Mountain Boys, Mike Stevens, Chubby Wise, J.D. Crowe and the New South, Country Gentlemen Reunion, Mac Wiseman, the Larry Stephenson Band, the Mayor and Buford, Lou Reid, Terry Baucom and Carolina, Bob Paisley & the Southern Grass, the Del McCoury Band, the Sand Mountain Boys, and the Lonesome River Band.

This music festival differs from most, since jam sessions are prevalent and a good number of audience members join in with the bands at any given time. As bluegrass lovers admit, this music represents a way of life.

In addition to an almost seamless stream of performances, the Bluegrass Festival offers arts and crafts booths, food and beverages, and CDs from all of the scheduled artists for sale before and after their shows.

Tickets are available at the gate and are sold at the convention center box office during the festival. Prices are undetermined as of this writing but vary as they are based on age, seating, number of days you are interested in attending, etc. Please call ahead for details.

December

North Strand

Christmas Tour of Homes
Throughout the North Strand
(843) 249-6449

Like its Georgetown cousin, this Christmas Tour of Homes gives one the chance to see stately homes dressed up for the Yuletide season. Sponsored by the North Myrtle Beach Women's Club, six abodes are opened to the public for one afternoon in December. Proceeds from the event help a mix of charities, such as Children's Hospice, the North Myrtle Beach Rescue Squad, the North Myrtle Beach Animal Shelter, and various scholarship funds.

Myrtle Beach

Springmaid Beach Craft Show
3200 South Ocean Boulevard, Myrtle Beach
(843) 315-7162

This early December event includes more than 300 booths, representing craftspeople and artists alike. Some 20,000 showgoers treated to an incredible array of quilts, jewelry, clothing, woodcrafts, baskets, stained-glass doll houses, and collectibles plus wreaths and decorations for the holiday season. The Springmaid Beach Craft Show is open to the public, with booths found both indoors and outdoors. Admission is free.

SCADA (North-South All-Star Football Game)
Doug Shaw Memorial Stadium, 33rd Avenue North and Oak Street, Myrtle Beach
(864) 573-7627

As the name implies, this mid-December game showcases the best young players from the northern and southern portions of South Carolina. The teams battle it out on the field, while college scouts get a good look at potential recruits. In the past, head coaches and representatives from Clemson University, the University of North Carolina, and Wake Forest University were on hand to assess the skills of 88 hopeful high schoolers. Tickets for the event cost $5.00 in advance and $7.00 at the gate.

Beach Ball Classic
Myrtle Beach Convention Center
(843) 213-0032
www.beachballclassic.com

Sponsored by an impressive variety of local businesses, the Beach Ball Classic in late December is always an exciting showcase of this country's best high-school basketball talent. Teams are rated and selected to play in this tournament before standing-room-only crowds of cheering fans, basketball enthusiasts, and college scouts. To give you an idea of the kind of talent to expect at the classic, check out this impressive list of former Beach Ball stars that wound up in the NBA: Kenny Anderson, Grant Hill, Jimmy Jackson, Don MacLean, Jerrod Mustaf, Billy Owens, Cherokee Parks, Rasheed Wallace, and Dontonio Wingfield.

The 20th Beach Ball Classic was played in 2000.

Games start each day at 3:30 P.M. and culminate around 10:00 P.M. An admission fee is announced close to tournament time.

South Strand

Nights of a Thousand Candles
Brookgreen Gardens, Murrells Inlet
(843) 235-6025, (843) 235-6016
www.brookgreen.org

Come enjoy three weekends of wonder and beauty as these beautiful gardens are decorated for the holidays in a natural style, complemented by luminaria along the paths and twinkle lights throughout. There are special dramatic and musical performances, a Lowcountry oyster roast, and more, all guaranteed to put you in a festive spirit. The cost is $8.00 for non-members. The event has been so successful that sell-out crowds are always anticipated, so do take time to call in advance or visit the Web site to reserve tickets for you and your family.

Georgetown County Festival of Trees
Litchfield Exchange Mall
(843) 546-3410

Delight in the true spirit of Christmas by attending the Hospice of Georgetown County's Festival of Trees. Breakfast with Santa kicks off festivities on a Saturday morning in early December, and attractions include a breathtaking display of uniquely decorated Fraser firs and a variety of music and entertainment. The Christmas Shop, Country Kitchen, and Santa's Shop offer lots of opportunities for shortening your shopping list, too. Call for a complete schedule.

Arts and Culture

In an area replete with state-of-the-art theaters built to show-case international headline stars, you would think that the Grand Strand's community arts scene would head for the beach to bury its proverbial head in the sand. Instead our native artists seem to have absorbed this main-stage professional energy and talent, launching more ambitious programs than ever before.

The loose Latin translation of the word amateur is "for the love of it." Never underestimate the momentum and power created by amateur talent that performs and presents out of pure joy, without pay for the hours invested.

The Grand Strand boasts a nationally recognized symphony orchestra, a row of art galleries, a true cafe society, resident artists whose works are being shown worldwide, legitimate entrance to the museum community, a Broadway-class method actor, and much more.

Not too surprisingly, when summer has packed the beach with tourists, the Grand Strand's arts and cultural organizations taper or curtail their activities. In fact most of these organizations' seasons run from September to March or April. Traditionally tourists have not provided large audiences for cultural offerings, and many of the organizations' volunteers are too busy working at their "real jobs" during the summer months to devote more than minimal time to their favorite artistic endeavors.

Arts Councils

Waccamaw Arts and Crafts Guild
(843) 238-4628

The Waccamaw Arts and Crafts Guild boasts more than 200 members and is dedicated to promoting interest and creativity in the visual arts. Approximately 75 percent of the members are artists. Most others are patrons or fans. Monthly meetings include demonstrations, slide presentations, social gatherings to exhibit members' recent works, and panel discussions on a variety of topics. The guild hosts a spring and fall show each year and has an art gallery at Myrtle Square Mall. Call the number listed if you are interested in joining the guild.

Wheelwright Council for the Arts
Coastal Carolina University, Conway
(843) 347-3161

This organization, composed of community members and Coastal Carolina University faculty and staff, supervises the use of Wheelwright Auditorium. The Wheelwright group coordinates the university's arts program, including a cultural arts series and student plays. The Wheelwright Council's stated function is to bring to the area high-caliber art performances that other groups are unable to secure. The council presents a Passport Series that offers experiences in film, dance, and the performing arts.

Wheelwright's upcoming playbill is ambitious, with performances of *In the Woods*, *The Complete Works of Shakespeare*, *Fabulas*, Broadway musical medleys, and more. Tickets at the door for student productions are $10.00 for adults, $5.00 for students younger than age 18, and free for Coastal Carolina students. Touring productions are about $15; ticket prices vary for other events.

South Strand

Cultural Council of Georgetown County
632 Prince Street, Georgetown
(843) 527–2822
www.ccgeorgetown.org

The Cultural Council of Georgetown County (CCGC) was established in 1997 as an umbrella organization for the area's growing lineup of cultural activities. The organization encompasses the performing, visual, and literary arts, as well as the allied areas in architecture, historic preservation, landscape architecture, industrial design, and production crafts. Its purpose is to provide educational opportunities and space for exhibitions and other art activities, and to encourage existing and fledgling cultural organizations to reach their potential. To that end the Arts Exchange—located most recently to 632 Prince Street in the historic Masonic Lodge—is an art gallery and cultural center. The CCGC currently has a membership of more than 500 members and 25 artist guilds. They sponsor an outdoor free concert during the month of May in addition to many educational opportunities. Each month more than 1,000 visitors come through the Art Exchange Gallery.

The Cultural Council offerings change and expand frequently, so please call or visit the Web site for up-to-the-minute details.

Auditoriums and Theaters

Myrtle Beach

Myrtle Beach High School Music and Arts Center
3300 Central Parkway, Myrtle Beach
(843) 448–7149
www.hcs.k12.sc.us/high/mbh/

The Myrtle Beach High School Auditorium is the area's largest auditorium, seating 2,000 people. The school district had planned to build a 1,000-seat venue, but Myrtle Beach residents convinced them to enlarge it so their city could attract bigger and better productions. Community-

raised funds helped pay for the increased cost of the exceptionally well-equipped if not particularly elegant auditorium.

South Strand

Strand Theatre
710 Front Street, Georgetown
(843) 527–2924

The Strand Theatre seats 160 people. Home to Georgetown's Swamp Fox Players (see subsequent entry), it's often called the Swamp Fox Theatre.

Beyond the Strand

McCown Auditorium
Corner of Ninth Avenue and Main Street, Conway
(843) 626–1211

This old auditorium was defunct for many years until Horry County bought it and transformed the entire building. Seating about 350 people, the auditorium is used for many community functions, including elementary-school plays and county board meetings. The building can be leased and rented for special events.

Wheelwright Auditorium
Coastal Carolina University,
U.S. Highway 501 East, Conway
(843) 347–3161

Wheelwright Auditorium, on the campus of Coastal Carolina University, roughly 10 miles west of Myrtle Beach off U.S. Highway 501, is an elegant facility that seats about 800 people. Among many performances (see the previous entry about the Wheelwright Council for the Arts),

Insiders' Tip
The *Sun News* publishes a special activities section called "kicks!" in its Friday editions.

Songwriter in the Round is an extraordinary event. Organized by George McCorkle of the Marshall Tucker Band (of Greenville, South Carolina), the event allows songwriters, who usually turn their work over to more famous performers, to explore their music with the audience.

Music and Song

Church Concert Series

Several churches along the Strand now offer quality concert series. They include North Myrtle Beach's Ocean Drive Presbyterian Church, (843) 249-2312, Myrtle Beach's Trinity Episcopal Church, (843) 448-8426, and First Presbyterian Church, (843) 448-4496. The concert series concept was brought here by Brown Bradley, minister of music at First Presbyterian, who participated in a successful series in New York before relocating to Myrtle Beach.

Trinity Performing Arts Series has been entertaining the Myrtle Beach community for more than a decade. Typical annual programming includes five primary concerts, a pipe organ series, and a kids' matinee. The series has featured artists including the Vienna Choir Boys, Peter Schickele of PDQ Bach fame, and the National Opera Company, as well as chamber music, oratorio, Gilbert and Sullivan productions, and Handel's "Messiah"—all with chamber orchestra accompaniment. Events are hosted by Trinity Episcopal Church, a performance venue that is acoustically ideal, visually elegant, and capable of seating in excess of 500 people. For information on upcoming events and season memberships, contact the series director at (843) 448-8426.

At the First Presbyterian Church, ticket holders are treated to a variety of featured vocalists and instrumentalists performing classical, pop, and Broadway selections. A popular past event featured the remarkable Dutch classic quartet Quink. Each year sellout performances of *The Best of Broadway* are presented. The FPC Players Drama Troupe spotlights local talent in family-friendly shows like *Dogs*, and in timeless Broadway hits like *Bells Are Ringing*. Season memberships are encouraged.

Since 1991 the Ocean Drive Presbyterian Church Concert Series has provided programming such as the Wheaton College Men's Choir, The Palmetto Brass, Frederico Hayler, and the Furman Singers. Season tickets may be purchased at a cost of $50 for two tickets and $100 for four tickets. Nonmembers may attend any concert for a suggested donation of $10.

Myrtle Beach

Coastal Concert Association
1107 48th Avenue North, Suite 211-L
(843) 449-7546
www.coastalconcert.com

Coastal Concert Association is a nonprofit arts organization that has been presenting concerts in the Grand Strand area for more than 25 years. Concerts range from brass ensembles to big band and Broadway musicals, symphonies, and dance groups. The aim is to present a variety each season starting in October and ending in April. Performances are held at the Myrtle Beach High School Music and Arts Center. Recent performances include the Broadway musical *Anything Goes*; the Dallas Brass; film and music composer Marvin Hamlisch; the Hungarian Symphony Orchestra; Pecs and Sandy Duncan Celebrates New York, a full concert evening of nonstop singing and dancing from Broadway's best musicals. Tickets are available at the door ($25.00 for adults for most performances and $5.00 for full-time students younger than age 21), but annual memberships ($60 to $75 for adults and $20 for students) are encouraged. Please call or visit the Web site for a current schedule.

Carolina Master Chorale
(843) 444-5774

Anyone who relishes the joy of singing is welcome to join the Carolina Master Chorale. This avid group of harmonizers, about 80 strong, offers concert performances for residents and visitors throughout the year. Since its founding in 1982, the chorale has continued to nurture the choral arts in our community. It offers four concerts during its annual season, including the concert for combined choruses at the Festival-By-The-Sea, a weekend-long choral workshop for invited choruses from the United States and Canada, featuring internationally known choral conductors. For the past two years, the Carolina Master Chorale has enjoyed its collaboration with the Long Bay Symphony Orchestra (LBSO). Tickets for Carolina Master Chorale concerts are $15 in advance.

The Long Bay Symphony
Long Bay Youth Orchestra
1551 21st Avenue North, Myrtle Beach
(843) 448–8379
www.longbaysymphony.com

The Long Bay Symphony performs a full season of classical, chamber, and POPS concerts, including playing the original scores during a silent film.

Many of the Long Bay Symphony members have performed with such respected organizations as the Metropolitan Opera in New York and the pop-infused Radio City Music Hall Orchestra. With this array of influences, the Long Bay group melds a variety of musical backgrounds, performing selections from classical to pop as well as full stage productions. It presents approximately 12 concerts each season.

Musicians range from high-school students to retirees, from points all along the Grand Strand. For concert information or season memberships, call the number listed.

The Long Bay Symphony promotes its approximately 60-member youth orchestra to spark youngsters' interest in "serious music" and to train older members for the symphony orchestra.

Adults who haven't played in years as well as those who are just learning to play can hone their skills with the youth symphony; the addition of adults has prompted some people to call the group the "Long Bay Orchestra for the Young and Youthful." Members of the youth orchestra also have a chance to be awarded scholarships for private lessons.

The Long Bay Symphony performs a variety of classical, chamber, and POPS concerts each year.
PHOTO: DANNY CHAMBLEE, THE LONG BAY SYMPHONY

Under the direction of Dr. Charles Evans, the youth orchestra performs two or three times a year, once with the symphony, and the symphony offers master classes for interested musicians.

Indigo Choral Society
(843) 237–3418

Founded in 1997 the Indigo Choral Society is a community chorus in every sense of the word. Drawing members from throughout Georgetown County, the forty- to fifty-voice chorus has evolved into a singing group that fosters true family spirit.

During the Annual Fourth of July Free Concert on the lawn of the Kaminski House on Front Street in Georgetown, families bring picnics, enjoy the scenery beside the Sampit River, and thrill to the patriotic and folk music the chorus sings.

At the Annual Christmas Concert, usually held in Georgetown's beautiful St. Mary's Catholic Church, holiday sounds fill the air. Accompanied by organ, piano, harp, oboe, and flute, the chorus renders old favorites as well as new pieces. A smaller group of madrigal singers blends voices in splendid historical offerings.

In the spring the chorus showcases a different theme each year. Previous works have ranged from Broadway show tunes to Handel's "Te Deum" to spirituals and Thomas Jefferson's writings set to music.

Information about joining the Indigo Choral Society can be obtained from the

Insiders' Tip

If you get the urge to paint or otherwise artistically express yourself while at the beach, visit Broadway Street near the Pavilion. This small shopping district includes artists supply stores, upscale salons, and galleries.

director, Chuck Gee, at (843) 237–3418. Requests for tickets for concerts should be directed to Production Director Jean Askew at (843) 546–1441.

Performing Arts

Myrtle Beach

Grand Strand
Seniors for the Performing Arts
1268 21st Avenue North, Myrtle Beach
(843) 626–3991

In 1991 several Horryites age 50 and older started playing with the idea of forming their own theater group. They decided to give it a try. And when *Send Me No Flowers* attracted 2,000 people over six performances, they figured they were on to something good.

With an influx of retiring talent from the North, this thespian group produces at least three shows a year. Tickets are $7.50 each. *Send Me No Flowers, Arsenic and Old Lace,* and *Fiddler on the Roof* are examples of the group's scope. Auditions for each play are publicized, and the cast is selected from the general public and the membership. Volunteers from the general membership handle scenery, publicity, lighting, costuming, makeup, sound, and stage work. Please call for a current schedule.

Theatre of the Republic
331 Main Street, Conway
(843) 488–0821

Housed within a beautifully renovated historical building on Main Street in downtown Conway, the Theatre of the Republic (TOR) has been entertaining Grand Strand audiences for 33 years. TOR is a nonprofit amateur theater group with a history of providing high-quality, affordable theater for the community. In addition to four main season shows, TOR produces musical revues, holiday shows, and children's theatre productions and presents classic works through the newly formed Theatre of the Republic Repertory Group. Theatre of the Republic was named the Official Theatre of Horry County in 1975. For schedule

Performers and artists of all kinds make their home along the Strand. PHOTO: COURTESY OF BROOKGREEN GARDENS

information please contact the Theatre of the Republic office Monday through Friday from 9:00 A.M. to 5:00 P.M.

Murrells Inlet Community Theatre
Intersection of Murrells Inlet Road and Vaux Hall Avenue, Murrells Inlet
(843) 651–4152

The Murrells Inlet Community Theatre (MICT), founded in April 1998, has established a strong presence in the South Strand. The troupe strives to present plays appealing to all ages. Productions have included romantic comedies, serious dramas, and musicals. The group has performed at The Blessing of the Inlet, (see the Annual Events chapter) and for a Readers' Theatre group that entertains at senior centers, schools, and libraries. MICT also offers free seminars on a variety of theatrical topics, including audi-

tion preparation, stagecraft, technical instruction in sound and lighting, and a children's acting workshop.

Membership in this dynamic, enthusiastic group is open to anyone with a love for live theatre and the desire to take part in the creation and production of stage plays. Dues are $10 annually, which allow members to work on all facets of production. Performance tickets are $8.00. For ticket information call the number listed above.

South Strand

Bill Oberst and His Experience Theatre
(843) 237–7681, (800) 239–7681

When Broadway and Hollywood actor Hal Holbrook took time off from his world-famous Mark Twain stage show, his manager called Pawleys Island to find

Thomas Davis

"I want to express worldwide that South Carolina is beautiful," artist and third-generation Grand Strander Thomas Davis explained. "The Lowcountry lifestyle and culture is not what is usually expected. I stayed in the South of France to paint, in the Rhone Delta, and it's almost the same there—they also have rice fields and the intense light we have here.

"In the 1770s Lafayette landed right here at North Island." Thomas poked the table we sat at as if it were sand on the beach. "He came here. Now I'm doing the reverse, to bring our cultures full circle. While I traveled, people asked me all about South Carolina, they wanted to know what Lowcountry is." His plans, for both his paintings and our beautiful Carolina seascape, seem to culminate in a Paris exhibit. Just imagine Myrtle Beach in Paris, sand in the Louvre, shag at the Centre Pompidou!

"My goal is to show expressions of this land by blending color with culture on canvas. The viewer needs to look beyond the modern era to view and relive lifestyles of a simpler time. Despite changing times and cultures, the wetlands have survived; today the struggle between development and conservation continues this cycle. My paintings are an attempt to preserve the history, romance and adventurous soul of South Carolina's beloved wetlands."

Excluding his French scenes, Thomas' paintings are filled with Lowcountry life. *Creek Critters* is a relaxing afternoon drifting down the river. *Prontopup* is taken from a ride at the historic Pavilion. *No Fake Smiles in Pawleys Today* enjoys the rigors of paddling. *Creekpeople,* which is from a shrimping expedition, won first round people's choice at the 1997 VIVACE! fine arts festival.

"You have to make it elsewhere to be appreciated here," Thomas remarked about the Myrtle Beach art scene. "But Myrtle Beach is growing, there's so much opportunity now," he said happily. "The beach is good at being a community. The Waccamaw Arts Guild is active, but it needs more youth. You don't have to be experienced or fancy—just send in some slides."

In return for the inspiration and success the Grand Strand community has allowed him thus far, Thomas is busy reinvesting his energies into the community, like so many permanent residents here do.

Thomas has also been asked to be a part

Davis's work is displayed in homes along the East Coast. PHOTO: ROBERT CLARK

of the Community Appearance Board to help monitor and enforce new codes that have to do with the appearance of new buildings and signage. "The main guideline is knowing that the committee is there," he stated, confident that as Myrtle Beach grows as a city, it will show more of its natural beauty.

Thomas' work can be viewed, along with other local artists', at the Collectors Cafe and Gallery in Myrtle Beach (see the Restaurant chapter for more details). His art is also working its way into homes up and down the East Coast. Who knows, maybe after a spicy Mediterranean dinner at Collectors Cafe, you could end up taking home a painting that might be known someday as "a Davis."

Now that he is back from his travels, "I think I'm going to paint some landscapes, get back to my roots," Thomas told us with satisfaction, sounding like he'd already started in on his favorite subject again.

Oberst as a replacement. The Grand Strand actor's own one-man Twain show has become truly legendary. His 1996 addition of *Jesus of Nazareth* and *The Senator* as well as his 1997 *John Kennedy* are all remarkable presentations.

Once the youngest chamber of commerce executive director in America, a former candidate for the United States Congress, and the marketing director who guided Calvin Gilmore's Carolina Opry empire, Oberst is a complex man who brings his vast experiences to the stage in a unique presentation he calls "Experience Theatre."

Experience Theatre is a concept that takes the audience into a personal, interactive encounter with an individual historical figure. In *Jesus of Nazareth*, the messiah walks among the audience members, responds to their questions (handed out on cards as they enter the theater), shares bread with them, and even washes the feet of unsuspecting audience members. For each Experience Theatre performance, the room is sprayed with scents of the epoch to complement its respective show (e.g. heavy leathers for Twain's study; damp linens for Jesus).

It is not uncommon to see audience members weeping as they leave an Oberst performance, feeling deeply touched by the historical character; it really is an experience.

Unfortunately Oberst spends most of the year on the road, performing or lecturing university students worldwide. When on the Strand, however, he does many shows—mainly for local charities. Call the number listed for a schedule and ticket prices.

Swamp Fox Players Inc.
710 Front Street, Georgetown
(843) 527-2924
www.seaportgeorgetown.com/swamp_fox_
players.htm

Established in the early 1970s, this amateur theatrical group coordinates at least four productions per year. Since the community seems to be particularly fond of musicals and comedy, many of the Swamp Fox productions are flavored accordingly. Recent shows included *A Sanders Family Christmas*, *The Exact Center of the Universe*, and *Opal*.

This group calls the Strand Theatre, on Front Street in Georgetown, "home." Tickets range in price. Please call to inquire.

Visual Arts

Myrtle Beach

Franklin G. Burroughs and Simeon B. Chapin Art Museum
3100 South Kings Highway, Myrtle Beach
(843) 238-2510

The Franklin G. Burroughs and Simeon B. Chapin Art Museum, a former two-story Springmaid beach home donated by Cox Construction Co., is Horry County's first art museum. "A New Home for the

Myrtle Beach's first art museum, the Frankin G. Burroughs and Simeon B. Chapin Art Museum, delights visitors with local and international exhibits. PHOTO: LISA TOMER RENTZ

Visual Arts" unveiled in June 1997. The museum features an art gallery, a gift shop, and an art education center.

The art gallery building is housed in the former Springmaid Villa, a 1920s beach house that was saved from demolition. Renovations created 10 galleries with a total 3,600 square feet of exhibition space, a tearoom, and a large seminar room. Exhibits in the gallery showcase local and regional artists and national art exhibits. The permanent exhibit is the Waccamaw Arts and Craft Guild Purchase Award Collection 1970–1983.

The new art education center building, which is attached to the art gallery building, provides ample space for an art library, studio classrooms, a gift shop, and storage space for the museum collection. Recent activities have included corporate functions, watercolor classes, and a Christmas ornament–making class.

Admission is free. Hours are Tuesday through Saturday 10:00 A.M. to 4:00 P.M. and Sunday 1:00 to 4:00 P.M.

Horry County Museum
428 Main Street, Conway
(843) 248–1542
www.horrycountymuseum.org

The Horry County Museum offers numerous exhibits on the history, prehistory, and natural history of Horry (pronounced oh-ree) County at the museum's main location, as well as through the presentation of outreach exhibits and programs in various locations throughout the county. The majority of the museum's collections are stored at the Main Street location and include a highly acclaimed photographic collection as well as hundreds of historic artifacts documenting the unique history and culture of Horry County. The museum is open Monday through Saturday from 9:00 A.M. to 5:00 P.M.

Brookgreen Gardens
U.S. Highway 17 South, Murrells Inlet
(843) 235–6000, (800) 849–1931
www.brookgreen.org

Since opening to the public seven decades ago, Brookgreen Gardens has introduced visitors to an enchanting and compelling showcase of art and nature. The gardens are set on a 300-acre parcel in the heart of a 9,100-acre preserve on the South Carolina coast stretching from the Atlantic Ocean to historic rice fields bordering the Waccamaw River. Ranging from the small and delicate to the truly monumental, the sculptures on display at Brookgreen Gardens represent the works of such prominent American artists as Marshall Fredericks, Daniel Chester French, Gutzon Borglum, Frederic Remington, Carl Milles, and Anna Hyatt Huntington.

Through the Center for American Sculpture, Brookgreen fosters an appreciation of the American Figurative Sculpture collection; some 900 works by 330 sculptors range from 1819 to the present. Offerings include an outdoor sculpture exhibition of 550 works in landscaped settings, changing thematic gallery exhibitions, interpretive tours, lectures, and publications, and an annual Sculpture

Insiders' Tip

If you are a student, make sure to travel with your student ID. Many venues offer a student discount when you show your card.

Symposium. The Garden Room for Children contains pieces from the Brookgreen sculpture collection that appeal to younger visitors and their families.

Brookgreen Gardens is open from 9:30 A.M. to 5:00 P.M. daily. Admission is $12 for adults age 19 and older, $10 for seniors age 65 and older, and $10 for students ages 13 to 18. Children age 12 and younger are free.

From golf courses to shoreline to everything in between, you'll never suffer from a lack of things to do when you visit the Myrtle Beach area. PHOTO: COURTESY OF THE LITCHFIELD COUNTRY CLUB

Parks and Recreation

Parks
Recreation
Spectator Sports

There is no debate about it: Some of the most abundant natural beauty in all the world is right here along the Grand Strand. And thanks to the Work Projects Administration (WPA) and the Civilian Conservation Corps (CCC)—federal agencies that were created as part of President Franklin Delano Roosevelt's New Deal program, which was enacted during the Great Depression to create employment by establishing and building parks— these natural resources are preserved today in their original splendor.

During the summertime, sunshine is hot and plentiful in the Carolina-blue sky. The water is cool and equally plentiful. Autumn is brilliant . . . crisp mornings and breezy afternoons are perfect for beach walks and surf fishing. Winter comes in bite-size pieces: a string of brisk, snappy days, with long warm stretches in between. And when spring quickly arrives bearing wisteria, daffodils, and bright-faced college kids, it's hard to believe another year has passed. This deliciously temperate climate enables tourists and residents to enjoy the great outdoors for most of the year.

So head for the parks and take advantage of the enviable climate and incredible store of natural resources. Myrtle Beach State Park and Huntington Beach State Park are known for being among the best locations on the East Coast for bird-watching. Both parks also feature an ever-changing array of programming for the young and the young at heart.

We've also included a Spectator Sports section for those times when you want to sit in the bleachers and root for the home team. Locals are especially proud of the Myrtle Beach Pelicans, our first professional sports team.

Parks

State Parks

Myrtle Beach
Myrtle Beach State Park
U.S. Highway 17 South, between Myrtle and Surfside Beaches
(843) 238–5325
www.discoversouthcarolina.com

Situated in the heart of the Grand Strand, Myrtle Beach State Park boasts one of the most popular public beaches along the Carolina coast. This 312-acre oceanfront park is one of the last remaining natural areas along the northern shores of South Carolina. Natural beauty reigns here and gives visitors a glimpse of the way the entire Strand looked long ago before its development as a glittery resort mecca.

Myrtle Beach State Park was developed by the Civilian Conservation Corps. During World War II, the U.S. military took over the park as a coastal defense staging area. In March 1945 the park was returned to the citizens of the state. It was the first state park opened to the public in South Carolina, and it also holds the distinction of having the first campground and fishing pier on the Grand Strand.

Park facilities include approximately 350 camping sites, rented on a first-come, first-served basis; 40 additional sites are available by reservation up to 14 days in advance. (See the Accommodations chapter.) The park also offers five cabins, two apartments, and picnic areas with shelters. In addition to the 730-foot pier, there's a nature trail and nature center. A park naturalist conducts activities year-round and interprets the natural history of the coast. Surf fishing and pier fishing are allowed. Swimmers can splash about in the ocean or in the park's pool. The park also provides a snack bar and playground equipment.

Park hours are 6:00 A.M. to 10:00 P.M. year-round. Office hours are 8:00 A.M. to 5:00 P.M. daily. In summer, admission to the park is $2.00 per person. Visitors age 15 and younger are admitted for free.

South Strand

Huntington Beach State Park
U.S. Highway 17 South (across from Brookgreen Gardens), Murrells Inlet
(843) 237–4440

Huntington Beach State Park, worth a visit even if you see nothing else on the Strand, offers the best-preserved beach on the Grand Strand and one of the best we have seen anywhere in the world. Observe the diverse coastal environment at the freshwater lagoon, salt marsh, nature trail, and along the wide, beautiful beach.

The park is also the site of the imposing Spanish-style castle Atalaya, the former winter home and studio of American sculptress Anna Hyatt Huntington. Mrs. Huntington and her husband, Archer, were the visionary founders of Brookgreen Gardens. Seasonal tours of Atalaya are available.

Park facilities include about 135 camping sites, picnic areas with shelters, a boardwalk, and a general store. Activities such as surf fishing, swimming, and crabbing are encouraged, and the park offers one of the finest bird-watching sites on the East Coast. Nature programs and playground equipment are available for the young and young at heart. Atalaya Arts & Crafts Festival, a prestigious juried arts and crafts show, attracts thousands of visitors to the park every fall (see the Annual Events chapter for details).

Park hours are 6:00 A.M. to 10:00 P.M. daily from April through September and 6:00 A.M. to 6:00 P.M. daily from October through March. Office hours are 9:00 A.M. to 5:00 P.M. Monday through Friday and 11:00 A.M. to noon on Saturday and Sunday year-round. Admission to the park is $4.00 for adults, $2.00 for kids age 12 or younger, and free for children younger than age 6.

Hampton Plantation State Historic Site
1950 Rutledge Road, McClellanville
(843) 546–9361
www.discoversouthcarolina.com

Southwest of Georgetown, Hampton

Consistent renourishment makes for beautiful beaches graced by dunes and sea oats. PHOTO: COURTESY OF MYRTLE BEACH AREA CHAMBER OF COMMERCE

The Strand boasts two state parks, Huntington Beach and the Myrtle Beach State Park. Both offer a wealth of ecotourism activities. PHOTO: COURTESY OF MYRTLE BEACH AREA CHAMBER OF COMMERCE

Plantation is not technically a part of the stretch of real estate we call the Grand Strand. However, Hampton offers a peek at one of the most impressive restored plantation homes in South Carolina and, therefore, is well worth the short drive.

Adjacent to the Santee River, this 322-acre property was once a coastal rice plantation and last served as the home of Archibald Rutledge, noted writer and South Carolina poet laureate. The state purchased the property from Mr. Rutledge in 1971.

A National Historic Landmark, the Hampton mansion stands as the centerpiece of the park and is a monument to the state's glorious rice empire. The man-

sion's colossal Adam-style portico is one of the finest and earliest examples of its kind in all of North America, while its interior—purposely unfurnished—highlights the structure's design and construction. Cutaway sections of walls and ceilings exhibit the building's evolution from a simple farmhouse to a grand mansion. Exposed timber framing, hand-carved mantels, and delicately wrought hinges and hardware reveal the eighteenth-century builder's craft.

The grounds surrounding the mansion offer a unique opportunity to examine the wildlife of the Carolina Lowcountry. Cypress swamps, abandoned rice fields, and pine and hardwood forests are home to a staggering variety of flora and fauna. From the massive live oaks to the wildflowers and shrubs, Hampton Plantation is a naturalist's and photographer's delight in every season.

In addition to the beautiful home, the park includes a picnic area and marked nature trails.

Park hours are 9:00 A.M. to 6:00 P.M. daily, year-round. From Labor Day to Memorial Day, mansion hours are 1:00 to 4:00 P.M. Thursday through Monday. (Beginning Memorial Day and running through Labor Day, the mansion is open 11:00 A.M. to 4:00 P.M.) Admission to the plantation grounds is free; house tours are $3.00 for ages 17 and older, $2.00 for children six to sixteen, and free for South Carolina senior citizens and kids age five and younger. Guided tours are offered at no extra charge. For current schedules and lots of outstanding programming, please contact the park directly.

City Parks

City parks pepper the Strand and are perfect for a little rest and relaxation. Several parks provide playground equipment, basketball courts, and running tracks for your use and enjoyment; others offer serene picnic areas complete with tables and rest rooms.

North Strand

For more information about the parks in North Myrtle Beach, call the recreation department at (843) 280–5570. There is no admission fee and the city parks are open 24 hours a day.

Central Park
1030 Possum Trot Road, North Myrtle Beach

This park is a kind of athlete's track and field course. It features four tennis courts, four baseball/softball fields, a soccer field, a quarter-mile running track, a paved basketball court, two playground areas, and a picnic area.

Hill Street Park
Hill Street, North Myrtle Beach

The one-acre spread showcases what might be the North Strand's best lighted tennis court and a complex of playground equipment in addition to the standard swings.

McLean Park
Second Avenue South, North Myrtle Beach

McLean Park is a couple of blocks from the ocean and is sometimes used for outdoor concerts, Easter egg hunts, and small local festivals. In addition to two tennis courts, a roller hockey court, and playground equipment, the park also features a picnic area, a small lake, and a baseball field. Rest room facilities are available as well.

Insiders' Tip

Myrtle Beach and North Myrtle Beach both have a beach-going wheelchair program to ensure that wheelchair-bound people get to enjoy the ocean, too. There is no charge, but there is a time limit of one hour to ensure that everybody gets a turn. The wheelchairs are sturdy, have large balloon tires that allow the chair to be pushed through the soft sand, and come equipped with umbrellas. Beach-going wheelchairs and handicapped parking are available at the following locations: First Avenue South, North Myrtle Beach, and in Myrtle Beach at 77th Avenue North, 72nd Avenue North, 54th Avenue North, 24th Avenue North, 5th Avenue North, 8th Avenue North, and 8th Avenue South.

Chapin Park is an oasis of green in the center of Myrtle Beach. PHOTO: LISA TOMER RENTZ

City Park on the Ocean
First Avenue South and South Ocean Boulevard, North Myrtle Beach

This cartoon-colored park serves as a convenient ingress and egress to the beach in the Ocean Drive section of North Myrtle Beach. Matching the pavement of nearby Main Street, the small park is constructed of brightly tinted concrete; the rest room facilities and concession stand are in a modern art-deco style suited to the beach, accented with palm trees, of course. The delightful design won national recognition from the National Recreation and Park Society in 1989. Amenities also include beach wheelchairs, boardwalks onto the sand, a parking lot, and an outdoor shower. The concession stand is open only in the summer from 9:00 A.M. to 5:00 P.M. and the rest rooms are locked for the night at 9:00 P.M. and "when it gets cold," explained city maintenance.

Yow Park
Windy Hill Road, North Myrtle Beach

This quaint neighborhood park features a basketball court, playground, picnic area,

rest room facilities, and a charming decorative archway made from branches. The parking lot for this park is hidden; drive around the corner to Eyerly Road then walk through the archway and trees to get to the playground.

Myrtle Beach

For more information about the parks in Myrtle Beach, call the recreation department at (843) 918–2280. There is no admission fee, and the city parks are open 24 hours a day.

Chapin Park
16th Avenue North and Kings Highway, Myrtle Beach

In the very hub of downtown traffic, everybody's favorite park offers an unbelievably tranquil setting featuring a beautiful arbor area, picnic tables, and garden swings. Local business folk seeking to escape the rat race frequent the calm of Chapin during lunch, especially in the spring and fall. The swings are ideal for reading the paper, eating a homemade sandwich, or simply for taking in the sights that surround you.

Political candidates, outdoor festivals, and a host of city functions favor the atmosphere and location of Chapin Park. Weekends bring a variety of activities including art shows, outdoor concerts, and small festivals. Also, more than a few couples have exchanged wedding vows in the two-story gazebo that sits in the heart of this pretty green space. The playground, favored by local parents, features wooden equipment and lots of sand.

Hurl Rock Park
20th Avenue South and Ocean Boulevard, Myrtle Beach

Wooden decks create a lovely trail through Hurl Rock Park, which features a spectacular view of the beach. This park is great for photo opportunities, hand holding, and people watching.

Midway Park
19th Avenue South and Kings Highway, Myrtle Beach

Tennis is the name of the game at Midway, with six lighted courts. But that's not all. You'll also find a lighted basketball court here complete with two goals as well as a rest area and bathroom facilities.

South Strand

For more information about the parks in the South Strand, call the recreation department at (843) 650-4131. There is no admission fee and the city parks are open 24 hours a day.

Fuller Park
Surfside and Myrtle Drives, Surfside Beach

Fuller Park is an ideal family destination, with two lighted tennis courts, two basketball courts, a playground, and a picnic area with bathroom facilities. The Horry County Memorial Library is immediately adjacent, so make time to stop there, too.

W. O. (Bill) Martin Park
Lakeside Drive and Eighth Avenue South, Surfside Beach

A great place for a family reunion, the W. O. (Bill) Martin Park—formerly Lakeside

Park—features a large picnic area and the Floral Clubhouse that can be rented by contacting the Town of Surfside Recreation Department, (843) 650-4131. A large, open area adjacent to the park is perfect for Frisbee tossing, kite flying, and informal baseball and football games.

All Children's Park
10th Avenue South and Hollywood Drive, Surfside Beach

This innovative playground, designed and equipped for both able-bodied and disabled children—hence its name—has set a nationwide example.

All Children's Park features "standard" equipment modified to suit the needs of challenged youngsters—without separating them from their peers. Specially designed equipment includes a slide with tiered ramp along its side, mesh-net swings, and an elevated tic-tac-toe board and sandbox. A landscaped, shaded area with picnic tables and an adult swing adjoins the park.

Residential Parks

The following parks are public residential facilities maintained by the city of Myrtle Beach.

Carefully manicured landscapes and multicolored blooms create a delightful series of green sanctuaries—retreats from the hustle and bustle of resort living. Read a book, take a nap, ponder the mysteries of life. For more information, call (843) 918-2280.

Pinner Place Park is at Pinner Place and Pridgen Road. You'll find Withers Park at Second Avenue South and Myrtle Street. Loblolly Park is on Loblolly Circle in the prestigious Dunes section. A personal favorite, Gray Park is a pretty little space on 45th Avenue North and Burchap Drive. Memorial Park, at Porcher Avenue and Haskell Circle, is a gem. Right around the corner, McMillan Park is on Haskell Circle and Ocean Boulevard. Another Boulevard park is Cameron Park at 28th Avenue North. You'll find Springs Park at Springs Avenue and Hampton Circle, and McLeod Park is on 61st Avenue North.

Recreation

Myrtle Beach offers visitors opportunities to participate in lots of healthy sports such as bicycling, kayaking, and beach volleyball as well as "thrill sports" such as parasailing, bungee jumping, and sky diving. Health and fitness clubs abound; recreation centers and leagues provide organized activities for kids and adults alike. Of course, you'll find plenty of tennis and golf opportunities at nearly every turn as well. Golf is so popular, in fact, we've devoted an entire chapter to it in lieu of discussing it in depth here.

Beach Volleyball

Setting and spiking on the inviting sands of the beach is a favored activity during the summer season. The level of competition ranges from that found at family picnics to competitive tournaments with skilled professionals.

In the summertime pickup games abound all along the beach from Surfside to North Myrtle. Public volleyball nets in Myrtle Beach are set up at Downwind Sails, 29th Avenue South (adjacent to Damon's restaurant), and at Kingston Plantation (see the Accommodations chapter), located on the beach near Restaurant Row.

Biking

Bicycle paths in Myrtle Beach are clearly marked along the beach and Ocean Boulevard, and the residential area north of 54th Avenue North features an outdoor fitness trail with exercise equipment along the beach. Bicycles and adult-size, laid-back tricycles can be rented from a variety of locations along the beach, including the following vendors.

North Myrtle Beach

The Bike Doctor
800 Sea Mountain Highway,
North Myrtle Beach
(843) 249-8152

This shop is a full-service and fully stocked bicycle outlet, just 2 blocks from the beach. Parking is provided, so you can leave your car and ride your new or rented bike. Rentals include beach cruisers, standard two-wheel bikes, three-wheelers, "funcycles," tandems, and four-wheel, four-passenger bikes. Fees start at $4.00 per hour per bike. Gear such as helmets and pads is not included in the rental rate.

The Bike Doctor is open Monday through Saturday from 9:30 A.M. to 5:00 P.M.

Myrtle Beach

Bicycles-N-Gear
515 Highway 501, Myrtle Beach
(843) 626-2453

Beach-cruiser bikes can be rented for $10 a day and you can rent in-line skates from this store for $15 per day. Both rentals include helmets and protective gear.

This bike outfitter is open every day from 10:00 A.M. to 7:00 P.M.

The Bike Shop
715 Broadway, Myrtle Beach
(843) 448–5335

Open 8:00 A.M. to 5:00 P.M. Monday through Saturday, The Bike Shop loans customers complimentary helmets, locks, and baskets with every rental. Beach cruisers cost $5.00 for a half-day rental and $10.00 for the whole day, and a whole day of mountain biking is $15.00.

Fitness Clubs

Fitness is a thriving industry along the Grand Strand, which probably stands to reason if you take into consideration the premium locally on firm bodies, male and female.

All of the area's gyms and fitness clubs welcome visitors at any time of the year. It's not unusual to see packed aerobic classes during peak tourist times when visitors pop in to get their exercise high while on vacation. That most of these clubs are so affordable might pleasantly surprise you. To join an aerobics class for an hour or so, rates usually run $4.00 to $6.00. Annual memberships to fitness centers average $35 to $60 per month, although some might charge an up-front initiation fee.

North Strand

Lifequest Swim & Fitness Club
4390 Spa Drive, Little River
(843) 399–2582

Lifequest has lined up a gamut of programs from step aerobics to karate. The Next Generation Nautilus machines fill the weight room, along with treadmills, steppers, a Skywalker, Lifecycles, and recumbent bikes. To accommodate the wetter side of a workout, Lifequest has indoor and outdoor pools (aqua-aerobics classes are available), a whirlpool, steam room, and sauna. If your workout leaves your muscles sore, massage therapy is available.

Lifequest is open Monday through Thursday from 5:30 A.M. to 10:00 P.M., Friday from 5:30 A.M. to 9:00 P.M., Saturday from 8:00 A.M. to 6:00 P.M., and Sunday from 1:00 to 5:00 P.M. The club offers a variety of rates and fees.

Myrtle Beach

American Athletic Club
S.C. Highway 544 (Socastee area) and 3901 North Kings Highway, Myrtle Beach
(843) 650–0271
www.americanathletic.com

The popular American Athletic Club in Socastee recently expanded with a second location in the heart of Myrtle Beach. Both clubs feature 20,000-plus square feet, and both offer services and equipment to address all your fitness needs. You'll appreciate fully equipped weight rooms, private aerobic studios, dry-heat saunas and nutrition centers with a juice bar. The Socastee location also has an indoor swimming pool.

American Athletic Club is open Monday through Friday from 5:30 to 9:00 P.M., Saturday from 7:00 A.M. to 7:00 P.M., and Sunday from 1:00 to 5:00 P.M.

Gold's Gym
951 Jason Boulevard (10th Avenue North and U.S. Highway 17 Bypass), Myrtle Beach
(843) 448–3939
www.goldsgym.com

Probably the longest-standing fitness outlet in the area, Gold's has been locally owned and operated by Ted and Nancy Capp since 1982.

This is a venue for serious workouts as evidenced by folks Olympic and power lifting in the weight room, where many competitive body builders come to pump up and shape their muscles. Besides free weights, complete StairMaster and BodyMaster systems are available. Warm up on treadmills, bikes, steppers, or a stair climber. The gym also has a full aerobics schedule and a boxing class. Operating schedules change seasonally, as do rates; but for the most part, Gold's is open from 5:00 A.M. to about 9:00 P.M. Monday through Thursday, Friday from 6:00 A.M. to 7:00 P.M., Saturday from 6:00 A.M. to 7:00 P.M., and Sunday from 1:00 to 7:00 P.M.

Ocean Dunes/Sand Dunes Fitness Center
74th Avenue North (on the oceanfront), Myrtle Beach
(843) 692–5245

As you might guess from its name and address, this health club is housed in one of the Grand Strand's largest oceanview resort properties. Ocean Dunes is open seven days a week, 24 hours a day. The pool is open from 6:00 A.M. to 10:00 P.M.

Aerobics classes are offered, in addition to a fully equipped workout-room that sports Nautilus, treadmills, Lifecycles and Universal bikes, stair climbers, rowing machines, and a heated indoor pool. To wind down après workout, Ocean Dunes has three Jacuzzis, a steam room, and a dry sauna. Call ahead for rates; daily, weekly, monthly, and yearly memberships are available.

World Gym
3302 Highway 17 South, North Myrtle Beach
(843) 361–9966
www.myrtlebeachgyms.com

World Gym & Fitness is a comprehensive fitness facility featuring equipment and service unique to the Grand Strand. Gym membership delivers full access to fitness facilities that include the acclaimed Group Exercise Program and a workout area featuring a modern, award-winning studio design, surrounded by a Cardio Theater Entertainment System. The 1200-square foot area consists of equipment arranged into convenient workout centers, featuring the best quality resistance strength-training and free-weight systems you'll find anywhere. Other popular features include Group Cycling (Spinning), Planet Sun "All Superbed" Tanning, and the award-winning Extreme Blendz Juice Bar. World Gym & Fitness is open Monday through Thursday from 5:30 A.M. to 10:00 P.M., Friday from 5:30 A.M. to 8:00 P.M., and Saturday and Sunday from 8:00 A.M. to 8:00 P.M.

The Sport & Health Club at Kingston Plantation
9760 Kings Road, Myrtle Beach
(843) 497–2444
www.kingstonplantation.com

This $4-million facility is perhaps the prettiest club along the Grand Strand, nestled amid the beautiful setting of Kingston Plantation. It has a complete cardiovascular center with Life Fitness Circuit (a computerized system) equipment for strength training. Aerobics and "aquacise" programs are scheduled daily.

On the grounds you'll find clay and hard-surface tennis courts as well as racquetball and volleyball courts. Other features of this club include indoor and outdoor pools, a whirlpool, sauna, tanning beds, and massage therapy. The Sport & Health Club is open from 6:30 A.M. to 10:00 P.M. Monday through Thursday, 6:30 A.M. to 9:00 P.M. on Friday, 7:30 A.M. to 9:00 P.M. on Saturday, and 7:30 A.M. to 6:00 P.M. on Sunday.

Fitness One-On-One
Galleria Shopping Center
9600 North Kings Highway, Myrtle Beach
(843) 449–6486

Whether you're a neophyte or seasoned in bodybuilding regimes, and no matter what your age, Fitness One-On-One promises to take you to the height of your fitness potential. This is the only one-on-one, personalized-training facility on the Grand Strand. All individually tailored programs combine a personal workout plan with nutrition advice, cardiovascular exercise, and weight training. Owner Herb MacDonald offers clients weight-loss programs, body toning, beginner and advanced bodybuilding, and spot training. And to make sure you're feeling and looking your best, One-On-One also offers tanning facilities.

South Strand

Grand Strand Fitness & Racquet
671 JamesTowne Drive, Garden City Beach
(843) 651–8428

Grand Strand boasts a complete Life Fitness cardiovascular-conditioning system that incorporates treadmills, bikes, life steppers, and rowers. You can pump it up with weight-training machines or free weights and dumbbells. The fitness center is open Monday through Thursday from 6:00 A.M. to 10:00 P.M., Friday from 6:00 A.M. to 8:00 P.M., Saturday from 7:00 A.M. to 7:00 P.M., and Sunday from 1:00 to 6:00 P.M.

The club has four racquetball courts and volleyball under its roof plus a large aerobics studio with a custom-built floor to reduce impact. Aerobics classes use steps, slides, and weights in the programs and are offered every day of the week. The aerobics sessions are scheduled at various times between 7:30 A.M. and 6:30 P.M. For beginners Grand Strand can help you determine your initial fitness level with body-composition and pre-exercise analyses. Personalized training is also an option here.

Amenities include steam rooms, supervised child care, tanning beds, and a video security system in the parking lot. Membership rates are just too complicated to list here; Grand Strand Fitness has a roster of different membership packages, depending on what part of the facility you want to use. It's best to call ahead or drop by.

Plantation Resort
Health & Swim Club
1250 U.S. Highway 17 North, Surfside Beach
(843) 913–5060

This fitness club is as comprehensive as it gets—even offering programs for those who suffer from arthritis. It's no surprise that Plantation Resort has a full Aqua Aerobics program, as the club sports a 70-foot-long heated pool and giant whirlpool. Amenities include men's and women's saunas and steam rooms, a children's playground, a fully equipped weight room, and an aerobic space with Exerflex floor, where aerobics, yoga, and karate classes are held.

Plantation Resort is open 6:00 A.M. to 10:00 P.M. Monday through Friday, 7:30 A.M. to 10:00 P.M. Saturday, and 9:30 A.M. to 10:00 P.M. Sunday. Membership fees vary, based on particular programs or full use of club facilities.

Horseback Riding

Horseback riding is another popular pastime, but not many Grand Strand stables have horses for rent. Please note: Horses are prohibited from the beach during the busy summer tourist season. See the Beach Information chapter for details.

Best View Farm
6129 Best Western Trail, Myrtle Beach
(843) 650–7522

Call and speak to Caroline to discuss boarding facilities or riding lessons. Best View Farm is nestled on 45 densely wooded acres. Full-service boarding is available for $250 a month, and rides are priced individually. Call ahead for details.

Peachtree Farms
NC Highway 57 (just off U.S. 17),
Calabash, NC
(910) 287–4790

Peachtree Farms is strictly a riding stable; boarding is not available. One-hour trail rides can be booked for $35 per person. Call Gloria or any of her staff to reserve a

Insiders' Tip

Skateboarding and in-line skating are prohibited in downtown Myrtle Beach, where the prime flat property is full of railings and curbs to hop but also, unfortunately, lots of people on the sidewalks to avoid. The city has come up with a solution: a skate park. The city built the park for the many enthusiasts the sport is attracting. It's built behind the Pepper Geddings Recreation Center, (843) 918-2280, and has all sorts of demanding obstacles and ramps for skaters and, of course, no pedestrians.

horse. (See the Kidstuff chapter for additional information.)

Kayaking

Kayaking has grown in popularity, both along the beach and in local rivers and swamps. The following places (see the Water Sports chapter for details) are worth investigating if you're interested in this up-and-coming sport.

Myrtle Beach

Sailing & Ski Connection
515 U.S. Highway 501, Myrtle Beach
(843) 626–SAIL

This outfitter bills its kayak tours as "the adventure of a lifetime." New tours are scheduled weekly, and some are customized to suit group interest. Safety is a top priority: Complete supervision is provided (if desired), and the rules of boating are stressed every step of the way. See the entry in the Water Sports chapter for rates and schedules.

Downwind Sails
29th Avenue South, Myrtle Beach
(843) 448–7245

Downwind Sails rents ocean kayaks for fun and frolic in the surf. This shop is open between April and September. Rates vary with the time of year and availability of equipment. See the entry in the Water Sports chapter for details.

South Strand

Black River Expeditions
U.S. Highway 701, Georgetown
(843) 546–4840
www.blackriveroutdoors.com

Black River Expeditions offers half-, full-, and multiday tours on the area's abundant marshes, rivers, and creeks. Explore the aptly named waters of the Black River, the tidal creeks leading to the secluded beaches of Huntington Beach State Park, and the deserted and mysterious Drunken Jack Island—reputed to hold treasures of the pirate Blackbeard. See the entry in the Water Sports chapter for details.

Miniature Golf

Serious golfers, forget about tee times, golf-cart fees, and buckets of lost balls! By playing any one of dozens of miniature golf courses along the Grand Strand, you can enjoy spirited competition with the kids (your own as well as those you might wander upon) and the joy of sinking a hole in one—without breaking the budget. Actually, miniature golf might be even more challenging than a professional course. After all, how many long-necked llamas, bearded pirates, or spooky caves have you tripped over on a fairway lately?

Several miniature courses are part of amusement parks as complete properties. Most courses are open from 9:00 A.M. to midnight and have snack bars or cold drink machines. Admission ranges from $2.00 to $8.00 per putter. Special prices are offered for all-day play, which means you can play for a while and then come back later to play some more.

North Strand

Hawaiian Rumble Miniature Golf
33rd Avenue South, U.S. Highway 17, North Myrtle Beach
(843) 272–7812
www.hawaiianrumble.com

Ranked by *GOLF Magazine* as the No. 1 miniature golf course in the United States, Hawaiian Rumble offers a challenging gambit of shots in a lush and expertly landscaped setting of tropical palms, hibiscus, and other plants. The course circles and climbs up around a rumbling volcano, leis in almost every color are handed out to the players, and gentle Hawaiian music plays in the background. Hawaiian Rumble also sponsors the Masters Putting Championship, with a purse of $20,000—definitely worth a shot!

Mayday Miniature Golf
U.S. Highway 17, North Myrtle Beach
(843) 280–3535
www.maydaygolf.com

Two 18-hole courses make up this extravaganza. The centerpiece of the course is an actual plane crash-landed in the jungle. It is your mission to herd your ball around the 18-hole Mayday Mountain Course and then, if you have the fortitude, escape the thundering waterfall and wild animal calls of the Rescue Falls course. The Rescue Falls course features 18 holes, is wheelchair-accessible, and uses premium putting carpet that's as fast as a pool table, the owners claim. Mayday does have all-day play until 5:00 P.M. Call ahead for all-day rates and daily specials.

Myrtle Beach

Captain Hook's Adventure Golf
2205 North Kings Highway, Myrtle Beach
(843) 626–1430
www.burroughschapin.com/minigolf
Based on the timeless story of Peter Pan, Captain Hook offers two imagination-inspiring 18-hole courses. Players can choose the Lost Boys' course or the more challenging Hook's course, which has uphill shots and includes water holes and sand traps.

Dragon's Lair Fantasy Golf
Broadway at the Beach, 1197 Celebrity Circle,
Myrtle Beach
(843) 444–3215
www.burroughschapin.com/minigolf
A favorite attraction at the huge Broadway at the Beach complex is the fire-breathing volcanic mountain for you to putt around, through, and inside. You'll also putt over water, through castle doors, and up hills. This huge multicourse indoor complex is touted by its owners as employing cutting-edge minigolf technology. Whether or not this is true, we can assure you that it is the only miniature complex amid the shopping, theatre, and dining action of the Broadway at the Beach complex.

Jungle Lagoon
Fifth Avenue South and Kings Highway,
Myrtle Beach
(843) 626–7894
www.junglelagoon.com
In this tropical jungle setting you might wish you had a machete instead of a putter. You'll have to contend with lots of uphill shots, fast downhill curves, and angles on both courses (18 holes each). Spe-

cial rates are offered for children age five and younger. All-day play is available.

Jurassic Golf
29th Avenue South and Kings Highway,
Myrtle Beach
(843) 448–2116
www.burroughschapin.com/minigolf
You guessed it—ferocious dinosaurs threaten your score. Choose from two 18-hole courses. Discounts are offered to children age five and younger. All-day play ends at 5:00 P.M.

Pirates Watch
1500 South Kings Highway, Myrtle Beach
(843) 448–8600
Enjoy 36 holes brimming with action-packed waterfalls, daunting pirates, water traps, and lagoons. All-day play is offered until 5:00 P.M., 9:00 P.M. in fall.

Rainbow Falls
Restaurant Row, 9850 U.S. Highway 17,
Myrtle Beach
(843) 497–2557
Tricky corners, animal caves, and fairy-tale castles make up 36 holes of these two courses. One or two uphill holes could throw your game. Special rates are offered to groups and children age four and younger. All-day play is available until 5:00 P.M.

SpyGlass
3800 North Kings Highway, Myrtle Beach
(843) 626–9309
This 18-hole course has a fun degree of difficulty and offers discounts to senior citizens, children, and groups. Waterfalls, uphill holes, and those bloody pirates are the main obstacles. All-day play ends at 6:00 P.M.

Treasure Island
48th Avenue North, Myrtle Beach
(843) 449–4754
A hole in one is not easy to come by on this 18-hole course, but the play at Treasure Island is definitely worth the challenge. Discounts are available for senior citizens, children, and groups. All-day play ends at 6:00 P.M.

South Strand

Adventure Falls
735 U.S. Highway 17, Surfside Beach
(843) 238–0168

Animals and castles overlook the 36 holes of two courses. Groups and children are offered discounts, and all-day play ends at 5:00 P.M.

Buccaneer Bay
6001 U.S. Highway 17 South, Surfside Beach
(843) 238–3811

Two courses filled with pirates and big boats—36 holes between them—will make you ache to walk the plank. Several holes feature difficult angles and tricky obstacles. All-day play ends at 5:00 P.M.

Parasailing

Parasailing has become a popular activity along the beach. Participants wear a parachute and are pulled by a towrope behind a speed boat. The parachute fills with air and lifts the parasailer to heights around 300 feet. Parasailing adventures are offered through the following businesses: Parasail Express, 4091 Highway 17 Business, Myrtle Beach, (843) 357-7777; Captain Dick's Marina, 4123 U.S. Highway 17 Business, (843) 651-3676, Murrells Inlet; and Marlin Quay Parasailing, 1508 South Waccamaw Drive, Garden City Beach, (843) 651-4444.

Recreation Centers/ Leagues

The recreation centers we've included in this section offer a smattering of leagues for kids. Call each respective center to find out about sign-up dates; parents often get upset if they miss a registration deadline.

North Strand

North Myrtle Beach Community Center
Possum Trot Road, North Myrtle Beach
(843) 280–5570

Serving the community for decades, the North Myrtle Beach Community Center offers four meeting rooms and a gymnasium/auditorium. Activities include classes for the young and young at heart. Just a few of the offerings include arts and crafts, clogging, sign language, karate, drama, and creative dance. Team sports include basketball, T-ball, softball, baseball, and volleyball. Other activities offered at the center are aerobics, seniors' toning classes, introduction to bridge, and bridge games. Nominal fees are set by each individual instructor or coach. You might pay $5.00 for a yoga class or $35.00 for six weeks of line dancing.

The center is open Monday through Friday. Operating hours hinge on activities, so please call for details.

Myrtle Beach

Grand Strand YMCA
904 65th Avenue North, Myrtle Beach
(843) 449–9622
www.gsfymca.org

Our local YMCA actively sponsors community events, many geared toward children. Kids enjoy T-ball, baseball, soccer, swim classes, after-school day care, and day camps. Adults can enjoy coed volleyball, basketball, shag and ballroom dancing, softball, and health-enhancement workshops. The center features a Nautilus and free-weights center, a selection of cardiovascular equipment, and aerobics classes. Fees are competitive, ranging from a $3.00 one-day fee to $380 per family per year—and numerous levels in between. Call for all the details.

Pepper Geddings Recreation Center
3205 Oak Street, Myrtle Beach
(843) 918–2280

The Pepper Geddings Recreation Center is the most complete recreation center in the area. This facility features a 25-yard heated indoor swimming pool that is fully accessible to the physically challenged. Programs include American Red Cross swimming lessons for all ages and abilities, a variety of water-exercise programs, and a swim team, as well as lifeguard-certification and water-safety classes. You can pump up in the weight room with free weights and Nautilus equipment under the supervision of a professional trainer.

Instructional classes include arts and crafts; a variety of dances such as ballroom, shag, and tap; and bridge and other card games. The Parks and Recreation Department also offers after-school care and a summer day camp.

City-sponsored aerobics, swimming, and team sports including basketball are coordinated through this center. In addition to meeting rooms and a game room, the complex is surrounded by softball, baseball, and football fields, three lighted tennis courts, and a picnic shelter with a grill and tables.

Fees for most classes are nominal, and annual passes for the weight room and swimming pool are available. The center is open six days a week: Monday through Thursday from 6:00 A.M. to 9:00 P.M.; Friday from 6:00 A.M. to 6:30 P.M.; and Saturday from 10:00 A.M. to 5:00 P.M.

South Strand

**Surfside Beach Recreation Department
H. Blue Huckabee Recreation Complex,
Spanish Oak Drive and Glenns Bay Road,
Surfside Beach
(843) 650–4131
Dick M. Johnson Civic Center, Pine Drive,
Surfside Beach
(843) 650–4131**

The Surfside Beach Recreation Department provides year-round recreational programs for all ages. Many of the sports activities are held at the H. Blue Huckabee complex, which boasts three ball fields. Instructional courses and seminars, held at the Johnson Civic Center, include arts and crafts, dance, aerobics, and more. Special events include Easter egg hunts, Sun Fun Volleyball competitions (see the Annual Events chapter), an Old-fashioned Family Festival in October, a Christmas Tree Lighting Ceremony, and a Santa Hotline.

Tennis

If spirited competition on the courts is what you love, you can slam an ace or volley for fun on any one of numerous tennis courts that span the length of the Grand Strand. We'll start with the freebies, available on a first-come, first-served (pardon the pun) basis. Pay-as-you-play courts require reservations, so call in advance.

North Strand

**Central Park
1030 Possum Trot Road (between 13th and 15th Avenues South), North Myrtle Beach
(843) 280–5570**

Central Park offers four outdoor, lighted asphalt courts. Lights-out is 11:00 P.M.

**Hill Street Park
Hill Street (off Sea Mountain Highway),
North Myrtle Beach
(843) 280–5570**

Be the first to grab the one lighted asphalt court. The lights go out at 11:00 P.M.

**McLean Park
First Avenue South, North Myrtle Beach
(843) 280–5570**

McLean offers two outdoor, lighted asphalt courts. Lights-out is 11:00 P.M.

**Ocean Creek Tennis Center
U.S. Highway 17 (Windy Hill section), North Myrtle Beach
(843) 272–7724, Extension 1011**

Ocean Creek Tennis Center offers eight courts—three with Har-tru surfaces, two lighted for evening play, and one devoted solely to practice. The hourly rate is $15 for hard courts and $20 for Har-tru courts. Lessons are available from the center's on-site professional.

Myrtle Beach

**Kingston Plantation Sport & Health Club
9760 Kings Road, Myrtle Beach
(843) 497–2444
www.kingstonplantation.com**

Past host of the GTE Tennis Festival, which featured pro players such as Pete Sampras, Michael Chang, Andre Agassi, and Jimmy Connors, this $4 million health club offers four outdoor clay courts and five Har-tru courts. All courts are lighted and lessons are available for a minimal fee. Call to schedule an appointment.

Local tennis courts provide lots of opportunity for spirited competition. PHOTO: COURTESY OF MYRTLE BEACH AREA CHAMBER OF COMMERCE

Myrtle Beach Public Courts
3200 Oak Street, Myrtle Beach
(843) 918-2280
U.S. Highway 17 and 20th Avenue South,
Myrtle Beach
No phone

The two outdoor, asphalt-surfaced courts on Oak Street are next door to the Myrtle Beach Recreation Center. Lights allow you to play all night; however, when the center closes at 9:00 P.M., so do the rest room facilities.

The 20th Avenue South complex has six lighted courts, along with rest rooms and outdoor water fountains. All courts are asphalt-covered.

Myrtle Beach Tennis & Swim Club
U.S. Highway 17 Bypass (across from Dixie Stampede), Myrtle Beach
(843) 449-4486

Two of the 10 composition courts are lighted. You can practice with the ball machines or at the free backboard area. Full-time tennis professionals offer adult and junior programs year-round. Courts cost $15.00 per player per hour for singles and $5.00 per player per hour for doubles. A match setup service and racquet stringing are available. There's also a pro shop.

Pan-American Resort
5300 North Ocean Boulevard, Myrtle Beach
(843) 449-7411
www.panamericanresort.com

Guests of the Pan-American can play any of the three outdoor Cushion-tex courts for free. Others pay $8.00 per hour for singles or $10.00 per hour for doubles.

Prestwick Health & Tennis Club
1375 McMaster Drive, Myrtle Beach
(843) 828-1000

Prestwick offers 11 clay courts, 3 lighted courts, and 2 lighted hard-surface courts. Nonmembers pay $15 an hour per court. Private lessons are available for $40 an hour from the head pro. If you're really in top form—or want to get there—you can have a videotape made of your match, to see just what needs improvement.

South Strand

Litchfield Racquet Club
Hawthorn Drive, Litchfield Beach
(843) 237–3411, (888) 766–4633
www.litchfieldbeach.com

The club maintains 17 Har-tru clay courts, 3 of which are lighted. Instruction is available from two full-time professionals. Ball machines are also available. Litchfield also offers a year-round tennis school.

Surfside Beach Public Courts
Surfside Drive, Surfside Beach
(843) 650–4131

All three of these outdoor lighted courts are treated with asphalt. Rest room facilities and water fountains are nearby.

Spectator Sports

Auto Racing

Myrtle Beach Speedway
4300 U.S. Highway 501, Myrtle Beach
(843) 236–0500

Amateur and professional drivers thrill racing fans as the roar of engines ricochets off the asphalt of the Myrtle Beach Speedway. With each wave of the checkered flag, this spectator sport draws increasingly larger crowds.

Races are held most Saturday nights and feature five divisions: ministock, late-model stock, street stock, chargers, and trucks.

The local racing season is highlighted by The Winston Racing Series and also includes the All-Pro, NASCAR Dash, Open Wheel Modified, and Busch Grand National touring series.

The roots of stock-car racing in this area can be traced back more than three decades, when dirt tracks were carved out of remote forests near modern-day downtown. The present speedway facility was built in 1958 and was known as the Rac-

ing Association of Myrtle Beach Inc. (RAMBI) Raceway. At that time racing fans were following the budding careers of Richard Petty, Ralph Earnhardt, Ned Jarrett, and David Pearson. After a decade of dirt-track racing, the speedway was paved in 1969.

The popularity of auto racing fell during the 1970s but produced a name to be reckoned with—the late Dale Earnhardt. In 1978 Earnhardt won the late-model sportsman championship at Myrtle Beach Speedway. A year later he joined the Winston Cup roster and won Rookie of the Year honors.

Since the mid-1980s, auto racing has gained momentum. It's not unusual that hot racers at Myrtle Beach Speedway become stars later.

Gates open at 4:00 P.M., and drivers take practice laps before the green flag drops on the first of five heats at 7:30 P.M.

Concession items are available, including beer, soft drinks, and snack food such as hot dogs, chips, and candy. Spectators are permitted to bring small hand-held coolers.

Seating is stadium style, so you might want to bring a blanket or a cushioned seat for comfort. Admission varies widely per race.

Baseball

Myrtle Beach Pelicans
Coastal Federal Field 1251
21st Avenue North, Myrtle Beach
(843) 918–6000
www.myrtlebeachpelicans.com

The Pelicans are an Atlanta Braves Class-A affiliate.

The $12 million Coastal Federal Field provides a suitable nest for the Pelicans and brings fans right into the fast-paced action of the game while providing a load of amenities. There are 2,676 box seats and 1,481 reserved seats originally from Fulton County Stadium, former home of the Atlanta Braves. There are lounges, suites, patio boxes, picnic areas with views of the field, and a wheelchair-accessible children's playground. Parking is free. Specials, such as dollar drafts, are often

Professional baseball came to the Grand Strand with Coastal Federal Field and the Pelicans, offering something fun to do away from the water. PHOTO: ROBERT GURGANIFS

announced, and entertainment such as the "Steel In Time" steel-drum band plays during halftime. Dinger the Home Run Dog also scores with some impressive maneuvers. Dinger, a sleek, yellow retriever, runs bases, shags fly balls, and retrieves bats. And of course, hot dogs and popcorn, in addition to a few Myrtle Beach specialties, are available, with plenty of napkins on hand.

The Pelicans are part of the Carolina League, which over the past years has turned out Muscle Shoals, Willie Duke, Woody Fair, Harvey Haddix, Crash Davis, Earl Weaver, Wade Boggs, Rod Carew, Dwight Evans, and Barry Bonds.

The current Pelicans team is composed of professional athletes playing hard for the chance to wear the A and the tomahawk of the Atlanta Braves. Besides the players mentioned earlier, the roster of future all-stars includes outfielder Jayson Bass of Alabama, center Scott Bronowicz of Pennsylvania, right-hand pitcher Jacob Shumate of Florence, South Carolina (just an hour and a half from the Strand), and center Steve Torrealba of Venezuela.

The home team has the advantage of a clubhouse designed to assist them in their strenuous struggle to the major leagues. To complement the Brave's modified strength and conditioning program, the workout room has Cybex weight equipment, a training room, whirlpools, and batting cages.

Box seating is $7.50, reserved seating is $6.50, and grass seating is $3.00.

Coastal Carolina University Sports

Sports fans may be interested in checking out events at Coastal Carolina University, about 14 miles west of Myrtle Beach on U.S. Highway 501.

During the academic year, Coastal Carolina University fields 8 men's and 9 women's teams that compete in 17 sporting events, all of which are open to the general public at the campus. As members of the NCAA's Division I Big South Conference, the Chanticleers play soccer, tennis, volleyball, basketball, golf, baseball, and, most recently, football. For specific details the sports section of the *Sun News* is a comprehensive resource. For complete schedules contact the athletic department at Coastal Carolina University at (843) 349-2820 or on the Internet at www.coastal.edu/athletics.

Coastal's latest athletic endeavor is women's cross-country running; in 1997 the women finished 24th in the nation after ranking 19th in the interim, which is the highest ranking ever of any team at Coastal. The team won three consecutive championships and five altogether in the 1997 conference, and finished second in the 1999 Big South Conference.

Coastal Carolina's men's basketball team won four Big South championships from 1987 to 1991 and advanced to the NCAA tournament in 1991 and 1993. The team plays in Kimbel Arena, 2 blocks east of campus on an unnamed dead-end road between U.S. Highways 501 and 544. Tickets are $5.00 for adults and $3.00 for students.

The men's baseball team won five conference championships between 1986 and 1992, and won the 2002 Big South regular season. The collegiate baseball season lasts from mid-February to May and the team plays at the Charles L. Watson Stadium.

The men's tennis team won conference championships in 1988, 1989, 1993, and 1994.

The men's soccer team won five conference championships from 1986 to 1995, and again in 2001, and has participated in two NCAA tournaments. The soccer season lasts from September to November.

The baseball, tennis, and soccer venues are on the Coastal Carolina campus.

Golf

The Grand Strand has established itself as a veritable golfing mecca.

A number of golf tournaments are played around the Grand Strand, mostly for charity. The Omar Shrine Clowns "One Club" Golf Tournament tees off every February at Whispering Pines Golf Club; contact Bob Cape, (843) 650-2800. Myrtle Beach National golf course (see the Golf chapter) hosts the Retired Military Golf Classic every May; call Jerry Cox, (843) 448-2308. The Mark Sloan Memorial Golf Tournament is played in August at Myrtlewood Golf Club, (843) 626-3638. And the Charles Tilghman Junior Tournament is set for December at The Surf Club; call Bill Campbell, (843) 249-1524.

For more information on myriad golfing opportunities—regulation, par-3, and minigolf courses—and tournaments, see the Golf chapter.

Golf

Tournaments

Grand Strand
  Golf Courses

Miniature Golf

Golf Driving
  Ranges

Par-3 Courses

"Fore."

"Five. Six. Seven. . . . " The old golf joke gets seriously out of hand on the Grand Strand, especially if you are counting golf courses instead of strokes. During the past 10 years, the course count has expanded to nearly 120, stretching Myrtle Beach's tradition of summer vacationers into the spring and fall, when the climate in the Carolinas yields the most enjoyable temperatures for golfing.

In 2001 golfers played nearly 4.3 million rounds here, making the Myrtle Beach area one of the world's most popular golf destinations. Though no one keeps a central count of how many actual golfers come here every year, it is projected—comparing those 4 million rounds with hotel occupancy figures—that approximately 1.4 million golfers come to the Grand Strand every year.

The average golfer comes to the Grand Strand with three other golfers, spends three days here, and is a 39.8-year-old male with a household income of about $52,000. Golf has ranked as the number two generator of tourism revenues here since 1996, pulling in players primarily during spring and fall.

Yes, golf is a big deal here. It's so big, in fact, that golfing legend Gary Player has commented, "If you do not have a high-profile presence in Myrtle Beach, you are not considered a serious player in the golf industry."

Most courses market either through hotel package deals or through an advertising co-op association; package deals usually include a welcome gift, breakfast, greens fees, and a cart. Recently heavy discounts in the off-season (summer for golf) have begun to bleed over into the once-inflated fall fees.

Although the sheer abundance of courses is staggering, perhaps more impressive than the quantity is the quality. This 60-mile stretch of real estate boasts a collection of the country's finest course layouts. Creations of golf-great architects such as Jones, Player, Nicklaus, Fazio, Palmer, Maples, and Dye, these courses offer a lot more than what you might expect—they're everything golf fantasies are made of.

Something you might not know about the Grand Strand is that the topography of the countryside is delightfully diverse. If you're a beachgoer, you might know and love the salt-scrubbed beaches, sand castles, sailboats, sea oats, and little else. But wander inland just a bit; you'll discover bountiful secrets in the corners of our counties. You'll find undulating river bluffs and panoramic river vistas, shadowy swamp lands, stately old oaks weeping silver moss, sandy pine forests, and seemingly unchanging marshlands. The assortment of ecosystems continues to provide golf-course architects with some of the richest natural resources in the world.

Mother Nature not only has given us an abundance of beautiful real estate, but also has blessed us with a subtropical climate that makes the outdoors pleasant almost every day of the year. Crisp days and aqua-blue skies make autumn and spring the favored seasons of many golfers. Still, lots of folks are learning the local secret that outrageous bargains abound during the summer and winter months. Since our weather is governed by cool Gulf Stream breezes when temperatures rise and warm Gulf Stream breezes when temperatures dip, golfing is a year-round delight.

Like everything else in our neck of the woods, golf offerings are eclectic, electric, and just plain fun. Provocative and dazzling new courses flourish, along with the vintage, time-tested tracks graced with history and tradition. Pine Lakes International Country

Club, a semiprivate layout designed by Robert White in 1927, launched golf's popularity in this area and today is appropriately known as "The Granddaddy." Myrtle Beach's highly regarded Dunes Golf and Beach Club, designed in 1948 by Robert Trent Jones, carried on the tradition. In decades following, a parade of splendid designs have come to maturation along the Strand. As the number of courses spirals well past 100, the area's reputation blossoms accordingly.

With so many courses, the Grand Strand is naturally host to many tournaments for any and every kind of golfer. One of the oldest and biggest golfing events along South Carolina's Grand Strand is the DuPont World Amateur Handicap Championship, billed as the world's largest on-site championship. *Golf Digest* dubbed the August event the "Everyman Open," and *Golf World* crowned it the "mother of all golf tournaments." Little wonder. For nearly 20 years, roughly 50,000 golfers from all over the world have participated in the four-day, matched-handicap competition. For information regarding participation, call (800) 833–8798.

The DuPont tournament is held at various courses, as are other tournaments hosted by Myrtle Beach Golf Holiday: the International Summer Family Golf Tournaments, the Veteran's Golf Classic, and the National Police Golf Championship.

Myrtle Beach Golf Holiday, founded in 1967, is a nonprofit association of accommodations and golf courses along "The Carolinas' Golden Golf Coast," from Georgetown, South Carolina, to Southport, North Carolina. The organization's mission is to increase consumer awareness of the advantages of a Myrtle Beach–area golf vacation and make it as easy as possible for a golfer to reserve accommodations of a preferred level of luxury or economy. Devised as an advertising co-op program and originally put together by the head of a local ad agency, the tax-exempt status of the organization has allowed hotels and golf courses to advertise at rates and in media that they could never initially afford; it is a brilliant promotional tool for Myrtle Beach golf.

Prospective vacationing golfers and travel agents can call (800) 845–4653 or visit www.golfholiday.com to receive a free vacation planner complete with information on 82 resorts and 96 golf courses, as well as travel tips and information on how to directly book a golf vacation with a member accommodation. There are also toll-free numbers to call from the UK, Finland, France, Germany, Ireland, Japan, The Netherlands, Norway, Sweden, and Switzerland.

The Classics of Myrtle Beach is an umbrella organization that represents 13 of the Grand Strand's top courses and 10 of its best resorts. Their collection demands strict standards of quality and offers deluxe amenities that include fine restaurants, exercise and relaxation facilities, and entertainment options. They have truly mastered the small details that ensure your golf vacation is first class. Booking a Classic package couldn't be easier. Just select a resort and the courses and tee times you want; they will take care of everything else. Visit www.myrtlebeachclassics.com for additional information.

Service-oriented Myrtle Beach caters to a golfer's every need; there are also more than a dozen golf schools in town, many with PGA instructors, great student-teacher ratios, and programs keyed to all levels of play. For a listing of these schools as well as more details on the entire golf scene, check out *Insiders' Guide to Golf in the Carolinas*, by far the best guide to Grand Strand golfing, available where you bought this guide and anywhere quality books are sold.

For the inside scoop regarding golf on the Strand, refer to the *Sun News'* monthly magazine, *Myrtle Beach Golf.* You'll discover scads of interesting editorial, dining, and entertainment tips, a directory of courses, maps, and much more. A subscription costs $12 per 12 issues or $24 for 24 issues. Write Myrtle Beach Golf, P.O. Box 406, Myrtle Beach, SC 29578, or call (800) 568–1800 to start your subscription.

From the air, the Grand Strand's 100-plus courses establish the area as a golfer's paradise. PHOTO: COURTESY OF MYRTLE BEACH AREA CHAMBER OF COMMERCE

Tournaments

With so many courses, the Grand Strand naturally hosts many tournaments—local, national, and international—for any and every kind of golfer, not just the pros. For instance, one of the oldest and biggest golfing events along South Carolina's Grand Strand, the DuPont World Amateur Handicap Championship (see subsequent entry), is billed as the world's largest on-site championship. Call (800) 845–4653 for information about MBGH-hosted events.

Of course many tournaments carry large cash purses, including sizable sums awarded to the winners. Spectators also win, as they are treated to some of the best golf played by some of the best golfers on the planet. But the real winners of all PGA (and Nike) tour events are charitable organizations. In 1997 the United Way of Horry County, Disabled American Veterans, Make-A-Wish Foundation, Mobile Meals in Myrtle Beach, Hook-A-Kid-On-Golf, and the Elizabeth Chapin Patterson Community Assistance Center shared $200,000. In 1999 the SENIOR PGA TOUR tournaments combined raised a record $11,050,000 in charitable donations. In 2002, Myrtle Beach Golf Holiday hosted a 9/11 Memorial Golf Ball Tournament. Firefighters from across the country came to Myrtle Beach to raise money for The Thomas Elsasser Fund, a charity backed by the United Firefighters Association (UFA) and designed to benefit families of fallen firefighters. The tournament provided an opportunity for firefighters, many of whom assisted in the recovery efforts at Ground Zero, to gather in the "Golf Capital of the World."

**DuPont CoolMax World Amateur
Handicap Championship
(800) 833–8798
www.worldamateur.com**

The venerable DuPont CoolMax World Amateur Handicap Championship, one of the oldest and biggest golfing events on the Strand, is billed as the world's largest on-site championship. *Golf Digest* magazine dubbed the August event the "Everyman Open," and *Golf World* magazine crowned it the "mother of all golf tournaments." Little wonder. During the past 19 years, well more than 45,000 golfers from all over the world have participated in the four-day, matched-handicap competition.

Jimmy D'Angelo Senior Golf Classic
(843) 236–8888, (800) 340–0072
www.belleterre.com
Belle Terre hosts the Jimmy D'Angelo Senior Golf Classic for players who have reached their 50th birthday by November 4 of the present year. The entry fee is $200, which includes three rounds of golf, a luncheon, prizes, and an awards banquet at the Dunes Club (see subsequent entry).

Grand Strand Golf Courses

With nearly 120 courses on the Grand Strand, there are far and away too many for us to tell you about more than a fraction. Nonetheless, here's a representative assortment featuring different styles, prices, and locales. You should also take into account that, for the full picture of Grand Strand golfing, we extend the Grand Strand beyond the state line to include the southern tip of North Carolina, as it touches the traditional Grand Strand. This "extension" of the Strand applies only to our look at golfing, and we do so because those North Carolina courses really are part of the local golfing community.

Area golf courses reserve the right to alter greens fees at any given time. It's almost a sure bet that rates will be higher from March 1 to May 1 and during September and October; these times of year feature prime golfing weather and golf-course conditions. Morning greens fees are usually highest, with rates dropping beginning around noon and continuing to fall as the day gets warmer. To give you a proper perspective on greens fees on Grand Strand courses, we include the highest greens fees (including a cart unless otherwise noted) during peak season (March to May) for each entry. We also state each course's policy on walking.

Yardage from the men's white tees and par are provided in the course description. Remember, although there are oodles of courses to choose from, tee times are precious, especially during prime seasons. Call well in advance—three months or more—to book reservations.

North Strand

Angels Trace Golf Links
1215 Angels Club Drive Southwest,
Sunset Beach, NC
(910) 579–2277, (800) 718–5733
www.golfangelstrace.com
Angels Trace opened two 18-hole courses, the North Course and the South Course, in November 1995. Tees, fairways, and rough are 419 Bermuda grass, and greens are bent grass. Gently rolling fairways, moderate mounding, and shallow bunkers lead to large greens. The course designs each submit to the natural lay of the land and feature natural streams and lakes bordered by oyster shells.

The North Course has designated No. 5 as its signature hole. The par-4 dogleg left requires a placement shot, then a carry over water. Each side of the fairway is lined with two sand traps, and the green is elevated and surrounded by oyster shells. This premier course was designed by

Clyde Johnston, measures 6,216 yards, and plays par 72. The 6,442-yard, par-72 South Course, also designed by Johnston, incorporates features similar to those of the North Course. Greens fees at Angels Trace are $80; no walking.

Brunswick Plantation and Golf Resort
U.S. Highway 17, Calabash, NC
(800) 848–0290, (800) 835–4533
www.brunswickplantation.com

Brunswick Plantation inhabits a convenient, central point between Myrtle Beach, South Carolina, and Wilmington, North Carolina (which is an hour north of Myrtle Beach) and lies just minutes from beautiful Carolina beaches.

The 27 holes of this course measure 6,200 yards and plays par 72 as the natural beauty of the terrain is emphasized by integrating quick bent-grass greens and beautiful lush fairways with the wooded Carolina Pines.

The first nine holes of the Magnolia Course draw from the historic links of Scotland. The extensive mounds and large sand and grass bunkers present the challenge of this nine. The second nine, the Azalea Course, is carved from thick Carolina woodlands. Water is the dominant theme on many of the holes, demanding thought and strategy on every shot. The fourth hole is an island green accessible by bridge and surrounded by beautiful oyster shells. The Dogwood Course, which composes the final nine, meanders along the historic Caw Caw Run among the dense hardwood trees. The No.-6 hole will provide you with another challenging island green, and you can look forward to the No.-7 hole, where you'll discover a 300-year-old cypress tree that's more than 10 feet in diameter!

Greens fees are $70; no walking.

Carolina Shores Golf & Country Club
99 Carolina Shores Drive, Calabash, NC
(910) 579–2181, (800) 579–8292
www.carolinashoresgolf.com

Not for the faint of heart, Carolina Shores has earned a reputation as a hazardous layout that absolutely demands accuracy. Little wonder, since there are (count 'em) 96 diabolically placed bunkers, a dozen natural crater lakes, tree-lined fairways reminiscent of roller-coaster layouts, and perhaps the most dramatic starting hole in Grand Strand golf.

Although Carolina Shores demands precision play, brute strength is not necessary. Bring your best game and put yourself to the test. What's the joy of life without a few genuine challenges? Greens fees for this 6,231-yard, par-72 layout are $70; no walking.

The Gauntlet
St. James Plantation, N.C. Highway 211, Southport, NC
(910) 253–3008, (800) 247–4806
www.stjamesgolf.net

Although relatively young (The Gauntlet opened in 1991), this course is already widely known as one of the most formidable challenges on the Grand Strand. Set on a 200-acre tract characterized by marsh, maritime woodlands, lakes, and the ever-beautiful Intracoastal Waterway, the 6,448-yard, par-72 Gauntlet provides a magnificent arena that pits a golfer against one of P. B. Dye's finest and most challenging courses.

A stunning clubhouse and a tennis and swimming center hint at The Gauntlet's cherished old-fashioned Southern flair. Greens fees are $93; no walking.

Glen Dornoch Waterway Golf Links
U.S. Highway 17 North, Little River
(843) 249–2541, (800) 717–8784
www.glendornoch.com

This 270-acre site along the Intracoastal Waterway was created as a tribute to Dornoch, Scotland, the birthplace of golf legend Donald Ross. The 18-hole, 6,035-yard, par-72 Clyde Johnston design, which opened in September 1996, is set amid pines, oaks, lakes, a river, marsh, and the Intracoastal. At least four holes flank the waterway, and dramatic elevation changes—you'll find some 35-foot drops to the water—are nothing short of spectacular. Bring your most accurate game—there are no wide-open fairways here.

Greens fees are $118; no walking. Glen Dornoch includes a self-contained resort with a hotel, condominiums, and an array of related facilities.

Heather Glen
4650 Heather Glen Way, North Myrtle Beach
(843) 249–9000, (800) 868–4536
www.heatherglen.com

Timeless oaks and stately pines stud the 400-acre historic setting of Heather Glen, a course reminiscent of the best Scotland has to offer. Designed by Willard Byrd and Clyde Johnston, this course was pegged a masterpiece as quickly as it opened for play. *Golf Digest* named it 1987's "Best New Public Course in America" and one of the "50 Best Public Courses in America" in 1990. In 2001, *Golf Digest* gave it a 4½-star rating.

Heather Glen made a great thing even better when it expanded from 18 to 27 holes. This allows golfers to personally design their rounds by picking two of three stellar sets of nine holes from among the Red (3,127 yards), White (3,198 yards), and Blue (3,183 yards) Courses, all par 72. Greens fees are $104; no walking.

Back at the eighteenth-century-style clubhouse, cap off your round in an authentic-style pub serving Bass Ale and grilled sandwiches.

Lion's Paw Golf Links
Ocean Ridge Plantation
351 Ocean Ridge Parkway Southwest, Sunset Beach, NC
(910) 287–1717, (800) 233–1801
www.lionspaw.com

Since opening in 1991, the untamed Lion has often been described as Willard Byrd's finest work. Given Byrd's résumé, that description heartily endorses Lion's Paw as a course worth considering. This masterful layout is simultaneously wild and peaceful.

Perhaps the most striking feature of Lion's Paw is the contrast between the front nine holes and the back nine. The front nine feature a traditional layout, with natural elevation changes and feature such as Carolina pine trees. The back nine, however, is links-style after the great courses of Great Britain, with low-lying, mounded farmland and no trees.

No. 3 is a par 3 requiring a carry over water. Oyster shells flank each side of the fairway. No. 18 has a water hazard in the second-shot landing area, and the green is a peninsula surrounded by water. In all, this par-72 course measures 6,457 yards.

The scenery is breathtaking, and your game will be memorable. Greens fees are $75; no walking.

The Long Bay Club
S.C. Highway 9, North Myrtle Beach
(843) 399–2222, (800) 344–5590

The fact that The Long Bay Club is a Jack Nicklaus "signature course" is reason enough to pen it in on your golfing schedule. Open since 1988, the course continually has ranked among the top courses in the country.

A typical Nicklaus design, the 6,565-yard, par-72 layout showcases deep pot bunkers and vast waste areas; challenges abound. If the definition of a great layout is "a course with holes that become etched in memory," then Long Bay is indisputably great. In fact, the 10th hole, which features a scalloped, horseshoe-shaped sand trap, is one of the most recognizable holes in the entire golf world.

Greens fees are $112; no walking.

Marsh Harbour
Marsh Harbour Road, Calabash, NC
(843) 236–9318, (800) 581–5922
www.legendsgolf.com

This Dan Maples course has an interesting claim to fame—some holes are in South Carolina and some are in North Carolina. Marsh Harbour covers wetland along an inlet and the Intracoastal Waterway, making the course every bit as enjoyable to look at as it is to play. The combination of manicured turf and sparkling water creates a green and blue backdrop that's nothing shy of spectacular. Upon opening in 1980, the 6,000-yard, par-72 Marsh Harbour was rated among *Golf Digest*'s "Top 25 Public Courses in America."

The course's signature hole is the 570-yard 17th. Marvelously terrifying, this par 5 has three landing areas, two of which sport water on three sides. No one leaves Marsh Harbour without talking about No. 17.

Greens fees are $100; no walking.

The Long Bay Club—a Jack Nicklaus "signature course"—is ranked by Golf Digest *as one of the "Top Ten Courses" in the state of South Carolina.* PHOTO: MICHAEL SLEAR, COURTESY OF BRANDON ADVERTISING

Meadowlands
350 Calabash Road, Calabash, NC
(910) 287–7529, (888) 287–7529
www.meadowlandsgolf.com

Meadowlands threw open the barn doors in September 1997 and ever since has been befriending golfers. The grounds that once were farmland have been carefully and patiently sculpted by Willard Byrd and have been compared to Dan Maples' Man O' War Course (see subsequent entry). Meadowlands is wide-open for your grazing pleasure, cultivates tidewater greens, and welcomes you with a 6,000-square-foot, two-story clubhouse in a turn-of-the-century-style farmhouse setting. Meadowlands has a few memorable spots, from the alligator sanctuary located behind the 17th green to the 5-foot vertical drop lurking beyond the 13th. Metal spikes are not permitted, nor is walking. This 6,000-yard, par-72 course costs $67 to play.

Oyster Bay
Lakeshore Drive, Sunset Beach, NC
(843) 236–9318, (800) 552–2660

Yet another Dan Maples design, Oyster Bay really does have it all—6,305 yards set amid pretty lakes, sweeping marshes, and the Intracoastal Waterway, teeming with wildlife. Expect to see all sorts of shorebirds, and don't be surprised if you glimpse an alligator basking in the Carolina sunshine. This par-70 course was rated the "Best New Resort Course in America" in 1983 by *Golf Digest*. In 1990 the magazine sang its praises again, rating it one of the "Best 50 Public Courses in America."

A lake flanks the entire right side of the 13th fairway, and the green is guarded by a cavernous bunker. The 15th and 17th holes are par 3s with island greens, the latter of which is built on a mountain of oyster shells.

Greens fees are $110; no walking.

Panther's Run Golf Links
Ocean Ridge Plantation,
351 Ocean Ridge Parkway Southwest,
Sunset Beach, NC
(910) 287–1717, (800) 233–1801
www.panthersrun.com

The 18-hole, 6,267-yard, par-72 Panther's Run was created to deliver a different kind of challenge—one some call a "wild breed of golf." You'd be hard-pressed to find a more incredible variety of elevation in one location. Add twisting fairways and the classic beauty of a nature preserve and marshlands, and you've got a course that's as memorable for its scenery as for its challenge. A signature hole at Panther's Run is No. 15, which flanks a lake for the length of its right side. Avid golfers swear this is one of the finest driving holes to play.

Wildlife abounds here, so you might want to bring your binoculars. Panther's Run golf shop was rated in the top 100 in 1997 by *Golf Digest*, so bring your wallet, too.

Greens fees are $85; no walking March through May.

The Pearl Golf Links
1300 Pearl Boulevard Southwest, Sunset Beach, NC
(910) 579–8132, (888) 947–3275
www.thepearlgolf.com

The omnipresent and magnificent Dan Maples strikes again with The Pearl's two courses. Both the East and West Courses easily qualify as some of the finest in all the nation. Both are ranked among the top courses in the Carolinas and have been nominated "Best New Public Courses in America" by *Golf Digest*.

The par-72 East Course, encompassing 6,543 yards, is the more traditional of the two. Carved from pristine maritime forest, it boasts a dramatic finishing hole along the Calabash River—a mid-length par 4, uphill off the tee and downhill to the green, with the river and salt marsh on the left.

The Pearl's 6,738-yard, par-72 West Course is links-style; lots of wide-open stretches complemented by thick displays of pampas grass. The 18th hole alone is worth the greens fee; it features a finishing

hole—in 1997, it was voted best finishing hole by *GOLF Magazine*—along bluffs that overlook the blue ribbon of Intracoastal Waterway. Attention to detail and meticulous grooming characterize this course, which has hosted a number of major tournaments.

Greens fees are $76; no walking.

Possum Trot Golf Club
U.S. Highway 17 North, North Myrtle Beach
(843) 272–5341, (800) 626–8768

Open since 1968, Possum Trot bills itself as "the friendliest course down South, where the guest is number one." Noted among locals and returning tourists for consistently excellent playing conditions, this 6,388-yard, par-72 course features wide fairways that make for a low-maintenance round whether you're an average golfer or a low handicapper.

Possum Trot also offers a unique 16-acre practice facility; a driving range complete with chipping, pitching, and putting greens; and a practice bunker. Greens fees are $71, and walking is allowed at times; call ahead.

River Hills Golf & Country Club
U.S. Highway 17 North, Little River
(843) 399–2100, (800) 264–3810
www.riverhillsgolf.com

Just one year after opening, River Hills was nominated by *Golf Digest* as its "Best New Course for 1989." Also in 1989, *Golf Week* named the course one of the Southeast's "Top 50."

A public resort facility in an impressive country-club setting, River Hills remains an outstanding course that offers a pleasing blend of old and new design features, frequent elevation changes (more than any course in the area), and championship conditioning. This 6,285-yard, par-72 course is definitely worth adding to your playing schedule. Greens fees are $70; no walking.

Sandpiper Bay
800 Sandpiper Bay Drive, Sunset Beach, NC
(910) 579–9120, (800) 356–5827
www.sandpiperbaygolf.com

With some of the best bent-grass greens on the Strand, Sandpiper Bay has been a locals' favorite for nearly a decade. A Dan Maples design, players consistently find this 6,020-yard, par-71 course in great shape. With six par 3s and five par 5s, it's a challenge for players of all skill levels. A magnificent clubhouse, set among wind-whispering pines and glassy lakes, reflects Sandpiper Bay's commitment to quality and exceptional service.

Greens fees are $90; no walking.

Sea Trail Plantation
211 Clubhouse Road, Sunset Beach, NC
(910) 287–1157, (888) 229–5747
www.seatrail.com

Sea Trail Plantation has three courses, designed by notable architects Dan Maples, Rees Jones, and Willard Byrd. (With those names, how could you go wrong?) Each course is manageable—not too easy, not too tough—the kind you'll remember fondly once you've returned home. Even so, the traditional design of the Rees Jones course stands out to golf aficionados. Wide fairways, elevated greens, large mounds, swales, pot bunkers, and fresh-water lakes add to its aesthetic beauty. But, rest assured, its good looks haven't softened its challenge.

All three courses are par 72. The 6,251-yard Byrd Course costs $85 to play; the 6,334-yard Jones Course is $100; and the 6,332-yard Maples Course, $85. Walking is not permitted, and golfers must wear spikeless shoes on all three courses.

Surf Club
1701 Springland Lane, North Myrtle Beach
(843) 249–1524, (800) 765–SURF
www.surfgolf.com

This club opened in 1960 and has been a popular golfing destination for nearly four decades. Recently all the greens were rebuilt to enhance this George Cobb classic. Those who knew and loved the Surf before the renovation will appreciate the way architect John LaFoy retained the course's classic appeal while adding new challenges for golfers of all abilities. One avid local golfer described the Surf simply: "Traditional design without gimmicks. Strong par 4s merit playing."

The 6,360-yard, par-72 Surf Club course costs $93 to play; no walking.

A surprisingly diverse topography has given rise to golf courses that feature everything from marsh and river views to pristine woodlands filled with wildlife. PHOTO: COURTESY OF MYRTLE BEACH AREA CHAMBER OF COMMERCE

Thistle Golf Club
8840 Old Georgetown Road Southwest, Sunset Beach, NC
(910) 575–8700, (800) 571–6710
www.thistlegolf.com

In a relatively short time, Thistle Golf Club has established itself among the best courses the Strand has to offer. Since opening in 1999, the 27-hole Tim Cates' Scottish-links design has been ranked among the "Top 100 Fairways in America" by *Golf For Women Magazine*. The course also earned four stars from *Golf Digest*'s "Places to Play." An engaging layout and complimentary range balls, yardage book, and bag tags, make this an enviable golf experience. The 6,997-yard, par-72 course boasts generous fairways, large bent-grass greens, 5 sets of tees, and 12-minute tee times. Golfers of all abilities will enjoy a day at Thistle. Greens fees are $105; walking is permitted.

Tidewater Golf Club & Plantation
4901 Little River Neck Road, North Myrtle Beach
(843) 249–3829, (800) 446–5363
www.tide-water.com

If scenic vistas showcasing water suit your taste, you'll fall in love with Tidewater in a hurry. Truly incredible views of the Intracoastal Waterway, saltwater marshes, and the Atlantic Ocean abound. At least one hole plays alongside Hogg Inlet (a popular fishing area for Cherry Grove residents), so you can watch anglers reel in a few as you plan your next shot. This fabulous course was named one of the best new public courses by both *Golf Digest* and *GOLF Magazine* in 1990.

Situated on 560 acres of seaside peninsula, Tidewater gives you plenty of elbow room and privacy. The only hole you can see at any given time is the one you're playing, which creates the feeling of absolute solitude. The course has five sets of tees, so golfers can select those that best suit their games. Depending on tee selection, you can stretch this par-72 course from 4,765 to 7,020 yards.

Tidewater is one of the Grand Strand's most expensive golf courses (greens fees are $145), but when you see it, you'll understand why. Hale Irwin, three-time U.S. Open champion, called Tidewater "one of the finest and most spectacular courses on the East Coast." This course is definitely not to be missed. Walking is permitted.

Myrtle Beach

Arcadian Shores Golf Club
(at Myrtle Beach Hilton) 701 Hilton Road, Myrtle Beach
(843) 449–5217

Rees Jones designed this course that opened in 1974. It features standard Bermuda-grass fairways and lush bent-grass greens. Surrounding the greens and sprinkled along the fairways, you'll find no fewer than 64 sand bunkers amid this 6,446-yard, par-72 track—just so you'll remember you're at the beach! A variety of picturesque natural lakes adds to the challenge. In 1993 the course was listed among *Golf Digest*'s "Top 50 Resort Courses." *GOLF Magazine*, too, has noted Arcadian Shores's outstanding design.

Greens fees are $83; no walking.

Arrowhead Country Club
1201 Burcale Road, Myrtle Beach
(843) 236–3243, (800) 236–3243

This Raymond Floyd–designed course continually garners rave reviews. Twenty-seven holes currently are open for play; each nine-hole course has its own name. The appropriately named Lakes Course meanders 3,119 yards through a pristine pine forest and features striking undulations in the fairways, numerous white sand bunkers, and abundant lakes. The 3,123-yard Cypress Course, in contrast, is set amid a beautiful stand of hardwoods, unique to the Myrtle Beach area. The Waterway Course, which opened in November 1995, stretches 3,060 yards through hardwoods to the Intracoastal Waterway and includes a liberal mix of mounds and lakes. The feel is similar to the Lakes and Cypress Courses but is enhanced by the waterway view. All three courses are par 72.

Arrowhead's design, masterminded in collaboration with Tom Jackson, offers the feeling of playing golf in the Carolina foothills. A beautiful clubhouse, large practice facility, and a well-stocked pro shop add to the quality of this course. Greens fees are $87; no walking.

Belle Terre Golf Course
4073 U.S. Highway 501, Myrtle Beach
(843) 236–8888, (800) 957–9786
www.belleterre.com

"Belle Terre" is French for "beautiful earth." The 701-acre golf complex was named from architect Rees Jones's description of the land when he called it, "the most beautiful earth I have ever seen." The 54-hole complex features the Championship Course and the Skins Course, which is a par-58 course.

As for the Championship Course, expect no gimmicks and no housing developments—just pure, unadulterated golf. This traditional par-72 layout measures 7,013 yards from the championship tees.

Belle Terre's 3,200-yard, 18-hole Skins Course is distinctive in that it offers the opportunity to either walk the course or ride along state-of-the-art concrete cart paths. Complete with 4 par 4s and 14 par 3s, this jewel packs a lot of great golf holes, including water hazards and bunkers, into its classic layout. Designed to be fast and fun—and to make golfers use every club in the bag—this course allows busy executives to squeeze in a game of golf even when schedules seem unyielding.

The greens fees for the Skins Course are $35 to walk, $42 including cart; for the Championship Course, $93, and walking is not allowed. The clubhouse features an outstanding pro shop and restaurant as well as complete dressing rooms with eight showers and lockers. Belle Terre hosts the Jimmy D'Angelo Senior Golf Classic (see the previous "Tournaments" section).

The Dunes Golf and Beach Club
9000 North Ocean Boulevard, Myrtle Beach
(843) 449–5914
www.dunesgolfandbeachclub.com

The Dunes Club is one of the area's oldest and best-loved courses. A par-72 Robert Trent Jones design, Dunes was only the second course built in Myrtle Beach—back in 1948. Recent renovations make it one of a handful of courses with PennLink bent-grass greens.

Through the years, the 6,174-yard course has achieved worldwide renown. The 13th hole, rated one of the best 18 holes in America as rated by *Sports Illustrated*, is particularly popular. *GOLF Magazine* included the 13th hole in its "100 Best Holes in America," and *Southern Living* named it one of the "18 Ultimate Golf Holes of the South," proclaiming:

> *If a single golf hole can be given credit for popularizing Myrtle Beach golf, this is it. Its crescent-shaped fairway winds around the former Singleton Swash, now a lake. A monstrous drive is advised, to be followed by a monstrous 3-wood, and you're still a strong iron from a round green. It's a par 6 for most of us.*

So few people have reached the 13th green in two shots that those who have are noted in The Dunes Club's history. The hole is known as Waterloo; don't let it be yours.

The rest of the course is fairly traditional, with wide-open fairways, deep bunkers, and elevated greens. The course's beauty is anything but ordinary. The Atlantic Ocean is the backdrop for several holes, while others wind around and through the marsh. Understandably, this course has a maturity that other Grand Strand courses envy.

Rest assured, when you wrap up at No. 18, you will have used every club in your bag. And you may be hungry. If so, drop by the grill for a quick bite or the elegant dining room for a formal dinner with a panoramic view of the beach.

The Dunes remains one of the Strand's most exclusive private clubs and is available to the guests of a few select member hotels: The Breakers, The Caravelle, The Caribbean, The Driftwood, The Dunes Village, and The South Wind. Tee times are scheduled through the hotels; greens fees are $160 if booked that way.

Grande Dunes, a spectacular golf course in North Myrtle Beach, is one of many memorable courses in the area. PHOTO: COURTESY OF LHWH

The Legends Complex
U.S. Highway 501, Myrtle Beach
(843) 236–9318, (800) 299–6187
www.legendsgolf.com

Since 1990 the Legends Complex has offered three distinctive courses along the Grand Strand: Parkland, Heathland, and Moorland. The newest, and arguably the best, of the three is Parkland. When members of the Carolinas PGA held a championship here, the pros pointed out similarities to New Jersey's highly acclaimed Pine Valley Course. Parkland requires the ability to draw or fade the ball, and accuracy is an absolute must. This complex is not a place for beginners. Don't try this par-72, 6,425-yard course unless you're up to the challenge; you'll only get frustrated and slow down play.

Heathland is one of the most unusual courses along the Grand Strand. It would seem more at home in the Scottish landscape, given its lack of trees, menacing winds, and rolling fairways. Pot bunkers appear more ominous than they are, so don't be intimidated. One of the more interesting holes requires golfers playing from the men's tees to drive straight over a grove of trees; the ladies' tees are positioned on the other side to bypass the grove. Upon opening, this Tom Doak design was immediately selected as one of *GOLF Magazine*'s "Top 10 New Courses." Par-72 Heathland measures 6,190 yards.

Rounding out The Legends Complex is Moorland, which features some of the most feared holes in Myrtle Beach; you'll either love or hate this 6,125-yard, par-72 P. B. Dye course. When Legends' owner Larry Young hired the renowned Dye to design the course, his instruction was simple: "Make it as hard as you can." And Dye did! It can be downright difficult in places, especially the short par 4 called "Hell's Half-Acre," although when the tees are placed forward, it isn't an impossible challenge even for average golfers. Ironically, the higher a player's handicap, the more the individual seems to enjoy Moorland.

The Legends has one of the most impressive clubhouses we've ever seen. It climbs skyward from the undulating green terrain like a Scottish castle. Inside, the tradition of elegance continues with an upscale pro shop, comfortable pub, and dining room. There is also a state-of-the-art driving range with greens and flags as targets, instead of the usual wide-open space with distance markers.

Greens fees are $109; no walking. You can also book tee times at The Heritage, Marsh Harbor, and Oyster Bay by calling the listed telephone numbers.

Man O' War
U.S. Highway 501, Myrtle Beach
(843) 236–8000
www.manowargolfcourse.com

World-famous architect Dan Maples definitely won the battle with this legendary new layout, created from the depths of—believe it or not—a 100-acre lake. This long-awaited 6,402-yard, par-72 course, which opened in January 1996, features a pair of back-to-back island greens (remember when one island green was im-

pressive?) plus an awesome island 9th hole that's surrounded by water from tee to green. Distinctive wide fairways, bent-grass greens, a practice range, and a unique marina clubhouse add intrigue to an already marvelous course. Greens fees are $91; no walking.

Myrtle Beach National
U.S. Highway 501, Myrtle Beach
(843) 448–2308, (800) 344–5590
www.mbn.com

You'll find an outstanding trio of impeccably conditioned courses at Myrtle Beach National, each bearing Arnold Palmer's special touch. (All three par-72 courses were designed by Frank Duane with input from the master himself.)

If you can take your pick, choose the North Course. One of the oldest and most requested on the beach, this course reopened in December 1995 following extensive renovations.

Enhancements to the 6,413-yard layout include reshaped and enlarged greens sodded with the new hybrid Crenshaw bent grass. Trees have been removed to open the course. Several of the Bermuda-grass fairways feature increased undulation, and bunkers and lakes have been dramatically reshaped. The famous par-3 No. 12, which includes sand traps shaped like the letters "SC," has bulkheads and a foot bridge. This is one of the most recognizable holes on the Strand.

If you can't get on the Kings North Course (greens fees are $109), don't despair; you'll enjoy playing the South Creek (6,089 yards; $60) or West (6,113 yards; $60) Courses, too. West is probably the easiest of the trio. All three offer gently rolling fairways, towering pines, and a few perilous lakes. Myrtle Beach National serves up the perfect opportunity for a multiround day. Walking is not allowed on any of the three courses here.

Pine Lakes International Country Club
Woodside Drive, Myrtle Beach
(843) 449–6459, (800) 446–6817
www.pinelakes.com

Affectionately hailed as "The Grand-daddy," this is quite literally where Myrtle Beach golf began. This course, the oldest in the area, was constructed in 1927 and was originally called the Ocean Forest Club. Course architect Robert White, first PGA president and a native of St. Andrews, Scotland, endowed the 6,176-yard, par-71 layout with a unique Scottish flair.

Today as always golfers are greeted by starters donning kilts, welcomed with hot chocolate or a cool mimosa on the first tee, refreshed with a cup of Lowcountry clam chowder near the turn, and comforted with a "crying towel" at the finish. The par-3 No. 7 is a favorite during the springtime when an ambrosia of azaleas are in full bloom. The effect is nothing short of breathtaking. "Granddaddy" can be tough, with bunkers flanking both sides of numerous fairways, but being a part of the legend is worth the heartache.

Greens fees are $110; no walking.

River Oaks Golf Plantation
831 River Oaks Drive, Myrtle Beach
(843) 236–2222, (800) 762–8813
www.riveroaksgolfplantation.com

Rated in the Top 5 on the Grand Strand by Golf Course Rankings of America, this course has something for everyone. You can't help but enjoy the 27 holes of undulating greens, mounded fairways, large lakes, and finger-shaped bunkers among the Bear (6,314 yards), Fox (6,345), and Otter (6,425) Courses, each of which is par 72. Greens fees are $75; no walking.

In addition, the natural beauty and abundance of wildlife make every golf experience a mini-adventure. A professional staff, excellent practice areas, and beautifully manicured fairways, greens, and tees have made River Oaks a popular choice. River Oaks offers the American Golf Academy to help you improve your game. The course's convenient location across from Fantasy Harbor is also appealing.

Waterway Hills
U.S. Highway 17 North, near Restaurant Row, Myrtle Beach
(843) 449–6488, (800) 344–5590
www.mbn.com

Robert Trent Jones, sometimes called the "Dean of Golf Architecture" (Donald Ross fans likely would argue that distinction), designed this gem of a course.

When you emerge from the enclosed tram that ferries you across the Intracoastal Waterway, you'll find 27 superbly maintained holes set amid woodland seclusion, with more than a few lakes for spice.

Traditional in design, Waterway Hills offers rolling terrain and a variety of strategically placed bunkers. The three beautiful courses—Oaks (3,080 yards), Lakes (3,001 yards), and Ravine (2,927 yards), which are all par 72 in pairs—are characterized by landscape challenges that make each course suitably named. The Oaks' 27 holes wind through trees, and its fairways are lined with large oaks. The Lakes features four holes with water hazards and meanders around five substantial bodies of water. And No. 3 at The Ravine is a par 5 with a harrowing hazard: a 60-foot chasm.

Greens fees are $72 for any 18-hole combination; walking is permitted in the afternoon.

Wild Wing Plantation
1000 Wild Wing Boulevard, off U.S. Highway 501, Myrtle Beach
(843) 347–9464, (800) 736–WING
www.wildwing.com

Wild Wing Plantation is a highly acclaimed, multicourse facility that delivers world-class golf in a world-class setting. With four award-winning courses that cover more than 1,050 acres, Wild Wing has gone to great lengths to preserve the property's natural beauty.

A special distinction at Wild Wing is computerized golf carts. These computers give exact yardages from the ball, wherever it lies, to the center of the green. The computers also offer helpful hints like "bunker on left" and "green slopes to the right." (Sounds a little like cheating, but you have to live with your conscience.)

The par-72 Falcon Course, a favorite among locals, was designed by Rees Jones. Measuring 6,697 yards and featuring mounding, narrow fairways, and small greens, the Falcon specializes in diversity and visual excitement. There are two lakes, each 20 acres or more, on this 18-hole course plus a 500-yard bunker that'll haunt your memory for a long time to come.

On opening, the *Sun News* named the Avocet "Best New Course in Myrtle Beach." Designed as a signature course by Jeff Brauer and two-time PGA Champion Larry Nelson, the Avocet will keep you seeing double; creative contouring presents a host of elevated tees and greens, double fairways, grass bunkers . . . even a double green. The par-72 course covers 6,614 yards. *Golf Digest* named the course a four-star winner in 2001.

The Wood Stork, Wild Wing's first course, has been open for play since 1991 and has had time to garner even more praise than her sister courses. *Southern Links* magazine called it "Best in the South" for course conditioning and presentation. *Golf Digest* listed Wood Stork in its "Top 100 Great Value Courses in America" and in its "Top 3 Value Courses in Myrtle Beach." Willard Byrd preserved the lay of the land, the natural vegetation, and water resources on this 6,598-yard, par-72 track. The first 8 holes play through pristine wetlands; the remaining 10 holes wind through the shade of a stately pine forest. *Golf Digest* gave this layout 4½ stars!

Byrd also designed the 6,310-yard, par-72 Hummingbird Course. Stands of love grass and other native grasses form the course's wetland perimeter. The lush Bermuda-grass fairways, strategically placed lakes, and an array of pot bunkers and waste areas create excitement and an undeniable challenge. It's little wonder the Hummingbird has racked up the same awards as her sister, the Wood Stork.

Greens fees are $129 for the Avocet, $111 for the Falcon, and $98 for Hummingbird and Wood Stork. Walking occasionally is allowed on the Falcon Course; call the number listed for details.

Don't miss WishBones, Wild Wing's restaurant, in the 33,000-square-foot clubhouse. ("Wows" are in order.) It's a favorite hangout for golfing and nongolfing locals alike. A 45,000-square-foot putting green, a practice green with a 138-yard practice hole, and a huge pro shop round out the amenities at this outstanding development.

The Witch
1900 SC Highway 544, East Conway
(843) 448–1300, (843) 347–2706
www.witchgolf.com

Just off the Strand, outside Myrtle Beach, The Witch serves up a spectacular 6,011-yard, 18-hole course that seems to rise from the earth like some kind of inexplicable magic; it's nothing short of beautiful. Dan Maples molded this par-71 course—complete with nearly 4,000 feet of bridges—from woodlands and mystery-shrouded wetlands without disturbing the enchanted nature of the setting.

Playing The Witch is like taking a nature walk through swamps, marshes, and forests, with pine, cypress, and live oak trees, deer, foxes, and ospreys. The par-4 No. 15 requires an uphill drive followed by a placement shot to a landing area surrounded by wetlands. The 9th green is an island surrounded by wetlands.

Deceptively beautiful, the hundreds of acres of wetlands are Mother Nature's perfect hazards. Challenge lurks 'round every bend of this unforgettable course. Greens fees are $91; walking is not permitted.

The Wizard
4601 Leeshire Boulevard, Myrtle Beach
(843) 236–9393
www.wizardgolfcourse.com

This Dan Maples design replicates an Old-World Scottish course, complete with a Celtic castlelike clubhouse that actually looks worn from age and battle.

Maples moved an astounding 800,000 cubic yards of earth to bring the flavor of mountain golf (complete with rock bridges) to our seaside paradise of Myrtle Beach. This miraculous transformation of landscape has delivered the Grand Strand a premier Scottish-links course. Players always comment on No. 13; its rolling hills on both sides of the fairway give the impression of the Scottish countryside. The par-71 Wizard measures 6,206 yards of Old-World charm and challenge.

Greens fees at The Wizard are $91; walking is not permitted.

South Strand

Blackmoor
SC Highway 707, Murrells Inlet
(866) 952–5555
www.blackmoor.com

Trite as it sounds, Blackmoor Golf Club at Longwood Plantation is unique. This beautiful design is Gary Player's first in the Myrtle Beach area. And what a debut! Player's experience as the world's most traveled golfer is evident in every hole.

Flanking the tea-colored waters of the Waccamaw River, Blackmoor's design takes full advantage of the naturally lovely terrain. No. 14 is a dogleg right with water on one side and sand traps lurking on either side of the fairway; gamblers go for the green, which is 285 yards from the tee. The 8th hole sports a split fairway, and thickets of trees flank both sides.

If you play from the left, you'll need a 347-yard drive; from the right side it's a straightaway (if you miss the trees!) 270 yards. *Golf for Women* magazine rated this course in the top 100 women-friendly courses in America. At 6,533 yards and par 72, Blackmoor is a challenge for everyone.

Greens fees are $98; no walking. This course is one of our favorites.

Caledonia Golf & Fish Club
King River Road, Pawleys Island
(843) 237–3675, (800) 483–6800
www.fishclub.com

Caledonia, constructed on the site of a former rice plantation along the black ribbon of the Waccamaw River, is dazzling. The oak-lined drive to the antebellum-style clubhouse sets the tone for the experience. It won't take you long to realize that no expense has been spared here. Even the bridges that connect one hole to another feature old Charleston brick. *Golf Digest* ranked Caledonia 31st of the top 75 upscale courses to play in 1997. From 1999 to 2001, Caledonia was the only Myrtle Beach–area course to be named among the Top 100 of "America's Best Modern Golf Courses."

Designed by up-and-coming architect Mike Strantz, this course is highlighted by huge oaks, shimmering natural lakes, broad expanses of long-abandoned rice fields, and more than an occasional glimpse of the area's rich wildlife. Caledonia Golf & Fish Club has been named one of the "Top 100 You Can Play" by *GOLF Magazine*, "Top 25 Courses in South Carolina" by *Golf Digest*, "Top 100 Modern Courses" by *Golfweek*, and "Top 100 Best Courses for Women" by *Golf for Women*.

Caledonia measures 6,104 yards and plays par 72. The picturesque 18th hole borders the plantation's old rice field, and it requires a precise tee shot that sets up a difficult second shot: a forced carry onto a green that is watched closely by the beautiful antebellum-style clubhouse.

Greens fees are $150; walking is permitted. When you've finished your round, take some time to hang around the clubhouse, a replica of an eighteenth-century Colonial plantation home. With its rocking chair–studded wraparound porch, old brick fireplace, soaring ceilings, and delicious food, it's a great place to reflect on your game . . . and watch the sun set. Don't miss this one.

Deer Track Golf Resort
1705 Platt Boulevard, Surfside Beach
(843) 650–2146, (800) 548–9186

Deer Track, a time-tested favorite, offers two 18-hole championship courses. The carefully crafted Toski Links—a 6,511-yard, par-72 layout—offers wide, tree-lined Bermuda-grass fairways, elevated bent-grass greens, and picturesque landscaping. The more modern par-71, 6,143-yard South Course features sculpted sand bunkers, dramatic bent-grass greens, and spectacular lakes and ponds. Greens fees at each course are $74, and walking is permitted in the afternoon.

Home of the Classic Swing Golf School, Deer Track has a natural turf driving range and putting greens. A bit of trivia for golf fanatics: Deer Track is owned and operated by Gary Schaal, former president of the PGA of America.

The Heritage Club
King River Road, Pawleys Island
(843) 237–3424, (800) 552–2660
www.legendsgolf.com

The Heritage Club's 6,565-yard, par-71 course, designed by Dan Maples, is built on the site of not one but two historic rice plantations. Here, overlooking the Waccamaw River, you'll feel a little like you've stepped onto the set of *Gone with the Wind*. The majestic tree-lined approach to the plantation-style clubhouse sets the stage. This grand avenue of 300-year-old oaks would impress even Rhett and Scarlett. In contrast to the historic atmosphere of the course, the Heritage also has a technological angle: A computerized yardage system accompanies all carts.

While you play, enjoy not only the captivating hole designs but also the breathtaking views of the scenic Waccamaw River, endless marshes, freshwater lakes, and towering oaks and magnolias. But take heed: The Heritage demands accuracy off the tee.

Greens fees are $110; no walking.

The pro shop, bar, and dining room are exquisitely appointed with rich wood paneling. Before your round, loosen up at the driving range or the practice putting green. Lessons are available.

Litchfield Country Club
U.S. Highway 17 South, Pawleys Island
(843) 237–3411, (800) 845–1897
www.litchfieldbeach.com

> ## Insiders' Tip
> The view from Greg Norman's Australian Grille in Barefoot Landing is Greg Norman's golf course (the "Norman Course") in Barefoot Resort. Only the Intracoastal Waterway separates the bent-grass greens from your salad bowl.

Litchfield, sculpted by Willard Byrd from yet another former rice plantation, was one of the first dozen courses built along the Grand Strand. Time has given the course a seldom-found maturity. Litchfield meanders lazily around an upscale neighborhood, and though technically private, the club allows a limited number of visiting golfers. The signature hole is No. 14, a straightaway par 4 with a stream to the right. Add two large traps and a preponderant tree to the left, and you have a murderously narrow hole.

For the most part, however, the 6,342-yard, par-72 course isn't noted for its difficulty, so your round here should provide a pleasant memory. Greens fees are $95; no walking.

The antebellum-style clubhouse, the tree-and-flower-lined approach—the entire ambiance of the club, in fact—will make you feel like you're "walking in high cotton." Actually you are. So why not continue the self-indulgence after your round? Stay for "supper" and sample the fare that locals love.

Pawleys Plantation
70 Tanglewood Drive, Pawleys Island
(843) 237–6200, (800) 367–9959
www.pawleysplantation.com

Pawleys Plantation is an upscale residential community of one- to three-bedroom

Pawleys Plantation winds through hardwood and pine forests and along the saltwater marsh that divides Pawleys Island from the mainland. PHOTO: COURTESY OF LHWH

villas surrounding a lush par-72 golf course, 6,127 yards set amongst coastal tidal plains, golden rice fields, and moss-draped oaks. It was the exquisite setting that ultimately drew Jack Nicklaus to Pawleys Plantation. "I have a particular fondness for the Lowcountry," says Nicklaus. "We used what's there without forcing or changing what Mother nature provided."

A few of the course highlights include the par-3, third hole, requiring a forced carry over water from tee to green; the par-5, fourteenth hole where you must negotiate the marsh off the tee shot to a split fairway just before the green; or the tremendous par-4, eighteenth hole that permits only a well-placed drive down a narrow fairway bordered by marsh, sprawling oaks, and pines. There's an elegant clubhouse with a grill room that's ideal for a little 19th-hole relaxation.

Greens fees are $125; no walking.

Prestwick Country Club
SC Highway 544, Surfside Beach
(843) 293–4100
www.prestwickcountryclub.com

Prestwick, a semiprivate course, is another jewel designed by Pete and P. B. Dye. A 20-acre lake created for the course separates the 9th and 18th holes in dramatic fashion and highlights the natural beauty of this masterful 6,347-yard, par-72 layout. An assortment of winding streams and ponds bring water directly into play on 8 of the course's 18 holes. Each hole has six different sets of tees to challenge any skill level. Dye-inspired features abound: undulating greens, seemingly bottomless pot bunkers, and railroad ties galore.

Greens fees are $110. Only members can walk this course during late afternoon.

TPC Myrtle Beach
U.S. Highway 17 Bypass, Murrells Inlet
(843) 357–3399
www.tpc.com

The opening of this course in the fall of 1998 had significant impact in the world of Myrtle Beach and golf everywhere. The course was number 100 for the Grand Strand, strengthening our position as the "Golf Capital of the World." Additionally, the course is a Tournament Players Club (TPC) endeavor, which means it was designed with PGA players in mind. The design incorporates easy spectator movement and stadium-style seating at key holes.

Recently chosen for a second consecutive year as "100 Top Golf Shops in America" by *Golf World Business*, the TPC continues to set the standard for customer service, inventive retailing, and business performance in the Myrtle Beach area. Also recently recognized by *Golf Week* magazine as among the Top Ten Courses in South Carolina, the TPC of Myrtle Beach has quickly become one of the most celebrated courses in the TPC Network, the PGA Tour's golf-course management division.

TPC is a 7,014 yard, par-72, 18-hole course. Tom Fazio and Tom Marzolf, of Fazio Golf Designers, created the course, complete with a grand clubhouse, nine lakes (one on the driving range) and L-39 bent-grass greens (some as large as 6,500 feet). The culmination of all their work is softly sculpted ridges that create unobtrusive promontories. Peripheral areas around the greens have been "feathered up" to blend in the spectator locations. The finishing hole is a par 5 with a winding "Wadkin's Creek" and a large lake, culminating at a two-tiered green near the 20,000-square-foot clubhouse. The course has five sets of tees with yardages ranging from just under 7,000 to around 5,100.

On days when the pros aren't playing, the greens fees are $165 including cart, and metal spike alternatives are encouraged.

The Tradition Club
U.S. Highway 17 South, Pawleys Island
(843) 237–5041, (877) 599–0888

The Tradition Club opened to accolades in fall 1995. Adjacent to the upscale Willbrook community, The Tradition Club boasts a legendary, time-tested course (6,508 yards, par 72) with the requisite classic features: large tees, wide fairways, and huge, well-placed greens. Five sets of tees serve golfers of all skill levels.

Course architect Ron Garl has designed courses that have hosted PGA tour events and have been honored by *Golf Digest* and *GOLF Magazine* as tops in their class. More of Garl's courses have been named to Florida's top-50 list than any other architect's. In addition, The Tradition is rated in the top 75 women-friendly courses by *Golf for Women*. Every indication is that The Tradition lives up to—even surpasses—Garl's own standard of excellence.

Greens fees are $103; no walking.

The Tradition features the most elaborate practice area anywhere along the Strand. It includes a 43,000-square-foot, clover-shaped putting green with four practice locations. The 18th green is guarded by an 8,000-square-foot clubhouse decorated with Italian marble, leather upholstery, imported designer furniture, and original European artwork. The Tradition is a must-see—certainly among the area's finest courses.

True Blue Golf Club
King's River Road, Pawleys Island
(843) 235–0900, (888) 483–6801

True Blue is Caledonia's sister course, strategically located across the street. Built on the acreage of a nineteenth-century indigo and rice plantation by the same name, this course features bent-grass greens and an 18-acre practice facility with a learning center.

All the appeal of True Blue comes from the preservation of the abundant nature in the Lowcountry: native grasses such as field rye, natural elevations, and sandy areas including waste bunkers. On the 14th hole, the tee box is nearly 50 feet above the green.

Greens fees are $130 for True Blue's 6,958 yards at a par 72. Walking is permitted.

Wachesaw Plantation East
U.S. Highway 17 Bypass, Murrells Inlet
(843) 357–2090, (888) 922–0027

This former rice plantation is about to take off as one of the centers of golfing on the Strand; it is directly adjacent to the new PGA TPC course that opened in November 1998.

Architect Clyde Johnston accented the course's traditional Scottish-links design with wetlands and lakes amid rolling woods. This 6,297-yard, par-72 course features five sets of tees for golfers of all abilities.

Greens fees are $102; no walking.

Wedgefield Plantation
129 Clubhouse Lane, Georgetown
(843) 546–8587

Another once-upon-a-time rice plantation, this beautiful course is on the very southern tip of the Grand Strand in historic Georgetown. Cited by *Golf Week* magazine as one of the top 50 golf courses in South Carolina, this course features fairways winding through live oaks and patches of wildflowers; keep an eye out for the abundant wildlife. Practice up for the 14th hole, where two precise shots are required to carry the lakes. Wedgefield's course measures 6,325 yards (par 72).

Greens fees are $55; no walking. This is a South Carolina golfing experience that you really should take in on your southern leg of Strand play.

Wicked Stick
U.S. Highway 17 Bypass, Surfside Beach
(843) 215–2500, (800) 79–STICK
www.wickedstick.com

With his first-ever signature course in the area, John Daly has brought his "grip it, rip it" style to the Grand Strand. Along with architect Clyde Johnston, Daly has created a stunning links-style course patterned after famed Scottish designs. Wide-open spaces feature expansive "dune fields," large sand waste areas with gorselike vegetation, deep (read bottomless) pot bunkers, and strategically placed water hazards. This par-72 course measures 6,080 yards (more than 7,000 yards from the championship tees!).

"Our main goal was to design and build a course that is fun for the average golfer to play," said Gary Schaal, former PGA president and a member of the partnership that owns the course. "Together, John and Clyde have mapped out a course that looks intimidating but encourages golfers to 'grip it and rip it.'"

Greens fees are $87. Golfers can walk in late afternoon if the course isn't too busy.

Willbrook Plantation Golf Club
U.S. Highway 17 South, Pawleys Island
(843) 237–4900, (800) 344–5590

Dan Maples carved Willbrook Plantation from the fertile forests and wetlands of two historic rice plantations. He calls the course "one of my best" . . . quite a statement considering his résumé. The course's scenery, design, and inherent challenge are as captivating as its history. In fact flora and fauna are so abundant here, the course is registered with the Audubon Society to preserve its wetlands and wildlife.

The ruins of an old plantation home are visible from No. 5, and historic markers along the course signify a slave cemetery near the 8th hole as well as an old slave settlement near the 4th green. You don't have to play great to score well; Willbrook is easy in some spots and tough in others, making it an ideal 6,124-yard, par-72 course for golfers of mixed abilities.

Greens fees are $115; no walking.

Miniature Golf

Driving to and from the more "serious" courses in the Grand Strand, you'll be sure to notice the abundance of colorful, special-effect-filled miniature golf courses. Although most of them are better suited to children, Spring Breakers, and those who haven't developed their power drive yet, there are a few that are worth the traditional golf enthusiast's attention, either to test your skill or to give you another shot at the elusive purse.

North Strand

Hawaiian Rumble Miniature Golf
33rd Avenue South, U.S. Highway 17, North Myrtle Beach
(843) 272–7812
www.hawaiianrumble.com

Ranked by *GOLF Magazine* as the No. 1 miniature golf course in the United States, Hawaiian Rumble offers a challenging gambit of shots in a lush and expertly landscaped setting of tropical palms, hibiscus, and other plants. The course circles and climbs up around a rumbling volcano, leis in almost every color are handed out to the players, and gentle Hawaiian music plays in the background. Hawaiian Rumble also sponsors the Masters Putting Championship, with a purse of $20,000—definitely worth a shot!

Golf Driving Ranges
Myrtle Beach

Cane Patch
72nd Avenue North, Myrtle Beach
(843) 449–2732
www.mbeachkeyattractions.com

Practice your swing year-round starting at 8:00 A.M. The range is lighted for night-time practice during summer. All you need is a club and putter, both of which are furnished. Buckets are $4.50 for 45 golf balls, $5.50 for 75, and $8.50 for 115.

Harbour View Golf Complex
901 Highway 17 North, Little River
(843) 249–9117
www.harbourviewgolfcomplex.com

The Harbour View Golf Complex offers great golf for the whole family. The entire facility is open year-round, and it's lighted for evening enjoyment. The driving range includes mat- and turf-hitting areas, target greens, sand bunkers, chipping areas, and putting green. Small, medium, and large buckets are sold for $4.00, $6.00, and $8.00 respectively.

South Strand

Harbor Light
701 U.S. Highway 17 North, Surfside Beach
(843) 238–8978

Half the tees at Harbor Light are covered. Buckets are $6.00 for about 75 golf balls. In springtime the range is lighted for night practice. During the summer season the range is open 8:00 A.M. to 11:00 P.M.; it closes earlier in the winter.

Par-3 Courses
Myrtle Beach

Cane Patch
72nd Avenue North, Myrtle Beach
(843) 449–6085

From March through Labor Day, nine holes cost $8.00 and 18 holes, $12.00. Those prices fall to $6.50 and $9.50, respectively, off-season. The yardages at the three nine-hole courses are 698, 672, and 653. Locals are always privy to discount

Insiders' Tip
A mulligan is a second shot, which mysteriously leaves no mark on a scorecard.

passes at Cane Patch. This course also organizes leagues that play members of other par-3 courses in town.

South Strand

Tupelo Bay Golf Center
1800 Highway 17 South, Garden City
(843) 215–7888, (800) 657–2680
www.tupelobay.com

If you're looking for a family-flavored golf course in the Surfside/Garden City area, Tupelo Bay Golf Center is the place for you. In addition to the par-3 golf course, Tupelo Bay offers an 18-hole Executive Golf Course, an award-winning driving range, golf lessons, golf-club rentals, and golf packages. The par-3 course is great fun for the entire family. It also provides a great short-game workout with holes ranging from 73 to 105 yards, and the course is lighted for evening play.

Club rental (four clubs and bag) is available for $1.00, and a pull cart is available for $2.00. The adult rate for nine holes is $9.00. Eighteen holes is $14. Kids age 12 and younger can play 9 holes for $6.00 and 18 holes for $10.00. Tupelo Bay is open from 7:00 A.M. to 11:00 P.M.

Fishing

We could have named this chapter "Everything you always wanted to know about fishing but didn't know who to ask." The first attempt at this subject got us as snarled up as fishing line gone haywire. Luckily, one of us had just the father-in-law to set us straight.

He loves to fish. In fact at least one day of his annual Myrtle Beach vacation is devoted to wetting a line. According to him most anglers want to know what species they can expect to find in which waters, what tackle to bring along, and where to find the fish at different times of the year.

We took his advice seriously. As a result we think this chapter should answer the who, what, where, when, and, often, the why questions about fishing along the Grand Strand. If you don't find the answers to your questions here, the South Carolina Department of Natural Resources, Marine Resources Division, in Charleston, is a wonderful resource; call (843) 762–5000 or visit them on-line at www.dnr.state.sc.us.

Surf Fishing

Surf fishing is the most "friendly" form of the sport, since you only need to bring a rod and reel to the edge of the Atlantic Ocean. With year-round access to the beach, common catches from the surf—which can be plentiful—include bluefish, flounder, whiting, spot, pompano, and channel bass. With a simple tackle rig and a bucket for bait and catch in hand, surf anglers can be spotted along the coastline at just about any time of the year. But if you're serious about snagging dinner for the family, the less humid fall months are best for this type of fishing, especially when the sea is relatively calm.

Experienced surf casters suggest using fresh shrimp, minnows, or whiting (not more than 3 inches long) as bait. For best results consult tide tables and hit the beach at low tide. Look along the shoreline for washed-out areas that resemble creek beds in the sand leading out to the ocean's breakers. If you can discern a slough, pool, or drop-off, cast into that area; it's often 2 feet or more deeper than the surrounding water. Now comes the fun part. . . . Just sit back, watch, and wait for the big bite.

Surfcasting for Pompano and Whiting

The delicate, fine-tasting pompano is relatively abundant during late summer. But to catch them you must be accurate in your fishing technique. Pompano frequent the surf zone, right where the waves break in "suds" on the beach. There they feast on tiny mole crabs before the crustaceans have time to burrow into the sand. Pompano anglers use a small #1 or #2 hook tied directly to the line (8-pound test is recommended)—no leader necessary. Flip the baited hook into the breakwater and allow it to drift with the current. A split shot (1/16- or 1/32-ounce) attached about 12 to 18 inches above the hook will keep it slightly down in the water column as it drifts.

Whiting, which feed on small worms, crabs, and shrimp, can be caught from the surf during the summer. Fish the areas around groins, sloughs, and cuts along open beaches. A two-leader rig with #1 or 1/0 hooks, baited with cut shrimp and fished on the incoming tide, frequently yields good results.

From boat, pier, or surf, the Grand Strand is a fisherman's delight. PHOTO: COURTESY OF MYRTLE BEACH AREA CHAMBER OF COMMERCE

Both pompano and whiting generally weigh less than a pound and don't put up much of a fight, but they are certainly excellent table fare.

Inshore Fishing

Nothing will acquaint you as graciously with the pulse, sounds, and smells of Lowcountry life along the Grand Strand as fishing its coastal waters, estuaries, and salt marshes. The slow-moving, dark, acrid waters offer up sweet mysteries of lively marine life for the avid angler. At the mercy of tidal change, inland waters can cover everything at high tide, then unmask an incredibly bustling sea-life community at low ebb.

Fishing inland waters provides an opportunity to snag crevalle jack, Florida pompano, sheeps-head, Southern flounder, black drum, spotted sea trout, king mackerel, Spanish mackerel, red drum,

and whiting. Inshore-fishing action usually slows with the heat and mosquitoes of summer—especially compared with spring and fall. But if you're so inclined, summer fishing can be thrilling too, as coastal waters teem with bait fish and shrimp—favorite meals for game fish.

Making the Most of Inshore Fishing

If spotted sea trout is your catch of choice, look in lower parts of estuaries during the summer and around oyster bars, rocks, and pilings in spring and fall, when tidal currents are running strong. Cooler periods of the year will be your best bet, though, as the fish form larger schools. When luring the sea trout around areas with a structure, fish your bait either on the bottom, with a slip sinker placed above a 20-pound-test monofilament leader attached to a 1/0 or 2/0 hook, or from a float rig. The recreational size limit for the sea trout is 13 inches, and only 10 can be kept per day in aggregate.

During July juvenile red drum leave shallow creeks and form schools in the main estuaries. They're easy to catch en masse at this time of year but are often smaller than the allowable minimum size in South Carolina—14 inches. Late summer is the time to catch adult drum (often between 20 and 30 pounds) around jetties and at the mouths of bays and sounds. Their favorite bait seems to be live menhaden and finger mullet bottom-fished with fish-finder rigs. Use a smaller (4/0) hook for live bait, so it can swim more naturally in the current. Five red drum a day is the legal keeper limit.

South Carolina fishing laws dictate that gigging red drum or spotted sea trout is prohibited from December through February. However, on a calm, hot summer's eve, while estuary waters are clear on an early incoming tide, flounder gigging can yield a hearty harvest. Shallow-draft boats are the best for this type of flounder

hunting; one person polls the boat while another stands on the bow and spears any flounder seen on the bottom.

Summer trolling for flounder around inlets is a favorite Grand Strand sport. Troll live bait, such as mud minnows, slowly along the bottom or adjacent to rock jetties. Flounder must be at least 12 inches long to keep, and 20 per day is an angler's limit.

Sheepshead like to hang out around jetties, piers, and bridge pilings during summer months. They're very fussy eaters and usually will not bite anything other than the favored fiddler crab or live shrimp. Successful sheepshead anglers suggest a 1/4- or 3/8-ounce split shot crimped to a 20-pound-test monofilament leader. Appropriate hook sizes for sheepshead are #1, 1/0, or 2/0.

Black drum are the bottom-feeding cousins of the red drum; they do not consume other fish and prefer to be around rocks, pilings, and piers. Whether 5 pounds or 40, the black drum cannot resist a large piece of blue crab. A tried-and-

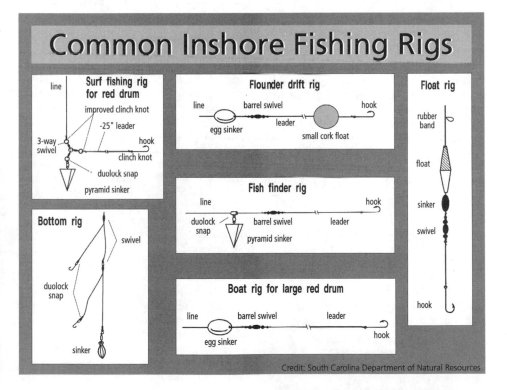

Credit: South Carolina Department of Natural Resources

true method of luring this fish is to pull the top shell from the crab and cut the meat into quarters. Thread a large piece onto a 5/0 to 9/0 hook tied onto a swivel with a 50-pound-test monofilament leader. Above the leader, which should be 18- to 24-inches long, attach a 2- to 3-ounce slip sinker to get the bait to the bottom. Black drum connoisseurs insist that a fish heavier than 15 pounds will have coarse flesh and be less tasty.

Although they don't make spectacular runs like a king mackerel or perform graceful jumps like the tarpon, the crevalle jack is considered one of the toughest fish you'll encounter around these parts. At night or at dusk, jacks lurk around rips during ebb tide, feeding on their favorite fish. Experienced anglers use a 20-pound-test line on a large-capacity reel and a moderately stout rod. Best baits for jacks are surface-popping plugs, such as the Striper Swiper, or swimming plugs by Redfin, Rebel, or Rapala. Sought after mostly for sport, jacks are not good eating and should be released.

Offshore Fishing

From sea bass hugging underwater reefs to blue marlin racing through the Gulf Stream, the Grand Strand is a point of departure for a variety of offshore fishing opportunities.

During the summer, sometimes following four or five consecutive days of flat, calm conditions, many of the area's blue-water fish move to within 15 miles of the coast. Of course in early spring, you'll have to travel by boat about 50 miles offshore to catch the same fish.

Offshore marine fishes in these waters include the blue marlin, yellowfin tuna, great barracuda, crevalle jack, wahoo, dolphin (the fish, not "Flipper"), king mackerel, little tunny, Spanish mackerel, white marlin, amberjack, and sailfish. Downriggers and planers are key elements to a successful offshore trip during the summer, especially during the steamy days of July and August. Summer heat polarizes much of the feeding activity of these fish into early morning and late afternoon, as they keep to deeper, cooler waters.

Avid offshore anglers continually argue the question of what bait is best for these fish. Natural baits offer real food—so if the fish strikes short, it will more than likely return for another nibble. On the other hand, artificial lures can be trolled faster, allowing more area to be fished, and don't require extra time to rig the bait.

Making the Most of Offshore Fishing

Blue- and white-marlin fishing is most productive in ocean depths of 300 to 1,200 feet during summer months and around 80 feet in cooler weather. Successful fishing for marlin usually calls for large bait—mullet, ballyhoo, ladyfish, and Spanish mackerel—rigged to skip across the surface or to swim. The bait often is dressed with brightly colored plastic skirts or attached to artificial lures.

Many blue marlin in local waters are in the 125- to 200-pound range—typically below the 99-inch minimum fork length for this species.

Sailfish reach peak abundance during July and August and may be caught only 10 miles off the beach, but many are below the legal minimum 63-inch fork length. Weed lines, current rips, and natural reefs in 120 to 300 feet of water are the best areas for these prized game fish. Averaging 35 to 45 pounds, sails prefer smaller baits than their larger marlin cousins. Effective trolling for sails requires small- to medium-size ballyhoo and mullet with a small artificial lure or colored skirt placed

Insiders' Tip

It's customary to tip a guide or charter mate about the same as you would tip a server in a restaurant—between 15 to 20 percent of your total bill.

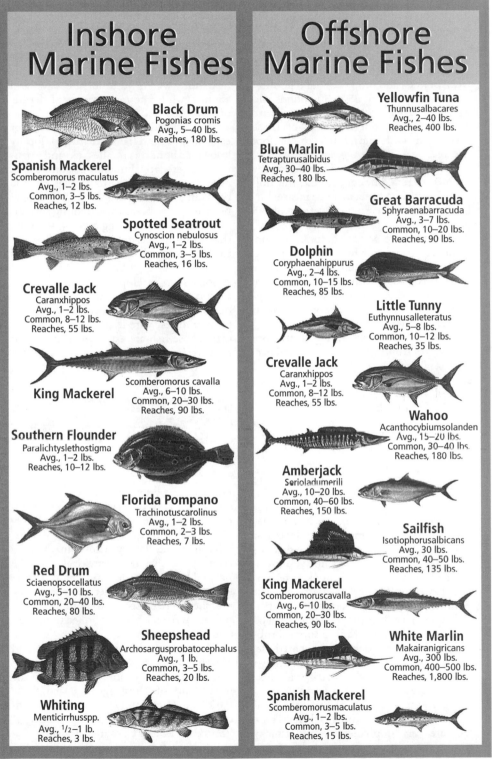

Inshore Marine Fishes

Black Drum
Pogonias cromis
Avg., 5–40 lbs.
Reaches, 180 lbs.

Spanish Mackerel
Scomberomorus maculatus
Avg., 1–2 lbs.
Common, 3–5 lbs.
Reaches, 12 lbs.

Spotted Seatrout
Cynoscion nebulosus
Avg., 1–2 lbs.
Common, 3–5 lbs.
Reaches, 16 lbs.

Crevalle Jack
Caranxhippos
Avg., 1–2 lbs.
Common, 8–12 lbs.
Reaches, 55 lbs.

King Mackerel
Scomberomorus cavalla
Avg., 6–10 lbs.
Common, 20–30 lbs.
Reaches, 90 lbs.

Southern Flounder
Paralichtyslethostigma
Avg., 1–2 lbs.
Reaches, 10–12 lbs.

Florida Pompano
Trachinotuscarolinus
Avg., 1–2 lbs.
Common, 2–3 lbs.
Reaches, 7 lbs.

Red Drum
Sciaenopsocellatus
Avg., 5–10 lbs.
Common, 20–40 lbs.
Reaches, 80 lbs.

Sheepshead
Archosargusprobatocephalus
Avg., 1 lb.
Common, 3–5 lbs.
Reaches, 20 lbs.

Whiting
Menticirrhusspp.
Avg., 1/2–1 lb.
Reaches, 3 lbs.

Offshore Marine Fishes

Yellowfin Tuna
Thunnusalbacares
Avg., 2–40 lbs.
Reaches, 400 lbs.

Blue Marlin
Tetrapturusalbidus
Avg., 30–40 lbs.
Reaches, 180 lbs.

Great Barracuda
Sphyraenabarracuda
Avg., 3–7 lbs.
Common, 10–20 lbs.
Reaches, 90 lbs.

Dolphin
Coryphaenahippurus
Avg., 2–4 lbs.
Common, 10–15 lbs.
Reaches, 85 lbs.

Little Tunny
Euthynnusalleteratus
Avg., 5–8 lbs.
Common, 10–12 lbs.
Reaches, 35 lbs.

Crevalle Jack
Caranxhippos
Avg., 1–2 lbs.
Common, 8–12 lbs.
Reaches, 55 lbs.

Wahoo
Acanthocybiumsolanden
Avg., 15–20 lbs.
Common, 30–40 lbs.
Reaches, 180 lbs.

Amberjack
Serioladumerili
Avg., 10–20 lbs.
Common, 40–60 lbs.
Reaches, 150 lbs.

Sailfish
Isotiophorusalbicans
Avg., 30 lbs.
Common, 40–50 lbs.
Reaches, 135 lbs.

King Mackerel
Scomberomoruscavalla
Avg., 6–10 lbs.
Common, 20–30 lbs.
Reaches, 90 lbs.

White Marlin
Makairanigricans
Avg., 300 lbs.
Common, 400–500 lbs.
Reaches, 1,800 lbs.

Spanish Mackerel
Scomberomorusmaculatus
Avg., 1–2 lbs.
Common, 3–5 lbs.
Reaches, 15 lbs.

Credit: South Carolina Department of Natural Resources

ahead of the bait. Sails have even been caught on spoons and plugs intended for king mackerel.

As summer progresses, the size of both dolphin and wahoo gradually declines. Dolphin, for instance, start summer at 10 to 20 pounds and drop to about 8 pounds, while wahoo start at 35 to 50 pounds and weigh in around 20 pounds by season's end. The best concentrations of these species can be found at 180- to 600-foot depths.

The same typically holds true for the yellowfin tuna, though, unlike the dolphin and wahoo, tuna increase in size during the summer to an average of 45 pounds.

Effective live bait for dolphin, wahoo, or tuna includes ballyhoo or mullet rigged with a small- to medium-size artificial lure or colored skirt. Although all baits are usually fished on the surface from outriggers, it is wise to run at least one line 60 to 70 feet deep via a downrigger.

For an action-packed day of offshore fishing, try trolling for amberjack and barracuda along artificial reefs and coastal shipwrecks. Tenacious fighters, these fish go out of their way to test an angler's equipment and skills.

Most anglers fish for amberjack with a 50-pound-class outfit, but for the ultimate experience, challenge the 'jack with 20- or 30-pound-test line. Wire leader is mandatory for barracuda (whose teeth are razor sharp), while heavy, 100- to 150-pound-test monofilament works well for the 'jacks. Large live baits, such as mullet up to 14 inches and menhaden, floated or free-lined down current, often are successful. Depending on the test line you use, a 5/0 to 8/0 extra strength hook is recommended—stainless steel, please, since most of these fish are released, not eaten. Artificial lures have also proven effective: The 'jack and 'cuda are partial to surgical rubber tubing colored dark green, chartreuse, and hot pink. They have also been known to get excited enough to strike at noisy surface lures.

Artificial and natural reefs are focal points for schools of king mackerel. These fish are very unpredictable and finicky during the summer months and frustrate anglers into wild goose chases with every bait and lure known. The only agreed-upon technique for summer king mackerel fishing is to pull in the rod and reel by 10:00 A.M., when macks seem to disappear. The larger female mackerel prefers nearshore waters just outside bays and sounds, while the males frequent depths of 60 to 120 feet.

Considered great game fish, but not esteemed as food fish, little tunny (locally known as bonito), crevalle jack, and Spanish mackerel are abundant in summer 15 miles from shore. One to 5 miles outside bays and sounds and around artificial reefs are prime areas for schooling fish. To determine prime casting areas, just locate the wheeling and diving terns feeding on the bait fish pushed to the surface by these voracious feeders. Small silver or gold spoons such as Hopkins, Clark, Captain Action, and Tony Accetta are the most productive; try fishing them on a 20-inch, 60-pound-test wire leader to prevent cutoffs. These fish are extremely fast, so you must retrieve your lure as quickly as possible or troll at a rapid pace.

The Lowcountry Tradition of Shellfishing

Oysters and Clams

Harvesting oysters and clams has been part of the Lowcountry culture for generations. From Hogg Inlet behind Cherry Grove Beach to the salt marshes of Murrells Inlet and Pawleys Creek, many Lowcountry families fed themselves with the natural bounty of shellfish. That all came to an end in 1987 when nearly all the marshes were closed to the public due to pollution from a bacteria linked to human and animal waste.

Today portions of Murrells Inlet and North Inlet are open in Georgetown County, and only one location, on the north end of Huntington Beach State Park (U.S. Highway 17), is accessible without a boat. Oyster and clam gathering is limited to South Carolina residents who have a bona fide saltwater fishing license.

South Carolinians can harvest only a reasonable amount of the shellfish—enough for personal consumption. In these authorized harvesting areas, no one can disturb oyster or clam beds between May 15 and September 1 of any year. The harvest limit is two bushels of oysters, a half bushel while wading in the water.

For specific questions and current shellfish bed closings, the local Department of Health and Environmental Control is a great resource; call (843) 448-1902.

Shrimping

If you like working with nets, you can try your hand at snaring shrimp, America's most popular seafood. The coastal marsh creeks are home to two penaeid shrimp species brown shrimp (*Penaeus aztecus*) and white shrimp (*Penaeus setiferus*). As shrimp become larger, they leave the brackish waters and move gradually toward the higher salinity of the ocean. Once they've reached about 4 inches in length, they inhabit coastal rivers and spend some time maturing, then move into the lower reaches of sounds, bays, and river mouths.

Recreational harvest of brown shrimp by cast nets and seines usually starts in early June in the tidal creeks. White shrimp initially are caught in these same creeks in late July or early August but disappear completely by late October. Harvesting by drop nets from docks and seawalls is most popular during the fall when larger white shrimp are moving seaward

Seines for shrimping cannot exceed 40 feet in length, and webbing must be a half-inch-square mesh or larger for nylon nets. Law also prohibits the blockage of more than one-half the width of any slough, creek, or other water-way on any tidal stage. Seines must be pulled by hand, not by any engine-powered boat or staked to poles. The most effective way to pull a seine is with the falling tide and along banks or sandbars, which provide areas to haul nets ashore and remove the shrimp. Less expensive and cumbersome than seines, cast nets are used more often for shrimping. Cast nets are also devoid of re-

Busy shrimp boats in Little River. PHOTO: LISA TOMER RENTZ

strictions on lengths or mesh sizes. Casting is popular in creeks with a mud bottom during low tide. Deeper areas of 3 or 4 feet or more often produce larger shrimp during the day, since the shrimp avoid light. A cast net can be used from a boat, creek bank, pier, or even while wading in the water. The lawful harvest of shrimp by cast net is limited to 60 days between September 1 and November 15.

Drop nets can be fished from bridges, docks, or seawalls and are almost exclusively used at night. Unlike the other meshed methods, drop nets require bait, and the best, we're told, is smoked herring. Drop netting typically doesn't yield large quantities of shrimp, but it sure is enjoyable and relaxing.

The legal daily limit for shrimp is 48 quarts (heads on) or 29 quarts (heads off) per boat or seining party.

Crabbing

Despite its fearsome appearance and aggressive nature, the blue crab is greatly cherished in the Lowcountry. Many gourmets prefer the blue crab's sweet meat to all other locally caught seafood.

Males of the species can be distinguished from females by the shape of the abdomen. The male has a T-shape abdomen, held tightly against the body until maturity, when it loosens. The immature female has a triangle-shaped abdomen that is sealed against the body, becoming rounded and loose after the final molt. Large males (often called "Jimmies") usually have brilliant blue claws and legs. Mature females or "sooks" show off the bright-orange tips on their claws.

South Carolina law allows individuals to fish two crab pots without a license if they are properly marked with floats bearing the owner's name. Be careful not to leave the pot in an area that exposes it and crabs at low tide, and check pots twice a day for the best yield. However, you must return a crab to the water if its point-to-point width is less than 5 inches or it is a female carrying an egg mass (sponge). Drop nets and collapsible traps (usually baited with herring) can be fished from docks and bridges. Or you can give "dipping" a try. Dipping involves a long-handled dip net, several yards of string, and a chicken neck or fish head for bait. Tie the bait to the string and throw out into the water. Once you feel a tug, pull the bait and crab close enough to quickly dip the crustacean from the water into a waiting bucket. Always keep crabs alive, cool, and dry prior to cooking. A refrigerator or cooler with a small amount of ice is the best storage method. Never put crabs in a container of water; they will die quickly from lack of oxygen.

Crabs become inactive in winter when water temperatures fall below 50 to 55 degrees. The best time of the year to harvest large, heavy crabs is usually from October through December. Mature females are typically found near the ocean, while large males are most common in rivers and creeks.

Fishing Charters

When casting into the world of deep-sea fishing, we feel the need to give you fair warning. If you have never been on an offshore fishing trip, take medication to relieve seasickness the night before you leave. Even some experienced sailors have been found writhing around the deck, begging for a quick and merciful death. Once a deep-sea fishing vessel is out on an excursion, it will not turn back to shore early for the sake of one or two heaving passengers. Most local pharmacies carry motion-sickness pills—available over the counter—as well as patches that affix behind the ear.

That said, get ready for some exhilarating fishing opportunities, both inshore and in the Gulf Stream. The following charters are good bets.

North Strand

Blackfish Charter Boat
Waterfront Drive, Little River
(843) 249–1379

With more than 40 years of experience fishing local waters, Captain Larry Long will take a party of six people on fishing excursions from spring through fall, specifically April through mid-November.

Insiders' Tip

If you're going to be fishing without a local captain or guide, check on current regulations before embarking on your fishing trip. Fines for illegal fish can be substantial.

Half- and full-day trips can be arranged, including shark fishing and trolling the Gulf Stream. As is typical for fishing charters, bait and tackle are included; food and drink are not. Trips on *The Blackfish* cost $450 for a half day and $700 for the whole day. A Gulf Stream adventure is $1,100 for approximately 12 hours. Bottom fishing, trolling, or shark fishing is available on each trip.

Ten-year-old Stephen Manser Jr. from Lake Norman, North Carolina, had the fishing trip of a lifetime aboard Long's *Blackfish* in July 1997. The "tug" on young Stephen's line turned out to be a 12-foot-long, 1,200-pound gray tiger shark that took everyone on the boat three hours to reel in.

Little River Fishing Fleet
4495 Minneola Avenue, Little River
(843) 249–1100
www.littleriverfleet.com

The Little River Fishing Fleet delivers fishing at its finest. Captain Danny Juel has 25 years experience as a commercial-fishing captain, head-boat captain, and private-charter captain. He has established a reputation for safe fishing trips and providing customers with the finest fishing expertise available for any type of fishing. Captain Juel's knowledge of the ocean and the best fishing grounds is impressive. Captain Bruce McFarland has 20 years experience as a boat captain, and his fishing knowledge extends from the Gulf of Mexico, around Florida, and up the Eastern seaboard.

Pride of the Carolina is a 90-foot aluminum all-purpose fishing boat, with an air-conditioned cabin, state-of-the-art fish-finding equipment, a full galley, clean rest rooms, and first-class mates. Half-day fishing and night fishing trips are $30 for adults and $25 for children ages 12 and younger. For Gulf Stream fishing, the cost is $70 for adults and $60 for children. Personal coolers are not permitted, but food, soft drinks, and beer are available on the boat.

The *Sundancer*, a 40-foot fiberglass boat, is fully equipped with state-of-the-

Deep-sea fishing is a favorite activity among those who visit the Grand Strand. PHOTO: COURTESY OF CAPTAIN DICK'S MARINA

art fish-finding electronics. This boat carries up to 15 people for bottom fishing and is also available for private full- and half-day charters—all the way to the Gulf Stream, if you like. Prices vary depending on season and number of people onboard. Call ahead to ask questions.

Bait and tackle (rod and reel) are supplied on all trips, and all necessary licenses are held by the Little River Fleet. Schedules may vary due to private charters, weather, or season, so be sure to call ahead.

South Carolina Saltwater Game-fish Records Caught in Grand Strand Waters

Common Name (AFS)—Weight (lbs.-oz.); Port, Year; Angler, Hometown

Amberjack—99-11; Georgetown, 1998; S. Kelly, North Myrtle Beach, SC

Barracuda, Great—65-0; Georgetown, 1948; Henry Shelor, Sumter, SC

Bonito, Atlantic—7-11; Little River, 1993; Charles Adams, Tabor City, NC

Drum, Red (Ch Bass)**—75-0; Murrells Inlet, 1965; A. J. Taylor, Conway. SC

Flounder, Summer—3-8; Murrells Inlet, 1982; J. Wallace, Charlotte, NC

Grouper, Snowy—30-0; Murrells Inlet, 1981; R. Perdue, Murrells Inlet, SC

Grouper, Speckled Hind—45-0; Little River, 1973; H. R. Murray, Little River, SC

Grouper, Warsaw—310-0; Murrells Inlet, 1976; C. D. Pratt, Knoxville, TN

Grouper, Yellowmouth—22-8; Murrells Inlet, 2001; Brian J. Ford, Murrells Inlet, SC

Grunt, Margate—18-8; Murrells Inlet, 1971; J. L. Flowers, Charlotte, NC

Hogfish—20-8; Murrells Inlet, 1988; J. Cline, Pawleys Island, SC

Houndfish—9-4; Murrells Inlet, 1974; W. Kirby, Pittsburg, PA

Kingfish (Whiting) (tie)—2-10; Pawleys Island, 1968; C. Micheau, Georgetown, SC

Mackerel, Spanish—11-0; Myrtle Beach, 1983; W. Deas, Jr., Myrtle Beach, SC

Porgy, Red **—10-8; Murrells Inlet, 1985; J. F. Duffer, Myrtle Beach, SC

Runner, Rainbow—14-14; Georgetown, 1985; W. D. Harder, Orangeburg, SC

Sailfish—75-0; Georgetown, 1968; G. A. Reid, Clinton, SC

Seatrout, Spotted—11-13; Murrells Inlet, 1976; A. Pendergrass, Murrells Inlet, SC

Shark, Shortfin Mako—302-12; Georgetown, 1978; L. F. Howell, Beaufort, SC

Shark, Tiger—1,780-0; Cherry Grove, 1964; W. Maxwell, Charlotte, NC

Snapper, Red—37-8; Little River, 1964; K. Henry, Rock Hill, SC

Swordfish—500-0; Georgetown, 1978; B. H. Peace III, Pawleys Island, SC

Tilefish, Blueline—14-6; Murrells Inlet, 1982; O. Cockerfield, Ft. Wayne, IN

Triggerfish, Gray*—13-9; Murrells Inlet, 1989; Jim Hilton, Lake Wylie, SC

Triggerfish, Queen—6-5; Murrells Inlet, 2000; Alicea Novak, Matthews, NC

Tuna, Blackfin—37-11; Georgetown, 2002; Charlie Byars, Central, SC

Tuna, Bluefin—332-6; Murrells Inlet, 1996; Michael E. Stone, Savannah, GA

Wahoo—130-5; Murrells Inlet, 1998; J. Moore, Valdese, NC

* Indicates a current world's record
** Not eligible for state record consideration due to state or federal restrictions
This info can be found on the Internet at www.dnr.state.sc.us/marine/saltrecs/saltrec.html

---

Hurricane Fishing Fleet
Hurricane Marina, The Waterfront at Calabash, Calabash, NC
(910) 579–3660, (800) 373–2004
www.hurricanefleet.com

Trips depart daily, March through December, from Calabash waters. Hurricane's armada includes the 90-foot *Hurricane II*, the 77-foot *Capt. Juel II*, the 45-foot *Cyclone*, and the 40-foot *Party Time*.

Bottom-fishing trips range from half day to full day in the Gulf Stream and include excursions specifically for snapper. Trolling and other sportfishing trips of 4½ to 12 hours can be arranged as well as nighttime shark fishing. Public and private charters are available. Costs start at $30 per person for adults and $25 for children, and reservations are recommended. Rod, reel, bait, and tackle are provided.

***Longway* Charter Fishing**
The Waterfront, 1898 North Twisted Oaks
Drive, Little River
(843) 249–7813
www.longwaycharters.com

Another boat that can accommodate parties of up to six people, *Longway* accepts both individual and group reservations. A five-hour trip costs $400; an eight-hour trip, $600; and a 12-hour Gulf Stream excursion, $1,000. All prices include gear and bait. Charters run from mid-April to mid-November.

South Strand

Captain Dick's Marina
4123 U.S. Highway 17 South, Murrells Inlet
(843) 651–3676, (866) 557–3474
www.captdicks.com

Enjoy deep-sea bottom fishing aboard the *New Capt. Bill, Capt. Bill III,* and *New Inlet Princess.* Trips range from 5 to 24 hours. Rods, manual reels, bait, and tackle are provided on the shorter trips; electric reels are only available for the much longer deep-sea voyages. Fishing licenses are provided for all anglers who charter from here. Air-conditioned cabins and full food service are featured on all of Captain Dick's vessels. Fishing excursions cost anywhere from $37 to $199 per adult. Special sportfishing junkets can be booked by individuals or groups of six for a half day, three-quarter day, or full day in Gulf Stream waters. Prices range from $499 to $1,199.

Georgetown Charters
Georgetown Landing Marina,
Marina Drive and U.S. Highway 17,
Georgetown
(843) 997–9842

Inshore, nearshore, flats, and jetty fishing excursions can be chartered year-round. Parties of two to four people can be accommodated for half-day trips for $375 to $475, three-quarter day trips for $350 to $450, and full day trips for $475 to $575.

Customized touring or shelling jaunts are also available. This company does not take individual reservations; you must organize your own party. See the Boating chapter for information about this marina's facilities and hours.

Real Crazy Charters
Marlin Quay Marina, 1398 South Waccamaw
Drive, Murrells Inlet
(843) 651–4444
www.marlinquay.com

This sportfishing headquarters offers charters any time of the year plus parasailing (see the Water Sports chapter for parasailing details). Vessels for charter include a 27-foot catamaran and a 38-foot Hatteras.

Half-, three-quarter-, and full-day as well as Gulf Stream adventures are available. Bait, tackle, and licenses are provided. Cost ranges from $445 to $1,200. Reservations are recommended.

The *Extreme Fisherman*
Pawleys Island
(843) 235–6347, (843) 439–0909
www.extremefisherman.com

Extreme Fisherman captain Pete Mercuro offers inshore, flats, surf, and nearshore fishing charters in and around the Myrtle Beach area. Whether light tackle or fly fishing, you can ride the wild edge where the big fish are found. Murrells Inlet, Litchfield Beach, Pawleys Island, and North Inlet and Winyah Bay in Georgetown are all favored destinations. For a lone fisherman, prices run around $225 for five hours or so. A full-day, or seven hour, excursion is $375 ($50 for additional anglers). Captain Mercuro generally accommodates parties of one to four people. Call ahead to ask about larger parties.

Insiders' Tip

Don't forget your camera—and plenty of film—when going out on a charter fishing trip. You'll want to record all those near misses and great catches.

Piers are made for fishing. PHOTO: COURTESY OF MYRTLE BEACH AREA CHAMBER OF COMMERCE

Fishing Piers

Believe it or not, fishing piers are a major business undertaking. Recently it was reported that a developer interested in adding a pier to North Myrtle Beach would spend between $3 million and $3.5 million just for construction. That's why a fishing pier is never merely a structure reaching into the sea from whence you cast a line. All piers on the Grand Strand offer a mixture of shops, arcades, restaurants, and water-sports outlets. There's enough to do to keep you occupied for a few hours or an entire day.

Make the most of your fall pier-fishing excursion by casting your line from the northernmost piers, from the north side. Southward migration occurs at this time as fish of all shapes and sizes respond to shorter days and lower sunlight intensity. They reach these northern piers on the north side first. September usually yields anglers a bountiful catch of king and Spanish mackerel, mullet, menhaden, pompano, spot, and bluefish.

North Strand

Cherry Grove Pier
3500 North Ocean Boulevard,
North Myrtle Beach
(843) 249–1625
www.cherrygrovepier.com

Daily admission is $6.50 for the first rod and $6.00 for each additional rod. Seasonal rates are available. Holiday House Motel guests are admitted free. Pier walkers are charged 50 cents.

This pier is 985 feet long and is lighted for night fishing. You'll find a full line of pier tackle plus a gift shop and restaurant. Cherry Grove is open 24 hours a day from March 1 through the Sunday following Thanksgiving.

Myrtle Beach

Apache Pier
Apache Campground, 9700 Kings Road, Myrtle Beach
(843) 497–6486
www.apachefamilycampground.com

Welcome to the longest pier anywhere along the East Coast—measuring 1,220 feet in length. Accents include a bait-and-tackle shop, arcade, restaurant, and aquariums filled with indigenous fish. Nightly entertainment is also part of the fun from May 30 through Labor Day weekend.

It will cost you $5.00 a day to fish from the pier or 50 cents to partake in the action as a spectator. Campers staying at Apache Campground (see the Accommodations chapter) pay only $4.00. Hours are 6:00 A.M. to midnight from spring through fall and 8:00 A.M. to 6:00 P.M. all winter.

Myrtle Beach State Park
4401 South Kings Highway, Myrtle Beach
(843) 238–5326
www.discoversouthcarolina.com

A $2.00 parking fee is levied to anyone entering the park, except from November 5 to mid-March. Regular admission cost is $4.50 per fishing pole, and season passes are available. Fishing rods can be rented for $4.00 a piece. The pier is open to the public whenever the park is—6:00 A.M. to 10:00 P.M. each day. Tackle, bait, ice, and a gift shop are on the premises.

Pier 14 Restaurant, Lounge & Fishing Pier
1306 North Ocean Boulevard, Myrtle Beach
(843) 448–4314

More popular for the fine dining at the restaurant than for the fishing allure, Pier 14 does its rod-and-reel business from the gift and tackle shop situated right next door. There is a $6.00 charge for fishing, but anyone can walk the pier or watch the angling free of charge. An arcade and an outdoor patio also are open to the public. Pier 14 is in full swing from 7:00 A.M. to midnight all summerlong, continuing through the end of November. This pier is closed during the winter months, mid-November until early February.

Second Avenue Pier & Restaurant
200 North Ocean Boulevard, Myrtle Beach
(843) 626–8480

Admission is $6.00 for a daily pass to fish, 50 cents for spectators; inquire about season passes. You'll find a full line of bait, tackle, rods, and reels here plus a gift shop, arcade, and full-service restaurant.

This lighted pier with T-shape end is 905 feet long. Hours are 7:00 A.M. to 11:00 P.M. daily from March 1 through the end of September or early October.

Springmaid Pier
3200 South Ocean Boulevard, Myrtle Beach
(843) 238–5189 Ext. 3008

Bait and ice are sold here, and tackle is available for rent or purchase. Admission price is $6.50 per angler (spectators are free), with special weekly and year-round rates offered.

Springmaid is open seven days a week year-round from 6:00 A.M. to midnight; the tackle shop closes at 10:00 P.M. during summer.

South Strand

The Pier at Garden City
110 Waccamaw Drive South, Garden City Beach
(843) 651–9700
www.pieratgardencity.com

The Pier at Garden City is generally open 7 days a week, 24 hours a day from March through December. Daily hours may vary, so it is best to call ahead. Daily admission to fish is $6.50, and spectators are admitted free. Season passes can be purchased for $75. Bait and rental gear are available from the tackle shop.

Stop by the arcade and oceanfront deck of the Pier Cafe for before- or after-fishing activities. The cafe itself usually closes from Christmas through April 1.

Surfside Pier
11 South Ocean Boulevard, Surfside Beach
(843) 238–0121

Admission to this 810-foot-long pier is $7.50 per angler. Spectators pay a 50 cent charge. Weekly and season passes are available. You'll find tackle, bait, and rod-

and-reel rentals on the pier along with a gift shop.

The biggest tarpon ever caught from a South Carolina pier (142 pounds) was landed here in September 1995. The tackle shop and pier are open 24 hours a day from March 1 through December 15.

Bait and Tackle Shops

Like any sport, you need the right equipment to complement technique. All Grand Strand piers and fishing venues offer a smattering of outlets where you can get your hands on a rod and reel and bait. But for the serious angler, the following bait and tackle venues offer years of experience, local tips, and top-quality gear.

North Strand

Boulineau's Foods Plus
318 Sea Mountain Highway, Cherry Grove
(843) 249–3556
Since 1948 Boulineau's has served as one of the area's most popular suppliers of fishing equipment, hardware, cut bait—and lots

and lots of free advice. The shop is open year-round from 6:00 A.M. to 11:00 P.M.

Johnny's Bait & Tackle
4377 Sea Mountain Highway
(SC Highway 9), Little River
(843) 249–1288
Cornell Williamson is proud of his decades-old business and is about as experienced an angler as you'll ever meet. He swears by his mud minnows to catch flounder and recommends ballyhoo and rig mullet to troll for king mackerel. Both offshore and freshwater tackle are available.

Saltwater, freshwater, and shrimping licenses can be purchased here. Johnny's is open every day of the year from 6:00 A.M. to 4:30 P.M.

Myrtle Beach

City Bait & Tackle
713 Eighth Avenue North and Alder Street,
Myrtle Beach
(843) 448–2543
This 30-year-old family business has earned a sterling reputation among local

Shrimp and worms are this fisherman's choice of bait on the Cherry Grove Pier. PHOTO: LISA TOMER RENTZ

fishing enthusiasts. Owner Roy Brigham will tell you in a heartbeat that the only advertising worth believing in is good customer service and word of mouth.

City Bait & Tackle keeps a steady supply of mullet, shrimp, and squid as preferred bait, as well as a wide range of tackle. Roy is always willing to inform customers where to cast their line for the catch of the day. This store is open 365 days a year from 6:00 A.M. to 7:00 P.M. Monday through Friday and 6:00 A.M. to noon on weekends.

South Strand

Cedar Hill Landing
5225 U.S. Highway 17 South Business, Murrells Inlet
(843) 651–8706

Cedar Hill is another bait-and-tackle shop owned by the Nance family with a full array of live bait—oysters, crabs, and shrimp—and all the equipment an angler needs to be completely outfitted. This fishing emporium is open year-round, seven days a week from 6:30 A.M. to 6:30 P.M. Johnboat rentals are available here, and we'll tell you more about that if you refer to the Boating chapter.

Fishing Tournaments

If you reckon yourself an astute angler and want to put your skills to the ultimate test, you've come to the right place. We've listed a handful of area tournaments that are open to all interested participants.

Boating tournaments, usually of the offshore variety, are relatively costly to enter, but prize purses are lucrative, typically totaling thousands of dollars. The pier-fishing contests tend to be cumulative events, lasting several months; awards are less extravagant and often involve goods rather than cold, hard cash.

Regardless of the form or nature of the brass ring, the following tournaments are competitive as well as a great excuse to ply the waters along the Grand Strand.

Insiders' Tip
When buying waders or boots, always buy them one and one-half sizes larger than your shoe size. The larger size will enable you to slip them off in the event that you fall overboard. Boots or waders filled with water will make you sink like a stone.

Boat Fishing

American Red Cross
Inshore Saltwater Fishing Tournament
(843) 546–5422 (Judith Bayer-Griffin)

This is an annual team competition, focused on reeling in the biggest spot tail bass, spotted sea trout, and flounder from Murrells Inlet to Charleston. Prizes are based on 80 percent entry fee payback, for the first 10 places, with a $1,000 minimum guaranteed to the first-place winner and $100 for the largest in each species. The tournament gets under way with a captain's dinner; fishing begins the next morning at daylight. Entry fee is $75 for early birds and $85 for others.

South Carolina Governor's Cup Billfishing Series
(843) 762–5036
www.dnr.state.sc.us

The South Carolina Governor's Cup Billfishing Series, in its 14th season in 2002, is an umbrella event encompassing billfishing tournaments along the state's coast. The series promotes coastal tourism and encourages tag-and-release angling, as well as conservation of South Carolina's marine resources. It has been recognized internationally for its efforts

One look at the smile on this fellow's face and you know it's hard to beat the singular pleasure of catching "the big one." PHOTO: COURTESY OF CAPTAIN DICK'S MARINA

to conserve billfish and other species through tag and release.

This Governor's Cup tournament involves marinas from Murrells Inlet to Edisto Island. Participants garner points during six fishing events for the biggest billfish caught; points also are awarded for the tag and release of blue and white marlin and sailfish, as well as tuna, dolphin, and wahoo. Each event sets its own price for entry. The average first-place purse for

this event is $12,000. Participating marinas usually include Marlin Quay Marina in Murrells Inlet, Georgetown Landing Marina in Georgetown, Bohicket in John's Island, Charleston Harbor Marina Resort in Charleston, and Edisto Marina in Edisto Beach. (See the Boating chapter for details about Grand Strand marinas.)

Besides receiving a cash prize, winners are invited to the governor's mansion for a celebratory dinner.

Tailwalkers King Sting
King Mackerel Classic
(843) 527–2495 (Stuart Ballard)
www.tailwalker.com

Always held the first weekend in August, this fishing competition is also a multi-inlet event, with boats departing from Georgetown. Based on the participation of at least 175 boats, the first-place catch wins a boat, motor, and trailer valued at nearly $50,000. The second-place angler receives $15,000 cash, and third place takes home $7,500. The rest of the prize money is divided evenly among anglers who claim the next 30-largest mackerels. This tournament costs $375 per boat to enter, but organizers promise that almost every contestant floats away a winner.

Pier Fishing

Grand Strand Fishing Rodeo
(843) 626–7444
www.myrtlebeachinfo.com

If you prefer to cast from one of the Grand Strand's piers, this annual tournament is for you. More than $10,000 in cash and prizes is awarded from April through October for the biggest "fish of the month." There's no fee to enter the tournament.

Pier King Mackerel Tournaments
(843) 626–7444

These mid-June and September pier tournaments are much like the Fishing Rodeo. Pay the $35 per person entry fee and cast from any pier along the Grand Strand to tempt the tenacious "kings." The total cash purse is based upon the collected entry fees and is allotted proportionally among the first- through fifth-place winners.

Official Weigh Stations

If you're a participant in one of these tournaments and want to throw your day's catch into the hat for competition, the following locations serve as official weigh stations.

On the North Strand: Cherry Grove Pier, North Ocean Boulevard.

In Myrtle Beach: Apache Pier, 9700 Kings Road; Second Avenue Pier, 200 North Ocean Boulevard; Myrtle Beach State Park, 4401 U.S. Highway 17 South; and Springmaid Beach Pier, 3200 South Ocean Boulevard.

On the South Strand: Surfside Pier, 11 South Ocean Boulevard; Marlin Quay Marina, 1398 South Waccamaw Drive; The Pier at Garden City, 110 Waccamaw Drive South; and Captain Dick's Marina, 4123 U.S. Highway 17 Business.

Boating

Rules of the Waterway
Public Boat Ramps
Public-Access Marinas
Boating Tours and
    Excursions
Boat Rentals

Boating the Grand Strand's waters is a bewitching alternative means of travel through this part of the country, foregone by most. What often gets missed in the wink-of-an-eye speeds of faster modes of transportation stretches out before you in a peaceful panorama when navigating rivers, marshes, and waterways. Like the persona of area natives, the Grand Strand's seaways seem slower-moving, easier . . . belying the churning eddy of activity just below the surface.

In this coastal area, water routes once were the main arteries for the lifeblood and growth of this region and today are steeped in the history of its people. When the marshy inlets of Calabash, Cherry Grove, Murrells Inlet, and Pawleys Island were fair game for anyone, their bulging beds of oysters and clams fed generations of families. There was a time when nets, pots, and traps were seen dangling from almost any dock or even a tree, containing the daily catch of blue crabs and shrimp. The deep, drifting Waccamaw River made rice planters some of the wealthiest people in the world during the 1850s, as its waters fed massive rice paddies along its banks. During summers in the mid-1800s, the river was alive with barges carrying whole families and their favorite furnishings from their inland plantation homes to seasonal abodes on Pawleys Island—a cooler clime and a safe haven from "summer fever" (malaria transmitted from mosquitoes).

The historical development of Grand Strand boating routes seems as murky as the water itself. All that we know for sure is that it was a generations-long process, most likely motivated by economic need or inspired by the discoveries of maverick explorers.

Sometimes referred to as the Inland Waterway, or even Watery Route 1, the Intracoastal Waterway stretches from 23 miles north of Boston to the Florida Keys. The Intracoastal is the domain of pleasure craft, small fishing vessels, and, at times, barges. It is a master of quick change: at one moment a narrow, banked channel; at the next turn a broad, hazy inland sea bounded by gold, green, and brown marsh grasses. Dredged to a 12-foot depth from Norfolk, Virginia, southward to Miami, the Intracoastal is famous for hidden sandbars along its path—the main reason smaller craft are recommended.

Because some of its northern sections are closed, mile 0 officially begins at Norfolk. The waterway's history is sketchy at best, but evidence shows it was used by Native Americans to travel the length of the coast. Around 1643 some Massachusetts colonists dug a half-mile-long canal linking the Anniquam River and Gloucester Harbor. President George Washington was responsible for surveying the Great Dismal Swamp, a 200,000-acre wilderness spanning parts of southeastern Virginia and northeastern North Carolina, in 1763. Thirty years later work finally began in the swamp to connect rivers in Virginia and North Carolina. The final portion was completed in 1936 when the federal government became involved and tied in the area between Little River and Winyah Bay in South Carolina.

Today when it comes to boating, the Grand Strand offers practically every imaginable type of waterway, including tea-colored rivers stained by the tannins of cypress roots, briny marshes, and the open waters of the Atlantic Ocean and aqua-blue Gulf Stream.

Boats of all shapes and sizes cruise the Intracoastal Waterway—often traveling from northern climes all the way south to Florida and back again. PHOTO: COURTESY OF MYRTLE BEACH AREA CHAMBER OF COMMERCE

Rules of the Waterway

Even though we know you wouldn't launch a boat without knowledge of safety methods and rules, we thought it important to outline your legal responsibilities as a boater. First and foremost, the operator of any vessel is required by law to file with local authorities a formal, written report of any accident. This can be accomplished simply by contacting the U.S. Coast Guard Boating Safety Hotline, (800) 368–5647, to make a verbal report and acquire a form.

Accident Reports

It is necessary to report damage to a vessel or its equipment, injury or loss of life, or any missing passenger. You must also file a report in the case of grounding, capsizing, someone falling overboard, colliding, sinking, striking a boat or propeller, swamping, flooding, fire, an explosion, or the disappearance of a craft. Injury to or the death or disappearance of an individual must be reported within 48 hours, while damage to a vessel or property must be disclosed within 10 days of the incident.

Approaching Vessels and Right-of-Way

When approaching another boat in open waters, each party must move to the right after a short (one-second) horn signal, answered by the other vessel. If crossing paths, the boat to your right from dead ahead to two points abaft your beam has the right-of-way. You should sound one short blast ("I'm altering course to starboard"), two short blasts ("…to port"), or three short blasts ("…to stern").

In all situations the boat being overtaken has the right-of-way, even if the overtaking ship enters your danger zone. The overtaking boat is required to sound two long and one short blast if it intends to pass on the right; two long, two short blasts if on the left. If you are being overtaken, respond with one long, one short, one long, and one short signal if you understand and agree.

Casting Off

Leaving a slip or dock dictates that you have no right-of-way until you are completely clear of the dock. It is every operator's responsibility to leave port without danger to other boats, and it's a good idea to sound one long blast as you are about to depart. All sailboats under sail alone (no motorized power) and fishing boats have the right-of-way and should be given wide berth. The only exception to this rule is when the sailboat is overtaking a motorboat, in which case the motorized craft maintains the right-of-way.

Common sense guides most boating regulations: Allow large ships with restricted maneuverability the right-of-way; stay away from docks, piers, and swimming areas; and take responsibility for damage caused by your wake.

Life Jackets

In boats less that 16 feet in length, a wearable life vest must be accessible for each person aboard. If the boat is more than 16 feet in length, wearable life vests must be accessible, in addition to a ring buoy or other safety device that can be thrown. All children younger than age 12 aboard a vessel less than 16 feet long are required to wear life jackets.

The Pilot

Anyone age 16 or older can legally pilot a boat. Those younger than age 16 can only run a vessel after taking a boater education course and passing a test. Courses are offered through the U.S. Coast Guard Auxiliary, U.S. Power Squadron, and the Department of Motor Vehicles. The DMV issues educational handbooks for study prior to testing.

Safety First

If the wind suddenly shifts, or if lightning and choppy water are evident, there's a good chance a storm is brewing; in that case, boating is not a good idea for the time being.

Before casting off into any waters, check your vessel for the following items: a portable radio to check weather reports, a flashlight, extra batteries, matches, a navigation map of the area, suntan lotion, a first-aid kit, sunglasses, a raincoat, and an extra length of tie-line. It's always best to tell someone where you're going, who is accompanying you, and how long you plan to be away. Before starting the engine, open hatches, run the blower, and, most importantly, sniff for gasoline fumes in the fuel and engine areas. Make sure all fishing and hunting gear is well packed—there's nothing like a loose fish hook to ruin a potentially great outing.

While cruising change seats carefully, especially if the craft is a small one. The rule is to stay low and near the center line. Use caution when passing a powerboat, and anchor from the bow with a line that is at least five times as long as the water's depth.

Public Boat Ramps

The following sites (listed geographically from north to south) are provided by Horry and Georgetown Counties to allow boaters access to waterways. None of them

Insiders' Tip
More than 1,000 people die in boating accidents every year. Fifty percent of those deaths involve alcohol. Fifty percent of drunk men who drown have their flies unzipped. Get the picture?

has been formally named, so we've provided the approximate location for each.

Hogg Inlet: in the North Myrtle Beach area between Little River and Cherry Grove Beach

North Myrtle Beach/Little River: under the bridge at S.C. Highway 9, on the Intracoastal Waterway

Ocean Drive Beach: in North Myrtle Beach, just west of U.S. Highway 17

Three in Socastee: Off S.C. Highway 544 turn into Rosewood Estates and follow the road until it ends; Peachtree Landing, located off S.C. Highway 544 at the old Socastee Bridge; and Enterprise Landing, located off S.C. Highway 707 just south of the Socastee bridges

Murrells Inlet: Highway 17 Business beside Belin United Methodist Church

Georgetown: follow U.S. Highway 701 to its southern end in Georgetown

Public-access Marinas

If you're lucky enough to own a sailing vessel, we think you'll find the following comprehensive list of area marinas useful in getting around the Strand by watercraft. It's always best to contact the marinas in advance, especially if you'll be arriving late at night or if your boat is experiencing mechanical trouble. Marina personnel usually will make sure someone is there to meet you and that the right equipment is available for repairs. All of the Grand Strand's public marinas listed here are open year-round, even if hours of operation vary from season to season.

North Strand

Anchor Marina
2200 Little River Neck Road, Little River
(843) 249-7899

"Do it yourself is always welcome" is the motto of Anchor Marina, where sailors are encouraged to pull in for repairs and supplies. A 35-ton travel lift is available, and mechanics are on call 24 hours a day to fix anything from a blister to a broken propeller shaft. Anchor's staff also offer bottom painting, fiberglass work, and power washing.

This 85-slip marina provides wet and dry storage, showers, bathrooms, a ship's store, restaurant, and lounge. General hours for the marina and store are 8:00 A.M. to 5:00 P.M. seven days a week; the restaurant and lounge are open from 11:00 A.M. until the wee hours of the morning.

B. W.'s Marina
4495 Mineola Avenue, Little River
(843) 280-8954

B. W.'s, managed by Michelle Coffey, officially opened for business in April 1996, taking over for the Pier at Little River. Ten slips are available for monthly rental. Water and 110- and 220-amp electrical hookups also are available, as well as gasoline and diesel fuels. This marina is open from 7:30 A.M. to 6:00 P.M. with extended hours during the summer.

Coquina Harbour Inc.
4208 Coquina Harbor Drive, Little River
(843) 249-9333, (866) 249-9333
www.coquinayachtclub.com

Russell Edwards manages this 113-slip marina that offers a bathhouse and self-service laundry facilities. Monthly and yearly slip leases can be negotiated. The marina is open year-round.

Crickett Cove Marina
4495 North Baker Street, Little River
(843) 249-7169
www.crickettcove.com

Crickett Cove opened in July 1997 and is the last such venture that will be permitted on saltwater marsh since those wetlands are a protected natural habitat. Concrete floating docks offer transient boat storage, and 90-plus wet slips are available for boats from 40 to 55 feet in length. Dry storage can accommodate 340 vessels as long as 35 feet. Two fueling depots, inside and outside, offer gas and diesel fuel pumps. Hookups include water, cable TV, telephone, and 30-, 50-, and 100-amp electricity. Crickett Cove serves guests with showers, bathrooms, and laundry facilities. Currents, (843) 280-3189, opened in February 1998 and serves lunch and dinner. Currents opens

Nautical Lingo

While by no means a complete list, the following glossary will help keep your common boating terminology shipshape from stem to stern.

ABEAM—At right angles to the boat's center line.
AFT—Toward the back.
ASTERN—At or toward the back of the boat.
BEAM—The boat at its widest part.
BILGE—Lower interior areas of the hull.
BOW—Front end of the boat.
BOW EYE—Where trailer cable is attached to the boat.
BROAD ON THE BOW—Between abeam and bow.
BROAD ON THE QUARTER—Halfway between abeam and astern.
BULKHEADS—Vertical partitions.
CENTERBOARD—Plate of metal or wood, raised or lowered on pivot to control sailboat's lateral resistance.
CHART—A boater's map. Never call it a map.
CLEAT—Fittings with horns to which a line is secured.
COME ABOUT—Changing direction by bringing bow through the wind.
CURRENT—River or tidal flow of water.
DEAD AHEAD—Straight ahead over bow.
DEAD ASTERN—Straight back over stern.
DRAFT—Depth of water needed to float the boat.

From shrimp boats to private yachts to state-of-the-art oceangoing vessels, area marinas sport a wide assortment of watercraft. PHOTO: COURTESY OF BRANDON ADVERTISING

EBB—Outgoing tide.

FATHOM—Six feet (a measure of depth).

FLOOD—Incoming tide.

FORE—Toward the front (bow) of the boat.

FORE AND AFT—An object that runs parallel to the keel.

GUNWALE—Upper part of the top plank of topsides.

GROUND TACKLE—All the gear used for anchoring.

HALYARD—A line to hoist a sail.

HEAD—Fore part of the boat; also, a seagoing toilet.

HELM—The steering mechanism of a boat.

HULL—Basic part of a boat consisting of the keel, frames, planking, and deck.

JIB—Triangular sail set between bow and foremast.

JIBE—Sailboat changes direction by bringing the stern through the wind. This maneuver can be dangerous.

KEEL—Major structural member of a hull.

KNOT—Measure of speed (=1 nautical mph).

LEEWARD—The side of a boat away from the wind.

LINE—Any rope that performs a function on the boat.

NAUTICAL MILE—A measure of distance (6,076.1 feet).

PORT—Left side of the boat.

REEF—Short lengths of line spaced horizontally on a sail. The sail is dropped to where the lines can be tied, thus shortening (reefing) the sail in a strong wind.

RODE—The anchor line.

RUDDER (RIGHT, LEFT)—The rudder positioned to the right or left. Often confused with right or left tiller. A tiller put to the right will move the rudder left.

SHEER—A line to control a sail's angle to the wind.

SLACK—Period between flood and ebb when the current is not flowing.

SPRINGLINE—A line leading from stern to forward (or on bow to aft) on dock to prevent boat from moving ahead or astern.

STARBOARD—The right side of the boat.

STEM—The near-vertical structural member at the bow.

STERN—The back of the boat.

TACK—Sailing as near to the wind as possible. Starboard tack, wind coming over the forward right side of the boat; port tack, wind coming over the forward left. Also for motorboats not heading directly into the wind.

TIDE—The rise or fall of water.

TILLER—A horizontal arm extending from the top of the rudder post that is used to steer the boat.

TRANSOM—Flat planking across the stern.

VEER—Wind direction shifts clockwise.

WINDWARD—Toward the wind.

YAW—Stern moved to either side by a following sea.

Source: *Boating Guide,* 3rd edition, Martin Frederick Inc., Snibbe Book Div.

daily at 11:30 A.M. Marina hours are 8:00 A.M. to sunset seven days a week.

Harbourgate Marina
2120 Sea Mountain Highway (SC Highway 9), North Myrtle Beach
(843) 249–8888

This marina, under the Little River Swing Bridge, offers a full range of services, including repairs. You'll find cable TV, laundry facilities, and showers on-site. Harbourgate also boasts a well-stocked ship's store on the premises. Harbourgate Marina is the location of a 100-room Hampton Inn, (843) 249–1997, that opened April 1, 1997. Guests of the Hampton Inn receive special privileges at the marina and a free continental breakfast every morning during their stay.

Marina at Dock Holidays/Vereen's Marina
1525 13th Avenue North, North Myrtle Beach
(843) 280–6354

Wet dockage is available at one of 102 slips here, as are laundry facilities, showers, a ship's store, cable TV, water, and phone hookups. Dock Holidays offers gas and diesel fuels. Five popular restaurants and lounges are located nearby. Thirty- and 50-amp shore power also is accessible. In 1997 Dock Holidays added a pump-out station for nautical guests. Hours of operation range from 8:00 A.M. to 7:00 P.M., depending on the season.

Myrtle Beach Yacht Club at Coquina Harbour
714 U.S. Highway 17 North, Little River
(843) 249–5376
www.myrtlebeachyachtclub.com

Many of this club's 153 slips are designated for transient use, and boaters can enjoy convenient access to both 30- and 50-amp power. There is a swimming pool, a pool bar and restaurant, as well as showers, bathrooms, laundry facilities, and water and cable TV hookups. The club offers diesel and gasoline fuels as well as a pump-out station. You'll find an on-site ship's store offering beer, wine, and ice, and a number of first-class restaurants are within walking distance. The black-and-white lighthouse at the mouth of Coquina Harbor marks the nautical route to the club. Hours of operation are always 8:00 A.M. to 6:30 P.M.

Especially during the winter, the Intracoastal Waterway is filled with boats of all shapes and sizes— many of which are headed south for warmer weather. PHOTO: COURTESY OF LOWCOUNTRY COMPANION

North Myrtle Beach Marina
4430 Kingsport Road, Little River
(843) 249-1000

This full-service marina offers dry storage and crane service that can accommodate any motorized watercraft or sailboat up to 65 feet in length. North Myrtle Beach Marina specializes in service and repairs. The ship's store at this marina stocks an extensive array of boat supplies and fishing tackle. Hours of operation are 8:00 A.M. to 6:00 P.M. daily.

Myrtle Beach

Hague Marina
#1 Hague Drive, off SC Highway 707, at the Intracoastal Waterway, Myrtle Beach
(843) 293-2141

George Russ manages this site. Hague offers yacht service and supplies and storage—wet or dry, covered or uncovered. Transient dockage is available for $1.00 per foot per night. Water and electric hookups plus a ship's store are available. Hague is open 8:00 A.M. to 6:00 P.M. daily spring through fall, until 5:30 P.M. during the winter months.

Osprey Marina
8400 Osprey Road, Myrtle Beach
(843) 215-5353
www.ospreymarina.com

Osprey opened in January 1997 next door to the Waccatee Zoo (see the Attractions and Kidstuff chapters). All of Osprey's 96 slips are rented by the year only. Dry storage is available, as are cable TV, phone, water, and 30- and 50-amp electric hookups. This marina provides a pump-out station as well as gasoline and diesel fuels. Amenities include showers, laundry facilities, and an on-site convenience store. Hours run 8:00 A.M. to 6:00 P.M.

South Strand

Belle Isle Marina
Belle Isle Road, Georgetown
(843) 546-8491

Sporting both floating and fixed docks, Belle Isle provides 120 slips, dry storage, laundry facilities, showers, and bathrooms and also offers diesel fuel or gasoline. Transportation into town is available at no charge. The marina also has a fully stocked ship's store.

In season the marina and store are open seven days a week from 7:00 A.M. to 7:00 P.M. When the weather gets cooler and things slow down, they operate from 9:00 A.M. to 5:00 P.M.

Georgetown Landing Marina
432 Marina Drive and U.S. Highway 17, Georgetown
(843) 546-1776
www.georgetownlandingmarina.com

This 150-slip deep-water marina has both floating and fixed docks, as well as a floating linear transient dock. Gas and diesel fuels are available. The property is home to the Lands End Restaurant, popular for years with locals who come to sample the daily seafood specials. Georgetown Landing is open 8:00 A.M. to 7:00 P.M. Sunday through Thursday and 8:00 A.M. to 8:00 P.M. on Friday and Saturday throughout summer. In the winter hours are 8:00 A.M. until dark. A 98-room Hampton Inn, (843) 545-5000, services this marina.

Marlin Quay Marina
1508 South Waccamaw Drive, Garden City Beach
(843) 651-4444, (877) 670-3474
www.marlinquay.com

Besides running an array of charters from this marina, owner Charles Stone offers boat dockage for long-term lease. Bathrooms, showers, laundry facilities, 30- and 50-amp power hookups, and a ship's store are available, as are gasoline and diesel fuel pumps. The marina does not allow "live aboards" (where people live on the boat year-round) or Jet Skis. It is open year-round—6:00 A.M. to 8:00 P.M. in the summer months and 8:00 A.M. to 5:00 P.M. during the winter after Daylight Savings Time kicks in.

Wacca-Wache Marina
1950 Wachesaw Road, Murrells Inlet
(843) 651-2994
www.waccawachemarina.com

Wacca-Wache maintains 108 floating slips, 12 of which are available for transient vessels. This marina also offers 120 dry-storage slips and a choice of 30-, 50-, or 100-amp electrical hookups. Additional services include cable TV hookups, a pump-out station, gasoline and diesel fuel, a ship's store, laundry facilities, and showers. A courtesy car is available to transient boaters for an hour at a time to boaters docked at the marina. Wacca-Wache is open from 8:00 A.M. to 8:00 P.M. during peak boating season, generally June through September.

Boating Tours and Excursions

If you don't have your own vessel and want to explore the Grand Strand from a watery point of view, check out one or more of the following trips. There is something for everybody, no matter what your age or particular interest.

North Strand

Great American Riverboats
Waccatee 200, Enterprise Road, Socastee
Barefoot Landing, U.S. Highway 17,
North Myrtle Beach
(843) 650–6600, (800) 685–6601
www.mbriverboat.com

The Great American Riverboat Company operates three well-appointed boats in the Myrtle Beach area. The *Queen Mary II*—an exquisite replica of the glamorous cruise liner built in the 1930s—operates from the Waccatee Zoo in the Socastee community on the south end of the Strand. The *Barefoot Princess II*—an enormous riverboat that traveled 3200 miles down the Mississippi, across the Gulf of Mexico, and back up the Waterway to its current home—operates from Barefoot Landing on the northern end of the Strand. Boarding locations vary for *The Jungle Princess,* the fleet's tropically-themed riverboat. In addition to outdoor decks, all three boats boast enclosed, climate-controlled decks-with snack bars,

comfortable seating, dance floors, and elegant dining areas.

Several daytime, sunset, and dinner cruises are offered along the Intracoastal Waterway. The daytime excursion lasts 1½ hours and costs $12.00 for adults and $6.00 for kids ages 6 to 16; it's free for children 5 and younger. The sunset cruise lasts two hours; admission is $14.00 for adults, $7.00 for children ages 6 to 16, and free for kids 5 and younger. Patrons on the 2½-hour dinner cruise have their choice of a prime rib or chicken dinner for $36.50 (tax and gratuity included). An early-bird dinner cruise and a one-hour sight-seeing tour are other popular offerings.

Hurricane Fishing Fleet
Hurricane Marina, The Waterfront at Calabash, Calabash, NC
(910) 579–3600, (800) 373–2004
www.hurricanefleet.com

"If you haven't experienced the charm of Myrtle Beach from the deck of one of our cruises, you haven't experienced Myrtle Beach," is the motto referring to the Hurricane's roster of sea tours.

Hurricane's Adventure Cruises encourage passengers to join the crew for an afternoon, setting a course for the Atlantic Ocean, where you'll meet up with a shrimp-boat fleet and watch them ply their trade. Shrimping and watching active marine life is the theme of this jaunt, which costs $18 per person age 12 and older and $15 per child age 11 and younger.

Call the number listed for reservations and schedules, because hours and types of cruises change periodically.

South Strand

Captain Bill's Fleet
Captain Dick's Marina,
4123 U.S. Highway 17 South Business,
Murrells Inlet
(843) 651–3676, (866) 557–3474
www.captdicks.com

Discover Murrells Inlet and the Atlantic Ocean from Captain Dick's located on the waterfront in Murrells Inlet. Make fishing memories and experience the real

Many of the area's most popular cruises never leave the calm waters of area creeks and inlets—making these outings an ideal choice for young and old. PHOTO: COURTESY OF CAPTAIN DICK'S MARINA

thrill of catching those big ones. Longer trips travel farther offshore to deeper water and produce a wider variety, greater quantity, and larger fish! From the half-day Sea Bass Fishing Adventure to the All Day Gulfstream Adventure to the Overnight Gulfstream Excursion, choices abound and range in price from $37 to $142 per person depending on age and which fishing adventure you choose.

Captain Dick's Saltwater Marsh Explorer Adventure has long remained one of their most popular tours. Discover the area's own marine wonderland in a 2½-hour boat journey guided by a marine biologist. Experience the vital, living habitat that is home to hundreds of fascinating and mysterious marine creatures. Not an artificial environment like a zoo or aquarium, this interactive tour delivers a glimpse of the real thing. Various nets and dredges are employed to retrieve specimens from beneath the water. Specimens go into onboard touch tanks where they can be seen, observed, and, when appropriate, touched and held. There is also a fishing demonstration and a beach walk

along a barrier island that is not accessible by car. Participants occasionally encounter bottle-nosed dolphins—an added delight! All Explorer vessels are rest room equipped.

"Cruisin' The Beach," an ocean sightseeing cruise, is a memorable excursion suitable for the entire family. This cruise departs from the historic inlet, passes through the tranquil natural beauty of the marsh, and ends up on the majestic Atlantic. Cruising the shoreline of the Grand Strand, the Myrtle Beach skyline is newly captivating. Call ahead for scheduling information. Rates are $16.00 per adult and $6.00 for children between the ages of 6 and 12. Children younger than age six are free.

Captain Dick's offers more than we have room to tell you about. Dozens of tours include ecology outings, fishing and sight-seeing excursions, and pirate adventures. The captain also offers boat rentals, Jet Ski rental, parasailing, and nearly anything else you can think of. Give the captain a call at the number listed or visit the Web site.

Black River Outdoors Center
U.S. Highway 701 North, Georgetown
(843) 546–4840
www.blackriveroutdoors.com

Unlike white water, the waterways along the Tideland Coast are "meandering, gentle, flowing," says naturalist and ecotourism enthusiast Bill Unger, owner of Black River Outdoors Center. Year-round, Unger and his professionally trained guides offer kayak tours upon the area's blackwater rivers, cypress-tupelo swamps, salt marshes, and rice plantation canals and creeks. A sampling of the guided explorations, designed for the adventurous types who love exploring, include the wildlife swamp preserves of the Black River, Waccamaw National Wildlife Refuge and Sandy Island, the creeks and canals of Chicora Wood Plantation, and the saltwater marshes of Murrells Inlet and Huntington Beach State Park.

The uninitiated are often surprised to learn that participation requires only a moderate level of physical fitness. Even first-timers have no trouble paddling the gentle waterways of the area. Reservations are required, and guided day tours of 3½ to 4 hours are priced at a very reasonable $45 (when accompanied by parents, children younger than age 13 are $25). Group rates are available.

If you are hungry for a bit of solitude, you can also rent kayaks and canoes to launch your own self-guided adventure. Life jackets, paddles, car-top carriers, and safety instruction are included.

Touring kayaks are available for the more experienced. Or you can rent a surf kayak to keep at your beach house for a day or a week!

Black River Outdoors Center also offers an impressive stock of kayaks, canoes, small-boat trailers, and paddling accessories at their retail store, open Monday through Saturday from 9:00 A.M. until 5:30 P.M.

Rover Tours
End of Broad Street, Downtown Boardwalk,
Georgetown
(843) 546–8822, (800) 705–9063
www.rovertours.com

Rover Tours is located on the Harborwalk downtown in historic Georgetown. The company operates two boats. The *Jolly Rover* is a tall-ship schooner, the same kind of vessel once used by shifty-eyed pirates to ply our Lowcountry waterways. This ship, a 79-foot, two-masted, gaff-rigged topsail schooner that can hold 49 passengers, is a carefully and lovingly crafted replica with modern features for which Blackbeard would have yearned: a steel hull, aluminum masts and nylon sails, modern rest-room facilities, an inboard engine, and safety lines around the deck to keep little pirates from falling overboard.

Throughout spring and summer, the *Jolly Rover* will feature three tours per day, Monday through Saturday. Two-hour "Pirate Adventures" at 10:00 A.M. and 1:00 P.M. feature folklore and stories told by a "real" pirate in period clothing. The young and young at heart will enjoy tales of plank walking and buried treasure. Enjoy the fine salt air on deck or relax "down below" as you sail around an uninhabited island and catch glimpses of bald eagles, sea birds, and maybe even a 'gator lurking on shore. At 6:00 P.M., also on Mondays through Saturdays, a 2½-hour "Romantic Evening Sail" gives lucky guests an opportunity to experience the romance and magic of daylight disappearing over darkening waters. This tour certainly makes for a memorable end to any day!

The *Jolly Rover* is operated by an experienced captain and crew. There's an onboard ship's store with light snacks, beverages, and *Jolly Rover* souvenirs.

The *Carolina Rover*, a 49-passenger pontoon boat, offers a different kind of tour. Monday through Saturdays, three-hour daily tours—at 9:00 A.M., 1:00 P.M., and 5:00 P.M.—focus on the Georgetown Lighthouse, shelling excursions, and the lush natural environment of the Carolina Lowcountry.

The ever-popular three-hour Adventure Cruise transports its guests a dozen miles or so over smooth inland waters into the mouth of Winyah Bay, where an uninhabited and wildlife-rich barrier island sports a historic old lighthouse—and more shells than most of you have ever seen. Participants are allowed to step right off the boat onto the sun-bleached shoreline to sun, stroll, and pick up shells. Plenty of time is allotted for the beach, so expect to spend roughly three hours blissfully removed from civilization.

The *Carolina Rover* features plenty of shade, snacks, beverages, and clean rest room facilities. An onboard naturalist's informative commentary is an added delight.

Cap'n Rod's Lowcountry Plantation Tours
Harborwalk, Georgetown
(843) 477–0287
www.lowcountrytours.com

For a delightful change of pace, Captain Rod offers a selection of relaxing, enjoyable, and educational tours. Comfortably seated aboard the canvas-covered, outboard-powered pontoon boat, you'll explore pockets of solitude in and around Winyah Bay, as well as in five surrounding

Riverboat cruises along the Intracoastal Waterway are a special treat. PHOTO: COURTESY OF MYRTLE BEACH AREA CHAMBER OF COMMERCE

rivers. Captain Rod, a longtime native and marvelous storyteller, delivers entertaining narrative that includes local lore, natural and American history tidbits, environmental issues, and a hearty helping of good old Southern humor and hospitality.

Daily plantation tours allow participants to cruise peaceful, slow-moving rivers past plantation mansions, long-abandoned rice fields, majestic old oaks, and a plethora of wildlife. Loved by history buffs and nature lovers, these three-hour tours are perennial favorites and attract lots of return clientele.

Lighthouse tours cruise to a remote barrier island—past Hobcaw Barony and over the sunken remains of the USS *Harvest Moon*—where Winyah Bay meets the wide, blue Atlantic. Explore a place where the sea spills its secrets and deposits an ever-changing array of shelling opportunities.

Plenty of snacks and beverages are available onboard, so bring a buck or two but you need not bring anything more. There are clean rest rooms, too.

Brookgreen Gardens
U.S. Highway 17 South, Murrells Inlet
(843) 235–6000, (800) 849–1931
www.brookgreen.com
Some of Brookgreen Gardens' most unspoiled vistas can be enjoyed aboard *The Springfield,* a 48-foot pontoon boat that offers an up-close look at some of the Lowcountry's native flora and fauna. Several times each day as the boat winds its way through the scenic waterways, a Brookgreen naturalist tells the story of the long-abandoned rice fields that once thrived in Georgetown County from the mid-eighteenth century until the Civil

War. These tours combine the marvels of nature, the thrill of discovery, and the intrigue of history. Wilderness lovers, bird-watchers, botanical enthusiasts, and history buffs will long remember this trip.

Boat Rentals

If you have a penchant to captain your own vessel or are looking to take a leisurely cruise on a pontoon boat, the following is a comprehensive listing of established, year-round outlets that offer this equipment. During the summer you can contact any of the public-access marinas listed earlier in this chapter. Many rent watercraft during the busy season but discontinue rentals right after Labor Day. If you are on the lookout for great kayaking and canoeing opportunities, please refer to the Water Sports chapter.

Myrtle Beach

Downwind Sails
2915 South Ocean Sails Boulevard,
Myrtle Beach
(843) 448–7245
Right on the beach, Downwind Sails rents 14- or 16-foot sailboats and Hobie Cats from April 1 through October 25. The general price is $35 per hour, but discounts often apply after Labor Day when business slows down. Lessons are highly recommended for novices and run $45 per hour. Downwind is open all summerlong from 8:00 A.M. to 8:00 P.M. Downwind Sails is closed during the off-season.

Myrtle Beach Water Sports Inc.
9915 North Kings Highway, Myrtle Beach
(843) 497–8848, (866) RENT–ATV
Little River waterfront
(843) 280–7777, (866) 4–SEA–DOO
These two locations rent pontoon boats, Jet Skis, and jet boats and also offer parasailing, island tours, and dolphin watches. Both locations are open seven days a week, 8:00 A.M. until 6:00 P.M. April through October. For more information, visit www.myrtlebeachwatersports.com.

The Sailing & Ski Connection
515B Highway 501, Myrtle Beach
(843) 626–7245

The Sailing & Ski Connection offers kayak rentals and tours. You'll pay $25 for a single kayak with life jacket and paddle and $30 for a tandem. If need be, Sailing & Ski will deliver your kayak to you. Call for delivery information and pricing. Visit the store to browse a wide variety of boating gear.

South Strand

Captain Dick's Marina
4123 U.S. Highway 17 Business,
Murrells Inlet
(843) 651–3676, (866) 557–3474
www.captdicks.com

For cruising or fishing the inlet only, Captain Dick's rents 15-foot fiberglass johnboats with 15-hp outboard motors. Each boat accommodates up to four people and rents for $69 per four hours, $89 for eight hours. Life jackets, fuel, safety equipment, and licenses are included in the rental package. For an additional charge, you can also rent a rod and reel for the trip. Johnboat rentals are offered Easter through Thanksgiving. Parasailing trips are an option, too.

Cedar Hill Landing
5225 U.S. Highway 17 Business,
Murrells Inlet
(843) 651–8706

Cedar Hill rents 14-foot johnboats with 6-hp and 15-hp motors for $55 per half day or $75 per full day of fishing or cruising. Fuel, fishing licenses, and life jackets are included in the rental fee. Rod and reels cost an additional $8.00 per rig. Rentals are available year-round.

Inlet Jet Ski and Marine
4491 Highway 17 South Business,
Murrells Inlet
(843) 651–3133
www.inletjetskiandmarine.com

Inlet Jet Ski and Marine has a variety of boat rentals to choose from for fishing, cruising, and sight-seeing on the area's much loved waterways. All boats are in top running condition and are equipped with Coast Guard regulation gear and necessary fishing licenses. Inlet Jet Ski will deliver boats to Murrells Inlet or to the Wacca Wache boat landing on the Intracoastal Waterway. Full-day (7:00 A.M. to 7:00 P.M.) and half-day (7:00 A.M. to 12:30 P.M. and 1:30 to 7:30 P.M.) rentals are available. Call for overnight and weekly rates.

For stress-free days by the sea, pack light: a small cooler, big towel, plenty of sunscreen, and a fat novel.
PHOTO: COURTESY OF MYRTLE BEACH AREA CHAMBER OF COMMERCE

Beach Information

With an average annual temperature of 64 degrees and 215 days of Carolina-blue skies and bright sunshine each year, the Grand Strand's mild, subtropical climate is a mecca for sun worshipers and beachcombers alike. Even when the summer temperatures and humidity chase the majority of people into air-conditioned shelter, the beach will always carry a soft, welcoming breeze that defies the heat. The wide ribbon of sandy coast stretches for 60 miles, and the Atlantic Ocean is usually less turbulent than its West Coast cousin, the Pacific Ocean. As hundreds of thousands of locals and visitors will attest, there's nothing like a glorious day at the beach!

A Friendly Reminder about Sun Exposure . . .

There are few things in life easier to acquire and more painful to live with than a bad sunburn, and around here you can turn a good stinging shade of pink in just 30 minutes to an hour. Longer doses of sun can send sunbathers to the hospital with blisters, nausea, and excruciating pain.

Don't be fooled by clouds or cool air: You can get a bad burn even on a day when you can't see the sun. Before you hit the Strand, pick up some good suntan lotion with a high sun protection factor (SPF). We suggest an SPF of 15 to begin the suntan process. Apply it an hour before you start swimming, walking, or bicycling and remember to reapply it after swimming or if you're perspiring—even if it's waterproof. Most experts recommend avoiding the sun during the hottest part of the day: between noon and 4:00 P.M. Even under the shade the sun can reflect off the water and sand, so you can still get a burn.

When it comes to SPFs and protecting your skin, there's safety in numbers. Ranging from 2 to 45, the SPF on a particular sunscreen tells you how many times longer (not how many hours longer) the lotion protects you from a sunburn, compared to the time it would take if you wore no sunscreen at all. So, if your skin normally reddens after 20 unprotected minutes in the sun, slathering on an SPF 15 will let you endure the rays for 5 hours (20 x 15 = 300 minutes). You can also make an educated SPF decision by keeping tabs on news reports of daily ultraviolet (UV) index numbers. These numbers range from 0 to 10+, depending on the season, cloud cover, and other atmospheric conditions. On a day with a moderate UV reading of 5, wear an SPF 15 lotion and a hat; if the reading is 10 or higher, aim for an SPF of 30 and cover up.

Be sure to wear something on your head. A visor is good to protect your face, but to shield your head and hair, a full hat with a brim that's at least 3-inches wide is best. Good sunglasses that filter out ultraviolet rays should also be part of your standard beach attire. If you've got young children or a baby with you, be sure to take extra care to protect their tender skin. Make them wear hats and reapply sunscreen every few minutes. If kids are determined to stay in the ocean for hours, put T-shirts on them. Some rafts and Boogie boards will cause mild rashes on unprotected stomachs anyway, so the T-shirts will serve two purposes.

If you want to dress to beat the heat, get wise to fabric and weaves. Unbleached cotton, satiny polyesters, and silk either absorb or reflect UV rays, while crepe, viscose, and bleached cottons allow UV rays to pass through, making a direct hit to your skin. Look for tightly woven materials, like cotton twill, that don't allow light to pass through, enhancing its sun protection power. And, while white and pastel shades of clothing may make you feel cooler, dark tones actually absorb UV rays better.

Ocean Swimming Safety

There is nothing quite so seductive as the gently rolling waves of the Atlantic Ocean. It beckons you to walk in and float amid its briny, undulating waters. And, all at once, you're in perfect commune with nature itself. We know how easily common sense can be forgotten while riding the folds of the ocean, but you must always remember that the forces of nature are not only majestic but also unpredictable—and, at times, downright dangerous. That's why swimming is not permitted beyond 50 yards from the beach or over shoulder depth.

Lucky for us all, Grand Strand beaches are prime tourist attractions overseen by trained lifeguards. As a visitor to the area or local resident, it is always a good idea to plant your beach chair near a lifeguard stand. Before you even get one toe into the surf, these watchdogs of the shoreline will let you know the current swimming conditions by posting colored flags: yellow means use extra caution; red means NO SWIMMING! Scoping out a lifeguard-protected area of the beach gives you the peace of mind that comes from knowing you're not swimming alone, your children have an extra pair of eyes locked on them, and, if anything untoward should happen, someone well-trained in rescue and CPR is on hand.

Undertow

That incredible force of water that pulls you oceanward when waves recede is an undertow. Depending on weather conditions, it can be very strong. If you find yourself caught in one, don't panic or try to fight it. Stay calm. Float with the waves and you will eventually be brought back to shore. If waves are bigger than usual, it's a good bet that the undertow will be stronger and it's best to stay in shallower waters.

Riptides

When you combine high waves, a full moon, and hurricanes or tropical storms brewing in the Atlantic Ocean, conditions are rife for dangerous riptides, or rip currents. "Rips" occur when two opposing currents meet, causing a swirling action that can carry swimmers from safer waters. These currents represent an overflow of water coming into shore that travels back into the ocean in a narrow current with considerable force and speed. Telltale signs of riptides are rough, choppy water that appears deeper and darker than normal, with swirling debris, kelp, or sand. Since 80 percent of ocean rescues are a result of swimmers finding themselves caught in a rip current, it's wise to know how to get out of such a force. As with a strong undertow, try to relax. It's useless to fight a rip current. Go along with it and then angle yourself to swim or float parallel to the shoreline. Waves at either side of the rip current will take you back to shore.

Beach Rules

Alcohol

All Grand Strand beaches forbid alcohol consumption and possession. All open containers with alcohol are forbidden. This rule applies to all public-access areas as well.

Attracting Sharks

No one is permitted to bait, fish for, or otherwise attract sharks to an area within a half mile of the beach.

Long, lazy days on the edge of the ocean are one of life's sweetest pleasures. PHOTO: COURTESY OF MYRTLE BEACH AREA CHAMBER OF COMMERCE

Cars on the Beach

Driving on the beach is no longer allowed on any portion of the Grand Strand beaches.

Distribution of Literature/Solicitation

You might have wondered why the only advertising along the beach is by airplane banner or a lighted boat. Well it's because other forms are against the law here. No one can distribute anything in the genre of pamphlets, advertisements, handbills, or circulars. It is also a "no-no" to conduct business of any kind on the beach, including promotional devices such as free samples or admission passes.

Fireworks

Unincorporated areas of Horry County are the only places where fireworks are permitted (they're not allowed within any city limits). Use is restricted to private property between the hours of 10:00 A.M. and 10:00 P.M.

Glass Containers

It is unlawful to take any glass bottle, drinking glass, or other glass containers to the beach with you.

Horses

Horses are not allowed on the Strand in North Myrtle Beach. Riders in Myrtle Beach must have a permit from the city clerk. In Surfside, horses are banned from the beach April 1 through November 1, and in Horry County, horses are banned from beaches March 1 through October 31.

Littering

Although you would never believe it, considering the mountains of trash collected along the Strand every fall during Beach Sweep, littering on the beach or in the water is against the law. This includes any glass, bottles, cans, paper, garbage, waste, or refuse.

Motorized Watercraft

In North Myrtle Beach motorized watercraft cannot be launched from the beach between 9:00 A.M. and 5:00 P.M. from May 15 through September 15. Vehicles must be kept at least 50 yards from swimmers. In Myrtle Beach, all motorized craft must be at least 50 yards beyond bathers; Jet Skis must be at least 100 yards away. No motorized boats are allowed at Surfside Beach.

All boats must be registered with a permit secured from a lifeguard. Boats must not be left unattended between 8:00 P.M. and 8:00 A.M. In Horry County, boaters cannot endanger swimmers and must be at least 400 feet from the shore and 500 feet from any fishing pier.

Animal Laws

In North Myrtle Beach, Myrtle Beach, and Surfside Beach, dogs in public must be kept on a leash at all times. From May 15 through September 15, no dogs are allowed on the beach between 9:00 A.M. and 5:00 P.M. In Myrtle Beach between 21st Avenue North and 13th Avenue South, no animals are allowed on the beach or on Ocean Boulevard at any time of year.

Rafts and Floats

In Myrtle Beach and in Horry County areas, rafts must be covered with fabric and have ropes attached to their entire perimeters.

Sand Dunes, Sea Oats, and Beach Grass

It is illegal to walk on sand dunes and to pick or otherwise damage sea oats, beach grass, or sand fencing.

Sleeping on the Beach

Myrtle Beach, North Myrtle Beach, and Horry County forbid sleeping on the beach between 9:00 P.M. and sunrise. In Surfside Beach people must not sleep in or around automobiles or motor vehicles on the street, in an alleyway, or at public accesses.

Swimming

Swimming in the ocean isn't the same as swimming in a lake, river, or pool, so don't expect it to be. Veteran ocean swimmers don't fear the ocean, its waves or currents, but they have a healthy respect for it. Caution and common sense are the keys.

One of the most important things to remember is that the lifeguard, young and good-looking though he or she might be, has trained rigorously for this job. Listen to the lifeguard.

All Grand Strand beaches set shoulder-deep and 50-yards-offshore limits for swimmers, but the lifeguard has the authority to keep you in closer if he or she believes conditions warrant it. Disobeying the lifeguard can result in arrest and charges; fines can run from $25 to $200.

Thong Bathing Suits/ Nudity

It is illegal to wear a thong bathing suit in North Myrtle Beach, Myrtle Beach, or Surfside Beach. Skinny-dippers and nudists, take note: You can be arrested for public nudity on the beach or at any beach-access point.

Off to conquer the next big wave! PHOTO: COURTESY OF MYRTLE BEACH AREA CHAMBER OF COMMERCE

Noise

It is a violation to play any radio or similar device loud enough to disturb persons in dwellings, hotels, or residences. This ordinance also includes vehicles and motorcycles with loud exhaust pipes.

Beach Wheelchairs

Beach wheelchairs are available for free to disabled persons in the Myrtle Beach area. The chairs are designed with oversize rubber wheels that make rolling on a sandy surface easy. The following beach services are responsible for the distribution and storage of the wheelchairs at the following locations:

Myrtle Beach Lifeguards, 76th Avenue North to 69th Avenue North; John's Beach Service, 63rd Avenue North to 23rd Avenue North; Boardwalk Beach Service,

Ninth Avenue North to the Myrtle Beach Pavilion; Huggins Beach Service, Seventh Avenue North to Third Avenue North; and Lack's Beach Service, 20th Avenue South to 29th Avenue South.

Members of the disabled public who wish to use one of the beachgoing wheelchairs can either contact the beach service of their choice or go to one of the aforementioned locations. In the off-season, call the police department for assistance. Although there is no fee for using the wheelchair, a one-hour limit is requested, unless no one else wishes to use it. Beachgoing wheelchairs must be pushed by a second party.

Jellyfish

Jellyfish visits are predictable when southeastern winds blow the live gooey masses into warm, shallow waters. Some are per-

The Grand Strand Beach Renourishment Project

Few would argue the fact that the Grand Strand's 60 miles of shoreline is the foundation of the area's status as a tourism mecca. Hundreds of thousands of people visit South Carolina's coast each year. In fact during the summer months, the population of Horry County swells to 10 times its winter population.

Unfortunately many beaches are threatened with the persistent problem of land loss. Population growth and increased development have created a situation in which beach erosion can have severe economic consequences. Estimates reveal that approximately $3 trillion of the nation's coastal development is vulnerable to erosion. It is also estimated that 70 percent of the world's beaches are undergoing erosion, with percentages approaching 90 percent along the Atlantic coastal plain.

There are two general categories of erosion control on sand beaches. The first type is hard stabilization, or armoring, where structures such as seawalls, groins, revetments, and off-shore breakwaters are built to help protect development along shorelines. But these structures can be destructive to recreational beaches. Accordingly, South Carolina adopted the Beachfront Management Act in 1988; state legislation now prevents further armorment of the Palmetto state's beaches.

Beach nourishment is a popular option for maintaining recreational beaches.

Beach nourishment, renourishment, and replenishment are interchangeable terms for the process of placing sand on an eroding shore in order to restore and/or maintain recreational beaches. More than 200 beaches in the United States have experienced some renourishment effort. At least nine beaches in South Carolina have been replenished at some point in their history. The state's earliest renourishment project occurred in 1954 on Edisto Island.

The Grand Strand has a history of renourishment projects. A major nourishment effort—covering an 8.6-mile stretch of beach—was undertaken during the mid-1980s.

Beach renourishment projects, which utilize sand pumped from the ocean floor, protect oceanfront property and keep our beaches wide and beautiful. PHOTO: COURTESY OF CITY OF MYRTLE BEACH

At the time the project was the second-largest nourishment ever performed in the United States using an inland source of sand. More than 853,000 cubic yards of sand were hauled 24 hours a day, 7 days per week. It took 59,539 truckloads of sand and the cost totaled $4.7 million. In 1989 Hurricane Hugo took a toll on the Grand Strand. The following spring more sand was added to the beach in an emergency nourishment effort.

In 1996 a second major nourishment project for the North Myrtle Beach area began in September and was completed in the fall of 1998. Several offshore sandbars served as the sediment sources, and sand was hydraulically pumped onshore, where it was spread with bulldozers. The total project length was about 25 miles and the cost was $54 million.

fectly harmless, but the stinging variety will produce a swelling welt similar to a wound caused by the lash of a whip. And don't be fooled! They can sting even after they wash up on shore. Common symptoms from the venom of a Portuguese man-of-war, for instance, can include nausea, vomiting, and muscle cramps. The man-of-war type is actually a colony of jellyfish contained below a 10-inch-long purple and blue float. Tentacles have been known to reach 20 feet and are described by experts as "self-contained, spring-loaded venom glands" that zap a swimmer or anything else that gets in the way. If you're frolicking in the ocean late in the summer and see a blue, football-shape mass floating around, get out of the way.

The sea nettle form of the medusa family is the least toxic, unless you're highly allergic to its formula of venom. Sea nettles are umbrella-shaped, usually spanning 6 inches in diameter and showing a red pigment. Their tentacles are 5- to 7-feet long, and even when beached, they can attack if their stinging cells are still wet.

Of greater concern to your general health and well-being is the small, box-shaped jellyfish called a sea wasp. It's clear, only about 3 inches long, and its tentacles hang from the side of the body, often unnoticed. Unlike the Portuguese man-of-war, no one has ever died from a sea nettle sting, but its toxins cause immense pain.

Cabbage head, or cannonball, jellyfish is the only generally harmless variety that descends upon Grand Strand shores.

Clear on top with red sides, they get their name from the fact that they resemble a head of cabbage.

Since the water-based toxins of jellyfish react to proteins, meat tenderizer is the most effective way to treat stings, and it should be the first line of treatment. If meat tenderizer is not on-hand, some people use vinegar. All area lifeguards carry a specially formulated ointment (cortisone, meat tenderizer, and Vaseline) for jellyfish stings and will be more than happy to share it with you. Most often, tentacles or nettles are left on the victim's skin and need to be removed. Always use tweezers or run the edge of a credit card along the area to remove nettles. Rinse the area with alcohol, then apply ointment or meat tenderizer.

Shell Collecting

Seashells are considered by many to be timeless art treasures. But unlike most objets d'art, they are created by Mother Nature, given to us by the sea, and the price is right—they're free. Since the beginning of recorded time, mankind has held a fascination with seashells. They are found in excavated ancient temples, graves, and sacred statues. Native American Indians used scallop shells as dishes and made weapons from the sharp lips of others. Shell cups and ornaments were used in religious and war ceremonies as well as to top Indian burial mounds.

How We Get Seashells

It is important to note that a shell is actually the splendidly built home of a living mollusk, fashioned from lime taken from the sea water. If you collect a shell that is empty, you are justifiably taking a discarded house. But if you snatch one from the beach that still holds a living organism, you are killing that mollusk. A mollusk's internal organs are covered by a sac of skin called a mantle, and this organ manufactures the shell by secreting a substance that mixes with lime taken from food. The richer the food source, the thicker and more colorful the shell. Shell homes are built, bit by bit, in layers. Color comes from a rhythm of pigments fed to the shell at particular times in its development. Sunlight and heat also influence color, which is why shells of the same species might vary greatly in pigment.

Collection Tips

Whenever there is turbulence in the sea from tropical storms or hurricanes, you can bet that shorelines will be stocked with shells. After Hurricane Fran thundered by the Grand Strand in September 1996, Huntington Beach State Park reported its jetties were knee-deep in whelks and Horse Conchs.

The Grand Strand beach has also kicked up 60-million-year-old fossils. It's true! In April 1997 a retired high-school teacher identified a strange object, found by the hundreds on a North Myrtle Beach section of beach, as 60-million-year-old casts of clam shells. They were mistaken by many as fossilized turtle heads. Richard E. Petit, a research associate with the Smithsonian Institute, checked them out and confirmed that the molds were formed inside Cucullaea, a mollusk that

Sandcastle building remains one of the quintessential summertime pleasures for the young and young at heart. PHOTO: COURTESY OF MYRTLE BEACH AREA CHAMBER OF COMMERCE

became extinct in this part of the world a little less than 60 million years ago. Petit explained that they look like miniature stone turtle heads due to the employ shell filling with fine silt that hardened over the millennia.

Normally the best time to search out shells is during a new or full moon and always at low tide. You'll discover the most abundant selection around jetties in Garden City Beach, Murrells Inlet, and Huntington Beach State Park. If you're a serious collector, a field trip to one of the barrier islands, such as Shell Island, will reveal a treasure trove of seashells, since these keys are uninhabited, virgin territory.

To take full advantage of your seashell collecting experience along the Strand, we suggest contacting Steve Roth at Huntington Beach State Park, (843) 235-8755, or Al Kaiser, president of the Grand Strand Shell Club, (843) 215-8695. Roth is a local expert on shells and heads up an entire program devoted to mollusks. His beachcombing programs at Huntington Beach include guided tours through the shell-heaped area, and he is as free as the ocean breeze with information and expertise. Beachcombing and shell-collecting romps are offered several times each week year-round and are free with paid admission to the park (refer to the Parks and Recreation chapter for details on Huntington Beach State Park).

The Grand Strand Shell Club has been in existence for more than 10 years, with the express purpose of educating the public and preserving shell species. If you would like to join the 150 members of this shelling club, an annual membership costs a mere $5.00 for an individual and $8.00 for your whole family. The group coordinates numerous field trips every year, a Seashell Auction (the main fund-raising event), and exhibitions at area malls. In conjunction with the city of Myrtle Beach, The Shell Club has created an extensive and fascinating shell display that is housed at the Myrtle Beach Convention Center. More than 500 shells are showcased, representing more than 150 species.

For a real treat, feast your eyes on a personal collection of more than 7,000 shells and fossils at the Nature Center established at Ocean Lakes Campground, 6001 U.S. Highway 17 South in Myrtle Beach. Retired minister Leonard Raker displays the result of his 40-year obsession with the sea's bounty.

Actually, it's a love story. When Raker was dating his wife, he found a beautiful and rare shell and gave it to her. She lost it. The young man has been combing beaches from Prince Edward Island, Canada, to Honolulu ever since for a replacement. To this day he hasn't found that particular shell anywhere, but he has amassed an impressive collection that includes microscopic species.

Leonard Raker receives no salary but shares his shells and fossils with the world and holds educational programs at the center. If you are not a guest at the campground, please call Mr. Raker at (843) 238-4908 to make an appointment to view his fascinating collection.

Species along the Strand

You're in shell-collecting heaven, with more than 700 species washing up regularly on Grand Strand shores, including a host of rare, sought-after varieties. The most common classes of shells to be found are pelecypods (bivalves)—two shells that have a hingelike closing—and gastropods (univalves), which are one-shelled creatures. Here you'll also find an abundance of sand dollars (echinoderms), relatives of the starfish. Because Gulf Stream currents come to us from Florida, you might be lucky enough to snap up a Florida Horse Conch, the largest known univalve that grows up to 24 inches. Another shelling jackpot that can be found along the Grand Strand is the Left-handed Lightening Whelk, considered a prize since it grows counterclockwise and can reach up to 18 inches in size. Bivalves from the cockle family that regularly visit our shores are the Lemon, Prickly, and Giant Atlantic shells. The Notated Clam, with its zigzag scrawling, is a fairly common find. Keep an eye out for South Carolina's state shell, the Lettered Olive. It's known for its glossy appearance caused by its owner embracing it before he or she leaves home. And our

Our long, blond beaches will always be the area's primary attraction. PHOTO: COURTESY OF BRANDON
ADVERTISING

neighbor North Carolina consistently releases its state shell to us—the very beautiful Scotch Bonnet.

Hurricanes: Don't Get Caught Blowin' in the Wind

Hurricanes, tornadoes, and gusty tropical storms are no strangers to Grand Stranders. Nearly every year the area is threatened to be directly hit by hurricanes. Each hurricane brings its own brand of wrath, whipping residents and businesses with high winds and teeming rains that raise roof shingles, blow away outdoor signs, and bend palm trees to the ground. With every one of these storms, thousands of residents are left without power for days at a time, and flooding sends riverfront homeowners to higher ground. State officials and locals alike take fast and strong measures to protect life and property when alerted to each impending hurricane, recalling the devastation wrought

when Hurricane Hugo hit the Strand in 1989. While many considered the mandatory evacuation order an extreme measure at the time, Hugo reminded folks why Hurricane Hazel claimed 95 lives in 1954, before advanced mass communication.

The September day Hugo arrived was not unlike any other beautiful fall day along the Grand Strand with blue Carolina skies, warm but not humid. Light swirls of wind blew around pieces of loose paper by late afternoon, but nothing noticeable foretold of the coming onslaught. Like many Myrtle Beach residents, I boarded and taped windows, brought in supplies, and settled down for a stormier-than-usual evening. By 10:00 P.M., calm naivete turned into abject terror as windows bowed inwards, power failure forced silent darkness, driving rains stung the skin, and attempts at walking outdoors proved futile. To add insult to injury, many of those who fled inland were followed by the devilish tornadoes spawned when Hugo made landfall. Those whirling dervishes were responsible for tossing around mobile homes, selectively demolishing beach houses, and snapping Carolina pines from the top, leaving behind nothing but seawater-burnt needles.

Be advised, the advent of a hurricane is nothing to fool around with. This special section has been included to give you all necessary information to keep yourself and your family as safe as possible in the face of such a natural disaster.

Hurricanes, Tropical Storms, and Tornadoes

Tropical storms and hurricanes that hit the eastern United States usually begin off the coast of Africa during late summer, when seas near the equator are unusually warm. A tropical depression is the first step in creating a full-fledged hurricane. Winds begin to rotate in a pattern, increasing to about 31 miles per hour as pressure drops near the center. Narrow bands of rainfall form, some resulting in heavy downpours. Tropical depressions are defined as organized, sustained winds of less than 40 MPH.

A definite circular wind pattern has developed by the time a tropical storm is upon us. Warm, moist air is pumped into the weather system by wind speeds of up to 74 mph, causing heavy rainfall and a pattern of squall lines. Tropical storms carry winds from 40 to 74 MPH.

Hurricanes are huge atmospheric heat pumps that pull in moist air from the ocean's surface to gain power. The air converges in the center and spirals upward. As it rises the air cools and thunderstorms form. The ocean surface under the spiral acts as a low-pressure area. Cool, dry air is cycled downward, where it is warmed by the sea and rises to continue the swirling cycle.

A hurricane's strength depends largely on the degree to which air is allowed to flow unhindered into and out of the central column, or eye. Hurricanes gain their classification when winds roar above 74 MPH.

Tornadoes are funnel clouds. Scientists cannot agree on exactly what causes such a phenomenon. Some claim the origin to be vigorous updrafts in a thunder-cloud; others think the cause is falling hail. In any case a spinning funnel cloud has been known to lift cars and rip apart buildings as its vacuum action sucks in air from the ground and carries it upward. The weakest type of tornado blows out from a thunderstorm, usually lasting less than five minutes with winds rarely exceeding 150 MPH. Large tornadoes can stir up enough wind to travel as fast as 300 MPH. In rare instances twisters have lasted for hours, measured a half-mile wide, and traveled more than 200 miles.

Advance Preparation: Surviving a Hurricane

When you live in a coastal area, you need to have an advance plan for hurricanes, just as you would for a house fire. Since inland motels fill up quickly with the warning of a hurricane, formulate some idea of where you will go if evacuation is necessary. Gather basic supplies required for securing your home and valuables now. Keep them stored in the garage or some other accessible room.

Items to keep on hand: plywood for boarding the outside of windows, tape, rain gear, batteries, rope, bottled water, canned foods (don't forget the can opener), flashlights, a battery-operated radio, candles, and first-aid supplies. All of these items sell out in a hurry when a storm is coming, so it's smart to always keep them in supply.

If both parents in a household work, and if you have children who work, develop a plan of communication in the event of a hurricane warning or evacuation order. Determine where you will meet and who is responsible for what facets of your preparedness plan. Think through how you will assist an invalid or disabled member of your family.

Evacuation shelters offer only the bare necessities. Store your valuables and irreplaceable keepsakes in empty appliances and put plastic bags over household goods such as televisions, lamps, and computers. Before you evacuate, let a friend or relative outside the area know of your intended destination.

cleanup supplies; toilet paper, paper towels, and pre-moistened towelettes.

Check mobile-home tie-downs and secure lawn furniture or other loose outdoor items. Moor small watercraft or move boats to safety. Tape, board, or shutter windows to help prevent glass from shattering and wedge sliding-glass doors to prevent them from lifting off their tracks. What will you do with the pets? Now is the time to determine whether you will leave them in the house or take them to a kennel. Evacuation shelters do not allow pets of any kind. For your pet's sake have the following necessities on hand: proper identification collar and rabies tag; carrier or cage; leash; water and food bowls; any medications; newspapers or cat litter; and proof of vaccinations.

What to Do during a Hurricane Warning

Hurricane warnings are issued when conditions are expected in your area within 24 hours or less. Stay tuned to radio or television for official bulletins and make sure everything is boarded and taped. If you decide to stay in your home during a hurricane, understand that emergency vehicles and personnel are taken off the roads when winds reach 55 mph or more. If any member of your family has special needs, make sure your local EMS has that information.

Stay on the downside of the house away from windows, skylights, and glass doors. Clean appropriate containers and your bathtub for storing water. Use the telephone only in an emergency. If you lose power, turn off major appliances to reduce damage and curtail a power surge when electricity is resumed. A hard and fast rule is never to stay in a mobile home or an area within a flood zone under any condition during a hurricane. Before you evacuate, shut off water and electricity at main stations and securely lock up.

What to Do during a Hurricane Watch

A hurricane watch is issued when there is a threat of such conditions in your area within 24 to 36 hours. Begin to monitor storm reports on various radio and television stations. Rely only on facts presented by the media and emergency officials. This is the time to refill any necessary prescriptions (we suggest two-weeks worth) and fill up your vehicle's gas tank. You could lose precious time waiting in line at the gas pump, and if electricity goes out, pumps won't operate. If you will need cash for travel, get it during the "watch" time frame. ATMs also will have waiting lines and do not work without electricity.

Specifically, have these items stocked in your home: canned food and juices; dried fruit; bread; cookies; crackers; peanut butter and jelly; coffee and tea; enough bottled water for a gallon per person per day for two weeks; ice to cool food and charcoal (for a hibachi or grill) to cook it; a water-purification kit; disposable plates, cups and utensils; infant-care items; a battery-operated radio, TV, and clock; mosquito repellent; ice chest; plastic trash bags; chlorinated bleach; fire extinguisher;

Hurricane Shelters

When evacuation is imminent, keep an ear cocked to local radio and television for updated shelter locations. Locations may change or become full during the course of a storm. As of this writing, the American Red Cross reports that the following two shelters will be opened within four hours after each school closes following a voluntary evacuation request from the state's governor: Conway High School at 2201 Church Street in Conway and Loris High School at 301 Heritage Road in Loris.

In the event of a mandatory evacuation, the following shelters will open as soon as possible: Aynor High School, 201 Jordanville Highway in Aynor; Carolina Forest Elementary, 285 East Perry Road off Highway 501 in Myrtle Beach; Forestbrook Elementary, 4000 Panthers Parkway off Forestbrook Road in Myrtle Beach; Green Sea-Floyds, 5265 Highway 9 in Green Sea; Loris Middle School, 3410 Church Street in Loris; Whittemore Park Middle, 1808 Rhue Street in Conway; North Myrtle Beach Middle School, 11240 Highway 90 in Little River; Forestbrook Middle School, 4430 Gator Lane off Forestbrook Road in Myrtle Beach; and, in Georgetown County, Pleasant Hill High School, Schoolhouse Drive in Hemingway.

Be prepared for shelter accommodations: You will be sleeping on the floor or a cot, food might not be available, there are no provisions for medical services, and pets are not allowed. Bring pillows, blankets, sleeping bags or air mattresses, extra clothing, shoes, eyeglasses, lightweight folding chairs and cots, and personal hygiene items. Have important papers and identification with you.

Contact the local Red Cross chapter at (843) 477-0020 for further information on disaster preparedness for your business and family.

From sailboats to Jet Skis to kayaks and canoes, there's a waterborne vessel just right for you.

PHOTO: COURTESY OF MYRTLE BEACH AREA CHAMBER OF COMMERCE

Water Sports

Surfing
Waterskiing
Scuba Diving
Water-Sports
Outlets

Worldwide, there are more exciting waters to explore, but for the sheer pleasure of participating in water sports, the Grand Strand has its fair share of fans. In fact our sun-kissed area is a perfect place to learn and practice the rudiments of a particular water sport. The Intracoastal Waterway and Black River offer calmer waters to test out waterskiing; there are plenty of scuba-diving courses available and some interesting underwater ledges and wrecks to explore; and the relatively less powerful breakers of the Atlantic Ocean have never discouraged a novice surfer.

Whether you're adept at a water sport or want to try one out, this chapter should send you in the right direction.

Surfing

South Carolina waters are not especially good for surfing except when a hurricane or other storm is approaching. Unlike the West Coast, our East Coast has a continental shelf more than 60 miles off the shore that forms a gradual upgrade toward the beach. By Mother Nature's design, wave swells start breaking when they hit the shelf, diminishing the seawater rollers as they travel inland.

Still the Grand Strand has its share of avid surfers. On just about any day, you'll see people waxing their boards and rushing to the water to ride the wall or hit the lip.

An active and proud community of surfers—an interesting mix of clergy, business owners, restaurant workers, and high-school and college students—is alive and well along the Strand. The well-established Grand Strand District of the Eastern Surfing Association now hails more than 200-plus members, ranging in age from 4 to 52 years old. The association holds competitions throughout the year along the Strand; local amateur surfers hoping to turn professional vie for points to help them get into meets around the country. For information call Denny Green at (843) 293–0200, or visit www.nscsurfing.com.

Grand Strand surfing enthusiasts all have slightly different reasons for their love of the sport: Some refer to surfing as a way of life; others cite the sport as a natural, addictive high; and some even wax spiritual that surfing is God's way of teaching love and respect for the ocean.

Whatever the motivation to engage in wave riding, the smaller, calmer swells along the Grand Strand give beginners a wonderful chance to learn the sport while developing the strength, flexibility, endurance, and balance needed to do it well.

Rules of Surfing

Surfing is restricted to certain areas and times on all Grand Strand beaches. All surfers are required to wear leashes. In Horry County surfers must not endanger swimmers and must not surf within 300 feet of a fishing pier.

In North Myrtle Beach surfing and skim boarding are forbidden between 9:00 A.M. and 4:00 P.M. from May 15 through September 15, except in four areas: near Cherry Grove Pier and at 13th Avenue South, 28th Avenue South, 38th Avenue South, and 6th Avenue North.

Surfboards are not allowed in Myrtle Beach between 9:00 A.M. and 5:00 P.M. from March 16 through September 15, except in four locations: 29th Avenue South, 41st Avenue North through 47th Avenue North, 82nd Avenue North to the city limits, and from the south side of 8th Avenue North to the north end of the public boardwalk. (Last location open only from October 1 to April 15.)

In Surfside Beach surfing is not allowed from 9:00 A.M. to 5:00 P.M. except in the area between 12th Avenue North to 14th Avenue North and 6th Avenue South to 9th Avenue South. For more information on regulations, call (843) 650-4131.

There are a number of shops along the Grand Strand that cater exclusively to the sport of surfing. All of these outlets carry a full line of accessories and apparel, including wet suits, booties, gloves, hoods, and, of course, swimwear.

North Strand

Bert's Surf Shop
806 21st Avenue, North Myrtle Beach
(843) 272-7458

Bert's can set you up with boards from the CB, Hobie, ProMotion, Robert August, and Hap Jacobs lines. You can rent surfboards for 5 to 10 hours at a cost between $15 and $20. Bert's offers a full line of men's and ladies clothing. The shop is generally open from 10:00 A.M. until 10:00 P.M., but seasonal schedules sometimes apply. Call ahead if you need to.

North Shore Surf Shop
201-C Sea Mountain Highway
(S.C. Highway 9), North Myrtle Beach
(843) 249-5169
110 U.S. Highway 17 South,
North Myrtle Beach
(843) 280-5071
www.northshoresurfshop.com

North Shore carries Wave Riding vehicles, as well as Action, Liar, and Lost boards. Kayaks, surfboards, and body boards can be rented from $3.00 an hour to $20.00 per day. Please note that the Sea Mountain Highway store is only open Friday, Saturday, and Sunday from October 1 to March 1.

Surf City
3300 U.S. Highway 17 South,
North Myrtle Beach
(843) 272-1090

Surf City stocks new and used surfboards,

skim boards, body boards, skateboards, and other related equipment. Rental rates range anywhere from $10 to $20 per day.

Myrtle Beach

Surf City
1103 North Kings Highway, Myrtle Beach
(843) 626-7919
Myrtle Square Mall, 2501 North Kings Highway, Myrtle Beach
(843) 626-5412

These locations of Surf City, like their North Myrtle Beach counterpart, sell and rent surfboards, body boards, skateboards, and related equipment.

South Strand

Surf the Earth
47 Da Gullah Way, Pawleys Island
(843) 235-3500, (800) 864-6752
www.surf-the-earth.com

Surf the Earth is Pawleys Island's only complete surf shop, offering surfboards, skates and skateboards, surfboats, kayaks of all shapes and sizes, and a full range of clothing. Kayaks and surfboards are available for rental. Surf and kayak lessons, kayak tours, and free local delivery on rentals are also available. The shop is open Monday through Saturday from 10:00 A.M. to 6:00 P.M.

Village Surf Shop
500 Atlantic Avenue, Garden City Beach
(843) 651-6396
2016 North Kings Highway, Myrtle Beach
(843) 651-8176
www.villagesurf.com

Established in 1969, Village Surf Shop is the oldest hard-core surf shop around. Besides crafting custom boards, this store carries Perfection, RipCurl, and Sharp Eye brands.

If your passion dictates a custom-made surfboard, and your wallet is willing, this is the one and only place to visit along the Strand. Besides fashioning custom boards, this store carries Perfection, Rusty, Spyder, JC Hawaii, Kechele, and Lost name brands.

Owner Kelly Richards is usually found next door to this shop, covered in Styrofoam dust with rock music blaring as he shapes one of his masterpieces, called Perfection Surfboards. For more than two decades, Richards has made boards that are better suited to surfing the East Coast, having a wider surface and heavier weight that allows for a longer ride on smaller waves. The Village also rents surfboards for $20 a day, $30 for two days.

Waterskiing

Especially along the Intracoastal Waterway on warm Sunday afternoons, the chugging and screeching of motors from powerboats is a familiar sound. This is when locals launch their vessels to socialize with friends, sunbathe, and partake in the exciting and fun sport of waterskiing.

The Black River in Georgetown is another popular waterskiing venue.

In South Carolina, waterskiing is prohibited between sunset and sunrise. It is considered a three-person operation:

• The boat operator ensures the safe navigation of the vessel and skiers. He or she monitors the boat's speed, adjusting it to the abilities or desires of the skier.

• The observer, who must be at least 12 years old, takes responsibility for the skier's safety by keeping a constant eye on the person skimming across the water, the tow rope, and the wakes. An alternative to an observer is a wide-angle rearview mirror adjusted so the operator can see the person in tow.

• The skier is responsible for not exceeding his or her abilities, helping to ensure the safe operation of the boat, and communicating with the operator of the vessel. A ski belt or PFD (personal flotation device) must be worn unless the skier has a first-class or higher rating with the American Water Ski Association. But even if the skier is not wearing such an apparatus, an extra PFD must be aboard.

For all waterskiing equipment and wet suits, visit The Sailing & Ski Connection at 515 U.S. Highway 501 in Myrtle Beach; or give them a call at (843) 626–SAIL.

> ## Insiders' Tip
> Always wear an effective waterproof sunscreen when playing any sport in local waters. Reapply the lotion or gel often, all over your body, even if you're wearing a shirt and shorts. When clothing gets wet, fibers relax and allow the sun a direct hit on your skin.

Scuba Diving

Exploring the ocean and discovering its treasures is an unquestionably exciting experience. However this sport, as much as any other, is inherently fraught with danger. Therefore we urge you to educate yourself well about the rules, regulations, and risks associated with scuba diving and receive proper training from a certified instructor before strapping on a tank and plunging into the ocean's depths.

No diving is allowed in any waters within the city limits of Myrtle Beach or near piers. The sport can be legally practiced in Surfside Beach, but only if the diver is equipped with a flag to mark his/her underwater location. In all cases you aren't allowed to scuba dive unless you are certified, and every body of water has restrictions on underwater hunting.

Wrecks

Along with artificial reefs—mostly created by intentionally sunken vessels—and live bottom ledges, the Grand Strand offers some fascinating dive sites. Many are historically significant. In 1942 the *Hebe*, a Dutch merchant ship, and the *St. Cathan*, a British submarine chaser, collided and sank; at the time the vessels crossed paths, the *St. Cathan* was under blackout conditions to avoid a U-boat. These two wrecks now rest a quarter-mile apart on the ocean floor, as they have for more than 50 years, providing refuge to myriad marine life. Experienced divers say it's a wonderful site to mingle with game fish and tropicals, search for historic artifacts, and take underwater photographs. Two unnamed wrecks occurred in Grand Strand waters in the 1800s, one of which is a copper-clad paddle-wheel steamer. Apparently the scattered wreckage from each is replete with historic artifacts.

In 1964 while under tow to the Virgin Islands to become a floating hotel and casino, the *Richmond*—a 261-foot, 5-deck passenger ship—sank off the coast of Georgetown during a storm. Most of the steel decks and the hull had remained intact since the accident until Hurricane Hugo hit in 1989, collapsing what remained of the hull. The wreckage is scattered but is still home to a wealth of fish species, including angels, butterflies, damsels, grouper, jacks, and spades.

Artificial Reefs

Since the briny waters of the Grand Strand area are underlaid by a sandy ocean floor that by nature offers little "live bottom" to attract sea life, the Grand Strand Saltwater Anglers Association, in conjunction with state and local fishing clubs, developed a program to create artificial reefs. These reefs have cultivated underwater forests where deserts formerly stood on the ocean's floor and turned salvage into ecological treasures. In short, artificial reefs provide abundant fishing and diving sites that are easily accessible to small craft.

One such reef, the Bill Perry—named in memory of a local young fisherman who died in a car accident—was built in 1992, 25 miles offshore. Sunken vessels at this spot include a shrimp boat, a tug boat, and two 115-foot military landing craft containing Polaris missiles, igniters, and control pads. In one year plant growth went wild. The site, a favorite for divers, resembles a thick, underwater forest with such dense fish activity that it is now

sometimes difficult to pinpoint the reef. Large ivory coral is the most abundant around Bill Perry Reef.

Creating an artificial reef is not as easy as just sinking a large piece of machinery or broken-down vessel. Whatever is sunk must meet guidelines set forth by the South Carolina Department of Natural Resources. It must be cleaned, environmentally safe, and stripped of all floatable material, plastic or oils. Then it must be hauled out to sea by barge and tug boat. Objects such as a cement mixer fall to the ocean floor on their own, but ships must have holes blasted in them to sink as well as to provide the new reef with ventilation and water flow. The Defense Department is the biggest contributor of materials for artificial reefs; it costs anywhere from $1,000 to a whopping $50,000 to properly prepare and sink them.

Other artificial sites that attract hundreds of divers each year include:

• the 10-mile Barge, where a 200-foot barge was sunk in 1972 in about 30 to 40 feet of water just off the Murrells Inlet coastline;

• the 11-mile Tug and Airplane, created using a 90-foot tug boat and, later, a Navy training plane;

• the BP-25, named after the 160-foot tanker *Bernard Perkins* that's sunk at the spot; and,

• the 468-foot-long WW II Amphibious Assault Troop Transport the USS *Vermilion*, which was sunk in 1988. The *Vermilion* was originally dropped in 107 feet of water, but the 1989 assault of Hurricane Hugo moved the wreck a quarter-mile into 130 feet of water.

The latest, greatest dive site to hit the Grand Strand is called Barracuda Alley! In cooperation with the SC Department of Natural Resources, this 150-foot barge—outfitted with structures of various shapes and designs that attract fish—was sunk in 63 feet of water early in 2000 alongside a group of 20 armored personnel carriers. With much of the structure rising 10 to 20 feet off the bottom, and with more than 100 feet of swim-throughs and a training platform, this is an excellent dive for everyone. Come and visit this site, about 10 miles from Little River Inlet, so you can see how it grows and changes throughout the years.

For further information on South Carolina's Artificial Reef Program, write to Artificial Reefs, P.O. Box 12559, Charleston, SC 29422-2559, call Bob Martore at (843) 762-5082, or visit www.dnr.state.sc.us.

Dive Shops

We suggest you contact or stop by the following dive shops to check out a good selection of scuba gear for sale or rent, to receive instruction and certification, or to book daily diving charters. All of the following shops offer PADI certification, and professional staff members can likely answer any questions you might have.

North Strand

Coastal Scuba
1501 U.S. Highway 17 South,
North Myrtle Beach
(800) 249-9388
www.coastalscuba.com

Coastal Scuba brings together many years of experience from its captains, instructors, and dive masters to make your diving experience the very best it can be. Every diver—from the newly certified to the seasoned veteran—will find a dive charter through Coastal Scuba; there are more than half a dozen to choose from and they range in price from $60 to $115. A variety of classes—from minicourses to accelerated "executive-style" classes to full

PADI certification and advanced instruction—are also offered.

The *Safari IV*, Coastal Scuba's dive vessel, is a 45-foot customized dive boat sleek enough to get to dive sites quickly and sturdy enough to offer stability against an occasionally unpredictable Atlantic. The boat is spacious and comfortable, complete with a full-size head (bathroom), two ice coolers for snacks, and a professional crew. She carries all Coast Guard–required equipment, including a first-aid kit and oxygen.

Demand for diving is high, especially during the summer and on weekends, so please book early. Visit the Web site for lots of additional information.

South Strand

Mermaid Diving Adventures
3552 U.S. Highway 17 Business,
Murrells Inlet
(843) 357-3483
www.mermaiddiving.com

Mermaid is the only Nitrox facility in the area. (Nitrox is oxygen-enriched air that provides for longer diving times, shorter surface intervals, and increased physical energy.) The PADI-certified instructors here boast that they can turn anyone onto scuba diving for life if given the chance. Individuals ages 12 to 79 have "graduated" from Mermaid's certification courses; the basic open-water course costs $165 a person.

Annual dive trips are coordinated to the Bahamas, Mexico, and Florida to meet the manatee face-to-face. Mermaid specializes in full-service Dacor and Oceanic equipment.

Dive charters can be booked at Mermaid on weekends during spring and fall and seven days a week during the summer months. Each junket can take along six passengers. Charters range from $75 to $110 per person.

Scuba Express
Highway 17 Business, Murrells Inlet
(843) 357–3337
www.expresswatersports.com
Scuba Express is the "South End's" largest dive boat. A 40-foot-long custom dive vessel, it is equipped with a bathroom, shower, four bunks and plenty of seating, an enclosed cabin, and a covered back deck to keep guests out of the elements. Of course it also features all related safety gear. A class for beginners costs $165.

Water-Sports Outlets

Whether or not you're nautically inclined, you shouldn't miss experiencing the incredible feeling of gliding across the waves on a windsurfer or Waverunner; paddling the back bays and estuaries of coastal inland waters in a sea kayak; or soaring, suspended in air, as you parasail above the salty ocean spray.

We include a few establishments that provide the equipment you'll need to participate in these exhilarating activities. Kayaking seems to be the new water sport of choice along the Grand Strand, following an impressive emergence of ecologically inclined tours. Kayaking is feasible for folks of almost any fitness and skill level, as it allows paddlers to explore waters and the surrounding landscape at a leisurely pace. If you're combing the area for equipment rentals during summer, you most likely will find more outlets than we've included here. That's because a number of independent business people set up rental stands at local marinas until the end of the summer. If there's a marina

close by, call ahead to see if it rents your favorite type of water buggy. (Refer to the Boating chapter for a listing of local marinas.) We mention only those venues that can be contacted yearlong and have an established location.

Kayaking

Myrtle Beach

Sailing & Ski Connection
515 U.S. Highway 501, Myrtle Beach
(843) 626–SAIL
Weather permitting, Sailing & Ski runs weekly, supervised kayak tours along the salt marshes of Murrells Inlet. If a group has a special interest, this outfitter will do everything it can to make that interest a reality. The regular salt-marsh trip—$40 per person—lasts three hours and includes munchies.

South Strand

Black River Expeditions Inc.
21 Garden Avenue, Georgetown
(843) 546–4840
www.blackriveroutdoors.com
By canoe or kayak, Black River Expeditions takes watery advantage of the tidelands of Georgetown, one of the largest estuarine systems on the East Coast. Hundreds of miles of waterways offer something new and exciting at every turn: the Black River's cypress swamps; saltwater tidal creeks of Pawleys Island and Huntington Marsh; rice plantation canals of the Great Pee Dee and Waccamaw Rivers; the Cape Romain National Wildlife Refuge; and the Francis Marion National Forest. All tours are guided and include all necessary equipment, safety instruction, and transportation. The waters are known to be slow-moving. Year-round, daily morning excursions last about four hours; evening paddle cruises—Tuesdays, Wednesdays, and Thursdays from April until Labor Day—last around 1½ hours.

Kayaking tours of tidal saltwater creeks start out at Huntington Beach State Park and proceed through cordgrass marshes and along sandy beaches of Murrells Inlet to the causeway. Half-day guided tours are $45 for adults and teens and $25 for those age 12 and younger. This same trip is offered at night around periods of the full moon for the same price as the daytime treks; bring along your own food, drinks, and a flashlight if going at night.

Kayak and canoe tours of the Black River follow the ancient watery route of commerce that served rice and indigo plantations from the 1700s. These treks explore the untouched blackwater cypress swamps, alive with ducks, wild turkeys, herons, alligators, and the swamp canary. Prices are the same as the previously mentioned saltwater creek trips.

Departing from East Bay Park Landing on the Sampit River in Georgetown, the Historic Harbor Paddle Cruise passes the Harborwalk, scores of fishing vessels, private yachts, the tall ship *Jolly Rover,* the Kaminski House and Clock Tower. This tour is offered on summer nights at a cost of $20 per person; children younger than age seven go for free.

If the history of rice planting intrigues you, the Chicora Wood Plantation "Creeks and Canals" trip will take you to the remains of antebellum dikes and trunk gates once used to flood rice paddies. Creeks and hand-dug canals interlace the Great Pee Dee and Waccamaw Rivers and showcase vast plantations that sustained an aristocratic society who made millions growing "Waccamaw Gold."

The daytime version of this trip includes a peek from the water at one of the plantation homes. This half-day excursion costs $45 for adults and teens, $20 for ages 12 and younger.

Jet Skiing, Parasailing, Wave Running, and More

In this section we include personal watercraft rentals where you are at the helm of fast and slick vessels. If it's a pontoon or sailboat you're specifically looking for, please refer to the Boating chapter for related information.

Myrtle Beach

Downwind Sails
2915 South Ocean Boulevard, Myrtle Beach
(843) 448–7245

Rentals, rides, and lessons for bananas, Jet Skis, and parasailers are available here. Prices vary depending on what equipment you want, the time of year, and what's in stock. It's a good bet, though, that you'll enjoy significant discounts after late August, when heavy tourist traffic dies down. Downwind Sails is open April to mid-October and is right on the beach. This is a great spot to hang out during the summer, with all of the boating action plus regular beach volleyball tournaments.

Myrtle Beach Water Sports, Inc.
9915 North Kings Highway, Myrtle Beach
(843) 497–8848, (866) RENT–ATV
www.myrtlebeachwatersports.com

This water-sports store rents Jet Skis, pontoons, and jetboats by the hour. Specials on rentals and tours are offered throughout the year, so be sure to inquire about any discounts you might be entitled to. This outlet is open 8:00 A.M. to 6:00 P.M. daily from March 1 through October.

Insiders' Tip

Personal watercraft have proven to be dangerous water-sports equipment in the hands of an inexperienced or impaired operator. Every year the Grand Strand mourns deaths caused by too young, too reckless, or too drunk personal watercraft drivers involved in boating accidents.

Nothing can beat parasailing for great views and sheer exhilaration. PHOTO: COURTESY OF MYRTLE BEACH AREA CHAMBER OF COMMERCE

South Strand

Captain Dick's Marina
4123 U.S. Highway 17 Business,
Murrells Inlet
(843) 651–3676, (866) 577–3474
www.captdicks.com

Parasailing flights are booked from this marina year-round, weather permitting. Bookings slow down considerably beginning in October and continuing throughout winter when winds are friskier and waters choppier. For about $50 you can enjoy a nearly two-hour boat trip and 12 to 15 minutes of soaring 200 to 300 feet above the ocean. Captain Dick's also rents genuine Yamaha Wave Runners. Cost is $69 for 45 minutes of riding inlet channels out into the ocean.

Marlin Quay Parasailing
Marlin Quay Marina,
1398 South Waccamaw Drive,
Garden City Beach
(843) 651–4444, (877) 670–3474
www.marlinquay.com

This high-flying experience includes a 1½- to 2-hour boat ride in the Atlantic Ocean plus a 15-minute flight at more than 200 feet in the air. There must be six people per boat to make the excursion. The cost is $42 plus tax per parasailer. Trips are scheduled from April through mid-October. Discounts for couples are available.

Myrtle Beach Water Sports of Little River
Little River Waterfront
(843) 280–7777, (866) SEA–DOO

Enjoy beautiful scenic views of Bird Island from your lofty parasail perch. Reservations are required. This water-sport resource also offers pontoons and Jet Skis. Open daily from 8:00 A.M. to 6:00 P.M., March through October.

Day Trips

Charleston
Conway
Indigo Farms, NC
Wilmington, NC

Once upon a time there were lulls of "what can we do today" for Grand Strand visitors. These were usually rainy days when the beach was less than pleasant, long days during too-long vacations that needed a break in the monotony, and those disastrous days when the sun had turned the skin too lobster to handle another burning. But with the most recent growth along the Grand Strand, it is nearly impossible to find a day without some suitable activity . . . no matter what your particular interest.

This chapter offers suggestions for day trips. Any one of them will give you an up-close look at Southern culture, a taste of the extraordinary beauty and history of the Carolinas' coastal region, and generally something to do if you wonder what is just beyond the Strand's offerings. Zip to Conway or Charleston in South Carolina, or Wilmington, just across the state line in North Carolina, to spend a day enjoying the sights and return; you'll be cozy in your bed before the lines shorten on Restaurant Row.

Charleston

Charleston. The very name of this beautiful city conjures up images of sprawling plantations, honey-dipped Southern belles, and the sweet bouquet of magnolia floating on the ocean breeze. Charleston, a synergy of charm and cosmopolitan flair, is steeped in a history that parallels the South itself—indeed the little city is a microcosm of the whole South. More distinctive than any other Southern city, Charleston has found its way into operas, novels, movies, television dramas, and even soap operas. Simply put there's no place like it in all the world, and you don't dare get as close as Myrtle Beach and miss out on the enchantment.

It will come as no surprise that Charleston boasts far too many enticements to mention even a respectable fraction in this chapter. If you want to know more, pick up a copy of *Insiders' Guide to Greater Charleston.* Cover to cover, it's packed with the particulars you'll need to know to enjoy this fascinating city to its fullest extent.

Any time is a great time to visit the area, but spring, as a whole, is remarkable, with warm days, crisp nights, and flowers galore. In May **Spoleto,** an international arts festival, exacts a welcome grip on the city. Consistently a huge success, Spoleto is a celebration of opera, jazz, theater, dance, and visual arts sometimes categorized as classical and sometimes modern enough to cause controversy. People from all over the globe return year after year, and the numbers keep growing. For more information about the festival, write P.O. Box 157, Charleston, South Carolina 29402, call (843) 722 2764, or visit www.spoletousa.org.

In September **The Charleston Preservation Society** opens many of the city's privately owned homes and gardens during its annual candlelight tour series. This is the second of our two favorite times to visit. Many of the tours include chamber music and champagne receptions, and all are imbued with an authentic sense of yesteryear. Learn more by calling (843) 722-4630, or visit them on-line at www.preservationsociety.org.

Many of Charleston's legendary plantations are open to the public. All of the gardens are memorable; some are outright unforgettable. The most popular and well-known of the lineup: **Drayton Hall,** (843) 769-2600, www.draytonhall.org; **Middleton Place,** (800) 782-3608, www.middletonplace.org; **Magnolia Plantation and Gardens,** (800) 367-3517, www.magnoliaplantation.com; **Cypress Gardens,**

The Lowcountry's signature sweet-grass baskets are still made by hand in Charleston. PHOTO: COURTESY OF CHARLESTON CONVENTION & VISITORS BUREAU

(843) 553-0515, www.cypressgardens.org, which was once part of Dean Hall Plantation; and Boone Hall, (843) 884-4371, www.boonehallplantation.com. Admission to the plantations and gardens is $12.50 for adults and $6.00 for children ages 6 to 12.

Charles Towne Landing, 1500 Old Towne Road, (843) 852-4200, a South Carolina state park, is also a former plantation. Today the park is dedicated to recreating and interpreting the first permanent English settlement in the Carolinas, on this site in 1670. There's a film about the history of the Lowcountry, an animal forest, a reproduction of a 17th-

century trading vessel, and a colonial area where visitors can observe candle making, open-fire cooking, woodworking, and the colony's first printing press. Bicycles, the best way to get around, are available for rent. Hours are 8:30 A.M. to 5:00 P.M. Admission is $5.00 for adults, $2.50 for children ages 6 through 14, and $2.50 for out-of-state seniors. In-state seniors, disabled visitors, and children younger than 6 are admitted free. Learn more at www.charlestonarea.com/ctlanding.htm.

Nearly every school child in South Carolina has been to the **Fort Sumter National Monument** in Charleston Harbor at least once. Many know the story by heart. In 1861 Confederate soldiers fired upon Union forces stationed at the fort, and the Civil War began. You can get to Fort Sumter by boat only, but that's a big part of the fun. Catch the tour at Charleston's City Marina on Lockwood Boulevard or at Patriots Point in Mount Pleasant. Call (843) 722-1691 for more information or visit www.nps.gov/fusu/fusu.htm.

Charleston is home to **The Citadel,** 171 Moultrie Street, (843) 953-5000, once an all-male state-supported military college that has recently been the center of much controversy over the court-ordered admittance of women. If you're headed to Charleston, plan your trip to include a Friday when school is in session so you can watch the weekly dress parade; it starts at 3:45 P.M. Visit The Citadel on-line at www.citadel.edu.

Charleston is chock-full of museums and carefully preserved historic homes, many of which are open to the public. The **Frances R. Edmunds Center for Historic Preservation,** 108 Meeting Street, (843) 724-8484, is a good place to start your visit. You can buy tickets here to most area attractions, and the staff will offer lots of friendly tourist advice. The center is open Monday through Saturday from 10:00 A.M. to 5:00 P.M., and Sunday from 2:00 to 5:00 P.M.

If you're looking for excellent shopping alternatives, Charleston sports a fine array. So if your day trip isn't full to overflowing, at least check out **King Street** and the **Old Market** area. The selections are overwhelming: old shops, new shops, food shops, open-air shops. It's something you'll have to experience to understand.

Charleston is a scenic two-hour trip from Myrtle Beach. Take U.S. Highway 17 South. Even the trip down to Charleston is a great experience. Driving through **Frances Marion National Park** shows you some of the finest coastal natural beauty in America ... and, alas, some of the most devastation to forest and wildlife areas by a hurricane (the centuries-old trees will never recover from the damage wrought by Hurricane Hugo, and the area shows the loss).

Insiders' Tip

If you decide to explore Charleston, be sure to leave plenty of time to stop along the way. If you are staying in Myrtle Beach, the two-hour drive south to Charleston is filled with diversions: a detour into Murrells Inlet or Pawleys Island, a tour of Hampton Plantation, roadside produce stands, historical markers. Watch for the signs!

The historic antebellum village of **McClellanville** (also devastated by Hugo, but well-recovered) is about halfway along the route and offers some of the finest white oak–lined streets and hanging moss in South Carolina. Just before you get to Charleston, the little village of Mt. Pleasant will amaze you with roadside huts set up to sell baskets, bowls, and other carriers woven from South Carolina sweet grass—an art developed by slaves and handed down through the generations to just a handful of old women who still remember the method. These beautiful objects are also among the most utilitarian pieces you can find. Museums pay fortunes for them; here and here alone you can find them on the roadside for what'll seem like a steal.

Conway

Conway is one of the prettiest little towns you'll ever stumble upon if you seek a typical southern small town; it's filled with friendly folks who can demonstrate the very essence of Southern hospitality. A mere 14 miles from Myrtle Beach, most people are introduced to Conway as they drive through it en route to Myrtle Beach.

Most people don't realize that a few blocks east of the congestion on U.S. Highway 501 Bypass, just beyond the choke of auto exhaust, is Conway's historic section. In addition to its rich history, thanks to the extensive planting and protection of trees, Conway has been designated a Tree City, USA. However the newest trees aren't the ones that impress visitors most; the enormous age-old oaks are what Conwayites and tourists love best. Local residents have gone to great lengths to preserve and protect their oaks. In some cases they have even constructed roads around the majestic trees! The reward is a cool canopy of shade unfurling across streets where lovely homes date from a century ago and more.

One of the first and finest oaks you'll see as you drive down Conway's Main Street is the **Wade Hampton Oak** in front of the Horry County Museum. A plaque on the oak commemorates the day in 1876 when Confederate general Wade Hampton brought his campaign for the governorship to Conway and addressed a crowd from beneath the tree. Many years later, when construction of a railroad threatened the historic hardwood, a spirited local lady, Mary Beaty, brandished a loaded shotgun and ordered workers, "Touch not a single bough."

Just across the street from the Horry County Museum, another stately oak spills shade in the yard of the First Methodist Church. Its gnarled branches stretch over the historic graves in the cemetery. Don't miss the oak on Elm Street at Fifth Avenue around which motorists have to maneuver their cars. On Sixth Avenue, near Elm Street, the road literally splits in half to go around another tree. A monument at the foot of this tree was erected in honor of soldiers who died defending the Confederacy. The blacktop makes way for another oak at the intersection of Seventh Avenue and Beaty Street. If time permits, allow yourself the leisure to mosey along nearby streets; you'll enjoy a veritable parade of the beautiful old trees that typify the South at its finest. The Conway Chamber of Commerce publishes *A Guide to Conway's Fine Oaks*, an illustrated booklet with facts, poems dedicated to the trees, and a self-guided tour.

But before you take off for a lazy amble beneath the trees, stop for an enlightening tour at the **Horry County Museum,** 201 Main Street, (843) 248-1282. Open 10:00 A.M. to 5:00 P.M. Monday through Saturday, one of the museum's most popular exhibits includes a variety of Lowcountry animals. Sadly, burgeoning development in the area has endangered many species. Those on display were accidentally killed (that's right, there is a "roadkill" display in the museum). In addition to birds, alligators, and more, you can see everybody's favorite: an enormous 300-pound black bear that was hit by a car on U.S. 501 many years ago. The central theme underlying all of the exhibits is the wide range of environmental conditions found in Horry County and how its inhabitants, from prehistoric times to the present, have adapted to these local conditions. Find out more at www.horrycountymuseum.org.

If yours is a spring vacation, Conway is a not-to-be-missed excursion. Flowers begin blooming as early as March and usually flourish throughout most of April. Tulip trees and Japanese magnolias are particular favorites. They're complemented by quince, daffodils, narcissus, goldenrod, white and purple wisteria, crape myrtle, flowering cherry trees, Bradford pear trees, pink and white dogwoods, and thousands of azaleas in vivid, delicious colors.

Conway is the county seat of Horry County. Plans for the town, originally known as Kingston Township, were drafted around 1734. The first settlers arrived a few years later. (It wasn't until the early 1900s that Conway residents began to build vacation cottages at New Town, the summer retreat now known as Myrtle Beach.) As the area's primary transportation route, the Waccamaw River was absolutely vital to early life in Conway. For many, many years, the town's economy centered on by-products gleaned from the thick pine forests that surrounded the city. Many businessmen found wealth selling lumber, tar, pitch, and turpentine.

Your best bet is to enter Conway over the Main Street Bridge. (The bridge has been restored to look like it did when it was first erected.) The **Conway Chamber** of Commerce, 203 Main Street, will be the first building on the left. Do yourself a favor and take a few minutes to stop and ask questions. And be sure to get a copy of the "Conway's Historic Tour" brochure so you won't miss a single one of the city's beautiful and significant buildings, many of which are on the National Register of Historic Buildings. The self-guided tour also features a number of distinctive homes including Snow Hill, at the corner of Kingston Lake and Lakeside Drives, and the Arthur Burroughs home just across the street.

Conway City Hall, on the left at the foot of the bridge, was designed by Robert Mills, who also masterminded the Washington Monument and several other public buildings in our nation's capital. Constructed in 1824 or 1825, the building was the area's first courthouse. The city clock, which has become a Conway trademark, was added more than a century later in 1939. In recent years, since the city became part of the Main Street USA program, Conway's once-sleepy downtown has been transformed by a host of extensive renovations. Buildings, most of which were built in the early 1900s, have been restored to their original appearances. Numerous businesses have opened and flourished since the restoration began more than a decade ago. A host of department stores, speciality shops, and antiques markets now line the historic streets.

For a town of modest size, Conway has a surprising number of excellent restaurants. A popular spot with locals is The Trestle, 308 Main Street, (843) 248-9896. Fresh pastries are featured every morning. A doughnut or a cinnamon twist with a cup of coffee will start your historic tour off right. Lunchtime fare includes stuffed potatoes, chicken salad, and a delectable club sandwich made extraordinary by fresh-baked sourdough bread. Other lunch suggestions include The Sidewheeler, 110 Main on the Riverfront, (843) 248-7048, and Chan's Garden, 1117 Third Avenue, (843) 248-9182. Wayne's Restaurant, 1127 Third Avenue, (843) 248-2951, a longtime local favorite, will serve up a sampling of the South's finest: Southern fried chicken, chicken bog (also known as chicken pilau, pronounced "per-low"), corn bread, Southern-style vegetables, collards, and creamy banana pudding.

Conway initiated development of its riverfront area several years ago, and the improvement has been phenomenal. For a change of pace, check out the boats at the city-owned Conway Marina at the end of Elm Street. Take a stroll along the scenic river on the updated 850-foot boardwalk. For an especially tranquil day, rent a canoe or pontoon boat at the marina and disappear down the river or into the swamp off Kingston Lake. Canoes and pontoons can be rented for a half day or full day. If you can, talk marina operator Dick Davis into serving as your guide. He also rents fishing boats and might be willing to show you where to catch "the big one."

Insiders' Tip

Though you can find sweet-grass baskets in many shops and markets around the Grand Strand, wait until you get to Charleston for the biggest selection of shapes and styles and so you can meet the craftspeople. In Mt. Pleasant, a suburb north of Charleston that you will drive through, the women who spend their days weaving the reeds set up roadside stands along U.S. Highway 17. Stands with baskets are also in the historic section of Charleston, convenient to the favorite walking paths of tourists and locals alike.

Another of the marina's options is to take a riverboat cruise on the *Kingston Lady*, and on several nights during the summer you can catch a live-play murder mystery on board, courtesy of the world-renowned Vagabond Players. Otherwise, a two to four hour tour down the uncharted Waccamaw is enhanced by a narrated history of the beautiful blackwater river that's estimated to be 5 million years old. You're sure to catch a glimpse of the river's abundant wildlife, including alligators, otters, turtles, and majestic blue herons. A two-hour sunset cruise is especially romantic and often features live entertainment. Call the Conway Marina and *Kingston Lady* at (843) 248-4033 or (800) 361-6058 to set up your river adventure. You can visit them on-line at www.kingstonlady.com.

Conway is the undisputed heart of Horry County's thriving tobacco industry. Each year, in a little more than three months, the Conway market pumps about $40 million into the economy. Many visitors to Conway enjoy the unique experience of a tobacco auction. The tobacco market typically opens in mid-July and closes toward the end of October. Conway's warehouses include **Coastal Farmer's** on Cultra Road off U.S. Highway 501 West at El Bethel, and **New Farmers** at 2401 Main Street. Tobacco isn't sold every day during the marketing season, and the order of the sale rotates. Before you head for the warehouses, get a sales schedule from the Conway Chamber of Commerce. The prattle of the auctioneer sounds like a strange language to the uninitiated, but any of the friendly farmers will be glad to give you a quick lesson in growing, grading, stabilization regulations, and "turning the tag."

Conway boasts several popular annual events. The **Rivertown Jazz Festival,** sponsored by the Conway Main Street program, draws thousands to the riverfront beneath Main Street Bridge. Usually scheduled for May or early June, this event showcases plenty of outrageously delicious food, jazzy toe-tapping tunes, entertainment for kids, and pretty river scenery to boot. Best of all the festival is free and appropriate for all ages, so bring lawn chairs or a big blanket, stretch out comfortably, and relegate your cares to some other day.

Riverfest is another much-anticipated annual event. Best wear your swimsuit; to truly enjoy this festival, you have to get wet. Events include Waccamaw raft races for all ages, crafts, concerts, lunch, and scads of children's games. The day's most unusual event is undoubtedly the Jell-O Jump. Adventuresome kids actually leap into a chilled vat of Jell-O to recover marked golf balls. Ball markings determine the prizes to be won, including items such as soft drinks and free passes to area attractions. But the grand-prize winner gets cold, hard cash. Riverfest is typically held on the Saturday that falls closest to the Fourth of July and features an explosive fireworks finale.

On the first weekend in December, the riverfront is the focus of another colorful event—the **Christmas Boat Parade.** In 1992 Conway had its first nighttime boat parade. The aquatic procession features boats of all sizes—bedecked in Christmas regalia. The 1992 occasion was an immediate hit, and it has become a much-loved annual event.

The Conway Area Chamber of Commerce offers popular bus tours of Conway's historical areas each year in conjunction with **Canadian-American Days Festival** in March (see the Annual Events chapter for details). Call (843) 248-2273 for more information. Another favorite Canadian-American event is the **Taste of Conway.** Not surprisingly, it's held along the riverfront and always draws eager crowds to sample the fine cuisine of Conway's restaurant owners and chefs. Delectable samples of appetizers, entrees, and desserts range from about $1.00 to $3.50.

To get to Conway, take U.S. 501 from Myrtle Beach, SC Highway 90 from North Myrtle Beach and SC Highway 544 (or U.S. 17 Bypass to SC 544) from the South Strand. Or, you might want to ride the Waccamaw Regional Transportation Authority's Lymo. Call (843) 488-0865 or visit www.golymo.com for schedules and fares. (See the Getting Here, Getting Around chapter for more information.)

For a wealth of information about Conway, the following Web sites are helpful: www.conwayscchamber.com and www. cityofconway.com.

Indigo Farms, NC

A day trip to Indigo Farms is a simple jaunt into the farm country that surrounds Myrtle Beach. The farm actually straddles the border between the Carolinas and gets its name from the blue crop that originally made this region famous. It's just a quick left and then a right out of North Myrtle Beach; take SC Highway 9 to Loris and turn right onto SC Highway 57 (Indigo Farms billboards will be around), then drive straight 'til you see the farm on the side of the road. Be sure to call (843) 399–6902 first for hours, which vary, and in-season crops, which vary, too.

For locals Indigo Farms is a gardening (especially for their large and priced-right ferns) and produce resource. Everything is grown on the actual farmhouse grounds or in the surrounding fields. The complex has an extensive greenhouse with a few permanent, beautiful specimens of palms growing against the roof (unfortunately, not for sale) among the lush geraniums, lantana, mandavilla, and everything else that's in season. The palms look like they've been around almost as long as the Bellamy family, who runs Indigo Farms, has worked this land. The storefront extends to include an eat-in bakery and cafe with pies galore, some locally made crafts that are on display, and the produce market, where the merchandise is meant to be squeezed and admired.

Still owned and operated by the latest generation of Bellamys (the exact count is in dispute by family members), on the day that we visited we found Mrs. Bellamy herself operating one of the cash registers in the produce market, helped out by one of her daughters-in-law. The Bellamys seem to want to share the best way to view a farm, which is from the middle of a field. At Indigo they grow quite a few pick-it-yourself crops, from strawberries and blueberries to tomatoes and peaches. Besides being a twist on the usual shopping experience, picking your own fruits and veggies brings out more flavor to enjoy.

As you would expect, fall harvest is a busy time at Indigo Farms. In addition to the usual farm activities, Indigo hosts two fests: **Farm Heritage Day** and **Pumpkin Day,** both in October. Both festivals turn the hard-working farm into something of a handmade amusement park that even the cows can enjoy.

Farm Heritage Day explores the area's original economic and domestic roots. Admission is free to events; children and adults alike can pet all the usual farm animals and some not-so-usual farm animals such as emus. Members of the Bellamy family and their friends provide demonstrations of crafts, usually something the demonstrator specializes in or just needs to get done: candle making or wool dyeing with indigo, which is actually another color before it hits the air and turns blue. There's a lot to learn. Traditional activities include apple bobbing, hay rides, scarecrow making, potbelly pig races, and tours of the farm facilities. Cornstalks are turned into mazes and tepees for the kids. Pumpkin Day is in preparation for Halloween, of course, and children are invited to draw on their pumpkins.

Throughout the year Indigo Farms is also available for school tours, picnics, open-air parties, and oyster roasts. The Bellamys are contemplating a Christmas event, so keep an eye peeled for their changing, seasonal schedule.

Wilmington, NC

Wilmington is a beautiful and historic seaport that affords residents and visitors the very finest opportunities for shopping, dining, culture, and art. Truth is, there's far too much to see and do in a single day, but if you choose carefully and plan your trip before leaving the Grand Strand, you can cover a lot of interesting territory in a short period of time. For a complete guide to this intriguing Southern city, buy yourself a copy of *Insiders' Guide to Wilmington and North Carolina's Southern Coast.* Additionally, you might give the folks at the **Cape Fear Coast**

The battleship USS North Carolina *is a must-see when you visit Wilmington.* PHOTO: JOE SWIFT

Convention and Visitors Bureau a ring, (800) 222-4757; they're well-equipped to answer any of your questions. Their Web site is helpful as well: www. cape-fear.nc.us.

Wilmington boasts the largest urban registered historic district in the entire state of North Carolina. Indeed, it boasts one of the largest districts listed on the National Register of Historic Places, with homes dating from as early as the mid-1700s. Meticulously restored Victorian, Georgian, Italianate, and antebellum homes—from grand mansions to cottages—attest to the perseverance of Wilmingtonians. The area considered historically significant covers 200 city blocks, but much of the fun and captivating charm of Wilmington is concentrated on and near the riverfront. An architecturally unique historic district highlights the downtown area, with a scenic riverfront park overlooking the USS *North Carolina* battleship.

Follow U.S. 17 North from the Grand Strand to Wilmington. Guide signs are posted to point you downtown where a deep harbor, restaurants, shops, and impressive homes await. The harbor itself offers surprises. With a little luck, a Coast Guard ship or other vessels will be docked there, allowing visitors to board and browse.

As in many historic Southern cities, a good way to begin your Wilmington adventure is with a horse-drawn carriage tour along the riverfront past stately mansions and beautifully restored homes. Various tours, including walking and boat tours, are available at the foot of Market Street by the river. They are well worth the reasonable prices as they provide lively narratives of the area's history and point out attractions you might want to return to on your own. Two popular boat tours on the Cape Fear River are aboard the *Cap-*

tain *J.M. Maffitt* and the *Henrietta II*. The *Henrietta II* bills itself as North Carolina's only true sternwheel paddleboat. Sightseeing cruises offer opportunities to view real plantations. The *Maffitt* also offers sight-seeing cruises on the Cape Fear River. Special fall cruises are a real treat.

During the summer months the *Maffitt* serves as a river taxi to ferry people to the battleship *North Carolina*. Once the most powerful battleship in the world, the *North Carolina* now rests majestically in the harbor and is easily seen from Water Street; but to drive to it, you have to go to U.S. 17 South and circle the city. (If you save the battleship for your last stop before heading back to the Grand Strand, it will be right on the way home.) If you want to stay downtown for shopping and supper, take the *Maffitt* instead of driving. For more information, call (800) 676–0162 or visit www.cfrboats.com.

Battleship *North Carolina*, a 15-story battleship that is 2 city blocks long, is Wilmington's most popular attraction. Dedicated to the 10,000 North Carolinians who sacrificed their lives during World War II, the battleship *North Carolina* participated in every major naval offensive in the Pacific Ocean. But here's a word of warning. If you have a physical handicap, claustrophobia, or any ailment that remotely resembles vertigo, tuck your greenbacks back in your pocket and move on. Only the main deck is wheelchair-accessible. One staircase after another requires careful maneuvering, and there are 5- to 6-inch ledges to finesse at every door. There are more than a few tight spots. Granted, you don't have to climb into the turrets, but if you tour the lower deck, you're already into the tight spots before you realize you need to turn back. The brave souls who decide to go ahead will enjoy a wonderful history lesson.

The adventure begins with an orientation film about the battleship and its escapades during World War II. After orientation, choose from two self-guided tours. One tour can take as long as two hours. Winding through the ship's bowels, you'll see the cobbler shop, sailors' quarters, officers' quarters, galley, bake shop, kitchen, dining areas, engine room,

laundry, print shop, dark room, a doctor's office and dispensary, an operating room, an isolation area, a financial section, a supply office, and more. It's awesome! A second tour eliminates much of the climbing and takes in fewer decks; it takes approximately an hour.

The ship is open daily from 8:00 A.M. until 8:00 P.M. May 6 through September 15 and until 5:00 P.M. for the rest of the year. Admission costs $8.00 for adults and $4.00 for children ages 6 to 11; kids younger than age 6 get in free. For more information call (910) 350–1817 or visit www.battleshipnc.com.

Let's head back downtown for some shopping. In most cases downtown stores are independent specialty stores that brim with surprises from upscale to whimsical. One of Wilmington's brightest stars is the recently revived **City Market.** (You can enter on South Front Street or Water Street.) The market has fresh fruit and vegetables, a variety of tempting home-baked treats, jellies, honey, and plenty of handmade crafts. On the northern end of the riverfront, The **Cotton Exchange,** www.shopcottonexchange.com, is another not-to-be-missed shopping stop. It's at the corner of Water and Grace Streets, (910) 343–9896. (You can also enter at 313 North Front.) An old cotton warehouse that's been converted into a mall of sorts, The Cotton Exchange houses more than 30 businesses on three levels. Even if you don't like to shop, it's worth the stop to see the displays of cotton bales, weighing equipment, and photographs that recount the building's evolution. At last count there were four restaurants at The Cotton Exchange, so don't worry when hunger assails you. **Chandler's Wharf,** an equally charming but smaller shopping complex, is on the extreme southern end of the riverfront. It, too, definitely merits a stop.

If there's any time left in your day, other attractions include **Louise Wells Cameron Art Museum,** 3201 South 17th Street, (910) 395–5999, www.cameronart museum.com, a 42,000-square-foot facility featuring a permanent collection of North Carolina and American art from the eighteenth century to the present; **Orton Plantation,** off N.C. Highway 133 at Winnabow, (910) 371-6851, www. ortongardens.com, an old rice plantation where the gardens are open to the public; and the **Wilmington Railroad Museum,** 501 Nutt Street, (910) 763-2634, www. wilmington.org/railroad, a kind of fun house for folks fascinated by trains and train culture.

Wilmington's biggest shindig of the year is the **Azalea Festival.** It's held in April and includes a parade, street fair, and home and garden tours. For more information about the area or the festival, call the Cape Fear Coast Convention and Visitors Bureau, (800) 222-4757 or visit azalea.wilmington.org.

And, one last note, you might want to call ahead to see if **Thalian Hall Center for the Performing Arts,** 310 Chestnut Street, (910) 343-3664, has a performance scheduled during your visit. Full-scale musicals, light opera, and internationally renowned dance companies are part of Thalian's consistently high-quality programming. Thalian Hall is the only surviving theater designed by John Montague Trumble, one of America's foremost nineteenth-century theater designers. Historic tours are offered. Call (910) 343-3664 or (800) 523-2820 in advance for reservations and exact tour schedules. The Web site is also helpful, www.thalianhall.com.

Because of the large international film industry headquartered in Wilmington (Coleco's DeLaurentis studio is there, and several major films have come from Wilmington, including *The Crow, Blue Velvet, Cape Fear, King Kong,* and others), there is a large artsy avant garde community. Walk along cobblestone Front Street any night to sip espresso at the coffeehouses, listen to live music in the bars, or enjoy New Age cuisine in one of the cozy little restaurants. Oh, and don't forget to smile and say hello to any of the visiting movie stars who might be there on location.

Real Estate

Residential
Developments

Real-Estate
Agencies

If you choose to visit the Grand Strand in the early spring,
you'll probably be surprised at how early the flowers blossom—and by how much construction is going on. For spring fix-up (as opposed to spring cleaning), Grand Stranders get out their hammers and wrenches, nail guns and compressors, bulldozers and cranes to prepare for the busy summer months ahead. Burgeoning growth is evidenced by a wealth of new construction, too. In fact the area is growing nine times faster than the national average.

The Strand's permanent population has tripled in the last 30 years. Horry County is one of the nation's fastest-growing retirement communities. In fact, nearly 20 percent of the population in both Horry and Georgetown Counties is older than 65. That figure can be compared to only 9 percent in 1980.

With a relatively low cost of living (despite regressive state sales tax on food, clothing, and housing), the Myrtle Beach area appeals to active retirees, singles, and new families. Residential opportunities abound: golf-course villas, country clubs, sprawling residences with amenities, smaller single-family neighborhoods, friendly mobile-home communities, and condominium villages.

As is the case in many resort areas, real-estate scams have posed problems in Myrtle Beach. Federal consumer watchdogs have done pretty well in helping to close down many real-estate shams in the past few years.

Do be careful before you sign on the dotted line. But don't fret; with a little research and homework, you should do fine. Take time to analyze your real-estate purchases carefully, whether for investment or permanent occupancy. You should consider the long-term potential of the property. Is high tide already lapping at the back deck? Is insurance a manageable expense? Is an oceanfront view worth it, or should you consider a purchase off the beach . . . on a lake, the Waccamaw River, or a golf course? Do zoning ordinances protect the long-term integrity of your investment? And don't forget to inquire about homeowner association fees; these are not included in your mortgage but are assessed monthly or annually—and can increase rather considerably, and unexpectedly, as well.

Myrtle Beach boasts many reputable and well-established communities. Historically these areas tended to be concentrated on the North Strand. That is changing, albeit slowly. Enduring communities such as The Dunes, Pine Lakes, and anything on Ocean Boulevard from 30th to 80th Avenues North will certainly prove a strong purchase. In these areas, zoning laws are already in place to protect the value of your purchase. As a result, such properties come with a hefty price tag. But there are plenty of newer developments all over the Strand that are well worth considering. One of the most exclusive addresses in America, with residents including Amy Vanderbilt, professional football player Michael Fox of the Carolina Panthers, the CEO of NationsBank, and other luminaries, is the South Strand neighborhood of DeBordieu (locally pronounced "debby-doo"). Remember, these days a place "at the beach" doesn't necessarily mean "on the beach."

The subsequently listed developments represent a few of our favorite communities. These are followed by a sampling of the dozens of real-estate agencies with strong reputations.

Residential Developments

North Strand

Barefoot Resort & Golf
North Myrtle Beach
(843) 390–1999, (877) 612–1418
www.bfresort.com

Barefoot Resort has united the experience and talent of four of golf's most recognized names— Greg Norman, Davis Love III, Tom Fazio, and Pete Dye—to create incredible golf surroundings. In addition to golf Barefoot Resort includes a selection of residential communities that features more than 1,000 homes and 2,600 multifamily units for primary, retirement, or second-home living.

At the heart of the resort is a town center planned to be reminiscent of Savannah's Riverfront and Charleston's Market, where residents and visitors stroll brick sidewalks past open-air cafes, retail stores, and service establishments. Amenities will eventually include a 174-slip marina, full-service resort accommodations, access to a private beach club, and specialty retail shops.

Within Barefoot, single-family communities have floor plans ranging from 1,000-square-foot patio homes to 3,500-square-foot estate homes. Homes with homesites are priced roughly from $150,000 to $500,000. Multifamily communities feature all shapes, sizes, and price ranges of condominium villas from $80,000 to around $500,000.

Hillsborough
Highway 90 between Highway 501 and
Highway 22, Conway
(843) 234–3232
www.coldwellbankerchicora.com

Hillsborough is located in a part of the Grand Strand that is developing quickly because of the easier access new roads are providing. This quiet country setting is convenient to both Myrtle Beach and Conway and is scarcely 10 minutes from the beach itself. This community offers three- and four-bedroom homes with two-car garages and spacious floor plans. Hillsborough also features a four-acre amenity center with a clubhouse, pool, recreation area, and walking and bike paths. Situated in a highly regarded school district, Hillsborough is an ideal community for families. Perhaps best of all, this community is extremely affordable, with prices starting around $130,000.

Lightkeeper's Village
U.S. Highway 17, Little River
(843) 249–5720, (800) 344–1604
www.lightkeepersvillage.com

Overlooking the Intracoastal Waterway and adjacent to Coquina Harbor, this 35-acre community offers three types of properties: Lighthouse Pointe, Watchmen's Cottages, and Yacht Club Villas.

Lighthouse Pointe, priced from $200,000, includes waterway villas. Three-bedroom floor plans prominently feature natural light. The neighborhood boasts a waterfront pool with spacious sundecks and a waterfront clubhouse with a bar, sitting areas, and a fitness room.

Watchmen's Cottages, priced from $120,000, feature elegant and finely detailed two- and three-bedroom homes. The single-level design was created specifically with retirees in mind.

The two-bedroom, two-bath Yacht Club Villas are priced from $130,000. Residents enjoy the tennis court, putting green, three pools, sundecks, two clubhouses, and Waterway and Harbour-side boardwalks. Boat slips also are available.

Tidewater Golf Club & Plantation
4901 Little River Neck Road,
North Myrtle Beach
(843) 249–1403, (800) 843–3234

Like more than a few residential communities in this area, Tidewater is probably best known for its golf course. This community offers homes on-course or off-course.

Developers at Tidewater carefully planned this community to preserve and protect the area's dense maritime forest and to offer homeowners spectacular views of saltwater marshes, freshwater ponds, and the Atlantic Ocean. You'll find luxurious condominium villas, custom-finished homes, and spacious courtyard

Insiders' Tip

If you're interested in buying a home in a planned community that assesses a monthly homeowner's fee, investigate the terms thoroughly. Such fees can be raised without notice at any given time. Find out the original and current fees. Ask if the fee covers home insurance, pest control, outside irrigation and lighting or landscape maintenance. If you're paying a hefty fee just to support ever-increasing liability insurance for the community pool that you rarely use, a home in that community might not be worth it to you.

houses. Each of the residential districts at Tidewater features its own distinct architectural style and landscaping. Villas range from $130,000 to $165,000, and homes with lots start at approximately $200,000 and range to more than half a million dollars.

Tidewater sports its own swim and racquet club with a junior Olympic-size pool, a kiddie pool, and tennis courts.

The Waterfront at Briarcliffe Commons
U.S. Highway 17, Briarcliffe
(843) 361–8877, (888) 272–8700

Briarcliffe is a pleasant stretch of tall pines between North Myrtle Beach and Restaurant Row that can be easily overlooked as you zoom by in your car on Highway 17. Residents like their community that way; green and relatively undisturbed.

The Waterfront at Briarcliffe Commons makes the most of this enticing location by offering 188 condominiums between Highway 17 and the Intracoastal Waterway. Buildings overlooking the waterway are five stories, and the lake-and-lagoon-view buildings have three levels. The development also includes a pool and hot-tub complex overlooking the waterway, two levels of terraced walkways, bridges, gazebos, fishing pier, and a secure entrance.

The floor plans offer three bedrooms (one as an alternate den/office), 9-foot or vaulted ceilings, walk-in closets, and large screened verandas. Prices start at $105,900 and extend to $159,000 for the prime waterway view.

The allure of this location is compounded by a highway front commercial center containing a Copeland's New Orleans restaurant, a Fuddruckers, and a Marriott Courtyard hotel. Not only is this center convenient for residents, but it also serves as a buffer to the gates of one of the North Strand's most enticing condominium communities.

Myrtle Beach

Dunes Golf and Beach Club
9000 North Ocean Boulevard, Myrtle Beach
inquire through local Realtors

If living among the local ruling class and the old money is important to you, this is the place to choose: There are not many *nouveau riche* here. The homes, sold through various Realtors, are quite beautiful—though many are older than you might expect. Appropriately the upscale Dunes Golf Club anchors this community. Many homes feature golf vistas; a precious few feature ocean views.

Buying a home here doesn't qualify you to enjoy the many amenities; memberships are additional, and the dues are steep. Home prices at Dunes start around $200,000 and climb upwards of $1,000,000.

Oceanfront highrises are highly coveted, but other real estate options on the Grand Strand abound.

PHOTO: COURTESY OF MYRTLE BEACH AREA CHAMBER OF COMMERCE

Seagate Village
Highway 17 Business South, Myrtle Beach
(843) 839–3909
www.chicora.com

Seagate is an affordable, conveniently located community located immediately across the highway from Myrtle Beach

State Park. Two-, three-, and four-bedroom homes are offered with a variety of different floor plans. Exterior features include carports, outside storage, and landscaping packages. The amenity package includes pools, cabanas, garden plots, boat & RV storage, exercise facilities, and miles of walking paths. Seagate is extremely convenient to shopping, restaurants, golf, and the beach. Condo ownership is also available at Seagate. Homes begin in the low $60,000s, making this one of the area's most affordable communities.

Kingston Plantation
9770 Kings Road, Myrtle Beach
(843) 449–6400, (800) 382–3332
www.kingstonplantationrealestate.com

Kingston Plantation is 145 heavily forested, parklike acres with freshwater lakes and a half mile of secluded beach. Expect to see wildlife, including black swans, egrets, mallard ducks, and sea turtles.

A $4.5 million health club features an indoor pool, three squash and racquetball courts, an aerobics studio, weight-training and cardiovascular equipment, a sauna, a whirlpool, and locker-room facilities. There's even a professional masseuse on staff. Outdoors you'll find a junior Olympic-size pool and exceptional tennis facilities. (See the Parks and Recreation chapter for related information.) In addition, each of Kingston's different communities typically feature unique amenities.

From luxury oceanfront residences to clusters of lakeside villas and town homes, Kingston has a home to suit virtually any taste, with 90 different floor plans in all. Prices vary dramatically—from roughly $120,000 to $450,000.

Plantation Point
3800 U.S. Highway 17 Bypass, Myrtle Beach
inquire through local Realtors
www.plantationpointmb.com

Plantation Point is well-known as one of the more expensive communities in the Myrtle Beach area. Just off the bypass in Myrtle Beach, it's right in the heart of the action. The Myrtlewood Golf Club wraps around the development. Some lots and homes flank the Intracoastal Waterway.

There are many different residential options at Plantation Point, and what you choose determines what amenities you may access. Charleston Place is the newest offering, with single-family brick homes fronting the course. Options in Plantation Point include lots, estate homes, single-family homes, and town-house communities in a range of prices—from around $115,000 for a modest town house to $400,000 or more for an estate home.

Southgate in Carolina Forest
Highway 501, Myrtle Beach
(843) 903–0182
www.chicora.com

Southgate is located in Carolina Forest, Myrtle Beach's only master planned community. International Paper Realty created Carolina Forest with areas for churches, schools, shopping, and a post office. The 11,000-square-acre community has the potential to accommodate a population of 40,000. Spacious three-bedroom homes include two-car garages and extra-large master bedroom suites. The community is literally minutes to numerous golf courses, restaurants, entertainment, shopping, and the award-winning Conway Hospital. In addition to Myrtle Beach's proximity, historic Conway and Coastal Carolina University are also close at hand. Three-bedroom homes are priced from the low $100,000s.

South Strand

DeBordieu
U.S. Highway 17,
Georgetown
(843) 546–4176, (843) 527–4321,
(800) 753–5597
www.privatecommunities.com

DeBordieu is a private oceanfront residential community encompassing 2,700 acres of age-old oaks and pines, tidal marshes, and creeks with access to the Atlantic Ocean. This might be the most prestigious address on the South Strand. Justifiably so, DeBordieu bills itself as a purveyor of "splendid isolation."

This community offers a variety of homesites and villas with ocean, forest, marsh, and fairway views, and all are served by central water and sewer systems and underground utilities.

DeBordieu Club's golf course has been nationally acclaimed as one of Pete Dye's best. The colonial-style clubhouse is spec-

Insiders' Tip

Unless you've lived along the Grand Strand for a while or visited often, don't jump into buying a home just because the market's hot and houses seem to sell quickly. Rent first to avoid making a hasty decision that you might later find difficult to live with. That will give you time to explore all the real-estate opportunities here.

tacular. The Beach Club, with its lovely pool overlooking the ocean, offers superb dining. And the Tennis Center boasts eight composition courts and an excellent pro shop. Access to DeBordieu is controlled by a security entrance that is staffed 24 hours a day.

Living here is a pricey proposition, but if money is not an object and you don't mind the half-hour drive to Myrtle Beach, there's no prettier place or better investment. Homesites range from one-half acre to five acres, with forest, creek, golf, and ocean views. Prices range from $120,000 to nearly a million dollars.

Heritage Plantation
U.S. Highway 17, Pawleys Island
(843) 237–9824, (800) 448–2010
www.heritageplantation.com

Blessed with a unique combination of 300-year-old oaks, giant magnolias, scenic rice fields, and Waccamaw River vistas, Heritage Plantation features a clubhouse with a 75-foot heated pool and Jacuzzi, lighted tennis courts, a fitness center, card room, and a social area for entertaining. Property owners enjoy abundant golfing opportunities, including special privileges on six of the Grand Strand's top-rated courses: Oyster Bay, Marsh Harbour, all three Legends courses, and The Heritage Club itself, where members get reserved tee times. The beaches of Pawleys Island are only 3 miles away.

Homesites at Heritage Plantation range from $40,000 to $290,000. Homes start around $180,000.

Indigo Creek
9557 Indigo Club Drive, off U.S. Highway 17 Bypass South, Murrells Inlet
(843) 650–9475, (800) 654–9202

Indigo Creek is rich in natural beauty, thick with forest, and sprinkled with lakes. It's a breeze to reach Myrtle Beach on U.S. Highway 17 Bypass from Indigo Creek, which is less than a five-minute drive from restaurants, entertainment, shopping, medical facilities, and beaches.

Indigo Creek boasts the features of a community committed to preserving long-term value: privacy, attractive landscaping, well-lighted streets with curbs and gutters, underground utilities, and an architectural review board. Even when the local real-estate market was sluggish and slow, Indigo Creek was setting sales records.

An 18-hole championship course designed by Willard Byrd offers an indisputably challenging game of golf. There's a private pool complex, too.

Lots at Indigo Creek are priced from $35,000, and homes begin at about $130,000.

Pebble Creek at the International Club
Tournament Boulevard, off Highway 707, Murrells Inlet
(843) 357–6004
www.chicora.com

New three- and four-bedroom single-family homes with scenic lake views are available along this championship 18-hole golf course. Floor plans of 1,600 to 2,500 square feet are designed to buyer specifications and include spacious master suites, as well as something rare to the area—a walk-up basement. Pebble Creek is situated next door to the highly acclaimed Tournament Player's Club. This community is minutes from the ocean, the Intracoastal Waterway, Inlet Square Mall, Brookgreen Gardens, Huntington Beach State Park, and all the beauty of historic Georgetown. Homes are priced from about $170,000 to around $200,000.

Litchfield by the Sea
U.S. Highway 17, Pawleys Island
(843) 237–4000, (800) 476–2861
www.thelitchfieldcompany.com

For more than 40 years, The Litchfield Company has been developing private seaside communities amid beaches, marshlands, and lush Lowcountry golf courses. Amenities include pools, spas, tennis and volleyball courts, bike paths, fishing opportunities, picnic areas, and three of the finest golf clubs in the Lowcountry.

Throughout this spacious resort, you can choose from homesites, single-family homes, and a variety of quality town homes or villas overlooking miles of clean, white sand beaches, marshland, lakes, or golf-course fairways. Prices range from around $125,000 to more than $1 million.

Pawleys Plantation
U.S. Highway 17, Pawleys Island
(843) 237–7884
www.pawleysplantation.com

Pawleys Plantation is a world-class golf and country club built on 582 acres of natural wetlands, salt marshes, lakes, and rolling green fairways. Bordered on the south by a 645-acre nature preserve, this private community offers homesites and golf villas for purchase as well as accommodations and golf packages for those who want to vacation in the country-club atmosphere. The Pawleys Plantation golf course is an 18-hole championship layout designed by Jack Nicklaus. Among its most unforgettable features are a tremendous double green, a dramatic split fairway, and breathtaking lake and marsh views. An antebellum-style clubhouse ranks with the finest club facilities in the Southeast. (See the Golf chapter for more detailed information.)

Neighborhoods of villas throughout the plantation offer comfortable year-round living or a perfect getaway house for the second-home buyer. Lots feature a variety of views. Homesites start at about $20,000, and villas start around $105,000.

Prestwick Country Club
1001 Links Road, Myrtle Beach
(843) 293–6000, (800) 521–8522
www.prestwickcountryclub.com

Prestwick is situated around a private, $6 million Pete and P. B. Dye–designed golf course (see the Golf chapter). Prestwick Country Club also boasts one of the Strand's finest tennis complexes—11 clay courts and 2 hard-surface courts. You'll also find a health-club facility with a sauna, whirlpool, exercise areas, and indoor and outdoor pools. Security is provided 24 hours a day.

Prestwick features condominiums and homes, with direct fairway or lake views, ranging from $120,000 to $400,000. Custom-built residences are also available. Homesites run from approximately $50,000 to $90,000. Patio homes are priced from $130,000 to more than $180,000.

Prince Creek
Highway 707, Murrells Inlet
(800) 476–2861
www.thelitchfieldcompany.com

This new community is getting lots of press for being the last master-planned community on the Waccamaw Neck, a finger of land that extends from Winyah Bay in Georgetown to the edge of Horry County.

Just 15 minutes south of Myrtle Beach, Prince Creek bills itself as being "next to nature but in the middle of it all." The nearby fishing village of Murrells Inlet offers restaurants, shopping, new schools, and state-of-the-art health-care facilities, including the brand-new Waccamaw Community Hospital.

Whether you are looking for a town home, villa, single-family home, or mansion, Prince Creek is likely to have an option for you.

Highwood offers homesites surrounding the PGA-owned Tournament Players Club. Showcasing golf and wetland and woodland views, these custom sites offer a gated community and amenities including a on-site pool and cabana.

The Bays is a gated community that integrates a variety of neighborhoods within 400 acres of natural beauty. Each neighborhood is distinct but linked by The Greenway, a tree-lined boulevard designed for vehicles and pedestrians alike. All communities within The Bays have access to The Park—a shared 10-acre recreation area.

John's Bay of Prince Creek, located within The Bays, is a town-home community. With five floor plans, John's Bay delivers a low-maintenance lifestyle that leaves time for enjoying the community's pool, workout room, park, golf, and more.

Wachesaw Plantation
Wachesaw Road, Murrells Inlet
(843) 357–1263, (800) 373–1263
www.wachesaw.com

Wachesaw Plantation has an interesting history: It's built on the site of old Native American burial grounds that later became flourishing rice plantations. Ancient moss-draped oaks characterize this private community.

Amenities include a clubhouse, equestrian center, eight tennis courts, a swim-

Insiders' Tip
Rentals, whether weekly, monthly, or annual, are big business on the Strand. If you're house shopping, consider letting next year's vacationers pay a good chunk of your mortgage—look into multifamily structures.

ming pool, and a Tom Fazio–designed private golf course. A beautiful dining facility offers expansive views of the Intracoastal Waterway. Homes are priced from $200,000; cottages from $130,000; homesites from $40,000.

Wachesaw Plantation East
U.S. Highway 17, Murrells Inlet
(843) 357–0346, (800) 451–0115
www.wachesaweast.com

Wachesaw Plantation East, a more recent development phase, offers a semiprivate golf course, a private residential community, and a host of amenities. Homes are carefully situated to capture views of the semiprivate golf course, lakes, and the natural beauty of the surrounding landscape. Though just a 15-minute drive south of Myrtle Beach, Wachesaw Plantation East remains worlds apart from Myrtle's fray yet is conveniently near shopping, dining, and medical facilities.

The Clyde Johnston–designed golf course, which opened for play in fall 1996, offers a hint of Scottish-links influence—accented by freshwater wetlands and lakes. (See the Golf chapter for details.)

The community features fitness and biking trails and a clubhouse complex that includes a health club, swimming pool, guest inn, and conference center.

Homes of 1,700 to 3,500 square feet are priced in the $150,000s. Condominiums—1,100 to 1,800 square feet—are priced from around $90,000.

Willbrook Plantation
U.S. Highway 17, Litchfield Beach
(843) 237–4000, (800) 476–2861

The natural profile of Willbrook Plantation has changed little since it operated as three colonial rice plantations. Deer and fowl remain abundant, as do towering cypress trees, Carolina pines and age-old oaks.

Half-acre lots, from about $70,000, are currently for sale throughout Willbrook Plantation. Single-family homes are available in a pleasant community called Allston Point.

Centex Builders developed the newest community within Willbrook. Called The

Tradition, this community is built around a new 18-hole championship golf course. Several different single-family floor plans are offered, starting at $130,000 (including homesites). Willbrook Golf and Country Club offers half-acre lots starting at $68,000.

In addition to swimming, tennis and the extensive clubhouse, all Willbrook residents can take advantage of the amenities at Litchfield By The Sea. Private beach access, a beach club, tennis and bike trails set the stage for a lifestyle that's tough to beat.

Real-Estate Agencies

As you drive along the Strand, it might seem that there's a real estate office on every corner. Since you have a plethora of choices, you should give much time and consideration to choosing your agent. More often than with many other occupations, people enter the real estate field from widely disparate backgrounds. Consequently, the first salesperson you stumble across might or might not be a good fit for you. Scan first, then narrow down. Interview different people and choose someone with whom you're truly comfortable. After all, this is probably one of the biggest investments you'll ever make, and you deserve someone you can speak with honestly, confide in frequently and respect without reservation. If you're coming from another area, speak with a real estate agent you know and trust back home. Often, agents have contacts in the industry that will help you zero in on the perfect person.

When looking for the perfect property, the *Sun News* can be a primary resource. In particular, every Sunday paper delivers a comprehensive insert called *Real Estate Plus*. It is estimated that at least a third of realty transactions begin with a newspaper ad. Realtors use it religiously—though not always to advertise their best buys. (Can't tip off the competition!) They usually advertise a broad and respectable selection of their listings, hoping to attract prospective buyers for the hidden bargains.

Listed subsequently are some area real estate agencies whose brokers can help with the purchase of a new residence or an investment property. Please consider that the Strand has dozens and dozens of professional Realtors, many of whom are not detailed here. This list is in no way meant to reflect upon the qualifications of the real estate professionals not included here. If you'd like further information about other companies in the area, call the Grand Strand Board of Realtors at (843) 272-6966, or the Association of Realtors, Inc., Myrtle Beach at (843) 626-3638.

North Strand

Century 21 Coastal Carolina Properties Inc.
1908 U.S. Highway 17 South, North Myrtle Beach
(843) 272-6754, (800) 568-9253
www.c21ccp.com

Coastal Carolina Properties was founded in August 1973 as a general brokerage and development agency. In 1978, a decision was made to concentrate on general brokerage, and Coastal Carolina Properties joined the renowned Century 21 system. It has grown to employ approximately 25 agents and staffs a property management division. In 1996 the company earned Century 21's Quality Service Award and was one of the top-21 producing companies in the Carolinas.

Crescent Realty
710 17th Avenue South, North Myrtle Beach
(843) 272-6753
www.crescent-realty.com

Crescent Realty takes its name from the beach community it has been operating from since 1977. Broker-in-charge Rachel S. Thompson and her associate, Helena Gray, have more than 49 years of combined experience in the business. Both Rachel and Helena live in North Myrtle Beach and thus have firsthand knowledge of that Grand Strand community.

Crescent Realty also works with North Carolina properties.

Many area real-estate companies also offer vacation rentals. PHOTO: COURTESY OF KIMBERLY ALLYSON DUNCAN

Elliott Realty/GMAC Real Estate
401 Sea Mountain Highway,
North Myrtle Beach
(843) 249–1406, (800) 525–0225
204 South Ocean Boulevard,
North Myrtle Beach
(843) 249–8307, (888) 293–7288
www.elliottgmac.com

Since its founding as an independent agency in 1959, Elliott Realty has been a leader in the way real estate is sold along the Grand Strand. More than 43 years later, the company still takes pride in offering clients and customers the most current and accurate information about the local real-estate market. In 2000 Elliott Realty affiliated with GMAC Home Services, becoming Elliott Realty/GMAC Real Estate. Each of this agency's knowledgeable, well-trained real-estate agents are full-time Realtors. The company's market area includes, but is not limited to, Little River, Cherry Grove, North Myrtle Beach, Atlantic Beach, Crescent Beach, Windy Hill, Loris, Longs, Chestnut Hill, Myrtle Beach, Surfside, Garden City, and Murrells Inlet.

RE/MAX Southern Shores
100 U.S. Highway 17 South,
North Myrtle Beach
(843) 249–5555, (800) 729–0064
www.myrtlebeachshores.com

With offices throughout North America, RE/MAX serves residential, commercial, and investment needs. The office, formed in 1988, has doubled in size since its founding. It is the oldest operating RE/MAX franchise on the Grand Strand. Currently, RE/MAX Southern Shores staff has 17 agents.

Myrtle Beach

Century 21 Boling & Associates
7722 North Kings Highway, Myrtle Beach
(843) 449–2121, (800) 634–2500
www.century21boling.com

This Century 21 office opened for business in 1986. In five years, Penny I. Boling, broker-in-charge, helped the company—at the time, one of the least productive in the region—become one of the leading Century 21 offices in South Carolina. Boling & Associates controls 200 or more listings at any given time, including condos and town homes, residential, commercial, and multifamily structures as well as land—all properties in various price ranges.

This agency thrives on a team-players concept. The majority of the sales associates have been with the company for more than five years. A property management division is available to coordinate annual rentals.

Century 21 Broadhurst & Associates Inc.
3405 North Kings Highway, Myrtle Beach
(843) 448–7169, (800) 845–2055

Century 21 Broadhurst & Associates, owned by Myrtle Beach City Councilwoman Rachel Broadhurst, is a full-service real-estate company with more than 30 professionally trained property specialists. In business since 1974, this firm is one of the largest Century 21 offices in the Carolinas, with agents in Murrells Inlet and Calabash as well as Myrtle Beach. Serving clients in all phases of real estate, Broadhurst & Associates offers one-stop shopping for residential, vacation, commercial, and investment properties. Broadhurst has received the Centurian Award six times. This is the highest honor presented by Century 21 International.

Coldwell Banker Chicora - Briarcliffe
Various Grand Strand locations
(843) 272–8700
www.chicora.com

Combining the two biggest companies on the Grand Strand, the Coldwell Banker Roberts Agency and Chicora Real Estate & Development, has created the largest company in the area. The two companies merged in 2000, and Coldwell Banker Chicora Real Estate was born. Today Coldwell Banker Chicora and affiliated companies have grown to more than 200 real-estate professionals responsible for planning, development, sales, financial management, and property supervision of more than 60 communities with nearly 8,000 dwellings. More than 1,700 individual properties with a value that approaches $250 million are currently listed.

Coldwell Banker Chicora has 30 locations from North Myrtle Beach to Georgetown. Their "Blue Ribbon Preferred" program is based on the concept of creating a pre-approved, buyer-ready home. Many tasks previously postponed until after the sale are now taken care of as soon as the property is listed. This means every sale is quick, professional, and hassle free.

Exit Grand Strand Properties
419 79th Avenue North, Suite 3,
Myrtle Beach
(843) 449–3948, (800) 410–EXIT (3948)
www.myrtlebeachexit.com

Exit Grand Strand Properties bills itself as "Your Source for Exceptional Real Estate Service!" With more than 20 sales associ-

---

Insiders' Tip
If you are relocating here from another state, many real estate agents advise that you start home-buying proceedings before you move and while you have an existing, long-term job. Banks are more likely to lend to someone with that security than to someone who has just moved.

ates, executives, and specialists, Exit makes it easy for buyers to find the right property. Visit the company's Web site for a variety of listings, area information, and home-buying tips.

Fitzgerald Realty Inc.
900 Gilead Drive, Suite 101A, Murrells Inlet
(843) 651–0003, (800) 395–6610
www.fitzgeraldrealty.com

Established in 1985, Fitzgerald Realty has approximately 20 full- and part-time agents. This real-estate firm specializes in residential and resort properties in the Grand Strand area.

The company prides itself on a "no surprises" sales process—from home selection through the final closing.

LITUS* Properties - Joe Garrell & Associates
1551 21st Avenue North, Suite 1,
Myrtle Beach
(843) 449–9000, (800) 285–5634

LITUS* Properties has been in business for more than 20 years, and its experience is renowned. LITUS* staffs more than 50 agents in numerous departments that handle commercial sales, business proper-

ties, resort properties, and general brokerage. The company is distinguished by a sales staff that collectively holds more certifications and accreditations in real estate and business-practice brokerage than any other agency in North America.

Pavilack Realty & Rental Corp.
603 North Kings Highway, Myrtle Beach
(843) 448–9471, (800) 868–9471
www.pavilack.com

Pavilack is a small company that offers clients personalized service in the sale or purchase of commercial real estate. Owner Harry Pavilack works closely with his associates, bringing his legal expertise to all transactions.

Robert E. Powell & Associates Realtors
4757 U.S. Highway 17 Bypass South,
Myrtle Beach
(843) 293–7778, (800) 868–7778
www.repowell.com

This firm has served the beach since 1976. Formerly Berry Realty, this agency's territory ranges from the North Carolina state line to Winyah Bay in Georgetown.

With approximately 15 agents, Powell specializes in residential properties—primary, secondary, and investment. This company also staffs a property-management division that orchestrates annual rentals and is particularly proud of its in-house training program.

The Prudential Burroughs & Chapin Realty Inc.
7421 North Kings Highway, Myrtle Beach
(843) 449–9444, (800) 277–7704
www.rockonthebeach.com

Anyone who knows anything about the history of Myrtle Beach will recognize the names Burroughs and Chapin. The parent company has been around for more than a century. With 24,000 acres, this company is one of the largest landowners in Horry County. The firm owns numerous office buildings and retail complexes, including Broadway at the Beach, Myrtle Square Mall, and Myrtle Beach Pavilion.

Recognized as No. 1 in Prudential Southern residential sales in 1996, Burroughs & Chapin Realty has more than 40

Insiders' Tip
The city planning offices of Myrtle and North Myrtle Beach are vaults of information for prospective homebuyers and current homeowners. City planners and building inspectors are on hand to offer advice concerning everything from flood zones to future developments. These factors and many more affect everything from your insurance rates to future land values.

agents. All have garnered more than $2 million in sales, making this one of the most productive firms in the Grand Strand area.

South Strand

Garden City Realty Inc.
608 Atlantic Avenue, Garden City Beach
(843) 651–0900, (866) 427–7253

Since 1973 Garden City Realty has been a focal point for South Strand real-estate deals and has earned a reputation for scrupulously fair dealing. This comprehensive agency's six agents can handle a range of real-estate needs—buying, selling, or renting. The experienced, well-trained staff has access to more than 4,500 listings of Myrtle Beach–area homes, condos, and land parcels. Garden City Realty offers nearly 400 rental properties on the South Strand.

Pawleys Island Realty Company
88 North Causeway, Pawleys Island
(843) 237–2431, (800) 937–7352
www.pawleysislandvacations.com

Pawleys Island Realty's professional associates can answer any questions you might have about any property in Georgetown County, including all the developments. The specialty at this agency is the resort real-estate market. Pawleys Island Realty also prides itself in being the largest vacation rental company in its area, with a large inventory of homes in Pawleys Island and Litchfield Beach.

Rose Real Estate
1711 U.S. Highway 17 South, Surfside Beach
(843) 650–9274, (800) 845–6706
www.rose-real-estate.com

Rose Realt Estate is the exclusive property-management company of the huge development known as Oceanside Village, a planned community of more than 900 modular beach homes and cottages; half are occupied by owners, and the others are available as rentals. Like the Ocean Lakes community of Myrtle Beach, residents of Oceanside Village get around in golf carts and enjoy the safety and security of 24-hour, on-site security systems. Amenities include swimming pools, lakes stocked with game fish, tennis courts, a volleyball court, softball diamond, huge clubhouse, and planned activities.

One important reason local retirees love the Strand is the fact that the area is rich with activities and attractions for grandkids and family members. PHOTO: COURTESY OF MYRTLE BEACH AREA CHAMBER OF COMMERCE

Senior Scene

The Grand Strand and retirees have a passionate love affair going. And this perfect coupling is not only compatible, but also seems to be intensifying every year as more and more active seniors come south to embrace the comfortable coastal lifestyle. In the past decade the number of adults age 65 and older has increased by almost 70 percent.

Who can blame them? They're finished with the workaday world but not with life. They come to get ultimate quality out of the golden years under the warm Carolina sunshine. Many of our retirees hail from colder regions to the north where they spent many a winter shoveling snow, wrapping kids in knitted scarves, and navigating icy roads. Here seniors can enjoy the freedom of a temperate climate, partake in the luxury of walking barefoot along a sandy coast, and, for the most part, get far more purchasing mileage out of their dollar.

In turn they have wooed and won the hearts of Grand Stranders with the skills and experience they apply to local civic groups, churches, the arts, and governmental entities. Retirees have become and will remain an integral part of this community. As one 69-year-old widow put it, "I moved to Myrtle Beach four months ago and have a busier schedule than ever before. No one needs to be lonely in Myrtle Beach. There's just too much to do." Echoing this sentiment, the Myrtle Beach area has been named by *Where to Retire* magazine as one of the 100 Best Retirement Towns in America. The Southeast Journal edition of the *Wall Street Journal* also ranked the Grand Strand as one of the dozen hottest retirement spots in six Southeast states: "If a community with 100 golf courses, 1,500 restaurants and 10 theaters featuring entertainers such as Johnny Mathis is NOT a retirement spot, something's wrong."

Many retired folks volunteer at area schools and hospitals. They serve on boards and councils, operate community projects, head up fund-raising drives, and participate in cultural programs. The Long Bay Symphony can credit its very existence to retirees who worked in the music business and performed with symphonies in larger cities. The over-55 set have their own acting troupe, the Grand Strand Players, which puts on three productions a year. The Waccamaw Carving Club, the Waccamaw Arts and Crafts Guild, the Grand Strand Concert Band, and the Long Bay Photography Club would all have slim membership rolls without retirees.

Horry's seniors have their own newspaper, *Fifty Plus;* their own annual trade show, The Lifestyles Expo, held each winter in the Myrtle Beach Convention Center (see the Annual Events chapter); and their own production company that puts together a 30-minute program each month for Cox Cable TV.

The Grand Strand also entices migrant retirees, usually referred to as "snowbirds," who follow the sunshine south to escape the harsh northern winters. They rent houses and apartments or stay in hotels, taking advantage of lower winter rates. Around March or April, when temperatures start to rise, they head home. No one seems to have a good grasp of just how many snowbirds winter along the Grand Strand, although estimates range upwards of 50,000.

The Carolinas are perfectly positioned to attract the new generation of retirees. Younger, more active seniors are choosing destinations like South Carolina because it is at least a day closer to their northern homes than Florida, offers a break from relentless heat and humidity, and provides plenty of activities beyond shuffleboard or a dip in the pool.

Jobs and entrepreneurial opportunity are also high on the list of desirable qualities, since many of today's retirees want to continue to work at least part-time or wish to start their own businesses.

The Single Senior Set

A recent census report tells us that 23 percent of Horry County's population is over the age of 65 and living alone. Many of these single seniors are satisfied with their new-found life of freedom and take up traveling and exercising lifelong passions that have lain dormant for years.

Of course tried and true ways to meet new friends are through attending your church or synagogue, becoming a member of a local senior center, enrolling in special interest courses, and joining volunteer organizations. But this section of the Insiders' Guide passes along some formal and informal settings guaranteed to put you in the mainstream of local, active seniors that you probably wouldn't find until you had lived here awhile.

One 68-year-old widow in Surfside Beach has taken up globe trotting and suggests booking on the annual group excursion coordinated every February by Surfside Travelers, 825-A Surfside Drive,

Insiders' Tip

If you're 55 years of age or older, always ask about available senior discounts whenever you shop, dine out, or purchase a good or service. Many Grand Strand businesses offer the senior set special price reductions.

(843) 238-2838. The trip is usually a cruise or other all-inclusive package. Past destinations have been Alaska, Cancun, Acapulco, and Puerto Rico. Although you don't have to be a senior to travel with this group, 95 percent of the group passengers are retired.

The VFW Post 10420, 4359 U.S. Highway 17 Bypass in Murrells Inlet, (843) 651-6900, is a hot spot for the older set when it comes to dining and dancing. It's open every day for lunch and dinner with live bands performing on Friday and Sunday nights from 6:30 to 10:30 P.M. Music ranges from Big Band tunes to beach music, and the dance floor is usually packed.

Mall-walking clubs have become serious programs for health and socializing among the 50-plus circle. Before stores open at 10:00 A.M., the empty aisles are alive with the sounds of chitchat and padding Reeboks as hundreds of participants log in mall-miles. All of the Grand Strand malls offer a walking club, and all are thriving. The Colonial Mallwalkers operate out of Colonial Mall, 10177 North Kings Highway, Myrtle Beach, and is sponsored by Grand Strand Regional Medical Center. Applications and flyers can be picked up anytime at the guest services booth near JCPenney and the food court, or call Hugh Brown or Dee Knight at the hospital, (843) 839-6015.

Applications for the Inlet Square Mall Walkers, U.S. Highway 17 Business in Murrells Inlet, are available near the entrance to JCPenney or by contacting Customer Service at (843) 651-6990. Grand Strand Regional also sponsors the Myrtle Square Milers at Myrtle Square Mall, 2501 North Kings Highway, Myrtle Beach. Flyers and applications are ready for you at the bulletin board near Kay-Bee Toys.

Active Senior Centers

To offer a central meeting spot and support to our ever-growing senior population along the Grand Strand, a number of centers have sprung up all along our shoreline. All are staffed by full-time activities personnel and operate Monday through Friday only. If you're a regular participant in these arenas of action, you'll need the weekends to rest up!

Myrtle Beach

Grand Strand Chapter of Senior Friends
Grand Strand Regional Medical Center
809 82nd Parkway, Myrtle Beach
(843) 692–1645, (843) 692–1634
www.grandstrandmed.com/seniorfriends.asp

The National Association of Senior Friends is a not-for-profit organization for anyone beyond the age of 50. Its goal is to funnel social and health benefits and opportunities through a single source. The local sponsor for the Grand Strand chapter is the Grand Strand Regional Medical Center. Activities include a monthly Dutch-treat luncheon and chapter meeting, a bowling league and brown-bag movie, day trips and overnight trips, an annual convention, a member-guest cookout, a birthday party, and a Christmas dance. Many benefits and discounts are available to members through the medical center. Membership is reasonably priced at only $15 a year.

Grand Strand Senior Center
1268 21st Avenue North, Myrtle Beach
(843) 626–3991

The Horry County Council On Aging realized the fruits of its labor in 1995 when this senior center opened its doors. This $1.4 million project offers seniors 16,000 square feet of space including an auditorium, kitchen, dressing rooms, and meeting chambers. Open Monday through Friday from 9:00 A.M. to 4:00 P.M., the senior center plays host to a dizzying schedule of events: arts and crafts, bridge, dance aerobics, yoga, mah-jongg (a game of Chinese origin similar to dominoes), bingo for prizes, health screening, ballroom dancing, art classes, chess, support groups, quilting . . . let us catch our breath . . . seminars, and tax-preparation instruction. You would have to have the energy of two preteens on summer vacation to keep up with all of the center's activities! The Seniors for the Performing Arts theatrical troupe performs full-production plays in the auditorium that have become very popular with senior-center members and locals alike. Regular luncheons are also part of the center's monthly agenda. Membership is $15 a person and allows access to all senior-center activities plus a monthly newsletter. New volunteers are always welcome.

South Strand

Georgetown Senior Center
2104 Lincoln Street, Georgetown
(843) 546–9410

The Georgetown center offers an agenda of things to do including crafts, exercise programs, quilting, card games, and day trips to such attractions as Brookgreen Gardens. There are about 30 active members. Lunch is served each day for 30 cents per person. You can join this senior center for a mere $2.00 a year. This program operates from 10:00 A.M. to 2:00 P.M.

South Strand Senior Center
1032 10th Avenue North (behind Giants Beachwear), Surfside Beach
(843) 238–3644

South Strand has 100 members with an average of 45 people coming to the center daily. A van service is available for seniors without transportation. A different roster of events is coordinated for each day, keeping things hopping with speakers, day trips, games, ceramics, and exercise. Hot lunches are served five days a week for donations. Membership cost is $4.00 a year. South Strand is open Monday through Friday from 9:00 A.M. to 2:00 P.M.

Educational Programs

Since the pursuit of knowledge spans every generation and one is never too young nor too old to learn, the Grand Strand has enjoyed a proliferation of educational programs that enroll seniors by the hundreds. With time on their hands and minds as sharp as tacks, many of our older citizens have quit marking off days on the calendar . . . they're too busy organizing their lives by semester.

CLASS
Art Works/Litchfield Exchange
Highway 17, Litchfield Beach
(843) 235–9600
www.artworksonline.net

Held year-round at Art Works in the Litchfield Exchanges, CLASS (Community Learning About Special Subjects) is an exciting addition to senior life for students from Myrtle Beach to Georgetown. Taught by talented and well-qualified instructors, classes range from single-day workshops to eight-week courses that meet once a week during the day and evening. Whether you are a native or new to the area, CLASS provides a casual environment for meeting people with common interests and for exploring subjects seniors may have been interested about but never had time to pursue.

As research findings continue to emphasize the importance of exercising the mind as well as the body, CLASS offers many programs that combine mental, sensory, and social stimulation. Subjects include cultural appreciation (art, music, film, literature), history (local and beyond), hands-on learning (computers, bridge, genealogy, cooking, herb gardening, handwriting analysis, creative writing, interior design), art instruction for beginners and accomplished artists in a variety of media (drawing, painting, portraiture, photography, stained glass), and a variety of personal-growth opportunities. Capping each week is *The Moveable Feast,* a series of literary luncheons featuring accomplished authors and held at different Waccamaw Neck restaurants.

The fall, winter, and spring terms include approximately sixty courses. Around thirty courses are planned during the summer months for short-term visitors. A complete schedule is available on the Web site.

Horry-Georgetown Technical College
Continuing Education
Conway Campus, 2050 Highway 501 East, Conway
(843) 347–3186
Grand Strand Campus, Woodlawn Park School, 743 Hemlock Avenue
(843) 477–0808
Georgetown Campus, 4003 South Frasier Street, Georgetown
(843) 546–8406
www.hor.tec.sc.us

All campus locations of Horry-Georgetown Technical College, including the Grand Strand campus on the former Myrtle Beach Air Force Base, encourage and support a wide range of courses and special programs that attract senior students due to their scope, convenience, and affordability. Every semester, a good number of continuing-education courses are designated as senior-citizen specials. If you are at least 60 years of age, a South Carolina resident, and neither yourself nor your spouse is employed full time, you may qualify to receive a total tuition waiver to take a particular course, or be eligible for a 50 percent discount of the tuition fee.

Continuing-education courses included topics such as financial and business training, computers and the Internet, construction and home repair, health and wellness, arts and crafts specialties, and languages.

The cost and hours of each course do vary. Each campus of Horry-Georgetown Technical College is happy to send you its current schedule and updates if you give them a call. Preregistration is required for all classes.

Lifelong Learning Society
Coastal Carolina University, Conway
(843) 349–2665

University faculty and professionals from the community teach a variety of intellectual, cultural, and social classes. No formal papers or exams are required of the senior students. A $29 membership fee to join the Lifelong program entitles participants to use of the campus facilities and student rates to University cultural events

With views like these, it's easy to understand why the Grand Strand's retirement population has more than doubled in the past decade. PHOTO: COURTESY OF LESNIK HIMMELSBACH WILSON HEARL & HIRSCH

and performances. Members also have the opportunity to attend special workshops, travel-study programs, and sessions at the university. A sampling of recent course offerings includes literature and film; computer classes; Political Science; History of China; The Aztecs; Heroes and Villains in American History; and Art and Music. There are also courses in ecology, marine science, genealogy, foreign languages, folklore, creative writing, and philosophy.

Course fees range from $20 to $59 and are normally offered Mondays through Saturdays.

Independent-Living Communities

Although there are several very nice residential areas exclusively for retirees, many choose to live amidst the rest of the population. In fact retirees can be found in just about every Grand Strand neighborhood. And if the residential community is governed by a homeowners' association, you can bet concerned and conscientious seniors will be involved. Here is a listing we put together of beautiful, safe, and active retirement-living communities.

North Strand

Country Lakes
4353 Erie Street, Little River
(843) 399–2333, (888) 716–9750
www.jensencommunities.com

The Jensen family's Country Lakes in the north end of the county is smaller than its Garden City cousin. A small pool and clubhouse grace the grounds. For security an electronic bar crosses the road to keep uninvited guests out and protect residents and their properties. There is an onsite sales office. Home costs run from the $70,000s to $120,000.

Myrtle Beach

Covenant Towers
5001 Little River Road, Myrtle Beach
(843) 449–2484
www.covenanttowers.com

Covenant Towers offers a simple and unique opportunity for independent adult living in an upscale development. Located in the residential north end next to prestigious Pine Lakes Golf Course, the nine acre campus has 159 independent-living condominium residences and even a few two-bedroom-plus den/study residences.

Occupants must be 55 years old or older and ownership is deeded fee simple. In addition to being equipped with an emergency call system, each residence boasts a balcony, full kitchen, and one, two, or three full baths. On-site amenities include a swimming pool, library, dining room, coffee shop, craft/game room, mail room, banking, beauty/barber shop, fish ponds, and gardens/grounds with walking paths. Nestled in a quiet, established residential neighborhood, Covenant Towers enjoys easy access to the beach, shopping, golf, restaurants, and all the wonderful opportunities the Grand Strand offers.

Numerous services and activities are available to homeowners. Dinner is available in the dining room Monday through Saturday evenings, and a full brunch is available on Sunday. A full-time activities staff coordinates recreational activities, i.e. water aerobics, sittercise, bridge, bowling, golf, bingo, crafts, etc., as well as opportunities to enjoy shows, concerts, lectures, shopping, and the many restaurants along the Grand Strand.

Residents also enjoy the convenience of housekeeping service, weekly linen service, water and sewerage, insurance coverage on the structures(s), and maintenance on the buildings and grounds included as well. The convenience of a small 30-bed, private, fully licensed, skilled nursing unit allows homeowners the comfort of a quick-skilled response to an emergency call or care by familiar professionals should a resident need respite or long-term care. Covenant Towers does not provide assisted-living services.

Homeowner residents elect the board of directors that govern the association with the guidance of a licensed administrator and professional property management company. They have proven themselves to be good stewards of their assets for nearly two decades and bring a wealth of professional and life experiences to this democratic process. Residences range in price from the low $40,000s to approximately $150,000 for the largest floor plan. Information is available on-site Monday through Friday and by appointment on the weekends.

Myrtle Trace South
506 Sand Ridge Road, East Conway
(843) 347–6637, (800) 227–0631
www.mbliving.com

As motorists pass the Myrtle Trace sign on U.S. Highway 501, they don't get a hint about the magnitude of what lies beyond that sign and the wooded area that buffers the community from traffic. But pull in and take a look around; you'll be stunned to find about 500 homes in three unique communities. Myrtle Trace is about 15 years old and has a maturity that some newer developments lack. It is immaculately manicured and features lakes, golf course lots, a clubhouse, and swimming pool.

Most of the people who buy at Myrtle Trace move in while they're still in their late 50s or early 60s, and they give new meaning to the words "active retirement." Residents band together to plan activities that range from all kinds of card games to theatrical performances. There is a bowling league, and of course, golf is king. Between 20 and 30 residents work several days a week at area golf courses as starters and rangers to earn a few dollars and, mostly, to secure golf privileges. About 50 of Myrtle Trace's women work as volunteers at nearby Conway Hospital.

Buyers can select a house design from 6 floor plans, and a staff designer is available to adjust the plans to suit the owner. A homesite and house range from $157,000 to $172,000, depending on the location and floor plan selected. Myrtle Trace is now within 1 mile of a shopping center off of U.S. 501, which offers a grocery store, pharmacy, shops, and restaurants. The sales office is on-site, and models are open every day except Sunday.

South Strand

Ocean Pines/Magnolia Grove
3196 Moonshadow Lane, Garden City
(843) 651–2520, (800) 238–6565
www.jensencommunities.com

In accordance with federal guidelines, Jensen's has restricted its manufactured-housing development to people age 55 and older. Initiated in the early 1970s, this development is currently home to about 575 families. At Jensen's, residents lease their lots and buy their own homes. A senior can move into a double-wide abode for between $60,000 and $95,000. There is also a section of homes closer to traditional mobile units that cost between $15,500 and $27,000. Jensen's is quiet and well-manicured and bubbles with small lakes and canals. Residents plan their own activities through the Jensen's Activity Club (JAC), which distributes a monthly newsletter chock-full of things to do. There's a sales office on-site.

Ocean Lakes
6001 U.S. Highway 17 South, Surfside Beach
(843) 238–3446, (800) 845–2229
www.oceanlakes.com

Ocean Lakes is billed as the largest oceanfront campground on the East Coast, and although it serves as a typical campground during the tourist season, it also has about 500 year-round residents, mostly retirees. In 1999 the National Association of RV Parks and Campgrounds nominated Ocean Lakes as the number-one large RV park in the United States. The campground is on the ocean and has a recreational building where residents can work on crafts or meet for a variety of activities. An indoor pool was recently added. An activities director makes sure residents stay busy with everything from shopping and trips, to miniature golf tournaments. A year-round chaplain works to meet residents' spiritual needs, providing Sunday worship services in an outdoor amphitheater when the weather permits and indoors when it doesn't.

Homes at Ocean Lakes are mostly small mobile units, some of which showcase a more permanent appearance with added rooms and porches. However, with the housing boom along the Grand Strand, a large number of two-story beach homes have been added to the landscape.

Ocean Lakes is a guarded community, and security staff stationed at the gate make sure only residents, their guests, registered campers, and people attending worship services get in. As added security, Ocean Lakes instituted a 24-hour patrol of the grounds.

Few people use their cars inside Ocean Lakes. Instead, you'll find their transportation much slower and more relaxed—golf carts work just fine, thank you! At any given time, there are about 130 sites for sale, ranging from $35,000 for a camper home to $300,000 for some oceanfront beach houses.

Assisted-Living Communities

Myrtle Beach

Myrtle Beach Estates
3620 Happy Woods Court, Myrtle Beach
(843) 293–8888
www.huntassistedliving.com

Myrtle Beach Estates takes great pride in providing gentle care and trained assistance for every resident. The community's atmosphere is created through a combination of a like-home environment and a professionally trained staff capable of providing skillful assistance on a moment's notice. The staff also coordinates all services provided by outside health professionals.

Residents enjoy a comfortable environment that is also secure—an environment that enhances well-being and ensures peace of mind. A full-time activity director provides a full slate of activities; residents can choose to do as much or as little as they prefer. Diet, exercise, and wellness programs are followed closely and managed to fit each resident's needs.

An ideal choice for independent, assisted living, Myrtle Beach Estates requires no entrance fees, endowments, or long-term leases, just one low, affordable monthly fee. This fee covers all services, features, and amenities, including a staff nurse on call 24 hours per day; three daily meals, daily housekeeping, and personal laundry services; weekly worship services; and a host of social, recreational, educational, and cultural activities. Fees range from $1,500 depending on the facilities and services selected.

The Lakes at Litchfield
120 Lakes at Litchfield Drive, Pawleys Island
(843) 235–9393, (800) 684–7866
www.lakes-litchfield.com

The Lakes at Litchfield is much more than a place to live. Residents and families take comfort in knowing the community offers a continuum of care that meets needs and provides a seamless transition as needs change. It's a community that takes pride in offering the setting, support, and services necessary to ensure residents' comfort and security.

The Lakes at Litchfield features a range of elegant residential choices that offers every comfort and convenience. Lovely two- and three-bedroom homes feature bright Carolina sunrooms, fireplaces, 9-foot ceilings, and quality appliances. Each home has its own garage, a cart for community travel, and a 24-hour emergency call system for safety. Meals in the elegant Charleston Dining Room, maid service, all maintenance, taxes, insurance, utilities, scheduled transportation, and more are all included in a reasonable occupancy fee. Plus, should you ever decide to leave The Lakes at Litchfield, a substantial amount of your initial investment will be returned. Spacious one- and two-bedroom apartments (with no up-front investment) are also affordable options. And the community is thoughtfully designed to embrace the natural charm of Pawleys Island with lakes, courtyards, and fountains, as well as a gazebo and clubhouse.

In addition to single-family homes, garden homes, and apartment homes, The Lakes at Litchfield Assisted Living and

Special Care Communities provide state-of-the-art services for those needing special attention and care. Per-month costs start at around $2,000 and go up to around $3,000 for dementia care. Both centers offer incomparable care in a truly caring community. See for yourself what makes The Lakes at Litchfield so special.

Myrtle Beach Manor by Marriott
9547 North Kings Highway, Myrtle Beach
(843) 449–5283
www.marriottsenior.com

Myrtle Beach Manor offers services for people in all phases of their senior years. There are 60 apartments, ranging from studios to one-bedroom units. These are rented on a monthly basis to people who want to live independently but like the security of knowing someone is nearby to watch out for them. The 104 beds in the health-care center are designed for those who need to be regularly looked in on. The manor also houses a secured Nursing Care Center and full rehabilitation department that includes occupational and physical therapy. An activities' director makes sure that residents have something to do seven days a week. The 35-year-old establishment has six lovely manicured acres, and a sunny day will bring many manor residents outside to enjoy the scenery and a view of the Intracoastal Waterway. Monthly costs at Myrtle Beach Manor begin at $1,950. A daily rate of $105 to $128 applies to those residents who require substantial health-care services.

Garden Manor
11951 Grandhaven Drive, Murrells Inlet
(843) 357–0200
www.gardenmanor.com

Garden Manor provides residents with multiple levels of care: independent care, care with assistance, extended care, and respite care. Garden Manor's professional staff demonstrates the true spirit of teamwork for the good of all residents.

Independent Care, which costs $1,750, is for seniors who desire the simplicity of living in safety and comfort while being released from the obligations of property taxes, maintenance, and repairs, as well as the fears of burglary, and the depreciation of property, companionship, and medical care.

Care with Assistance, which ranges from $1,900 to $2,500, is for seniors who need 24-hour protective care, including assistance in critical areas like diet and medications, but not the service of a nurse on a daily basis.

The Extended Care option, costing $2,500 to $3,000, is for seniors who have progressed beyond the normal ranges of assisted living/residential care but still do not require nursing care on a 24-hour basis.

The center also provides respite care, a service with prices that begin at $100 per day. A full-time staff is always on duty to assist those with medical difficulties. Additionally, activities and recreational events are planned to promote the happiness and physical stability of each resident. Cost of residency includes an unfurnished room, three meals and two snacks each day, housekeeping, laundry, an activity program, medication control and disbursement, and religious and counseling services.

In-Home Health-Care Options

When a parent, aunt, or other older relative becomes ill or infirm, it's not surprising that concerned family members look to a nursing home for care. But according to the South Carolina Budget and Control Board, Office of Insurance Services, a nursing home is often the most extreme option.

In order to keep loved ones in their own homes with their pride intact, there are other options to consider. We discuss some of those options in the following section, outlining the positive and negative aspects of each in a realistic manner.

Family Home Care

If you, your siblings, or other caring relatives live within reach, you could consider family home care. Modifications to the ailing person's home may be needed, modifications like installing a ramp near the entrance for wheelchair access and rearranging furniture to accommodate the chair or a walker. It might also be necessary to rent or purchase special equipment such as a hospital bed or oxygen tank. Everyone involved should decide who will do the cooking, cleaning, laundry, and shopping. And most of all, each helper must honestly evaluate his or her ability to do these chores.

The positive side to this arrangement is that it costs nothing but time, and in many cases, patients recover best in the comfort of familiar surroundings. It can also be a way to strengthen family relationships, providing the time required does not become a strain.

On the negative side, family members usually are not health-care professionals. Albeit with the best intentions, family members might tend to pamper a relative, rather than insisting, for example, on a prescribed daily walk.

Private Nursing

This arrangement intrudes the least on the lives of other family members, including a spouse. A private nurse can be hired to care for someone in the comfort of home. Private nurses can be found through nursing-placement services, home-health agencies, or discharge services of a hospital. Every hospital staffs a discharge nurse who can provide this information.

Some private nursing fees are covered by Medicare or the sick relative's supplemental insurance. For the most part, however, this is a very expensive care option, since most private nurses charge by the hour.

Home–Care Services

Overall, this care option compromises between the relatively high cost of a private nurse and the difficult task of being sole caretaker of a sick relative.

Generally you arrange for a nurse to stop in for a few hours, two or three times a week, depending on the person's needs.

Fine food is one of the many reasons visitors flock to the Strand. PHOTO: COURTESY OF MYRTLE BEACH AREA CHAMBER OF COMMERCE

Along with this, a nurse's aid is hired to come in on a particular schedule to bathe and groom the relative. Physical or occupational therapists can also be attained. Discharge services at your hospital can usually provide you with a list of qualified professionals or, in some cases, make all of the arrangements for you.

Medicare covers the costs of an agency-approved visiting nurse, nurse's aid, and therapist for up to eight hours a day for 21 consecutive days or as long as the relative's doctor deems necessary. Medicare coverage stops when the doctor says the nurse is no longer needed for care. At that point if you want the nurse's aid to continue, you foot the bill.

Care Management

This is a variation on home-care services, usually employed by relatives who don't live near the person requiring help. An elder-care agency or geriatric-care manager evaluates what the patient needs, develops an appropriate health-care plan, and hires the necessary personnel. The program is overseen by the manager, who is available 24 hours a day to handle problems or emergencies. Care managers usually receive $150 to $300 an hour for the initial consultation and to monitor the person's care regularly. You must also pay the fees for all personnel hired to care for the relative. Medicare and supplemental coverage does kick in for this service, but every condition is different.

Besides the Eldercare Locator number listed in this chapter's subsequent "Senior Service Directory" section, you can also contact the National Association of Professional Geriatric Care Managers in Tucson, Arizona, (520) 881-8008 or www.caremanager.org. This association publishes a directory of geriatric-care managers nationwide. For additional information contact the local chapter of the AARP (refer to the "Senior Service Directory") and ask for the free booklet *Care Management: Arranging for Long-term Care*.

Senior Services Directory

The following agencies and information clearinghouses could come in handy as resources for seniors.

North Strand

North Strand Senior Health Center
4237 River Hills Drive, Little River
(843) 281-2778
www.grandstrandmed.com

As an outpatient department of Grand Strand Regional Medical Center designed to meet and simplify the health-care process for seniors, the brand-new North Strand Senior Health Center targets the needs of the senior population. The staff has been specially trained in the needs of senior citizens and will help patients assess, manage, and prevent health-related problems. On-site services include medical exams, lab work, and EKGs. The center welcomes Medicare assignments.

Nonhealth services include assistance in locating community resources to addressing legal, financial, and housing concerns.

Myrtle Beach

Grand Strand Retirement Club
(843) 448-5670, (843) 237-5417

For $10 a year, any permanent and retired resident living east of the Intracoastal Waterway can join this social club, which meets regularly for lunch. Members perform some charity work but primarily meet to network. Please call ahead for reservations.

Senior Advisory Committee of Myrtle Beach
City Hall, 937 Broadway Street, Myrtle Beach
(843) 918-1014

This committee was organized through the city of Myrtle Beach to address specific needs of senior citizens, such as larger print on road signs, longer crosswalk signals, and noise ordinances.

Service Corps of Retired Executives (SCORE)
(843) 918-1079
www.sba.gov

Calling all retired business people and executives . . . This volunteer corps offers free counsel to individuals who want to

---

Insiders' Tip

If you're retired and an avid golfer, you can save a lot of money on tee times if you're willing to do a little work. A number of area golf courses trade out playing privileges with seniors who relieve the regular staff by working golf carts or acting as starters.

go into business as well as to businesses experiencing problems. Retired executives and professionals are encouraged to donate their skills and background to the cause.

Senior Golfers Association and *Senior Golf Journal*
3013 Church Street, Myrtle Beach
(843) 626–8100, (800) 337–0047
www.seniorgolfersamerica.com

The Senior Golfers Association and its publication, *Senior Golf Journal,* include members and subscriptions from virtually every town and city across the United States. Golf tournaments and the journal are coordinated here, but interest is national.

South Strand

Fifty-Five Alive Mature Driving
2061 Glenn's Bay Road, Surfside
1268 21st Avenue North, Myrtle Beach
(843) 626–3991

This refresher course consists of eight hours of classroom instruction that stresses safe, defensive driving skills. Those who take the course get a 10 to 15 percent discount on auto insurance. Cost is $10 per person. The program is sponsored by Trinity Presbyterian Church.

Fifty Plus
1432 Seahouse Court, Surfside
(843) 215–4118
www.fiftyplus.com

This newspaper, expressly printed to suit senior citizens and retirees, is published monthly and distributed all along the Grand Strand from the North Carolina border to Georgetown and Conway, South Carolina. For home delivery, subscriptions cost $18 per year; or pick up a free copy at newsstands.

Georgetown County Council on Aging
Georgetown
(843) 546–8539
www.scmatureadults.org

This agency can provide referral services for local seniors.

Surfside Beach Fifties-Plus Group
Surfside Civic Center, 829 Pine Drive, Surfside Beach
(843) 913–6339

This active social group is for older couples and singles. Fifties-Plus members get together for a meeting on the third Monday each month. A potluck luncheon is held the first Monday of each month, and planned activities range from bowling to games to trips.

Beyond the Strand

American Association of Retired Persons (AARP)
(800) 424–3410,
www.aarp.org/scsep

Devoted to the needs of senior adults, the AARP sponsors an employment program that includes job training and, in some cases, placement for older workers with limited incomes. Call the office nearest you and ask about the Senior Community Service Employment Program (SCSEP).

Elderhostel
Coastal Carolina University, Conway
(843) 349–2665, (877) 426–8056
www.elderhostel.org

Participants in this exciting program get an opportunity to take up to three noncredit courses in liberal arts and sciences from a host institution in the United States or abroad. This program is offered at more than 1,600 locations internationally.

Horry County Council on Aging Inc.
2213 North Main Street, Conway
(843) 248–5523
www.scmatureadults.org

The Council on Aging acts as an information and referral service for all senior citizens and their families. Staff provide up-to-date information on everything from home-delivered meals to living wills. This agency also performs the daunting task of managing eight area senior centers. In September 1997, this agency began publishing the monthly *Senior Life & Times* tabloid, which is distributed through the Council on Aging membership and its senior centers. *Life & Times* is full of tips, medical advice, and event calendars. To contact the publication, call (843) 236–5151.

Horry County Veterans Affairs Office
211 Beaty Street, Conway
(843) 248–1291
www.horrycounty.org

This agency provides services to veterans and their dependents or survivors. It also operates as an intermediary between veteran patients and the VA hospital.

Seniors Helping Seniors
(843) 449–5373
www.sos-healthcare.com

A division of Senior Peer Counseling Service, this agency is a marvelous resource for the senior set.

Social Security Administration
1316 Third Avenue, Conway
(843) 248–4271, (800) 325–0778,
(800) 772–1213
www.ssa.gov

This agency provides information on social security benefits, including Supplemental Security Income (SSI) and disability. According to a recent report from SSI, retirees younger than 65 may earn $8,640 a year before their Social Security benefits would be reduced. Those between the ages of 65 and 69 years may earn as much as $13,500. There is no limit on those 70 or more years old.

Office hours are 9:00 A.M. to 4:00 P.M. Monday through Friday.

SC Employment Security Commission
Coastal Workforce Center
200-A Victory Lane, Conway
(843) 234–WORK (9675)
www.sces.org

Many Grand Strand companies readily employ older citizens. Contact the center about job opportunities and a variety of training and educational programs in both Horry and Georgetown Counties.

South Carolina Services Information Systems
(888) 539–8796

Any senior who endures the misfortune of being disabled should call this toll-free number. South Carolina Services provides information on a variety of specialized resources for those in need.

Child Care and Education

Grand Stranders take great pride in their reputation as a beach community where family concerns receive their full attention. For example, parents here take education very seriously. In fact 83 percent of parents and guardians recently attended a personalized learning conference on behalf of their children, and 78 percent of parents and guardians officially pledged to be active in their child's education.

The fine schools of the Grand Strand—from private religious schools to technical academies—make good use of the amazing resources available in this area. For example, Horry Telephone Cooperative, a local connectivity provider, helped get the schools online. The tools are in place for the next generation of Grand Stranders to be able to read, write, and compete with their peers nationwide. As a result, Horry County school district was chosen to be a recipient of the "What Parents Want" award, as presented by School Match, an independent educational consulting firm. More than 60,000 parents were surveyed nationally to determine the criteria for this designation, and only 14 percent of schools nationwide qualified.

The Horry County school system serves more than 30,000 students. Horry County ranks first in the state for in-migration; by 2003 enrollment is expected to reach 30,542, representing an 11 percent increase from 1998. While South Carolina schools as a whole have not ranked very high in the nation, Horry County scholastic statistics rate higher and are improving. A $173 million building program currently under way will add 10 new schools and accomplish additions and renovations to 9 others. This comes on the heels of a $102 million building program that was completed in 1998, which added nine new schools and renovated four others.

The Horry County school district is the third largest of 85 state districts, and it still maintains a relatively low dropout rate of 1.8 percent, with 80 percent of graduates going on to higher education. Of the county's 1,982 classroom teachers, 1,496 hold advanced degrees. The board of education is elected democratically, hires a superintendent, and works with the National Education Association. Class sizes in grades kindergarten through eighth have been limited to 25 or less, and four schools in the area have been named National Blue Ribbon Schools by the U.S. Department of Education. Students have consistently scored above state average on the SAT. A plan is in place to raise the average SAT and ACT scores to national averages by 2003. A new literacy model helped Horry County students top the state average in English language arts. Efforts also include such practical measures as placing a school resource officer or a security guard on campus, and full-time drug and weapon canine surveillance teams in all high schools, middle schools, and career centers.

The first portion of this chapter discusses child care for the youngest of your gang. Then we move on to discuss primary- and secondary-education options.

Child Care

Day-Care Options

Although word of mouth has always been one of the best ways to zero in on reliable child care, newcomers don't have the benefit of an established network of reliable parents and other adults for advice. So if you're new to our area, we suggest you request information from the Family Information Network. This computer database, part of the Clemson University Extension Service system, provides information about day-care centers, including adult care, throughout the state. Extension offices are at 1949 Industrial Park Road, Conway, (843) 365-6715, and at 1837 North Frasier Street, Georgetown, (843) 546-4481. The Web site is www.clemson.edu/fin.

The Family Information Network can provide data on pricing and child-to-staff ratios as well as information about meals, transportation services, and other specifics you'll want to know about any center you're considering. It can also offer helpful hints on selecting the right day-care option for your child. Get the complete scoop on child-care laws and child-service agencies, too. If you'd like to use the computer yourself, call for an appointment. If convenience is important to you, just call and ask for county agent Debbie Strickland in the Conway office or Barbara Lambert in Georgetown. They'll be happy to sift through a veritable mountain of information and mail you a print-out of the centers in your area as well as any additional data you request. Best of all, there is absolutely no charge for this service.

The South Carolina Department of Social Services is responsible for licensing all day-care centers in the state. The Conway office, 1951 Industrial Park Road, (843) 365-5565, can provide you with a list of approved centers, including for-profit and nonprofit centers, as well as the names of individuals licensed to keep children in their homes. You can visit the Web site at www.state.us/dss.

Increasingly popular AuPairCare is an option. AuPairCare matches American families with child-care providers from all over the world, ages 18 to 26, who are interested in spending a year in the United States. Au pairs are thoroughly screened, and host families can choose for themselves a provider who best suits their personal needs and collective personality.

Unlike a paid employee for whom you have to report income, an au pair essentially becomes a member of the family: The individual lives in your home, participates in household chores, and shares your meals and your celebrations. In exchange for room, board, and a salarylike weekly allowance, the au pair offers con-

Numerous private schools flourish along the Grand Strand. PHOTO: KIMBERLY ALLYSON DUNCAN

stant care for one or more children. During the program year, local or regional AuPairCare counselors provide support to both the families and the au pair. For more information, call (800) 428-7247 or visit www.aupaircare.com.

Mother's Day Out (MDO) is a "playgroup" program offered by the First Presbyterian Church in Myrtle Beach that allows mothers to "escape" from their little ones for a few hours without resorting to an all-day day-care situation. The program is always up and running from May through September. Frequent special summer programs are available as well. There are always at least four staff members on duty.

The program operates weekdays from 9:00 A.M. until noon, with extended care offered until 5:00 P.M. Mornings are reserved for children from just-walking age through three years old. In the afternoons all children age five and younger are welcome to participate. Director Sherry Clardy describes the program as "semistructured play time." There's time for crafts, videos, snacks, reading, and more.

Although the program is church sponsored, parents do not have to be church members to use the service; however they should expect Christian values and education. MDO has met with such success,

> ## Insiders' Tip
> The mall-size Barnes & Noble bookstore on U.S. Highway 17 Bypass is the perfect place to take the kids. In addition to a truly staggering collection of children's literature, there are frequent storytelling hours and other activities for tykes. Call (843) 444-4046 for details.

parents must contend with a long waiting list. Preregistration is held in February for church members and the first week of March for the public, but you can call Ms. Clardy anytime, (843) 626-3883, to get your name on the waiting list.

St. Philip's Lutheran Church in Myrtle Beach also offers a Mother's Morning Out program that runs through May and June to supplement their extensive day-care program, which includes kinder-music and gymnastics. Contact Jeanie Stetzer, (843) 449-4322, for an application.

Be sure to read the Kidstuff and Attractions chapters for fun and educational activities to occupy your brood's time.

Baby-Sitting Services for Visitors

With the heavy influx of families visiting this area, there are frequent inquiries about baby-sitting services available to nonresidents. After all, time-starved moms and dads deserve a break from the family rat race every now and again!

If you'd consider leaving your child with a sitting service, read on. The following businesses cater primarily to the tourist market but serve a few locals as well. Although they can sometimes accommodate parents on short notice, officials suggest calling at least 24 hours in advance, especially during the busy summer season. Most of the sitters are mature women, many of whom are age 30 or older. All are thoroughly screened. Sitters provide their own transportation and will accept jobs from North Myrtle Beach to Garden City Beach.

The Kiddie Park Learning Center in Myrtle Beach is a service that caters to shoppers, beachgoers, and partygoers. In business for more than 35 years, Kiddie Park is open Monday through Saturday from 6:45 A.M. until 12:30 A.M. Patrons will pay $3.00 an hour. A full nine hours of service is $20. Call (843) 488-3413 for an appointment.

Many hotels and resorts also provide baby-sitting. Ask about availability of services—and rates—when making reservations.

Education

Public Schools

The Horry County School District's student services begin with an early-childhood program for four-year-olds with developmental and learning difficulties. Kindergarten for five-year-olds is a standard part of the statewide school curriculum and is available throughout the district.

The Horry County School District Web site, www.hcs.k12.sc.us, offers activity calendars so families can help their children continue learning during the summer. Activities can be adapted to suit the age, learning style, and progress of each child.

Every elementary school offers the PELICAN program for gifted and talented students. PELICAN provides enrichment activities one day a week that foster critical-thinking skills and encourage creativity.

Middle schools offer basic classes as well as honors programs. Similarly, all seven Horry County high schools provide a basic curriculum plus college-preparatory and honors classes. Advanced Placement classes afford students who pass standardized tests possible exemption from certain introductory college classes.

One unique feature of the Horry County schools is Playcard Environmental Center, a nature preserve in the western portion of the county. The center not only gives urban and suburban kids a taste of rural life, but also teaches all children a healthy respect for the earth's resources. Students learn about Native American and pioneer cultures and the ecosystems of a thriving blackwater swamp. The pristine preserve features a collection of farm and domestic animals, a nature trail with labeled flora and fauna, an old rope swing in a forested area, and a real beaver dam.

School officials assert that Playcard is unique in South Carolina and perhaps the United States. The 200-acre preserve also provides a site for observation and study in various scientific disciplines. The program is sponsored by both the community and the school district and is governed by an advisory board made up of representatives from Coastal Carolina University, Horry-Georgetown Technical College, and community and business members.

Conway is the district's largest high school, with more than 2,000 students. Socastee, the South Strand's high school, ranks second.

The Aynor/Conway Adult Education Center, the Loris, Socastee, and North Myrtle Beach Adult Education Centers, and the Academy of Arts, Science and Technology collectively provide vocational, technical, occupational, and academic training. The Conway School of Nursing, housed at the Aynor/Conway Adult Education Center, is a two-year program that prepares students for careers as licensed practical nurses (LPNs). The Academy of Arts, Science and Technology offers instruction in new programs such as graphics, video/audio technology, pre-engineering, golf course technology (that's right, the academic study of golf courses!), dance, and hospitality services (also known as hotel management).

For more information, contact Horry County Schools at (843) 448–6700.

Private Schools

With the exception of some day-care centers and preschools, all of Horry's private schools are church affiliated and basically Christian, reflecting a regional tradition of fundamental Christian morality, beliefs, and culture (see the Worship chapter).

North Strand

Risen Christ Lutheran School
10595 U.S. Highway 17 North,
North Myrtle Beach
(843) 272–8163

Risen Christ was established with the primary stated goal "of preparing each child for a happy and fruitful life." In keeping with their interpretation of such a lofty goal, a number of developmental categories are emphasized: intellectual, spiritual, emotional, social, and physical. Risen Christ staff believe that administering to students on these levels helps children grow into well-rounded and successful adults.

Local attractions like Brookgreen Gardens offer a variety of programs that combine pleasure and education. PHOTO: COURTESY OF LHWH

Risen Christ is dedicated to bringing up children "in the way of the Lord" (which presumably does not mean that all the students become carpenters and deliver impromptu speeches in temples). Along with providing spiritual training, Risen Christ strives to maintain high academic standards. The school belongs to the Lutheran Education Association and is one of more than 2,000 Lutheran schools in the United States. Curricular areas of study include religion, English, spelling, writing, math, social studies, science, computers, art, music, physical education, and Spanish (grades 6, 7, and 8).

Risen Christ offers pre-kindergarten and kindergarten classes as well as primary grades 1 through 8. Additionally, it offers before- and after-school child care

for pre-kindergartners through 5th graders. A summer camp also is offered for students.

Myrtle Beach

Calvary Christian School
SC Highway 544, Myrtle Beach
(843) 650–2829
www.calvarychristiansch.com

A ministry of Calvary Bible Church, Calvary offers preschool programs for youngsters three through five years of age and regular classes for 1st through 12th graders in a distinctly religious setting. In its second decade of operation, this is the Strand's oldest Christian school, although officially all denominations are welcome in a student body of approximately 335. The elementary classes are known for their strong phonics program. According to standardized achievement test results, Calvary rates more than a year ahead of national grade-level averages. Similarly, SAT scores rank ahead of both the state and the national average.

Cathedral Hall Academy
803 Howard Parkway, Myrtle Beach
(843) 477-1448
Sponsored by the Cathedral Bible College (also profiled in this chapter), Grand Strand Academy is a school with strong academics and a strong religious emphasis. The academy uses the advanced A Beka curriculum for 4-year-olds through 12th graders. The school's active fine arts program includes chorus, orchestra, art appreciation, even Latin and Greek on the high-school level.

St. Andrew Catholic School
3601 North Kings Highway, Myrtle Beach
(843) 448-6062
This school is supported by tuition and parish subsidies. Class sizes range from 25 to 30 students, and faculty positions total approximately 14. The program is enhanced by an active PTO and Mother's Club. Consequently, parent volunteers contribute significantly to the overall quality of their children's educational experience.

Christian education at St. Andrew is designed to educate the child as a whole—intellectually, morally, physically, emotionally, and socially. Students enjoy a high level of interaction with teachers and classmates. St. Andrew strives to develop leadership through classroom activities, school worship, liturgies, and extracurricular activities. The educational program is designed to foster academic excellence, emphasizing basic skills as a strong foundation. And the program's success is evident in standardized test results and in the number of students admitted to advanced-placement high-school programs.

Classes are offered from kindergarten (5-year-olds) through 8th grade, and afterschool care is available for students.

South Strand
Pawleys Island Montessori Day School
236 Commerce Drive, Pawleys Island
(843) 237-9015
www.pimds.org
Approximately 50 students, from 18-month-olds to 6th graders, attend Pawleys Island Montessori Day School. The curriculum, as the name indicates, is based on the world-renowned Montessori philosophy of education, where instructors respect each child's pace of learning and encourage students to follow their own interests. Emphasizing "concrete manipulations" (a.k.a. hands-on activities), the school has a student-teacher ratio of 10 to 1 or less. Established 17 years ago, the school operates nine months of the year, has playground facilities, is developing expansion plans, and welcomes new students. Contact Kim Oakley at the listed number for an application.

Beyond the Strand
ATC Christian School
1672 SC Highway 905, Conway
(843) 365-6803
An affiliate of The Prayer Center, ATCCS offers A Beka classes for 4-year-olds through 8th-graders. A preschool program for 2- and 3-year-olds is also available. Education is administered in a Christian environment, which school officials believe is vital not only for developing character through moral training but also for reaching an outstanding level of academic excellence.

Conway Christian School
1200 Medlen Parkway, Conway
(843) 365-2005
www.conwaychristian.com
The primary goal of Conway Christian School is to provide quality education with a Biblical perspective in a distinctly Christian atmosphere of discipline. The school's academic priority is teaching fundamental skills. An affiliate of Grace Presbyterian Church, Conway Christian offers preschool classes for 4- and 5-year-olds and uses the A Beka curriculum, including French and Spanish, for students in the 1st through 12th grades.

Higher Education

Myrtle Beach

Cathedral Bible College
803 Howard Parkway, Myrtle Beach
(843) 477-1448

Cathedral Bible College offers a Master of Theology degree, with majors in ministry, missions, Christian education, church administration, counseling, and music. The college, which occupies the site of a former U.S. Air Force base, enrolls approximately 100 students.

Fortune School of Real Estate
734 Hemlock Avenue, Myrtle Beach
(843) 236-1131, (843) 477-0808
www.re-school.com

Located with Horry-Georgetown Technical College, Fortune School of Real Estate trains new agents, existing agents, and aspiring brokers in preparation for the state licensing exam.

Webster University
4589 Oleander Drive, Myrtle Beach
(843) 497-3677
www.webster.edu

Webster University is an independent, nondenominational, multicampus international business college offering a graduate program at its Myrtle Beach campus. Webster prides itself on offering degree programs that many schools in the area

do not, including Management, Human Resources, and Counseling. Classes are conveniently scheduled to attract students from up to 2 hours away as well as working professionals. In response to increasing enrollment, Webster built a new and upgraded facility in 1997.

Graduate programs in business, human resources development, management, and clinical counseling are all accredited by the North Central Association of Colleges and Schools. Admission to the MA and MBA programs is open to all students who hold an undergraduate degree from a regionally accredited college or university.

In a nutshell, Webster offers education tailored to busy professionals. The distinction of Webster's whole approach is that of its commitment to education and to the community. This motto has created distinct advantages for adult students—fulfilling the wish list of anyone who wants to change careers, retool in the wake of cutbacks or closings, or advance in his or her current situation.

Beyond the Strand

Coastal Carolina University
U.S. Highway 501 East, Conway
(843) 347-3161
www.coastal.edu

Coastal Carolina is a comprehensive liberal arts institution offering baccalaureate degrees in 36 major fields of study as well as master's degrees in education. The university is committed to excellence in teaching, research, and public service.

Canvassing 260 wooded acres just minutes from the Atlantic Ocean and the resort area of Myrtle Beach, the Coastal Carolina campus is home to more than 5,800 students from South Carolina and 46 other states as well as 49 foreign countries.

A Coastal Carolina education offers a hands-on, personal educational experience. Approximately 200 faculty members bring impressive credentials from universities throughout the nation. Select faculty have been awarded Fulbright grants for research projects and study in such countries as New Zealand, Kenya, Colombia, Poland, and China. In addition, students can interact with worldwide experts on a variety of topical issues through the advanced technologies of long-distance education and on-line computer services.

Coastal Carolina's academic programs often are supplemented with field experiences and "real world" applications. Students have the chance to participate in faculty-led travel to a pristine barrier island on the South Carolina coast, the Grand Canyon, archaeological digs in surrounding historical settings, Fortune 500 companies, the marbled chambers of the United States Supreme Court, Oxford University, and East Africa.

A reciprocal student-exchange program with Nene College in North Hampton, England, has been established through the Palmetto Partnership for International Exchange, a partnership headed by Coastal Carolina with the College of Charleston and Lander and Winthrop Universities.

The university's four applied-research centers help students realize the practical applications of classroom theory and the importance of university-community relations.

University programs that serve the community include continuing education; Lifelong Learning Society, an academic program for those age 50 and older (see the Senior Scene chapter); and cultural events including live arts performances.

Coastal Carolina athletes participate in NCAA Division I, with 17 varsity teams competing in the Big South Conference.

Coastal Carolina is accredited by the Commission of the Southern Association of Colleges and Schools to award the baccalaureate degree and the master's degree in education.

In 1954, when a group of concerned citizens met in the Horry County Memorial Library to discuss the creation of a local college, the foundation was laid for Coastal Carolina to provide quality education for its students. For more than 40 years, the university has been building a tradition of excellence. In 1994 it broke from the University of South Carolina system in a major political battle over endowments; it seems that Coastal officials felt that they were at the bottom of the priorities list for fund-raising expenditures. Since the split, Coastal Carolina has begun major expansion, and the Golf Course Management program has come to be recognized as one of the nation's finest. In 2002 the largest freshman class ever began their college careers at Coastal and enrollment is up 19 percent in 2003.

Horry-Georgetown Technical College
2050 U.S. Highway 501 East, Conway
(843) 347-3186
www.hor.tec.sc.us

Horry-Georgetown Technical College, established in 1966, currently boasts an annual student enrollment of more than 4,200. Combined with the Continuing Education Division of HGTC, which provides skill enhancement and specialized job training, that number reaches 14,000. The college continues to grow and prosper while serving Horry and Georgetown Counties as well as surrounding communities.

Insiders' Tip
Horry-Georgetown Technical College offers a degree in golf course management. The two-year program is highly acclaimed.

HGTC is in the business of cultivating excellence across three campuses, with convenient sites in Conway, Myrtle Beach (now also on the former Air Force base), and Georgetown. The college offers more than 60 degrees, diplomas, and certificates—from Associate in Arts and Associate in Science to a varied technical and business curriculum. In addition to the two-year degrees, HGTC has several transfer agreements with other South Carolina colleges and universities that allow students to obtain four-year degrees. Furthermore, HGTC has 74 courses guaranteed to transfer for full credit to any public higher-education institution in South Carolina. Its thriving Continuing Education program and intensive on-site industrial training program—serving more than 75 businesses, industries, and organizations each year—round out HGTC's educational opportunities.

Horry-Georgetown Technical College is accredited by the Commission on Colleges of the Southern Association of Colleges and Schools.

North American Institute of Aviation
1700 Airport Road, Conway
(843) 397–3776, (800) 327–6242
www.naia.tr

This private international institute operates out of the Conway/Horry County Airport. Students—approaching nearly 100 at any given time—train to become commercial airline pilots. After a six-month course, pilots return to their home countries to accumulate flight time. Once they have logged 1,500 flight hours, they return to Conway to earn an Airline Transport Pilot designation.

Most of the students come from Scandinavian countries and live in dormitories at the airport.

The school moved to Conway from the Northeast about 18 years ago because officials preferred the area's geography and mild weather.

Health Care

Referrals and Free Advice

Regional Health-care Facilities

For the benefit of any visitor to the Grand Strand, this chapter will give you pertinent information about regional medical services, clinics, and hospitals. Health-care services listed here should be able to handle anything from a severe sunburn to debilitating pain.

The Grand Strand has recently witnessed an incredible growth in health-care services and specialists. Rapid growth, ideal locations for golf and attractions, and what one physician called "a doctor-friendly environment" have brought a weighty influx of medical expertise to the area.

In November 2002 the newest member of the Georgetown Hospital family opened its doors. Waccamaw Community Hospital, a 40-bed inpatient facility, accommodates the needs of an exploding population in the northern section of Georgetown Memorial Hospital's current service area.

Besides the less stressful lifestyle and heralded Southern hospitality enjoyed by many of these practitioners, the need for doctors who practice geriatrics, rheumatology, and endocrinology has soared in direct proportion with the number of senior citizens relocating to the Grand Strand.

If you are about to become a resident or have just moved into our area, the referral services can quickly put you in touch with a new family doctor or specialist.

Referrals and Free Advice

Physicians Referral Service
(843) 716–7000 EXT. 6401

Sponsored by Loris Community Hospital, referral to conveniently located physicians who meet a person's medical needs can be accessed by this service.

Doctors Referral Service is available Monday through Friday from 8:30 A.M. to 5:00 P.M.

Physician Referral Source
(843) 692–1052
www.grandstrandmed.com

Especially if a medical specialist is needed, this service will give you all the necessary referral information, including a doctor's hours. Physician Referral represents more than 275 physicians on Grand Strand Regional Medical Center's staff and more than 30 medical specialties and sub-specialties. This service is available 9:00 A.M. to 5:00 P.M., Monday through Friday.

Regional Health-care Facilities

Walk-in Clinics

Visitors who need to see a doctor but aren't sick enough to go to a hospital emergency room can save themselves time and money by seeking care at one of the Grand Strand's walk-in medical clinics.

These clinics take patients without appointments, but most of them don't take insurance, Medicaid, or Medicare, so be prepared to pay when you go. Costs run anywhere from $55 to $75 for an average visit, and some health-care providers accept traveler's checks, in-state personal checks, or credit cards as methods of payment (as noted in each write-up).

Clinic doctors routinely treat sunburn, heat rash, heat exhaustion, cuts, sprains, broken bones, jellyfish stings, and sore throats. And some facilities offer more complex services, including X rays and stabilization of patients who have had heart attacks. Here is a listing of walk-in clinics representing each area of the Strand.

North Strand

Access Medical Care
3816 U.S. Highway 17 South, North Myrtle Beach
(843) 272–1411

Access Medical Care offers minor surgery, X rays, electrocardiograms, and complete laboratory services, as well as a pharmacy. With the exception of Blue Cross/Blue Shield, insurance is not accepted, but office workers will fill out Medicare and Medicaid papers for people who live in South and North Carolina. Access will file workers' compensation claims. The clinic is open Monday through Friday from 8:00 A.M. to 7:00 P.M., and on Saturday and Sunday from 9:00 A.M. to 3:00 P.M.

Doctor's Care North Myrtle Beach
1714 U.S. Highway 17 South,
North Myrtle Beach
(843) 361–0705

Doctor's Care medical clinic provides primary and urgent care, including X rays, stitches, and stabilization of heart attack patients. The clinic accepts regular patients for family practice and can also handle minor lab work. Emergencies will be sent to the nearest hospital. The cost for a typical nonemergency office visit ranges from $59 to $65. The North Myrtle Beach clinic is open extended hours seven days a week.

Myrtle Beach

Access Medical Care
4810 North Kings Highway, Myrtle Beach
(843) 497–7131

Access Medical offers minor surgery, X rays, electrocardiograms, and complete lab services. Access also operates a limited-medications pharmacy. Insurance is not accepted (except Blue Cross/Blue Shield), but office workers will fill out Medicare and Medicaid papers for people who live in South and North Carolina. Access will file workers' compensation in-

jury claims. The clinic is open Monday through Friday from 8:00 A.M. to 7:00 P.M.

Care Express
Grand Strand Regional Medical Center
809 82nd Parkway, Myrtle Beach
(843) 692–1770
www.grandstrandmed.com

For minor emergency health-care situations requiring expert care, Grand Strand Regional Medical Center's Care Express can provide it immediately—around the clock, seven days every week. Care Express is a self-contained, urgent-care clinic within the Emergency Department. This setup facilitates examination by hospital specialists in a prompt, convenient, and private manner, without red tape and long waits. For unexpected emergencies, Care Express has access to the full range of specialist and technological support of an ultramodern Emergency Department.

Doctor's Care Myrtle Beach
1220 21st Avenue North, Myrtle Beach
(843) 626–9379

The Doctor's Care medical clinics provide primary and urgent care, including X rays, stitches, and stabilization of heart attack patients. Doctors here accept regular patients for family practice. The clinics also handle minor lab work. Emergencies are sent to the nearest hospital. The center is open extended hours seven days a week. The cost for a typical nonemergency office visit ranges from $59 to $65; if you return to the clinic, the cost is reduced. Doctor's Care dispenses common medications to its patients.

South Strand

Doctor's Care
Surfside Medical Center, 1600 U.S. Highway 17 North, Surfside Beach
(843) 238–1461

This Doctor's Care clinic, like its counterparts in North Myrtle Beach and Myrtle Beach (see previous entries for details), provides primary and urgent care and handles minor lab work. The Surfside Beach clinic is open seven days a week from 8:00 A.M. to 8:00 P.M.

South Strand Family Clinic
2347 U.S. Highway 17 Business, Garden City
(843) 357–2443
Resident physician and clinic owner Dr. James Turek takes care of patients here. This walk-in clinic, across from Garden City Furniture, also serves regular patients by appointment.

The clinic conducts allergy tests as well as bone-density tests to determine early signs of osteoporosis.

It is open Monday through Friday from 8:00 A.M. to 8:00 P.M., and on Saturday from 9:00 A.M. to 1:00 P.M. The cost of a first-time urgent-care visit starts at $55, while established patients pay $44.

Hospitals

It's heart-wrenching when you, a loved one, or friend needs hospital attention, but you can take comfort in the care and professionalism found at the following medical facilities. Scanning through this section, you should be able to get a good idea of the specialty services offered by each, just in case you need to make a quick decision about where to take someone for medical attention.

North Strand

Loris Healthcare System
3655 Mitchell Street, Loris
(843) 716–7000
www.lorishealthcaresystem.com
Some visitors at the northern end of the Grand Strand might find it quickest to visit Loris, an acute-care, nonprofit community hospital. Loris has a capacity of 105 patients, all in private rooms. The hospital also runs a separate 88-bed, skilled nursing assisted facility known as the Loris Healthcare System Extended Care Center.

Loris Hospital offers 24-hour emergency service, cardiac rehabilitation services, same-day surgery, a modern intensive-care unit, ultrasound, magnetic resonance imaging (MRI), a CT scanner, nuclear medicine, extensive outpatient services, an obstetrics unit with childbirth and breast-feeding classes, and nutritional counseling.

A 26,000-square-foot center for health and fitness houses cardiac rehabilitation, physical therapy, hydrotherapy, exercise programs, and meeting facilities. Regular classes focus on smoking cessation, weight loss, and low-fat cooking. Unlike other hospital-sponsored wellness programs, Loris Community offers use of its fitness facility to the public in an effort to keep people out of its beds through prevention.

The fitness center offers a variety of aerobic classes including Seniorcize and water aerobics, plus cardiovascular and strength-building equipment. In fact the center quickly earned a local reputation as an "unofficial" community spot, being selected by community members as the site for wedding receptions, gatherings, and programs.

Loris Healthcare System has constructed Seacoast Medical Center. Located in Little River, this 24-hour emergency

Insiders' Tip

Nearly all Grand Strand hospitals now have impressive wellness centers with exercise equipment, aerobics classes, swimming pools, and a host of heath-related programs. Membership is open to the public, making them an alternative workout spot to gyms, aerobics studios, and fitness venues. Trained professional staff is a must for all hospital wellness programs.

and same-day surgery facility makes health-care services more easily accessible to the communities of Longs, Little River, North Myrtle Beach, and Calabash.

Loris Healthcare System has also opened a full complement of medical offices, including Calabash Imaging and Diagnostic Center; Extended Care Center; Family Health Centers in Loris and Mt. Olive; and Rainbow Pediatrics in Loris and Little River.

Loris Healthcare System continues to enhance health services in the region by providing new services and renovations to existing facilities, including the open MRI services conveniently available at Seacoast Medical Center and enhanced Women's Services with the addition of new Labor, Delivery, and Recovery suites.

Myrtle Beach

Grand Strand Regional Medical Center
809 82nd Parkway, Myrtle Beach
(843) 692–1000
www.grandstrandmed.com

Grand Strand Regional Medical Center is a 219-bed acute-care facility that offers an array of medical services on both an inpatient and outpatient basis. The medical staff numbers more than 900 with more than 275 physicians on call.

Grand Strand Regional was named as one of the Top 100 hospitals in the country for cardiovascular care, with two operating rooms dedicated solely to open-heart surgery, angioplasty, and other heart-related procedures. The hospital is noted for its state-of-the-art cardiac catheterization and diagnostic laboratory, stents, and cardiac rehabilitation. A rehabilitation center now houses exercise equipment and supervised programs for cardiac patients that includes fitness, nutritional counseling, education, and risk education.

In 2001, 405 cardiac surgeries were performed with success rates exceeding state and national averages. The need for local services was apparent: Heart disease is the leading cause of death in South Carolina and accounts for 40 percent of all deaths statewide. Grand Strand Regional Medical Center in Myrtle Beach answered

that need by building a 14,600-square-foot, $5.9 million surgical addition to the hospital that includes an eight-bed surgical intensive-care unit and two new operating suites. A satellite pharmacy services the operating rooms and the surgical intensive-care unit.

The Emergency Department is a designated trauma center using electronic technology that includes a hyperbaric chamber commonly used in treating diving accidents, wounds, and burns. Emergency also offers Care Express to treat minor injuries and illnesses for anyone without a local physician. Care Express is open to new residents and visitors alike. Grand Strand Regional emergency services is also the proud owner of HeartLink, a cardiac transport ambulance for those in need of acute care. All of Grand Strand's emergency department physicians are board certified in emergency medicine. For added convenience, an outpatient pharmacy is open to the public from 7:00 A.M. to 7:00 P.M. every day of the week.

Grand Strand Hospital operates an accredited community cancer program in Horry and Georgetown Counties. It is also a member of the National Consortium of Breast Centers and oncology physicians and nurses are board certified. Mammography is available at the hospital and at diagnostic centers in Little River and Surfside Beach. Radiation therapy is available at a nearby facility and a cancer registry is employed to track patient treatments and follow-up through a national data bank. Grand Strand Medical utilizes minimally invasive breast biopsy (MIBB) and a Sentinel node biopsy program.

Grand Strand Regional Medical Center has six affiliates throughout the Grand Strand to provide quality, convenient health care. These include the Grand Strand Regional Diagnostic & Women's Center, South Strand Ambulatory Care Center, Grand Strand Regional Medical Center Wound Care Program, North Strand Diagnostic Center, North Strand Senior Health Center, and the South Strand Senior Health Center on the campus of Community Medical Center–South Strand.

Hospital officials work especially hard at preventive care and community education through an annual health fair held on the first Saturday in February, and a cardiac wellness program that includes the Mall Walkers' Club, the Cardiac Lifelong Program, and ongoing community cholesterol screenings.

Other community programs include prostate cancer screening and a teddy bear clinic for children—an annual event at Grand Strand Regional aimed at allaying children's fears of hospitals. Preschoolers bring their "injured" teddy bears into the emergency room where doctors and nurses apply bandages, splints, stitches, and the odd button.

South Strand

Georgetown Memorial Hospital
606 Black River Road, Georgetown
(843) 527–7000, (843) 626–9040 (from
Myrtle Beach)

This is a private, nonprofit acute-care medical facility that is currently licensed for 142 beds. More than 50 physicians representing 20 areas of specialty practice are members of the active medical staff.

Medical services include ambulatory surgery; birthing suites; cardiac diagnostics, catheterization, and rehabilitation; full emergency and lab services; MRI; pathology; radiology; renal dialysis; and respiratory therapy. The hospital also offers cholesterol screenings, dietary consultation, and discharge planning. Throughout any given year, Georgetown Memorial holds various educational programs and events.

Established in 1950, Georgetown Memorial has consistently expanded services to keep up with the needs of the community. Most recently the hospital added pre-op bays, a fifth surgical suite and a diagnostic imaging center.

Waccamaw Community Hospital
4070 Highway 17 Bypass, Murrells Inlet
(843) 357–5100
www.gmhsc.com

The newest member of the Georgetown Hospital Family opened its doors in late 2002. Waccamaw Community Hospital, a 40-bed inpatient facility, accommodates the needs of a growing population in northern Georgetown County and southern Horry County. The three-story building is comprised of nearly 187,000 square feet of interior space. Twenty-four-hour emergency services, obstetrics, inpatient and outpatient surgery, and medical/surgical units are offered at the new hospital. In addition a 29-bed acute-care rehabilitation facility is located on the same site. It is designed to serve as a short-term, interim step for patients who have been discharged from an inpatient facility. Rehabilitation therapy services, including physical, occupational, and speech therapy, are available to acute rehab inpatients.

Beyond the Strand

Conway Hospital
300 Singleton Ridge Road, Conway
(843) 347–7111
www.conwayhospital.com

Conway Hospital, a private, nonprofit institution, was in downtown Conway for more than a half century before a large, modern facility was built outside the city limits between Conway and Myrtle Beach.

The hospital opened in 1982, and today approximately 125 physicians make rounds among 160 modern, private rooms. The building itself has three stories, with patient rooms occupying the top two floors. Conway Hospital has 80 medical/surgical beds, 29 obstetrical/gynecological beds, 18 pediatrics beds, and 10 beds equipped for intensive and coronary care.

Services include 24-hour emergency and urgent-care, one-day surgery, chemotherapy, CT scanning, MRI, lithotripsy, maternity care, pediatric care, mammography, cardiac rehabilitation, nuclear medicine, physical therapy, respiratory therapy, home health care, surgical care, ultrasound, intensive care, and progressive care. A new generation of echocardiographic equipment, as well as CT scanning, MRI, digital substraction angiography, blood gas analysis, impedance plethysmography, advanced telemetry techniques, and cardiac catheterization allows for state-of-the-art diagnostic and treatment capabilities. The hospital

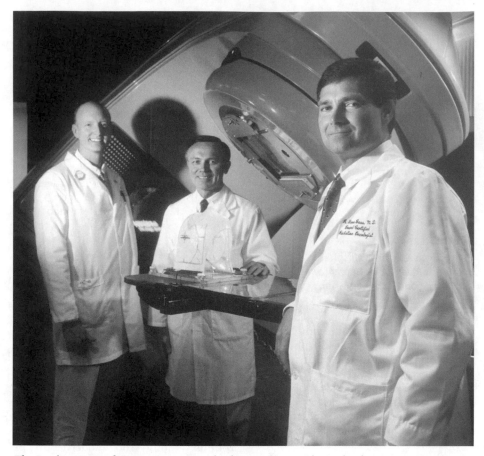

The Carolina Regional Cancer Center provides the region's most advanced radiation treatment therapy. PHOTO: COURTESY OF LHWH

is also certified as a Level III trauma center as well as Level II perinatal center.

Conway Hospital was the world's first to receive the Spectron Hip Reconstruction system. In August 1996, Dr. James Yates performed the sixth autologous chondrocyte transplant in the United States at Conway Hospital. The procedure is noted for producing remarkable results for young patients suffering from knee cartilage injury.

Patients requiring dialysis during their hospital stay are served at the facility through an inpatient dialysis unit. In addition, the adjoining Medstar subacute care building provides care to individuals in transition from intensive services to home, at a significantly reduced cost.

Adjacent to Conway Hospital is Kingston Nursing Center, an 88-bed long-term nursing home owned and operated by the hospital. And, through the efforts of a joint venture, Conway Hospital works with American Home Patient, a company that supplies home infusion services, home respiratory services and home medical equipment.

In spring 1996 Conway Hospital opened its 39,000-square-foot wellness and fitness center. This center includes a swimming pool, racquetball courts, an indoor track, basketball court, weight room, his and hers saunas, and locker rooms. Aerobics classes are scheduled as well. Memberships to the wellness facility are open to individuals, patients, and corporations, and a variety of rate packages is available. For more information, call (843) 347-1515.

In 1997 the AVX Corporation provided Conway Hospital with a $100,000 grant to put a 24-foot mobile health van on the road. Now health-screening services are available throughout Horry County to meet the needs of medically underserved people in the area.

Other Regional Facilities

McLeod Regional Medical Center
555 East Cheves Street, Florence
(843) 777-2000
www.mcleodhealth.org

About 75 miles from Myrtle Beach is McLeod Regional Hospital, a regional referral center for 12 counties in southeastern South Carolina. McLeod was established in 1906 as a small infirmary; today it's a large high-tech medical center, with 331 beds and a variety of services. Many Horry County residents depend on McLeod's neonatal intensive-care unit to tend to premature babies and full-term babies born with special problems.

The hospital's breast-imaging center helps doctors detect breast cancer in its early stages. McLeod had the state's first permanent MRI system, a high-tech machine that uses a magnetic field to see into the body in a much clearer way than other scanning machines allow.

McLeod also provides comprehensive inpatient, outpatient, and diagnostic facilities, including an extensive 24-hour laboratory, computerized tomography, angiography, computer-enhanced nuclear medicine, ultrasound, echocardiography, mammography, EEG, EKG, a vascular laboratory, osteoporosis screening, a sleep center, and 24-hour emergency care. The Florence hospital is the state-designated regional trauma center.

The facility added a five-story freestanding Women's Pavilion connected to McLeod. The pavilion houses a mammography unit, outpatient surgery rooms, and a special section for labor and delivery or Caesarean section.

McLeod Children's Hospital provides the highest level of pediatric care and technology available in the region. The Child Life Activity Center offers a place for relaxed play and distraction from illness or injury, and Child Life Specialists are assigned to work with children and their families to make the hospital stay easier. In 1994 McLeod opened the region's only five-bed Pediatric Intensive Care Unit (PICU). In 1997 the PICU was upgraded to a six-bed unit and is under the direction of two board-certified pediatric specialists. McLeod has five pediatric sub-specialists of pediatric cardiology, endocrinology, gastroenterology, and critical care.

A range of support departments buttress the hospital's services. These include rehabilitative services, pain management, cardiac rehabilitation, respiratory services, counseling and discharge planning, hospice, infection control, pastoral services, patient representatives, volunteer services, computer services, and marketing.

Mental Health/Addictions

South Strand
The Waccamaw Center for Mental Health
164 Waccamaw Medical Park Drive, Conway
(843) 347-4888
525 Lafayette Circle, Georgetown
(843) 546-6107
www.state.sc.us/dmh

The Waccamaw Center is a public, nonprofit agency that handles any sort of mental-health issue on an outpatient basis. Fees are established on a sliding scale; you pay only what you can afford based on income and expenses, and most insurances are accepted. Staff is on call 24 hours a day, seven days a week to respond to emergencies and crises. Both clinics offer adult services, child and adolescent therapy, alcohol and drug abuse counseling, programs for the chronically mentally ill, and emergency stabilization.

The center is continuously developing special community programs to institute prevention of growing mental-health problems. The school-based program operates out of a number of Grand Strand schools, offering on-site help to children and their families. An Employee Assistance Program offers mental-health services to business and industry on a contractual basis. The Waccamaw Center also will refer clients to an appropriate inpatient facility if it is necessary.

Beyond the Strand
Shoreline Behavioral Health Services
2404 Wise Road, Conway
(843) 365–8884
www.shorelinebhs.org

Shoreline Behavioral Health Services works with the South Carolina Department of Alcohol, other drug abuse services, and numerous local individuals, agencies, and organizations to reduce and control problems related to the use of alcohol and other drugs. They accomplish this through a variety of primary prevention, intervention, and treatment services. The agency strives to provide affordable and accessible quality services to the general public, as well as to special and high-risk populations. Services include a 10-bed Psychoactive Substance Abuse Dependency facility (PSAD), day and evening counseling services, employee assistance programs, a DUI education program, and lots more. Fees are based on services received, and a variety of payment plans are available.

Health-Related Associations and Support Groups

Arthritis Foundation
1330 West Peachtree Street, Atlanta, GA
(800) 283–7800
www.arthritis.org

The Arthritis Foundation provides a toll-free number to answer questions about various types of arthritis and, when appropriate, refers callers to community organizations. The foundation is also prepared to help clients and their families with financial support.

Better Breathers Club
Grand Strand Regional Medical Center
809 82nd Parkway, Myrtle Beach
(843) 692–1885
www.grandstrandmed.com

This group, supporting individuals who suffer from breathing difficulties, meets on the third Thursday of each month at 3:00 P.M. Meetings are free and open to the public. The group usually meets in the Cardiac Rehabilitation classroom. To be sure, please call the number listed to confirm the location.

Cancer Support Group
Georgetown Memorial Hospital
606 Black River Road, Georgetown
(843) 527–7448
www.gmhsc.com

The Cancer Support Group is open to anyone affected by cancer. The group meets monthly at the Georgetown Hospital Education Center. Other area groups include Breast Cancer Support, (843) 213-0333, and Grand Strand Prostate Cancer support group, (843) 272-1537.

Community Seminar
5046 Highway 17 Bypass, Myrtle Beach

Informative, educational community-health seminars are presented monthly, usually at a 10:00 A.M. meeting, at the South Strand Senior Health Center Community Room, Suite 101. Seminars feature local health-care professionals discussing a variety of health topics. The community health-care seminars are free and open to the public. Call ahead for a schedule.

Department of Health and Environmental Control
303 Hazzard Street, Georgetown
(843) 546–5593
101 Elm Street, Conway
(843) 248–1500
107 Highway 57 North, Little River
(843) 399–5553

DHEC provides pregnancy tests, blood tests, immunizations, family planning, and tuberculosis screening. The agency can provide health care to the home-bound, depending upon the particular circumstances. This department is always happy to provide the larger community and schools with health promotion and educational programs.

Department of Social Services (DSS)
330 Dozier Street, Georgetown
(843) 546–5134
1951 Industrial Park Road, Conway
(843) 365–5565
www.state.sc.us/dss

The mission of the South Carolina Department of Social Services is to ensure the health and safety of children and adults who cannot protect themselves; to help people in need of financial assistance reach their highest level of social and economic self-sufficiency, and to help parents and caregivers provide nurturing homes. In short the agency states its goal as helping people to live better lives. From child support services to elder care, DSS provides a wealth of health- and human-services information.

Diabetes Education Group
Grand Strand Senior Center
1268 21st Avenue North, Myrtle Beach
(843) 692–9526
www.grandstrandmed.com

This group meets on the fourth Wednesday of each month at 6:30 P.M. for the purpose of educating diabetes patients and their family members. Special diabetes management programs and speakers from health-care providers are featured. Time is also allotted for question-and-answer sessions. Meetings are free and open to the public. For further information call Grand Strand Regional Medical Center's Diabetes Management Program coordinator, Mary Ellen Rogers Scarborough, at the number listed above.

Diabetic Outreach/Multiple Sclerosis Support Group
300 Singleton Ridge Road, Conway
(843) 347–8108

A registered nurse and dietician are on hand for this group's monthly meetings, held the first Thursday of every month at 2:00 P.M. in the Finlayson Classroom of Conway Hospital. In the hospital's auditorium, on the second Wednesday of each month, the Multiple Sclerosis group meets from 7:00 to 9:00 P.M.

Joint Replacement Education Group
300 Singleton Ridge Road, Conway
(843) 347–7111

If you're anticipating knee-replacement surgery, you may just want to look this group up for information. Meetings are held on the first Tuesday of the month from 10:00 to 11:30 A.M. at the Conway Hospital Wellness & Fitness Center. Topics covered during the meeting include preparation for surgery and what to expect during the operation, during recovery, and during rehabilitation.

Mended Hearts Support Group
Grand Strand Regional Medical Center, 809 82nd Parkway, Myrtle Beach
(843) 692–1885
www.grandstrandmed.com

Individuals with heart problems—heart attack, angioplasty, or bypass—should attend this meeting on the second Thursday of the month at 7:00 P.M. Meetings are held in the Grand Strand Regional Medical Center Cardiac Rehabilitation classroom and are free and open to the public.

Murrells Inlet Alzheimer's Support Group
Belin Methodist Church, Murrells Inlet
(843) 527–7105

This group meets on the second and fourth Wednesday of each month at 10:00 A.M. and is cosponsored by Coastal Carolina Alzheimer's Chapter. Groups provide a listening ear, encouragement, coping techniques, moral support, and information. The Georgetown Alzheimer's Support Group can be reached at (843) 527-3111. Meetings are also held at Myrtle Beach Manor. Call (843) 449-5283 for details.

Media

Newspapers
Magazines
Radio Stations
Television Stations

Grand Stranders could not live without the media. Literally. When Hurricane Hugo thundered into town in September 1989, the radio became our nearest, dearest, and most trusted friend. We found ourselves again beholden to the radio during fall 1996 with stormy visits from Hurricanes Bertha and Fran. Even when power outages shrouded us in darkness and rudely shut off the television set, local radio stations such as WYAV-FM and WYAK-FM kept us informed. A number of local radio and television newscasters braved the swirling, high winds on Ocean Boulevard to give us up-to-the-minute reports, while newspaper reporters left the safety of their own homes to get the story from shelters and police outposts.

Besides comforting us through natural disasters, the media helps us digest the burgeoning amount of local goings-on. The Grand Strand has become a veritable boomtown. Without media reports and newspapers, we would have one heck of a time keeping up with the daily opening and closing of businesses, entertainment venues, new housing developments, and retailers.

In an area that is frenetically attracting national franchises, recording artists, and movie stars, the sense of the Grand Strand as a community would be lost in the shuffle without media stories about the people we know—our neighbors.

One thing is sure: The Grand Strand media will keep you in touch and up-to-date. Figuring out where to go on the weekend is easy when you pick up a copy of the *Sun News* on Fridays and rifle through the "kicks!" insert. Every festival, arts event, feature movie, new restaurant, entertainer, and venue is listed.

You can even start making plans while driving into town by surfing the channels of your car radio. Especially from March through September, radio airwaves are packed with announcements from nightclubs, restaurants, and shops. Nightclubs generally advertise what's happening that evening for entertainment plus food and drink specials. In fact your night's itinerary can be set even before you check into your hotel room.

With that in mind, get in touch with the Grand Strand by lending your eyes and ears to the local media.

Newspapers

Dailies

Sun News
914 Frontage Road East, Myrtle Beach
(843) 626–8555
www.myrtlebeachonline.com

Established in 1961, the *Sun News* is the only daily newspaper along the Grand Strand. It provides comprehensive local and international news, stock market reports, weather forecasts, and a classified advertising section. On Fridays the paper includes the "kicks!" section, which offers information about upcoming entertainment as well as reviews. In 1997 the *Sun News* began a Saturday insert magazine, rotating the subjects of Health & Fitness, Senior Living, Outdoors, Technology & Computers, and Homes & Gardens. The Sunday edition is chock-full of extras, including a separate real estate section, TV guide, coupons, and *Parade* magazine. Daily circulation is nearly 45,000.

Daily delivery subscriptions for a full year are $147 or $116 if you just want delivery on Friday, Saturday, and Sunday. A 13-week daily subscription runs $40.80; for weekend editions only the cost is $29.

Non-dailies

Myrtle Beach Herald
(843) 626–3131
www.myrtlebeachherald.com

Found mainly in area bookstores and grocery stores, this broadsheet newspaper comes out every Thursday morning. Editorial coverage investigates the Grand Strand from Little River to Murrells Inlet. A newcomer to the area, the *Herald* started rolling the presses in 1994. Individual issues are 50 cents a copy. Subscriptions within Horry County cost $25 a year; out-of-state subscriptions are $30.

North Myrtle Beach Times
(843) 249–3525

Published on Wednesdays, the *Times* attempts to zero in on Grand Strand–related issues, such as the local option sales tax and further development of the local transportation infrastructure. You can find it at bookstores and in brochure racks at local restaurants and businesses for 50 cents each. Subscriptions run $30 for the year.

Coastal Observer
(843) 237–8438
www.coastalobserver.com

This weekly newspaper hits the streets on Thursdays and covers the region known as the Waccamaw Neck: DeBordieu, Pawleys Island, Murrells Inlet, Litchfield Beach, and Garden City Beach. The *Observer* has been the recipient of numerous awards presented by the South Carolina Press Association for feature writing, sports coverage, layout, and design. It can be found in businesses and boxes throughout the Waccamaw Neck region at a cost of 25 cents per issue. Subscriptions are $14 a year.

Georgetown Times
(843) 546–4148
www.gtowntimes.com

A well-established local newspaper, the *Georgetown Times* is published on Mondays, Wednesdays, and Fridays and covers events in Georgetown and its surrounding communities. Special and favorite sections that come out in the *Times* at least once a year include the "Newcomer's Guide," "Bridal Guide," and "Hunting Guide." You'll find copies in news racks throughout the county for 25 cents apiece. Local subscriptions run $24 per year.

Magazines

Alternatives NewsMagazine
(843) 444–5556

Alternatives is considered a magazine by content only, since an issue is actually slightly smaller and glossier than a broadsheet newspaper. Articles focus more on ideas or concepts than on reporting news. Local cultural events are always listed thoroughly in *Alternatives*. The publication features a roster of eclectic columnists who give opinions on various subjects. *Alternatives* is a freebie and is available all over the Grand Strand—in offices, businesses, magazine racks, and restaurants. It's published twice a month, every other Thursday.

Lowcountry Companion
(843) 237–3899

Lowcountry Companion is a free distribution, tabloid-sized publication devoted to

...ing the South Carolina Lowcoun-
...ring 10 years of consistent publica-
...owcountry Companion has featured a
...variety of articles exploring all sorts
...nique subjects that relate to the rich
...toric and natural heritage of the re-
...on. The magazine strives to promote
...co-friendly tourism—tourism that utilizes natural resources without depleting
them. Each of three annual issues includes the area's most comprehensive calendar of events, as well as a restaurant
guide, a golf guide, and a comprehensive
directory of eco-friendly things to do. Annual subscriptions are available for $10.

Radio Stations

As in most any area with a largely
tourism-driven economy, the Grand
Strand's world of radio is an ever-changing, volatile industry. Local radio personalities are in a constant state of flux: in
and out of town, changing stations,
switching formats, and showing up
ferent time drives. On any given day your
favorite country-music DJ might disappear from the airwaves, only to be heard
further down the dial hawking the latest
rap tunes.

But if you're here long enough, you
can place a face to almost every voice you
hear on the radio. Businesses, restaurants,
nightclubs, and entertainment theaters
are always booking radio personalities to
perform on-site "remotes." These are
hard-working people, ladies and gentlemen. Many local radio personnel start
their days on-air at 5:00 A.M., then spend
the evening promoting a club act.

A 1997 study independently con-
ducted by Young & Rubicam found that
radio rules in the Myrtle Beach and Florence markets. The analysis set out to determine how much time American adults
spend watching television, reading newspapers and magazines, and listening to
the radio. Out of the 211 markets across
the nation used in the study, Myrtle Beach

Radio stations provide coverage and often sponsor local events and fundraisers. PHOTO: COURTESY OF
WWXM-FM 97.7

...u Florence ranked No. 7 for radio loyalty. Apparently our adult population listens to the radio an average of 3 hours and 26 minutes each day. The national average for tuning into the radio is 3 hours and 9 minutes each day.

We are confident that you will find the music that you love to listen to on at least one of the stations listed here.

Adult Contemporary
WMYB-FM 92.1 (Soft rock)
WNMB-FM 105.9

Adult Urban Contemporary
WDAI-FM 98.5
WXJY-FM 93.7

Contemporary Hits
WWXM-FM 97.7

Country
WEGX-FM 92.9
WGTR-FM 107.9
WYAK-FM 103.1
WLSC-AM 1240

Easy Listening
WJYR-AM 1450

Gospel
WLMC-AM 1470
WPJS-AM 1330

Jazz
WLGI-FM 90.9

Oldies
WSYN-FM 106.5
WVCO-FM 94.9
COOL-FM 104.9
WGTN-FM 100.7

Rock
WYAV-FM 104.1
WKZQ-FM 101.7
WSCA-FM 93.7
WWSK-FM 107.1

Talk Radio
WRNN-FM 99.5
WHMC-FM 90.1 (NPR)

Television Stations

First things first. In order to find you... vorite program on a particular netwo... you need to know which cable company servicing your area. TV guides will gi... you a lineup of what channel you shoul... turn to, in accordance with the designated cable delivery company you're hooked up to. This listing should set your remote control straight. Warning: If you're a channel surfer, ignore this section and simply proceed as usual.

North Strand

Horry Telephone Cooperative
3480 Highway 701, Conway
(843) 365–2151
www.htcinc.net

This cable provider jumps around Horry County, but exclusively services the northern Longs region and its surrounding communities, including Carolina Forest, Little River Inn, The Spa at Little River, The Preserve, and Colonial Charters.

Myrtle Beach

Time Warner Cable
1901 Oak Street, Myrtle Beach
(843) 913–7941
www.twcsc.com

You are in Time Warner country if you are living or staying in Myrtle Beach proper, Little River, Atlantic Beach, North Myrtle Beach, Briarcliffe, or any Myrtle Beach hotel or condominium. TV guides use "TG" to designate the Time Warner service in the areas of Georgetown and Andrews.

Time Warner officially acquired Jones Intercable in mid-1998. This cable company serves three-fourths of all customers in Horry and Georgetown Counties. At the same time, its delivery system was recently upgraded, at a cost of $15 million, to install fiber-optic cable and new converters. To the customer this means greater channel capacity, improved picture and sound quality, and increased reliabil-

gh-speed cable modems will offer
...et access.

...etwork Affiliates and
...ocal Satellites

ABC Affiliates

WWAY-TV 3
WCIV-TV 4
Local Satellite: WPDE–TV 15
Founders Center, 2411 Oak Street, Suite 206,
Myrtle Beach
(843) 234–WPDE
(843) 946–6689 (Weather Center)
www.wpdetv.com

News channel 15 boasts an impressive weather and environmental team and offers newscasts at 5:30 A.M., noon, 5:00 and 11:00 P.M. Chief Meteorologist Ed Piotrowski has been voted the state's No. 1 weathercaster by the Associated Press of South Carolina and was nominated for the National Hurricane Center's media award for outstanding efforts to educate and inform the public about hurricanes and hurricane preparedness. WPDE is the only area station to broadcast line lottery drawings nightly at 6:58 P.M. All of our ABC stations bring you *Good Morning America* at 7:00 A.M. and air *All My Children, One Life to Live,* and *General Hospital* from 1:00 through 4:00 P.M. Other ABC programming varies from channel to channel during the time blocks of morning talk shows and evening sitcoms.

Subscribers to Time Warner Cable can access ABC programming on Channel 9. TV 4 is on Channel 4. Horry Telephone service is on Channel 9 as well. Cablevision airs Channel 4 on Channel 57; Channel 9 stays the same.

CBS Affiliates

WCSC-TV 5
Local Satellite: WBTW-TV 13
101 McDonald Court, Myrtle Beach
(843) 293–1301
www.wbtw.com

Like the weather team of WPDE-TV 15, WBTW Chief Meteorologist Don Leuhrs has received accolades from public and press alike for his outstanding coverage of weather conditions during Hur... Fran in September 1996. TV 13 offers a local segment during its morning news broadcast that is one of the best venues for exposure in town. Approximately 31,000 viewers from the Grand Strand and as far away as Florence, South Carolina, tune in regularly. All CBS affiliates air the news at 5:00 and 6:00 P.M. Between 12:30 and 5:00 P.M. CBS offers an impressive lineup of soaps: *The Young and the Restless, The Bold and the Beautiful, As the World Turns,* and *Guiding Light.* Daytime programming ends with the *Oprah Winfrey Show.*

CBS carries tried-and-true shows, such as *60 Minutes,* as well as new hit programming like *Survivor* and *CSI.*

TV 13 has originated news and programming from the Myrtle Beach area for more than 15 years now and prides itself on being an integral part of the Grand Strand community. During Halloween, the station works with local Holiday Inns to provide barrier-free trick or treating to special-needs children. WBTW TV-13 also sponsors a Senior Fair each year and projects that honor outstanding local teachers, students, and athletes. Joining forces with Crime Stoppers and regional law enforcement, Channel 13 airs *Carolina's Most Wanted* every Sunday at noon. This program has been responsible for apprehending 60 percent of the criminals featured since viewers are able to give information and tips anonymously.

All CBS programming is found on Channel 13 for Time Warner customers and Horry Telephone viewers. HTC customers may select either channel 5 or 13.

NBC Affiliates

WECT-TV 6, www.wect.com
WIS-TV 10, www.wis.com
WCBD-TV 2, www.wcbd.com

These NBC stations offer a popular programming roster. *Days of Our Lives, Another World, Montel Williams,* and *Oprah Winfrey* round out daytime viewing from 1:00 to 5:00 P.M. Two hours of award-winning news follows, and then come some of the best sitcoms TV has to offer, including *Home Improvement, Friends, Seinfeld, Caro-*

...in The City, Frasier, and _Mad About You._ NBC introduced us to new shows such as _3rd Rock From the Sun, Men Behaving Badly,_ and _Suddenly Susan._ These affiliates also bring you the _Tonight Show_ every night of the week plus _ER, The Pretender,_ and _Profiler._

Time Warner Cable gives you NBC on channels 6 and 10 as does Horry Telephone. The network is found on channels 6 and 62 with Cablevision.

Fox Affiliates

WFXB-TV 43, www.wfxb.com
WTAT-TV 24, www.wtat24.com

A deal cut in October 1996 officially awarded Myrtle Beach's only independent television station, WGSE-TV 43, the Fox Broadcasting Company affiliation for the Florence and Myrtle Beach markets. Fox programming began on WFXB in January 1997, right around the date of the Super Bowl, which the station carried. Until then, WGSE-TV 43 aired only family and religious programming.

Besides major sporting events, Fox's programming includes _That '70s Show, The Simpsons, 24,_ and _Boston Public._ Fox programming can be found on Time Warner Channel 4. Cablevision airs Fox on channels 24 and 26 and Horry Telephone subscribers need to switch to Channel 7.

United Paramount Affiliate

WWMB-TV 21, www.upn.com

No matter what local cable service you subscribe to, WWMB programming is found on Channel 16.

This is the only network affiliate on the Grand Strand that airs the popular series _Enterprise, The Twilight Zone,_ and _WWE Smackdown._

Educational

WITV-TV 7, www.scetv.org
WHMC-TV 23, www.scetv.org
WJPM-TV 33, www.scetv.org
WUNJ-TV 39, www.unctv.org

All of these education-oriented stations offer programming for the entire family. All are good morning channels for kids; catch _Arthur_ and _Clifford the Big Red Dog._

The _NewsHour_ with Jim Lehrer airs every evening at 6:00 P.M., followed _..._ riety of instructional and invest... programming.

Time Warner customers can find _..._ TV 23, and TV 33 on local Channel _..._ while WUNJ-TV 39 is on Channel 3. _..._ you're staying in a Myrtle Beach hotel, t... channel will be 21. The Horry Telephon... channel is 8.

Scroll Channels

Time Warner Cable and Waccamaw Cable

Scroll channels offer a constant listing of local information and public-service announcements accompanied by easy-listening music. These channels are widely accessed by hotel guests since they supply Grand Strand visitors with plenty of updated information and complete community calendars.

Local Feature Shows

The talk show _Southern Style_ has featured local guests since its inception in 1985. "Hostess with the mostest" Diane DeVaughn Stokes invites a variety of people with stories and passions to her hourlong program, which airs twice daily at 10:00 A.M. and 7:30 P.M. on Time Warner Cable, Channel 5. Diane's spots are always upbeat, like the hostess herself—whether on or off the air. Time Warner also produces _Now This Week In Coastal Entertainment,_ hosted by Richard Green, that highlights some aspect of local living. _This Week_ is cablecast on Channel 5 four times a week—Sunday and Thursday at 2:00 P.M. and Saturday and Tuesday at 8:00 P.M. And if you're looking for a home along the Grand Strand, tune in to _Coastal Carolina Real Estate,_ which airs on Channel 5 at 7:00 A.M., 11:00 A.M., 6:30 P.M., and 1:00 A.M. every day.

Both the Travel Vision Group, Beach TV 45 of South Carolina, and _Grand Strand Video Magazine_ offer viewers cable programs that speak specifically to the tourism market. Programs take you to attractions, restaurants, and theaters—and even provide golf tips.

olunteer
Opportunities

Want to get the pulse on a seemingly erratic resort area in a hurry? Become a volunteer! We highly recommend a volunteer pastime as one of the best ways to become entrenched in the community. Whether you're a newcomer to the Grand Strand or have chosen this sandy coast as your retirement home, joining a volunteer corps can open an insightful window to local politics, culture, and people.

For those who are coming into town to tackle a new job assignment or career, a number of area businesses encourage volunteer activity by paying club membership dues for their employees. Civic, which means "of citizenship," organizations can often plug you right into a networking circuit of business contacts. Even *Fortune 500* magazine cites volunteer experience as a highlight many American corporations look for on resumes.

On a purely social level, civic involvement in a specific club will serve you up a slice of local life. Each organization presents its own microcosm or cross-section of Grand Strand citizenry, where you're bound to meet an interesting friend or two and, perhaps, the man or woman of your dreams. For singles, we can assure you that meeting locals through volunteer activities will beat a werewolf lifestyle of moonlight bar stalking.

Volunteer opportunities abound up and down the Grand Strand strip and in its pockets of subcommunities. To get a fairly comprehensive listing of volunteer outlets, we suggest dropping into the main office of the Myrtle Beach Area Chamber of Commerce on Oak Street to pick up the free-to-the-public guide *Civic & Service Organizations of the Myrtle Beach Area.* You can also get updated volunteer information from the *Sun News:* Civic and support-group meetings are announced in Sunday's "Coastal Living" section.

Included here are some volunteer organizations we know would gratefully welcome your help and/or participation.

Countywide

**Big Brothers and Big Sisters of Horry County
(843) 248-0164
www.bbbsa.org**

Big Brothers and Big Sisters is a nationwide, not-for-profit youth service organization. The mission of Big Brothers and Big Sisters is to "make a big difference, one child at a time" in the lives of at-risk children through professionally supported, primarily one-to-one mentoring relationships with caring adults, and to assist the children in achieving their highest potential as they grow to become confident, competent, and caring individuals. Big Brothers and Big Sisters of America

has matched millions of children in need with caring adult mentors since 1904. Research shows that children with Big Brothers and Big Sisters are less likely to use drugs and alcohol, skip school, or exhibit violent behavior.

Big Brothers and Big Sisters are caring adults who are mentors to children, often from single-parent homes. Men and women from all backgrounds help guide their little brothers and little sisters toward bright futures by sharing life experiences. "Bigs" and "Littles" enjoy school work, sports, recreational activities, movies, museums, and just talking together. In a nutshell, a "Big" is a friend.

Scouts, Carolina Low Country
(843) 527–6967
www.girlscoutsclc.org

Girl Scouts is the world's preeminent organization dedicated solely to girls. Girl Scouts aims to provide an accepting and nurturing environment where girls can build character and skills for success in the real world. Girl Scouting would not be possible without a league of dedicated adult volunteers. Opportunities exist for those willing and able to help once a week, once a month, or once a year. Volunteer opportunities include troop leader or committee member, trainer/workshop coordinator, mentor/advisor, chaperone, fund-raiser, camp staff, event director, nature consultant, cultural awareness instructor, and more.

Horry-Georgetown County Guardian Ad Litem Program
Horry County Offices, Third Avenue, Conway
(843) 248–7374
www.govoepp.state.sc.us

Volunteers in this program are specially trained to become advocates for abused and neglected children, representing the child's best interests through the Family Court system. This is interesting, work and a wonderful opportuni learn the legal system firsthand w helping a child in need.

Virtually anyone over the age of 21 w has an interest in children and the desir and time to serve can become a Guardian Ad Litem. Volunteers come from all professions and backgrounds, from stay-at-home moms to corporate executives. They conduct interviews with the child and other sources deemed necessary to a case, collect records and documents, seek recommendations and advice from experts, and monitor agencies and persons who provide care or service to the child. All of this data is reported as findings to the court.

We must tell you that the situations guardians encounter are often not at all pleasant, and some cases of abuse and neglect are downright ugly.

This program asks for a one-year commitment from its volunteers to handle one or more cases at a time, depending on your available time to give. You must apply and undergo a criminal check through the State Law Enforcement Division and the central registry at the Department of Social Services. Volunteers initially receive 30 hours of free training

Brookgreen Gardens boasts a very active volunteer program. PHOTO: COURTESY OF BROOKGREEN GARDENS

must observe a court hearing. Ongoing training is constantly in the works.

Literacy Council of Horry County
(843) 248–6140

How can you measure the contribution to a life when you teach someone who is illiterate how to read? The Literary Council is always eager to recruit volunteers to this task and offers a comprehensive training program. Teaching materials are given to every volunteer, and placement with a wishful reader is almost immediate. Literacy tutor training is held almost every other month at different locations around the county.

Mercy Hospice of Horry County
(843) 347–5500
www.conwayhospital.com

Hospice volunteers lend an extra pair of hands to help, extra ears to listen, and a heart to love and console. A training course is required to become a Hospice volunteer, since you will be working with a person suffering from a terminal, incurable condition and with his or her family. Volunteers are considered to be dedicated, loving friends who often provide relief for the caregiver. Volunteers also assist Hospice with office duties and fund-raising activities. The program is sponsored by Conway Hospital, Grand Strand Regional Medical Center, and Loris Healthcare System.

Mobile Meals
(843) 650–6310

"Waste not, want not" is the motto of this group, and its active volunteers don't believe in squandering a minute when it comes to delivering food to hungry people in need. Dozens of volunteers race hot lunches every day of the week—regardless of weather—to homebound citizens from the state line in Little River as far south as Brookgreen Gardens in Murrells Inlet. More than 40,000 meals are delivered. These volunteers are so dedicated, they even made deliveries on Christmas Day and New Year's Day. With so many meals to deliver to so many needy folks, Mobile Meals more than welcomes another pair of helping hands.

Optimist Clubs
(800) 500–8130
www.optimist.org

If you are searching for an outlet to help the community and the opportunity to develop and demonstrate your own leadership skills, you'll find what you're looking for in your local Optimist Club. Optimist Clubs conduct many exciting youth-oriented special events and promotions, including a youth safety program, childhood cancer campaign, and an "Always Buckle Children in the Back Seat" auto safety program. The Grand Strand club meets in Myrtle Beach and the North Strand chapter meets in North Myrtle Beach.

Volunteer Rescue Squads
In Myrtle Beach
(843) 626–7352
In Murrells Inlet
(843) 651–9170
In North Myrtle Beach
(843) 272–3144

Yes, the Grand Strand has a complete emergency ambulance service run solely

---

Insiders' Tip

Becoming a volunteer often uncovers hidden talents in people. Through civic participation and community projects, we've seen meek personalities turn into strong leaders, tongue-tied stutterers become inspiring public speakers, and people struggling with insecurities leave dead-end jobs to start their own businesses.

...teers. Not one paid employee works at any of the area rescue squads. They operate from 7:00 P.M. to 7:00 A.M., seven days a week, responding to emergency 911 calls dispatched from police departments. Volunteers serve as drivers, crews, and trained medical assistants. You must be 18 or older to volunteer.

Myrtle Beach

American Red Cross
2795 Pampas Drive, Myrtle Beach
(843) 477–0020
www.horrycounty.redcross.org
537 Lafayette Circle, Georgetown
(843) 546–5422
www.georgetown.redcross.org

If you prefer hands-on, in-the-trenches work, volunteering with the Red Cross could be just the ticket. This national community-assistance organization needs people to teach CPR courses, assist with Bloodmobiles, work in hurricane shelters, train for emergency disaster relief, and help to coordinate the annual Community Christmas Dinner.

City of Myrtle Beach
921-A Oak Street, Myrtle Beach
(843) 918–1000
www.cityofmyrtlebeach.com

If you want to get right in the thick of things, consider volunteering for the city. Take surveys, coach a youth sports team, or perform a number of office duties. Volunteer positions are available in the departments of planning, construction, police, finance, engineering, public services, and parks and recreation, so you can certainly find a suitable and enjoyable alternative. The city of Myrtle Beach also recruits active volunteers by the score for Chapin Library. Each department and facility accepts, screens, and trains volunteers to its specifications.

The Community Coalition of Horry County
(843) 349–2526
www.cchc.net

The Community Coalition of Horry County (CCHC) is a broad coalition of agencies, businesses, nonprofit o... tions, and individuals. The organiz... mission is to build collaboration... maximize community assets in an e... to strengthen the health and well-bei... Horry County families and neighb... hoods. Community initiatives include t... Family Friendly Business Initiative; Firs... Book, which has provided more than 10,000 books to children in Horry County; A Father's Place; Positive Voices—Safe & Drug Free Communities and Schools, and an active Youth Leadership Council. For more information contact Margene Willis, executive director.

Grand Strand Regional
Medical Center Auxiliary
(843) 692–1634
www.grandstrandmed.com

Volunteers are used in every department and on every floor of this major hospital. An orientation session is held monthly, at which time all guidelines, rules, and regulations are discussed. Individuals are matched to particular positions at the hospital according to their backgrounds and skills. Orientation and training are provided. Talk to Gay Cooke, CDVS, to get involved.

Grand Strand Humane Society
10th Avenue North Extension, Myrtle Beach
(843) 448–5891, (843) 448–9151
409 Bay Street, North Myrtle Beach
(843) 249–4948

This is definitely the right place for animal lovers to donate their time and energy. People are needed to assist in the care of animals in the North Myrtle Beach and Myrtle Beach shelters and to help with fund-raising and community-awareness programs. Volunteer coordinator Sue White can be reached at (843) 448–4904.

Grand Strand YMCA
904 65th Avenue North, Myrtle Beach
(843) 449–9622
www.gsfymca.org

YMCA volunteers are the lifeblood of the Grand Strand Family YMCA. As a volunteer in programs—a volunteer position aptly known as a VIP—you can spearhead

Many local businesses welcome volunteer contributions. PHOTO: COURTESY OF MYRTLE BEACH AREA CHAMBER OF COMMERCE

activities, act as a role model for a variety of young people, serve in the office, provide care for infants and toddlers, assist with special events, coach youth sports, chaperone trips, serve on various committees, and so much more. What you offer will be determined by your own interests and expertise. No matter how you help, you can make a big difference. In recognition of your time, support, and commitment, all VIPs are provided with special training, equipment, fellowship, and privileges.

Habitat for Humanity of Horry County
(843) 916–8815
www.habitatmb.org

Dedicated to providing adequate housing for needy families, this local chapter of Habitat for Humanity works in partnership with people in need to build and renovate decent, affordable housing. Volunteers for Habitat assist in a variety of ways: The entire construction of a home is done by volunteers and the soon-to-be-homeowners; others help to raise money for the organization through Habitat's thrift shop, concession stands at major events, and gift wrapping at local malls during the Christmas shopping season. All Habitat committees, including Site Selection, Family Selection, Legal Affairs, and Surveying, are composed of volunteers. The only restriction is that a volunteer must be at least 14 years of age to work on a construction site. Call Gail Olive at the number above if you want to pick up a hammer and join.

Kiwanis International
(843) 448–5123
www.kiwanis.org

A group for men and women age 18 and older, Kiwanis clubs worldwide are mandated to serve their communities. They run four or five major fund-raisers each year, and all monies raised must be donated or spent in the hometown. The group does a fine job supporting many area services such as Helping Hand and Meals on Wheels. Franklin Long will answer other questions you may have.

South Strand

Fire Departments
Surfside Beach Fire Department
115 U.S. Highway 17 North, Surfside Beach
(843) 913–6366
Murrells Inlet Fire Department
3641 U.S. Highway 17 South, Murrells Inlet
(843) 651–5143

Here's your chance to live out that childhood dream of riding along in a screeching fire-engine, wearing a shiny red hat and big boots, with your arm slung around a Dalmatian . . . OK, it's not really all fun and games. But volunteer fighters are always needed, and the partment requires no previous experien. training is provided.

United Way
515 Front Street, Georgetown
(843) 546–6317
www.unitedway.org

Nationally, United Way of America is dedicated to making a measurable impact in every community across America. The United Way movement includes approximately 1,400 community-based United Way organizations. Each is independent, separately incorporated, and governed by local volunteers. Volunteers are needed to assist with such office duties as typing, mail coordination, and filing. Volunteers are also needed to assist with various special events and activities. The Georgetown-area United Way is especially active and well respected. Year after year some of the community's most powerful business people take a pivotal role in this local chapter—which makes this United Way a great opportunity for networking and making a difference in the lives of others.

Worship

One local, albeit cynical, restaurant owner once commented to us, "Visitors don't come here to think, they don't come to read, and they certainly don't come here to go to church." He, of course, was alluding to the party-all-the-time image so often associated with Myrtle Beach. But despite his analysis and pronouncement, the Grand Strand is part of, and the vast majority of its visitors are from, the heart of the God-fearing Bible Belt. And one thing about Southerners is that regardless of how hard they party, they tend to be spiritual with the same vigor.

Consequently the denominational makeup of the area traditionally has been largely Protestant and more than a little fundamentalist in nature; South Carolina voters elected the only Christian Coalition–affiliated governor in the nation. Furthermore, this region's churches reflect its history: All Saints Episcopal Church on Pawleys Island celebrated its 235th birthday in 2002, and Prince George Winyah Church in Georgetown is one of South Carolina's few original colonial church buildings still in use. Conway's historic district is home to two more distinctive churches—Kingston Presbyterian and First United Methodist.

Nonetheless, with the large numbers of northern retirees and a more diverse population becoming year-round Grand Strand residents, the religious scene has come to in-

All Saints Episcopal Church in Pawleys Island is more than 230 years old. PHOTO: COURTESY OF BROOKGREEN GARDENS

Index

About the Authors

Kimberly Allyson Duncan

A native of the Carolina Lowcountry, Kimberly Allyson Duncan graduated from the University of South Carolina. She is president and owner of The Altman Group, a business communications firm that provides outsourcing solutions for a wide variety of marketing and public-relations needs. Located on Pawleys Island, the firm specializes in providing marketing-support services such as copywriting, public relations, and special-event planning. Kimberly also co-publishes *Lowcountry Companion,* a popular magazine that showcases the area's wealth of art, history, and natural resources.

Lisa Tomer Rentz

Transplanted to South Carolina when she was seventeen, Lisa Tomer Rentz has since eaten her weight in hushpuppies, walked miles of Strand with her dogs, and married a true Southern gentleman. Her background in marketing and her husband's family's hundred-year-old beach house in Ocean Drive drew her to the Grand Strand, where Lisa works as a freelance writer.